Tahiti
& French Polynesia

The Marquesas
p166

Bora Bora
p120

Maupiti
p136

Huahine
p94

Ra'iatea &
Taha'a
p105

Mo'orea
p75

Tahiti
p48

The Tuamotus
p143

The Australs
p193

The Gambier
Archipelago
p193

THIS EDITION WRITTEN AND RESEARCHED BY
Celeste Brash, Jean-Bernard Carillet

Contents

PLAN YOUR TRIP

Welcome to Tahiti
& French Polynesia......4

Tahiti & French
Polynesia Map..........6

Tahiti & French
Polynesia's Top 15 8

Need to Know 16

If You Like....... 18

Month By Month.......21

Itineraries 24

Which Island?......... 28

Diving................. 33

Travel with Children.....41

Regions at a Glance.... 44

ON THE ROAD

TAHITI 48
Pape'ete 51
Around Tahiti Nui 63
West Coast 63
East Coast 68
Taravao & Tahiti Iti..... 70

MO'OREA 75

HUAHINE 94

RA'IATEA &
TAHA'A 105
Ra'iatea 106
Taha'a 115

BORA BORA....... 120

MAUPITI.......... 136

THE TUAMOTUS... 143
Rangiroa............. 145
Tikehau............. 154
Mataiva 157
Fakarava............. 159
Ahe 164

THE MARQUESAS .. 166
Nuku Hiva 168
Taiohae............. 169
Hakaui Valley.......... 174

POLYNESIAN TATTOO P221

TROPICAL FLOWERS,
PAPE'ETE P51

Contents

Toovii Plateau 175
Taipivai 175
Hatiheu 175
'Ua Huka. **176**
'Ua Pou. **180**
Hakahau. 180
Hakahetau. 182
Hakamaii 182
Hohoi 182
Hiva Oa. **182**
Atuona & Around 183
Taaoa 187
Puamau 188
Hanapaaoa 188
Hanaiapa 188

Tahuata **189**
Fatu Hiva **191**

THE AUSTRALS
& THE GAMBIER
ARCHIPELAGO 193
The Australs **194**
Rururu 194
Tubuai. 197
Raivavae. 198
**The Gambier
Archipelago** **201**
Mangareva. 201

UNDERSTAND

Tahiti & French
Polynesia Today 204
History 206
Environment 215
Islander Life 218
French Polynesia in
Popular Culture 222
Food & Drink 224

SURVIVAL GUIDE

Directory A–Z 228
Transport 233
Health. 239
Language 242
Index. 249
Map Legend. 255

OVERWATER BUNGALOWS,
TIKEHAU P154

SPECIAL FEATURES

Which Island?. 28
Diving. 33
Travel with
Children. 41
Polynesian
Food & Drink. 224

Welcome to Tahiti & French Polynesia

Sculpted by sky-piercing, moss-green peaks and lined with vivid turquoise lagoons, sultry French Polynesia is a place to take it slow and experience warm, laid-back island culture.

The Dream

Tahiti: just the word conjures up centuries' worth of images: hibiscus flowers; grass skirts; a humid breeze over turquoise sea. The islands of French Polynesia became legend the minute European explorers reached home with tales of a heaven on earth where the soil was fertile, life was simple and lust was guilt-free. While the stereotypes are outdated, French Polynesia is still as dreamy as reality gets. The lagoons are just as blue, but there are now freeways, more conservative values and nine-to-five jobs. It's not the untainted paradise of explorer lore, but at least there's internet.

Polynesian Culture

Slowly, and particularly since the 1980s, islanders are bringing their culture back. Once forbidden, Reo Maohi (the Tahitian language) is now taught to university level; traditional tattoos are all the rage; and Tahitian dancing is the highlight of any party or festival. You'll see national pride swell during the Hawaiki Nui outrigger canoe race in November, the Miss Tahiti pageant in June and the highlight of the year, the Heiva festivals in July. So tuck a *tiare* (gardenia flower) behind your ear, smile and say *mauruuru* (thank you) for this time of revival.

Lagoon Spectacular

The slim stretches of white-, pink- and black-sand beaches in French Polynesia are really just pretty springboards into the real draw: the lagoons. Most high islands are surrounded by fringing reef that creates a protected swimming pool of the most intense aqua imaginable. Coral atolls have this same calibre of lagoon minus the big island in the middle. Fish, dolphins, rays, sharks, turtles and more inhabit these clear-water coral gardens that are as excellent for snorkelling as they are for diving and swimming. Surfers ride glassy wave faces at reef passes while kitesurfers fly across the water with the trade winds.

To Luxe or Not to Luxe

Over-the-top indulgence has become French Polynesia's – more specifically Bora Bora's – signature, and it often overshadows what the rest of the country has to offer. Resorts on the 'Pearl of the Pacific' are a honey-mooner's dream, with private overwater bungalows and views of the island's iconic, square-topped peak. But if this isn't your cup of coconut water, or not in your budget, don't let that dissuade you from visiting French Polynesia. Small, family-run lodgings offer a closer-to-the-culture experience for considerably less financial output.

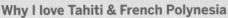

Why I love Tahiti & French Polynesia

By Celeste Brash, Lonely Planet Writer

It's not just because it's the most beautiful place on Earth. No, really. I love French Polynesia for the sound of rain on a tin roof, the smell of *tiare taina* gardenias in November, the floral taste of a perfect mango, the silky warmth of the ocean, a sea turtle swimming peacefully below me, the gift of a flower *hei* (flower necklace) from a friend, the tapping of a *toere* (hollowed-out piece of wood) drum in the distance and simply, the way islands slow the pulse and make the world feel like a softer, better place.

For more about our writers, see page 256

Above: Polynesian children wearing *hei* (floral necklaces)

Tahiti & French Polynesia

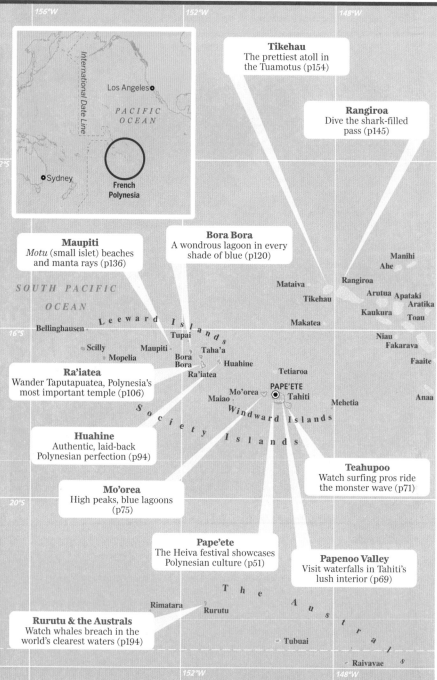

Tikehau
The prettiest atoll in the Tuamotus (p154)

Rangiroa
Dive the shark-filled pass (p145)

Maupiti
Motu (small islet) beaches and manta rays (p136)

Bora Bora
A wondrous lagoon in every shade of blue (p120)

Ra'iatea
Wander Taputapuatea, Polynesia's most important temple (p106)

Huahine
Authentic, laid-back Polynesian perfection (p94)

Mo'orea
High peaks, blue lagoons (p75)

Teahupoo
Watch surfing pros ride the monster wave (p71)

Pape'ete
The Heiva festival showcases Polynesian culture (p51)

Papenoo Valley
Visit waterfalls in Tahiti's lush interior (p69)

Rurutu & the Australs
Watch whales breach in the world's clearest waters (p194)

Los Angeles

PACIFIC OCEAN

International Date Line

Sydney

French Polynesia

SOUTH PACIFIC OCEAN

Bellinghausen

Scilly
Mopelia

Tupai
Maupiti
Bora Bora
Ra'iatea

Taha'a
Huahine

Leeward Islands

Mataiva
Tikehau
Makatea

Rangiroa
Arutua
Kaukura

Manihi
Ahe
Apataki
Aratika
Toau

Niau
Fakarava
Faaite

Tetiaroa

Mo'orea
Maiao

PAPE'ETE
Tahiti

Mehetia

Anaa

Society Islands

Windward Islands

Rimatara
Rururu

The Australs

Tubuai

Raivavae

0 — 200 km
0 — 100 miles
N

144°W
136°W

The Marquesas
Take the iconic *Aranui* through
these rugged islands (p166)

Motu One
Hatutu
Nuku Hiva
'Ua Huka
'Ua Pou
Hiva Oa
Tahuata
Fatu Hiva

The Marquesas

12°S

SOUTH
PACIFIC
OCEAN

Disappointment Islands

Tepoto Nord   Napuka

The

Takaroa
Takapoto
Tikei

Puka Puka

Taiaro
Kauehi

Takume   Fangatau
Fakahina

T   u

16°S

Raraka   Taenga   Raroia
Katiu
Nihiru   Rekareka
Makemo   Tauere
Marutea Nord
Tahanea
Motutunga   Tekokota   Tatakoto
Haraiki   Hikueru
Reitoru   Amanu
Marokau
Ravahere   Hao   Pukarua
Nengonengo   Akiaki   Reao
Vahitahi
Paraoa   Nukutavake
Manuhangi   Pinaki
Hereheretue   Vairaatea
Ahunui

a   m   o   t   u   s

20°S

Duke of Gloucester Islands

Anuanuraro
Anuanurunga
Nukutepipi   Vanavana   Tureia

Tenararo   Tenarunga
Vahanga   Marutea Sud
Tematangi   Matureivavao
Moruroa   Maria
Island

SOUTH PACIFIC
OCEAN
Fangataufa

The Gambier
Archipelago

Gambier Archipelago
Eerie but beautiful church
relics (p201)

Morane   Mangareva

Tropic of Capricorn   Temoe

144°W
140°W
136°W
24°S

Tahiti &
French Polynesia's
Top 15

Bora Bora's Lagoon

1 As the plane begins to descend, a magical scene comes into view: a perfect Morse-code ring of *motu* (small islets), mop-topped with palms, separating the indigo of the ocean from the crisp palette of lagoon blues. Bora Bora (p120) is a hot favourite for honeymooners – but we feel certain you didn't come all this way just to crack open a bottle of champagne. Get in that water via mask, fin and snorkel, on a SUP, with a scuba tank or even just splashing around on a beach. Below: Bora Bora lagoon, with view of Mt Otemanu

Heiva i Tahiti

2 During the annual Heiva (p220) festival in July, the whole country goes full tilt: the best dancers compete in decadent competitions wearing little more than palm fronds while they wiggle their hips at warp speed; outrigger-canoe racing ignites the lagoons; and traditional sports such as coconut husking go pro. This is the best time to experience the gentle, unpretentiously sophisticated Polynesian culture at its fieriest. The festival takes place on other islands including Bora Bora. If you arrive in June, you'll find dancers practising in nearly every village.

Mo'orea

3 Mo'orea (p75) is a tropical-island cliché brought to life. If you've been dreaming of a holiday-brochure turquoise lagoon, coral beaches, vertical peaks and lush landscapes, you'd be hard-pressed to find better than this gem of an island. Mo'orea has something for everyone. A startling variety of adventure options await: there are mountains to climb, coral gardens to snorkel, scenic areas to quad bike, waves to surf and sloping reefs to dive. But if all you want to do is unwind, a couple of lovely expanses of coral sand beckon.

Rangiroa's Tiputa Pass

4 French Polynesia's warm, tropical waters hold some of the greatest varieties of sea life in the South Pacific and you can find most of them in one spot at Tiputa Pass (p37) in Rangiroa. Mingle with grey reef sharks, manta rays, dolphins and sharks alongside loads of reef species including stingrays, jacks and clouds of butterfly fish (pictured, right). The lagoon also caters to snorkellers, with some of the clearest waters in the world and healthy coral gardens.

SHALAMOV / GETTY IMAGES ©

SEAPHOTOART / SHUTTERSTOCK ©

MATTEO COLOMBO / GETTY IMAGES ©

FRILET PATRICK / HEMIS.FR / GETTY IMAGES ©

Huahine

5 Boasting some of the best beaches in the country and a snoozy Polynesian charm, Huahine (p94) is the perfect spot to recharge the batteries. If you've got energy to burn, there's a slew of activities available, from hiking in the lush interior to snorkelling fabulous coral gardens. Culture buffs will also love Maeva, one of the most extensive complexes of pre-European *marae* (traditional temples) in French Polynesia. Huahine is refreshingly void of bling and large-scale development. It's all about ecotravel, and this is why it's gaining in popularity.

Tahiti's Waterfall Valleys

6 Take an island with high mountains and 90-degree cliffs, douse it with tropical rainfall and give it a few million years to erode into magnificent forms – and what do you get? Waterfalls. Lots of them. You could walk up any river in Tahiti and find myriad cascades, but you're best sticking with known trails or going with a guide. Try the trodden (though near-empty) paths to Papenoo (p69), Fautaua or take a boat ride to Tahiti Iti's Fenua Aihere for falls right on the coast.
Above: Waterfall, Tahiti

7

JENS KUHFS / GETTY IMAGES ©

8

ULRIKE MAIER / GETTY IMAGES ©

The Aranui

7 Snaggle-toothed volcanic peaks, deep ravines, waterfalls, secret bays and forests that could hold their own in a BBC documentary all await on this iconic boat voyage through the six inhabited islands of the Marquesas Archipelago. Part cargo ship, part cruise liner, the Aranui (p172) is a huge event at each island and you get to be there for the unloading of the supplies. The festive voyage also involves plenty of dance performances, local meals and a guide to explain the extraordinary culture and archaeological remains.

Surfing Teahupoo

8 The fearsome wave at Teahupoo (p71) may be beyond many surfers' level, but watching the pros tackle it during the Billabong Pro is one of the greatest live sporting events you may ever get to see. But here are plenty of other spots for the less warrior-like to surf: with warm water and swell from all directions beginners can paddle out to shore breaks, while more advanced surfers will be spoiled with hollow reef waves year-round. There are secret spots everywhere if you're willing to look.

Maupiti

9 Rising out of the lagoon like a mini Bora Bora, Maupiti (p136) has as many of the tropical-island-fantasy attributes as its larger neighbour, but only a fraction of the hype. Be ready to say hello to every friendly islander you pass in the village and to explore the magical white sand *motu*, deep blue lagoon and manta ray–filled passes. Don't expect big resorts here – digs are in adorable and intimate family-run hotels and *pensions*. Rent a kayak, strap on a scuba bottle, hike the mountain or just lounge on the beach in untainted, simple bliss.

Tattoos

10 Both beautiful and raw, dark geometric patterns against bronzed skin have made a comeback all over French Polynesia. The Marquesas are known for perfecting the art (p187), but the best island to get a tattoo is Tahiti where there are the most artists (many are from the Marquesas). In pre-European times, tattoos acted as a map to a person's social status and achievements, but today they are simply for beautification. Many of the ancient patterns have been copied or provide inspiration for new designs.

Tikehau

11 Best explored by boat, this watery landscape holds empty white- and pink-sand beaches, sea-bird nesting grounds and some of the best spots in the world to dive in with a mask and snorkel. Atolls are basically lagoons without the island and Tikehau (p154) is arguably the prettiest one in the country, with its scalloped bays and thriving pass. What little land mass there is peeks up only several metres above the surface and encircles lagoons so blue and thriving that high-island lagoons look meek in comparison.

Tahitian Pearl Farms

12 Forget diamonds, black pearls are a Tahitian gal's best friend. Pearls come in silvery white, black and every colour in between, so it's easy to get seduced by these sea gems' soothing hues. Don't miss visiting a farm (our favourite spots are on Taha'a, p115), where you'll see how the oysters are raised and harvested, and maybe even get to see a technician performing the culturing operation (called a 'graft'). Afterwards, you'll get to drool over lustrous jewellery and hopefully get a great deal on a special souvenir.

MAX SHEN / GETTY IMAGES ©

MATTEO COLOMBO / GETTY IMAGES ©

Whale-Watching

13 French Polynesia is an important breeding ground for humpback whales, which migrate to Polynesian waters between July and October. It's one of the best places in the world to see these magnificent creatures. They can be observed caring for new calves and engaging in elaborate mating rituals. The best areas to spot them are Mo'orea, Tahiti and Rurutu (p195), where operators organise whale-watching trips.

Marae Taputapuatea

14 The most important *marae* in French Polynesia – and possibly all of Polynesia – is Marae Taputapuatea (p106) on Ra'iatea, which has been extensively restored. *Marae* are religious sites built from basalt blocks placed side by side and piled up. In pre-European times, they were places of worship, burial and human sacrifice. Taputapuatea is shrouded with a palpable aura. It's worth going on a guided tour of Ra'iatea for explanations on the *marae* since otherwise there's little in the way of visitor information.

The Churches of the Gambier

15 French Polynesia's eeriest vestiges are churches, nunneries and other grand religious structures built from coral blocks in the late 19th century. Today, cracked, whitewashed churches with room for up to 1200 worshippers sit mutely, yet with an austere beauty, on islands with only a scattering of residents. They exist thanks to Father Honoré Laval, who history portrays as either an overzealous slave driver or a beacon of faith who inspired the islanders to build these amazing, yet out of place, European-style monuments (p201).

Need to Know

For more information, see Survival Guide (p227)

Currency

Cours de franc Pacifique (CFP; Pacific franc)

Language

French and Reo Maohi (Tahitian)

Visas

Most nationalities can stay one to three months without a visa.

Money

ATMs are found on main islands. Credit cards are accepted at hotels and restaurants on main islands, but not at family *pensions* or on remote islands.

Mobile Phones

Local SIM cards can be used in unlocked GSM-compatible phones. Other phones can be set to roaming.

Time

Hawaiian Standard Time (GMT/UTC minus 10 hours); the Marquesas Islands are a half-hour ahead of the rest of the islands.

When to Go

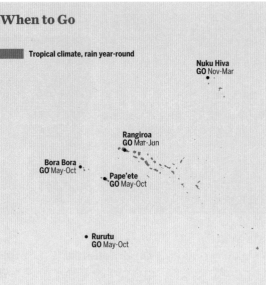

Tropical climate, rain year-round

Nuku Hiva
GO Nov-Mar

Rangiroa
GO Mar-Jun

Bora Bora
GO May-Oct

Pape'ete
GO May-Oct

Rurutu
GO May-Oct

High Season
(Jun–Aug, Dec & Jan)

➡ June to August are usually the coolest and driest months.

➡ December and January have plenty of sun and cooling showers.

➡ Festival month in July, with Heiva i Tahiti the highlight.

Shoulder
(Feb, May & Sep)

➡ February is one of the hottest months; May and September are mild.

➡ Off-season discounts for accommodation

➡ Flights and accommodation can be hard to find; book in advance.

Low Season
(Mar, Apr, Oct & Nov)

➡ March and April are hot and rainy.

➡ Pleasant in October and November.

➡ Watch for frequent school holidays when inter-island flights can be hard to book.

Websites

Tahiti Tourisme
(www.tahiti-tourisme.com)
Official tourism website.

Lonely Planet
(www.lonelyplanet.com/tahiti-and-french-polynesia)
Destination info, hotel bookings and more.

Ia Ora
(www.tahiti-pensions.com)
Info on small hotels and *pensions*.

Tahiti Traveler
(www.thetahititraveler.com)
Range of info, from history to local sights.

Important Numbers

There are no area codes in French Polynesia.

Country code	☎689
International access code	☎00
Ambulance	☎15
Fire	☎120
Police	☎20

Exchange Rates

Australia	A$1	79 CFP
Canada	C$1	79 CFP
Euro zone	€1	119 CFP
Japan	¥100	90 CFP
New Zealand	NZ$1	74 CFP
UK	UK£1	164 CFP
US	US$1	108 CFP

For current exchange rates, see www.xe.com

Daily Costs

Budget: Less than 12,000 CFP

➡ Room at basic family *pension*: 7000 CFP

➡ Baguette sandwich from grocer: 350 CFP

➡ Bicycle hire per day: 1500 CFP

Midrange: 12,000–40,000 CFP

➡ Room at upscale *pension* or boutique hotel: 22,000 CFP

➡ Main dish at a local *snack* bar: 1200 CFP

➡ All-day lagoon tour with lunch: 8000 CFP

Top End: More than 40,000 CFP

➡ Overwater bungalow (Bora Bora): 80,000 CFP

➡ Dance show and buffet at a Tahitian resort: 8500 CFP

➡ Single dive: 8000 CFP

Opening Hours

Opening hours vary. On Tahiti, businesses are less likely to close for lunch (although some do).

Banks 8–11.30am and 1–4pm Monday to Friday

Restaurants 11.30am–2pm and 6.30–9pm

Bars & Clubs 9pm–2am

Shops 8am–noon and 1.30–5pm

Arriving in Tahiti

Faa'a International Airport (Pape'ete; p233) All international flights arrive here.

Hotel shuttle Most hotels and *pensions* offer free or paid airport pickup if you've prebooked.

Buses Run about every half-hour from 5am to 6pm.

Taxis A taxi to downtown Pape'ete costs around 1800 CFP (2500 CFP between 8pm and 6am).

Car hire Rental agencies inside the airport open for arriving flights if they have clients who have prebooked.

Getting Around

Car There's little to no public transport in French Polynesia, depending on the island, so most visitors rent cars. Drive on the right.

Boat To get to more remote locations and between some islands; often used in tours.

Bus Only Pape'ete and its environs have frequent service.

Bicycles Best on the quieter roads of smaller islands; rentals are ubiquitous.

For much more on **getting around**, see p234

If You Like...

Diving, Snorkelling & Wildlife-Watching

Been searching for the world's most intense shade of aqua? What's below the surface is even more spectacular: sharks, coral gardens, turtles, rays, dolphins, humpback whales, clouds of fish...

Tiputa Pass It's shark week! Or more like shark century. This is French Polynesia's fauna-heavy diving capital. (p37)

Manta Point A manta-ray cleaning station makes sightings likely, but human crowds are rare. (p37)

Rurutu Spot humpbacks breaching near your boat. (p194)

Mo'orea Dolphins, whales, stingrays and sharks all star in a stunning lagoon. (p75)

Fakarava Dive in a Unesco biosphere reserve in and around the country's second largest lagoon. (p159)

Motu Tau Tau Some of the best coral gardens for snorkelling in the high islands. (p35)

Luxury Pampering

Live *la vie en bleu* while lounging poolside with exotic cocktails, soaking in tropical-flower-filled baths or getting your muscles

soothed with hot volcanic stones.

The Brando On stunning, Tetiaroa atoll, offers the highest level of eco-opulence. (p56)

St Regis Resort Overwater-bungalow bliss and a full-throttle celebrity magnet. (p130)

Le Taha'a Private Island & Spa Offers glamour, luxe and views of Bora Bora minus the hype. (p118)

Sofitel la Ora Moorea Beach Resort Chic decadence and chock-full of activities. (p90)

Tikehau Pearl Beach Resort Get your spa treatments in a remote paradise worthy of an adventure novel. (p157)

Kia Ora Resort & Spa Lets you lounge near town or whisks you to a Crusoe-chic private island. (p151)

History & Archaeology

Spirituality has always been paramount to Polynesian people and the historical vestiges you'll find in the islands are testament to this. Stone temples and Europe-worthy churches are highlights.

Marae Taputapuatea Arguably the most important ancient Polynesian place of worship in the world. (p106)

Opunohu Valley Tumbled remains of archery platforms, dwellings and temples wend up a jungle hill. (p81)

Gambier Archipelago In the 1880s, Father Honoré Laval led islanders to build coral block churches & cathedrals that seat thousands. (p201)

Kamuihei, Tahakia & Teiipoka Villages of stone rubble shaded by grand banyan trees on Nuku Hiva. (p175)

Iipona Five impressive stone *tiki* dominate this well-preserved site. (p188)

Maeva Walk along the lagoon and up the hill through the remains of this ancient village. (p97)

Hiking & Walking

Imagine waterfalls tumbling down fern-carpeted cliffs, wild passionfruit vines draped over beach hibiscus trees, and dark caves, each with an ancient legend. Choose from short walks through botanical gardens to multiday treks far from the modern world.

Te Pari & Fenua Aihere Coastal trail of waterfalls, caves, petroglyphs and leaping dolphins. (p72)

Vaipahi Spring Gardens Stroll the waterfall gardens or trek up the hill through chestnut trees. (p64)

Opunohu Valley Loop From a lush valley, through archaeological sites to one of the most spectacular viewpoints in the country. (p83)

Temehani Plateau Hike this high plateau in search of the *tiare apetahi,* one of the planet's most rarest flowers. (p111)

Nuku Hiva An island with a myriad spectacular treks along ridges, into waterfall valleys and along the coast. (p168)

Papenoo Valley Delve into the deep, lush interior of Tahiti with archaeological remains and myriad trails. (p69)

Art, Music & Dance

Hips that move like rippling water, men dancing in palm-leaf loincloths and percussion that stirs the primordial soul are reason enough to visit French Polynesia. Upping the ante are woodcarvings, basketry, local paintings and tattoo ink on bronzed skin.

Heiva, Tahiti The country's biggest festival of dance, song and traditional sports. It's also celebrated countrywide. (p51)

Marama Tattoo Marquesan designs are the most popular, but you'll find talented tattoo artists throughout the islands. (p134)

Marche de Pape'ete Find everything from woven hats to pearl jewellery and bright *pareu* (sarong-style garment). (p51)

'Ua Huka The wood-carving capital, although you can pick up finely worked pieces in most tourist areas. (p176)

Jean & Nadine Oberlin Marquesan tapa with a modern twist. (p189)

Top: Overwater bungalows at Le Taha'a Island Resort & Spa (p118), Motu Tau Tau
Bottom: Giving *hei* (floral necklaces) is the traditional welcome to visitors

Beaches

French Polynesia is home to svelte strips of white, pink and black sand that act as launching pads into the lagoons. Think intimate, palm-lined and pretty rather than flat or expansive.

Matira Beach Chic enough for designer bikinis but laid-back and spacious enough to bring the kids. (p122)

Temae An exceptionally wide, white-sand Mo'orea beach fronted by a turquoise swimming pool of ocean. (p77)

Jardin de Corail An easy-access yet empty white beach on Huahine with fantastic snorkelling. (p98)

Pink Sand Beach, Fakarava Sparkling pink sands contrast with intense blue water. (p159)

Blue Lagoon One of the most beautiful beach and blue-water spots in the world. (p146)

Plage de Taharuu Beautiful black sand and fun surf. (p64)

Surfing & Kitesurfing

The land of monster reef-breaking Teahupoo barrels also has softer beach waves, perfect for beginners; kitesurfers will also find plenty of stretches of windy lagoon. Whatever your level, all you need are the guts to get out there.

Teahupoo The big one, the one you've seen photos of that made you gasp. Watch the pros surf it in August during the Billabong Pro. (p71)

Papara A very powerful wave that breaks on sand consistently most of the year. (p64)

Haapiti The star of Mo'orea surf spots with powerful, deep waves over sand. (p83)

Mo'orea's Lagoon Kitesurfers should fly their gear on the tradewind-catching lagoon in front of Temae or the Beach-comber Intercontinental Resort. (p83)

Tubuai The windiest lagoon in the country offers an obstacle-free course of pure kitesurfing thrills – but you'll need your own gear. (p197)

Getting off the Beaten Path

With 118 islands and more than 68% of the country's population on Tahiti, it's not hard to go 'Crusoe' in French Polynesia. Or, if you want company, head to small isles where Polynesian culture still reigns and welcomes are warm.

Ahe A coral atoll of nesting sea birds, pearl farms, lovely lodging and few visitors. (p164)

Raivavae Rivals Bora Bora for beauty but has retained its taro farming and pandanus-weaving culture as well as its isolation. (p198)

The Gambier Archipelago A stunning archipelago surrounded by a single lagoon and graced with eerie deserted churches. (p201)

'Ua Huka Gorge on mangoes, visit woodcarving studios and explore the hills on horseback – all with the locals. (p176)

Taha'a Quietly sitting in the middle of the busy Society Islands, the wooded 'Vanilla Island' is one of the most laid-back places on the planet. (p115)

Tahiti Iti The quiet side of Tahiti has a surprising range of great lodging and restaurants. (p70)

Great Food & Drink

Relish local ingredients (fish, taro, fruits) prepared every which way. Try savoury vanilla sauces, Chinese specialities, gratins and some 1001 ways to eat coconut.

Roulottes Mobile food vans (found country-wide) serve the cheapest eats and offer the most local atmosphere. (p132)

Plage de Maui, Tahiti Try the seafood and local vegies steamed in a banana leaf while admiring the aqua lagoon. (p74)

Chez Tara, Huahine Traditional Tahitian food plus seafood dishes with a French twist. (p103)

Restaurant Matira Beach Beachside restaurant with million-dollar views; French dishes, local ingredients and Japanese specialities. (p133)

Distillery Huahine Passion Fruits so exotic you've never heard of them (plus all the well-known favourites) distilled into fantastic liquors. (p98)

Snack Mahana Fresh, big portions, smiling Polynesian service, plastic tables and a lagoon view. (p91),

Month by Month

February

It's hot and it might be raining, so tuck in and see a sure-to-impress documentary film or, if you're more masochistic, run a marathon. The rest of us will be cooling off in the water.

⚜ Chinese New Year

The date changes each year (it's based on the lunar calendar and is sometimes in January), but the two-week long celebrations always include dancing, martial-arts displays and fireworks. The most action is found at the Kanti Chinese Temple (Ave Georges Clemenceau) in Pape'ete.

☆ Fifo Pacific International Documentary Film Festival

In early February comes this festival with screenings (many in English) of the year's best Pacific documentary films, from Australia to Hawai'i.

🏃 International Mo'orea Marathon

This annual marathon tackles half of the island of Mo'orea. There is also a shorter half-marathon (21km) and an 800m 'family run'. The race finishes at Temae Beach where runners can cool off in the lagoon.

March

The heat is still on in March and rain is still likely, although less so than in the few months prior.

⚜ Arrival of the First Missionaries

On 5 March large religious festivities take place in churches all over the country to commemorate the arrival of the first Protestant missionaries in 1797. Polynesian families piously and enthusiastically celebrate this arrival of Christianity.

April

It's still balmy but cooling down a bit. April can be a lovely time to visit and you'll beat the high season by a month or so.

⚜ International Tattoo Convention

Thousands of locals and international tattoo enthusiasts show up for this five-day, early-April event where artists flaunt their skills and the human canvases flaunt their decorated skin. It's held on Tahiti in a new location each year.

May

Although the biggest festivals are in July, things softly kick off in May. Follow the rhythm of toere (traditional drums) to find people practising for the Heiva festival. The weather is mild and the tourist season has yet to begin.

🏃 Taapuna Masters

A lively surfing and bodyboarding competition at the Taapuna Pass break, for locals and international pros. Prizes go to the best tube ride and best aerial.

🏃 Tu'aro Ma'ohi Traditional Sports Championship

This annual competition takes place at several venues around Tahiti and usually runs from late April to mid-June. Sports include javelin throwing, rock lifting, fruit carrying, outrigger canoeing, coconut-tree climbing and coconut husking.

🏃 Tahiti Pearl Regatta

Sailboats, yachts and outrigger canoes from all over the world compete en masse in this regatta (www.tahitipearlregatta.org.pf) between Ra'iatea, Taha'a and Huahine. Although a sporting event, everyone takes plenty of time to relax on the white-sand islets dotting the lagoons.

🎉 Beauty Contests

Local beauty pageants for each district (plus Miss Dragon for Chinese Tahitians and Miss Popa'a for European Tahitians) are held with great enthusiasm around the Society Islands in April and May, leading up to the bigger Miss Tahiti and Miss Heiva i Tahiti contests.

🎉 Matari'i i Raro

One of the most important dates on the Polynesian calendar in ancient times, the beginning of the dry period on 18 May is starting to be celebrated again, although something different happens every year. The wet season begins for Matari'i i Ni'a in November.

June

There's a lot going on in June as everyone prepares for festival month. Plenty of cultural activities are on offer, the weather is fine and the crowds haven't yet arrived.

☆ Dance School Heiva

Tahitian dance schools from around the country perform at To'ata Amphitheater in well-rehearsed, often huge shows, with gorgeous costumes. It's not as professional as the Heiva i Tahiti but very lively and fun.

🔒 Heiva Rima'i

From mid-June to mid-July, artists from all over French Polynesia gather for this crafts fair at Salle Aora'i Tinihau in Pape'ete. Expect jewellery, woven pandanus items, wooden sculptures and other creative pieces.

🎉 Miss Tahiti

Tahiti has been known for its beautiful women for centuries. But the winner must have more than great looks – she must exemplify the Polynesian traditions that this flashy show highlights. It's a cultural treat and huge event.

July

Here it is, festival month, and everywhere you look there are dance performances, music shows, parades and sports competitions. This is the most vibrant and busy time to visit, and the weather is usually cool and dry.

🎉 Heiva i Tahiti

Held in Pape'ete, French Polynesia's most important festival lasts an entire month and is so impressive it's almost worth timing your trip around. The best dancers and singers perform and there are parades and traditional sports competitions.

🎉 Heiva i Bora Bora

Bora Bora runs its Heiva festival, chock full of singing and dancing competitions, from the end of June to mid-July. This is a smaller but arguably more personable festival than the bigger hoopla happening on Tahiti.

🎉 Bastille Day

It's still widely celebrated and businesses close, but nowadays the French national holiday gets overshadowed by the lively Polynesian festivals going on. But don't let that stop you from toasting *vive la France* with a bottle of Bordeaux.

August

Early in August is a great time to catch performances by winners of the Heiva i Tahiti dance competitions. The weather is often warm and dry and it's peak holiday season for European visitors.

🏃 Super Aito Vaa

A huge solo outrigger race around Tahiti. The 200 best rowers in the country compete in this gruelling yet colorful race that departs from Point Venus.

🏃 Tahiti Billabong Pro

This is one of the biggest events in surfing because the wave at Teahupoo is as beautiful as it is scary. Including the trials, the event (www.billabongpro.com) spans about a month – you can get a boat ride to watch surfers bold the tube.

✨ Miss Vahine Tane

Don't miss this vampy, cross-dressing beauty pageant with its tears, outrageous dresses and sky-high heels. It usually takes place on Tahiti in August or September and there's no official website; ask at your hotel.

September

The weather is usually warm and dry, and school holidays are over, so this can be a lovely, quiet time to visit.

🔒 Salon des Australes

If you love basketry, hats and mats, don't miss this artisans fair. Beautiful items, mostly woven from pandanus and all handmade in the Austral Islands, are offered for sale at the Territorial Assembly building in Pape'ete.

October

There's a two-week school vacation mid-October, so book your flights early and expect happy company from holidaying locals around the islands – especially at family pensions.

🏃 Stone-Fishing Contests

This is how Polynesians used to fish – herding fish with their canoes and stones. This traditional contest takes place on Bora Bora during the first half of October and you can find similar events on neighbouring Maupiti.

November

Pessimists call this the beginning of the rainy season, but Polynesians celebrate it as the 'season of abundance'. The fishing is great and most fruits start to come into season.

🏃 Hawaiki Nui Canoe Race

French Polynesia's major sporting event of the year, this is a three-day *pirogue* (canoe) race from Huahine to Ra'iatea, Taha'a and Bora Bora. Expect lots of people, ringside events on the beaches and a fun ambience (see www.hawaikinuivaa.pf, in French).

✨ Matari'i i Ni'a

Late November marks the beginning of the Polynesian 'season of abundance', which is essentially Polynesian New Year. It's a newly resurrected observance – expect cultural ceremonies at *marae* (traditional temples) in Tahiti.

December

French Polynesians are fervent about celebrating Christmas and this month is marked by heavy shopping and lots of church-going. It's a busy time for tourism, too, even though the wet season is taking hold.

✨ Marquesas Arts Festival

This outrageously visceral arts festival celebrating Marquesan art and identity is held every four years; the next one is in 2019. Fortunately, there are usually 'mini' festivals in between and the next is scheduled for December 2017.

⭐ Hura Tapairu

In an intimate setting at the Maison de la Culture on Pape'ete's waterfront, see up-and-coming traditional dance troupes give their all at this beautiful and inventive competition. It usually takes place during the first week of the month.

🔒 Salon Artisanal te Noera a te Rima'i

Where do Tahitians do their Christmas shopping? At this crafts fair of course. Find *tifaifai* (quilts), sculptures, handmade jewellery and plenty of plastic toys made in China. It's at Aorai Tinihau Centre in Pirae till 24 December.

Itineraries

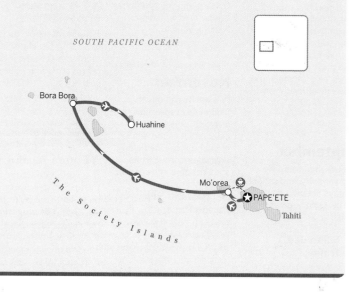

 A Glimpse of Paradise

From Pape'ete, fly or sail straight to **Mo'orea**, and stay for at least two nights. Mo'orea boasts soaring peaks, lush verdant hillsides and aqua waters, and is considered by many to be the most beautiful of the Society Islands. Cycle around magnificent Cook's Bay and Opunohu Bay, explore the island's archaeological sites or simply soak up the sun and splash around in the lagoon.

From Mo'orea, fly to **Bora Bora**. Live it up for a night or more (depending on your budget) in an overwater bungalow or partake in a variety of water excursions on the vast, blue lagoon. Dine by candlelight, relax in a spa and look out for celebrities.

From Bora Bora, it's a short flight to much more low-key **Huahine**, where you can end your holiday with two days of complete relaxation and a taste of authentic Polynesian culture. Go diving or snorkelling, take an island tour, enjoy near-empty beaches and don't miss trying *ma'a Tahiti* (traditional-style food) at Chez Tara.

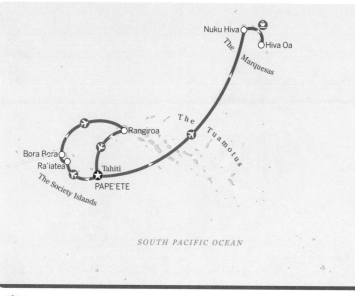

Polynesian Passage

Explore French Polynesia's myriad welcoming cultures as well as its natural beauty. Start with a day or more on **Tahiti**, where you can take an island tour or hire a car to explore Marché de Pape'ete (Pape'ete Market) and the waterfalls, roadside caves and hidden beaches around the island. At night, catch a dance performance at one of the resorts or (if it's a Friday or Saturday) go out for a wild night in **Pape'ete**.

Next get on a plane to **Ra'iatea** to see the impressive Marae Taputapuatea, one of the most important spiritual sites of ancient Polynesia. Hike up the Temehani Plateau in search of the *tiare apetahi,* one of the world's rarest flowers. Dive or snorkel the lagoon and be sure to take a picnic tour out to one of the island's fringing white-sand islets or kayak up Faaroa River, the only navigable river in French Polynesia. From here, take a short flight to **Bora Bora** to snorkel the lagoon, swoon at the island's square silhouette and live *la vida jet set* for a day or two. Then take a flight to **Rangiroa**, the largest coral atoll in the country. Dive with sharks, live in your swimsuit and quench your thirst with coconuts. Don't miss a tour of the immense lagoon to see pink-sand beaches and the surreally beautiful Lagon Bleu (Blue Lagoon), a lagoon within a lagoon. At sunset, watch dolphins frolic in Tiputa Pass.

Change cultures entirely when you fly on to the **Marquesas** (via Tahiti). Travelling here is like stepping back in time. You'll start in **Nuku Hiva**, where you can hike across windswept ridges into ancient volcanic craters before checking out the island's array of eerie archaeological sites, including Hikokua, Kamuihei and Tahakia. Take a plane to follow Paul Gauguin's trail to **Hiva Oa** to see the artist's tomb at Calvaire Cemetery and visit the Espace Culturel Paul Gauguin. Don't miss the giant stone *tiki* (sacred statues) at Iipona and several other ancient sites on the island. Alternatively, you could visit all of the Marquesas Islands by taking the *Aranui* cargo ship for one of the world's most unique cruises focusing on culture and archaeology.

BWZENITH / GETTY IMAGES ©

MACDUFF EVERTON / GETTY IMAGES ©

Top: Resort pool and beach, Mo'orea (p75)

Bottom: Fruit and vegetable stall at Marché de Pape'ete (p51), Tahiti

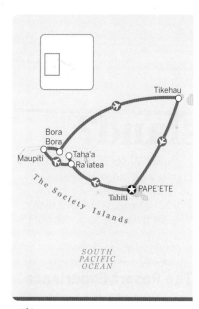

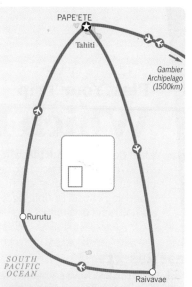

The Ultimate Honeymoon
10 DAYS

The ultimate honeymoon skips the main islands and brings you to our favourite spots for privacy and romance.

Fly to Ra'iatea from Pape'ete, then take a boat to a resort at one of **Taha'a's** *motu* (small islets), which look out over the turquoise lagoon and the awe-inspiring outline of Bora Bora. Kayak, take an island tour to visit pearl farms and vanilla plantations, and lounge in your own private paradise.

Sail back to Ra'iatea, from where you can catch a flight to **Maupiti**, a more isolated and rustic version of Bora Bora. Digs are Polynesian-style bungalows on the beach – nothing fancy, but perfect for snuggling.

From Maupiti, take a boat or fly to Bora Bora where you can catch a flight to **Tikehau** to pamper yourselves at the secluded Tikehau Pearl Beach Resort or at the artistic ecochic Ninamu resort, both on their own private islets. Virtually live in the glass-clear lagoon: dive, snorkel, frolic. Then dine on fabulous food, and drink cocktails as the sun sets. Of course, you could also pick just one of these islands and chill for a week or more.

Roads Less Travelled
8–10 DAYS

Pack a sweater and socks for this voyage since it dips below the Tropic of Capricorn for some chillier temperatures.

Take a flight to **Raivavae**, which has a similar form and magnificent blue lagoon to Bora Bora; only here you'll only find family-run *pensions* and a slow, traditional Polynesian pace of life. Spend two nights here. Follow goats to mountain vistas, explore the near-neon lagoon and meet the locals before taking another flight to **Rurutu** for three nights. If it's between May and October, this is one of the best islands for sighting humpback whales. Otherwise explore caves, take a horseback ride through coffee plantations and enjoy the unique uplifted coral landscapes.

Fly back to **Tahiti** before taking another flight to the **Gambier Archipelago** and its many islands encircled by one gigantic lagoon, for three nights. Explore the strange, majestic and mostly abandoned coral churches built in the 1800s and ogle the pearls farmed here, known as the most beautiful in the country. This is all doable in the time frame, but you'll have to plan well since some of these flights only run once or twice per week.

Plan Your Trip
Which Island?

Most people assume that a Tahitian holiday means staying at a resort, however, French Polynesia has a wide range of sleeping options, from camping, dorms, and upwards, depending on the island you chose. Double-occupancy bungalows, either at a resort, a small hotel or a family-run pension, are the most common option.

Best Resorts

Intercontinental Bora Bora Resort & Thalasso Spa (p130) Overwater bliss on a turquoise lagoon.

Ninamu (p156) Eclectic, naturalistic luxury on a sublime private island.

Sofitel la Ora Moorea Beach Resort (p90) Great-value over-the-water bungalows, fine dining and service.

Kia Ora Resort & Spa (p151) Comfort and style overlooking the country's largest lagoon.

Maitai Lapita Village (p101) Massive lakeside bungalows steps away from an electric blue lagoon and alabaster beach.

Best Pensions

Vanira Lodge (p73) Unique bungalows inspired by nature on a jungle-clad hilltop near legendary waves.

Sunset Hill Lodge (p127) Tiny bungalows at bargain prices with views over Vaitape Bay.

Maupiti Résidence (p141) Sitting pretty on one of the most stunning beaches on an island you can explore on your own.

Pension Atger (p117) Simple and great value, where a family welcomes you to their private islet.

Chez Raita (p165) Warm Polynesian welcome and all the white sand and blue water you need.

The Resort Experience

If you are ever going to pamper yourself silly, French Polynesia is a great place to do it. The luxury hotels often manage to blend their opulent bungalows into the natural setting, be they perched over a blue lagoon or settled back into lush gardens. Many of the top hotels are on isolated *motu* (islets), and can only be reached by boat.

Island by Island

While Bora Bora is undoubtedly French Polynesia's hot spot for resorts and over-the-water bungalows, its price tag is not for everyone. Here's the low-down on resort destinations around the country.

Tahiti

Most people stay at resorts on Tahiti as a stopover to farther-flung islands. Rooms are comfortable, there will inevitably be a stunning swimming pool and great restaurants, but the beach may be artificial. Resorts are all located near but outside of the capital, Pape'ete.

Mo'orea

Got kids? Mo'orea is the best family resort destination in the country; although it also caters well to active honeymooners and seekers of good value. It's arguably as beautiful as Bora Bora, but the resorts have remained more low-key and thus lower-priced.

Huahine

Huahine has some fine, very laid-back resorts far from the jet set. You'll find some overwater bungalows, a great-value beach-side boutique resort and lots of warm Polynesian charm. Come here for complete relaxation.

Ra'iatea & Taha'a

Each island has one or more resorts that are far from the tourist hustle. Taha'a has resorts that rival the luxury of Bora Bora. Ra'iatea's resorts are unpretentious with a natural plantation or nautical feel to them. Both places have the advantage of letting you enjoy the perks of a fabulous resort while having the opportunity to explore a relatively untouristy Polynesian island.

Bora Bora

You'll pay more for less out here – a resort holiday isn't going to be much fun on this island if you have to worry about money. If you've got cash to burn, however, this is the Pacific's most opulent pyre. Private islands and over-the-water bungalows are the signature offering as well as sightings of the rich and famous. Beyond top-notch choices, there are midrange options near or on a main island beach.

The Tuamotus

Coral atolls are the ideal destination for divers, snorkellers and anyone who really wants to get away from it all. Rangiroa, Manihi and Tikehau all have sublime resorts. On Rangiroa, you'll be in the main village and between other hotels and houses unless you stay at Kia Ora Sauvage. The romantic resorts on Tikehau and Manihi are more isolated with their own private beaches and regular shuttle boats to explore the villages.

The Marquesas

The two resorts in the Marquesas (one on Nuku Hiva and one on Hiva Oa) are both hilltop retreats offering swimming pools and fine dining before guests hit the jungles and dirt roads via 4WD. The resorts are reasonably comfortable, but this is a destination for those seeking outdoors, archaeology, history, culture and art – not the beach.

PRICE RANGES

The following price ranges refer to a double room with bathroom in high season unless otherwise specified. Prices include all taxes.

$ less than 10,000 CFP

$$ 10,000–20,000 CFP

$$$ more than 20,000 CFP

What to Expect

You can expect restaurants, bars, a swimming pool, a shop or two and a well organised activities desk. Glass-bottomed coffee tables, which look straight down into the lagoon, have become standard features of the overwater bungalows. Most will also have terraces.

You'll be met at the airport by your resort representative, offered a flower *hei* (necklace) and then be transferred to your resort – either by a waiting speedboat, airplane or van. After registration, often done while sipping a fresh, chilled glass of fruit juice, you'll be given the choice to partake in organised activities or just chill and explore the island on your own.

Food & Drink

All resorts will have at least one restaurant that will serve a mix of Western, Polynesian, Asian and fusion specialties, usually prepared by an international chef. The bar will be stocked and a good wine selection will be available. Most of the bigger hotels put on a Polynesian dance

CAMPING & HOSTELS

Camping options come and go, but generally it's a matter of *pensions* having areas where you can pitch your tent and use their facilities; you'll pay anywhere from around 1200 CFP to 2500 CFP per person. You'll find camping on Tahiti, Mo'orea, Huahine, Ra'iatea, Bora Bora, Maupiti, Rangiroa, Tikehau and Mataiva. A scant number of guesthouses (on Tahiti, Mo'orea, Bora Bora, Rangiroa and Huahine) have dorm beds ranging from 2000 CFP to 3500 CFP per person per night.

HOLIDAY RENTALS

Holiday rentals (private homes or rooms rented by an individual) are becoming more popular in French Polynesia, particularly on Mo'orea, although there are also some good options on Tahiti. These often have self-catering options and can be fun and economical for families or people travelling in larger groups who plan on staying in one place for more than a night or two.

To search further, good sites include the following:

➡ www.airbnb.com
➡ www.homeaway.com
➡ www.vrbo.com

performance, often with buffet meal, a few times a week. Breakfast is often a buffet and at other times meals will be à la carte, with more simple options such as burgers and sandwiches available at lunch. Dinners can be real gastronomic extravaganzas with multicourse tasting menus served with French wines – or you can always order à la carte. For more simple dinners at more reasonable prices, you may have to leave the resort.

The Pension or Small Hotel Experience

Pensions are a godsend for travellers who baulk at the prices of the big hotels and enjoy more independence and contact with local culture. These little establishments, generally family-run affairs, are great places to meet locals and other travellers. Upmarket versions can be private and quite luxurious, and have lots of amenities. At the lower end of the scale, brace yourself for cold showers, lumpy pillows and thin walls, but lap up the charm and culture.

Think ahead in terms of money, as many *pensions* do not take credit cards.

Island by Island

Pensions are found throughout French Polynesia and allow you to explore some very remote islands if you're up for an adventure. Small hotels are found mostly on the more touristed islands. The main difference between the two is the level of contact you're likely to have with the management; at *pensions* the owners usually take care of their guests almost like family, while small hotels will offer you services but leave you on your own and expect you to be more independent. *Pensions* may have private bungalows or rooms in a house with either private or shared bathrooms, while small hotels usually offer en-suite rooms in a building.

Tahiti

There are small hotels and *pensions* all around Tahiti, from vaguely tacky waterfront business hotels to artistic French-run hilltop bungalows, to surf lodges and Balinese-style villas.

Mo'orea

Mo'orea is one of the few islands that has a handful of backpacker-style accommodation and camping. It also has some very homey local-run places that will treat you like family, some midrange bargains right on the beach and even some extremely high-end villas on private *motu*.

Huahine

Huahine is swarming with wonderful homey *pensions*, many beachfront, and is also home to Chez Guynette, one of the best backpacker hangouts in the country.

Ra'iatea & Taha'a

Ra'iatea has some excellent choices on beaches and hilltops. Taha'a has mostly more chic, upmarket choices that include meals and activities.

Bora Bora

The *pensions* on Bora Bora don't give much bang for your buck and there are a scant few, so book in advance if you want to snag a good room. Fortunately, most are around Matira Point, one of the best beaches.

Maupiti

This is one of the world's most beautiful islands and you can choose to stay on a dreamy white-sand *motu* or the charming main island. There are no resorts here, so it's a very low-key sort of traveller vibe.

The Tuamotus

Life on poor soil with little fresh water is a bit rough, but many higher-end places will buffer you from that – still, you'll see firsthand how the locals live. Most places will include meals.

The Marquesas

If you're staying outside of Nuku Hiva and Hiva Oa you'll have no choice but to stay at a *pension*. Choices range from bare-bones to very comfortable, and most places will include two or three meals per day in the price. The welcome in these islands is particularly warm.

The Australs & Gambier

Rurutu has one relatively swanky hotel, while on the rest of these islands a *pension* will be the only option. These range from a musty room in the back of grandma's house to professionally run bungalow operations offering plenty of tourist support and excursions.

What to Expect

Some *pensions* on main islands have aircon; many will be fan-cooled and provide mosquito nets and mosquito coils. Few have pools. All should have towels and linens. Most places will pick you up at the airport if you've arranged it in advance.

On the main islands, some pensions are more like boutique hotels. On the more remote islands, however, you may encounter faulty plumbing, cold showers, unreliable electricity and a rustic set-up. If you need wi-fi or internet, check in advance to make sure your place will have it.

Expect to meet other travellers (often European), chat a bit with your host family, play with their kids and pet their dogs.

Food & Drink

Many *pensions* offer (and sometimes insist upon) half-board (or *demi-pension*), which usually means breakfast and dinner eaten with the family and other guests. Full board means all meals are included. In many cases, the food is a mix of French, Chinese and Tahitian and, on less touristy islands, there might not be other eating options available anyway.

Small hotels often have breakfast included in their tariff and may have a restaurant for lunch and dinner as well.

> **TOP SPAS**
>
> → **Intercontinental Bora Bora Resort & Thalasso Spa** (p130)
> → **Hilton Moorea Lagoon Resort & Spa** (p86)
> → **St Régis Resort, Bora Bora** (p130)
> → **Sofitel Bora Bora Private Island** (p130)

These restaurants are usually of high quality and popular with locals. You'll dine at your own table and order à la carte with a range of offerings.

If there's no restaurant, many small hotels and *pensions* offer transport to nearby options.

Activities

If you're staying at a *pension* on a remote island it's a good idea to organise activities before you go, or at least to let your hosts know that you'll be interested in what's on offer. Resorts and upscale *pensions* will always have plenty of activities available for their guests or work with independent operators they know and trust.

Lagoon Tours

Lagoon tours are the best means to see an island. Picnics are often included – this might mean *poisson cru* (raw fish in coconut milk) and other foods prepared for the day, or it might mean a seafood barbecue on the beach. Whatever the case, cruising around the lagoon in a speedboat with a bunch of food and drink is the way most Polynesians like to spend their weekends – so, even though you'll feel like a tourist, you'll actually be acting like a local.

The length and price of the tour will depend on where you're going, but you can expect a half-day to cost 3000 CFP to 5000 CFP, and a full day to cost 7000 CFP to 10,000 CFP. Resorts often run their own tours while there are also usually independent tours available; the latter will usually be cheaper and a more local experience.

Diving

Many resorts have dive centres, and *pensions* will always hook you up with diving if it's available on the island.

Spa Treatments

Almost all top-end resorts have a spa. Therapies make the most of the local bounty and can include luxuries such as black-pearl and vanilla scrubs, coconut-based *monoi* massage oils, Polynesian healer–inspired remedies and baths full of fragrant tropical flowers. The best take advantage of the view – for example the Deep Ocean Spa at the Intercontinental Bora Bora Resort & Thalasso Spa lets you gaze at the island's iconic peak and look through glass floor panels at the fish while enjoying their signature sea-based treatments.

Some *pensions* work with local massage therapists who will come and give you a rub down on-site, but for a real spa experience you'll have to book something at a resort.

Water Sports

Most resorts have a water-sports centre (but not all, so make sure you check before booking). These vary enormously – some offer the most basic array of kayaks and snorkel gear, while others run the gamut from waterskiing to kiteboarding and SUPs (stand-up paddle boarding).

Only the biggest *pensions* will have water-sports centres, but even smaller mom-and-pop places may have old windsurfers or kayaks – ask in advance.

Wildlife-Watching

Dive centres on many islands offer whale- and dolphin-watching – some of these places are affiliated with resorts. There are also plenty of independent dolphin- and whale-watching tours.

Planning & Choosing

Independent Travel

Outside of high season (June through August and mid-December to mid-January) you could arrive in French Polynesia without any idea of where you're going or what you're doing and have an amazing trip. During the seasonal rush, however, the better places will be booked so it's wise to plan in advance.

A good place to start planning your adventure is the website of Air Tahiti (p233) to see where it flies, its schedules and its prices. If you've got lots of time and don't mind seriously roughing it, check the supply-ship schedules available daily in the *La Dêpeche* newspaper.

Package Tours

French Polynesia lends itself to the package tour. Given the high price of flights to the region, and the often astronomical price of accommodation once there, a package tour can work out to be a financial blessing. On the downside, package tours don't give much leeway to explore at will. Although most tours offer the opportunity to visit more than one island, you will have to prebook one hotel or *pension* for each destination before departure (meaning you can't swap resorts halfway through if you're not happy).

There's a variety of tour packages available from travel agents and online booking agencies in all Western countries. If you want more than a straightforward combo package, a good travel agent is essential – they can negotiate better prices at the larger hotels and handle Air Tahiti bookings for your domestic flights once in French Polynesia. In addition to the traditional travel operators, there are agencies that specialise in diving tours – these packages typically include flights, accommodation and diving excursions.

Where to Book a Package

A great list of packages available from several different agencies with departures from around the world is available on the Air Tahiti Nui (p233) website. A list of travel agents specialising in French Polynesia can be found on the Tahiti Tourism website (www.tahiti-tourisme.com).

Note that most packages quote double-occupancy pricing. Solo travellers have to pay a 'single-person supplement'. Extra people can usually share a room, but there's a charge for the extra bed, which varies enormously from resort to resort.

Plan Your Trip
Diving

Diving in French Polynesia is a life-altering experience. One of the best destinations in the South Pacific, it offers seasoned and novice divers the full slate: jaw-dropping topography; gin-clear visibility; warm waters year-round; glittering blue seas; gorgeous reefs ablaze with technicolour tropical fish; high-voltage drift dives; and close encounters with sharks, manta rays and dolphins.

When to Go

There are regularly optimal diving conditions through most of the year, except when the trade wind blows, from June to August, producing choppy seas. Water temperatures range from a low of 26°C to a high of 29°C on most islands. You won't need anything more than a thin neoprene wetsuit. Current conditions vary a lot, from imperceptible to strong.

Island by Island

From Fakarava in the Tuamotus to Nuku Hiva in the Marquesas, you'll be spoilt for choice. Just as the individual islands have their distinct personalities, so too the dive sites have their own hallmarks. Just take your pick!

Tahiti

Although less charismatic than other French Polynesian islands, Tahiti shouldn't be overlooked, with about 20 lagoon and ocean sites between Arue and Pa'ea, plus the odd wreck.

The Aquarium (Map p52) Multihued tropicals flitting among coral boulders scattered on a sandy floor in less than 10m, as well as three minor wrecks (an old Cessna aircraft and two cargo boat hulls), make this site exciting for beginners. Off Faa'a airport's runway.

Best for Diving

Whatever your expectations and level of ability, there's a dive for you in French Polynesia.

Best for Certification
Tahiti, Mo'orea, Huahine, Bora Bora

Best Drift Dives
Tiputa Pass (Rangiroa), Garuae Pass (Fakarava)

Best Manta-Ray Encounters
Anau (Bora Bora), Manta Point (Maupiti), La Ferme aux Mantas (Tikehau)

Best Shark Encounters
Tuheiava Pass (Tikehau), Tiputa Pass (Rangiroa), Tumakohua Pass (Fakarava)

Best for Snorkelling
La Ferme aux Mantas (Tikehau), Motu Nuhi Nuhi (Rangiroa), Aquarium (Tahiti), Anau (Bora Bora)

Best for Corals
Roses (Mo'orea), Faa Miti (Huahine), Coral Garden (Maupiti), Motu Nuhi Nuhi/the Aquarium (Rangiroa)

Best for Wreck Diving
The Nordby (Ra'iatea), Cargo Ship & Catalina (Tahiti Nui)

Best Drop-Offs
St Etienne Drop-Off (Tahiti Nui), Le Tombant de Papeari (Tahiti Iti)

Cargo Ship & Catalina (Map p60) This great lagoon dive suitable for novices refers to a shipwreck and an aircraft wreck. Of particular interest is the *Catalina*, a twin-engine WWII flying boat that was scuttled in 1962. Its right wing tip rests on the seabed at 20m. Off the airport in Faa'a.

Faults of Arue (Map p60) On the north coast near Matavai Bay. This area features a good mix of gentle coral plateaus and steep drop-offs broken up by a series of fissures.

The Spring (La Source; Map p52) A very atmospheric site featuring three towering coral mounts and a couple of freshwater springs bubbling up from the ocean floor. Sea turtles and eagle rays are frequently observed in the area. Off Puna'auia on the west coast.

St Etienne Drop-Off (Map p52) A perfect wall dive just outside the reef at Puna'auia.

Tahiti Iti

For those willing to experience something different, Tahiti Iti boasts numerous pristine sites that are only used by one dive centre. The underwater natural formations are the main draw, with a profusion of steep drop-offs, canyons, arches and caves.

Hole in the Lagoon (Le Trou du Lagon; Map p52) Features a large circular basin inside the lagoon, off the south coast of Tahiti Iti. Stingrays and garden eels can often be seen on the sandy floor.

Marado (Map p52) The best dive off Tahiti Iti. Renowned for its abundance of gorgonians, which decorate a steep drop-off peppered with overhangs and crevices. Finish the dive on the plateau, which is alive with small tropicals.

Le Tombant de Papeari (Map p52) One of Tahiti Iti's most stunning dives, Le Tombant de Papeari is full of action. Here the reef plunges into an incredible abyss along a steep slope decorated with large gorgonians, but you don't need to go deep – parrotfish, Napoleon wrasses, red snappers, soldierfish, fusiliers, sea chubs and anthias are frequently observed in less than 20m.

Les Tables de Taravao (Map p52) This wonderfully scenic drop-off is topped with huge coral tables that look like big open jaws. They shelter hosts of small colourful fish that provide photographers with great opportunities in clear water.

Mo'orea

Mo'orea is a perfect place to hone your diving skills before tackling some more challenging dive sites in the Tuamotus. It offers easy, relaxed diving, with a good balance of reef dives and shark dives. Most diving is focused at the entrances to Cook's Bay and Opunohu Bay, and off the northwestern corner of the island. Unlike those in neighbouring Tahiti, the reefs here do not drop off steeply, but slope gently away in a series of canyons and valleys. Sadly, corals are in bad shape, due to the crown-of-thorns starfish, which caused great damage to the reefs several years ago.

Vaiare Pass (Map p78) Lemon sharks and blacktip sharks are commonly seen patrolling around this pass on the east coast.

Tiki Because of the site's long history of fish feeding (though it's a practice that no longer continues), you'll have a reasonable chance of seeing blacktip, grey and lemon sharks.

Temae (Map p78) A special site: on a sandy slope, conger eels wave in the current like some strange vegetation.

Taotoi (Map p87) This hot favourite on the north coast offers a pleasant seascape. Watch for eagle rays passing through a nearby channel.

Opunohu Canyons/Eden Park (Map p78) Famous for the many bulky lemon sharks (up to seven individuals) that regularly patrol the area, in about 20m. Sightings can't be guaranteed, though. On the north coast.

Roses (Map p78) This site features a vast expanse of *Montipora* coral that stretches as far as the eye can see. You might descend to 40m to hover over this gorgeous field for a closer look at the coral.

Huahine

If you want relaxed diving, Huahine will appeal to you. Novice divers in particular will feel comfortable – conditions are less challenging than anywhere else but still offer excellent fish action. There are some superb reef dives off Fare, near the airport (to the north of the island). Huahine Iti also boasts great sites but they're not offered by the local dive centres.

Faa Miti (Map p96) Just before the airstrip, Faa Miti features a series of atmospheric coral boulders laced with sand valleys at around 25m. Keep your eyes peeled for moray eels hiding in the recesses, stingrays buried in the sand, soldierfish, perches, surgeonfish and several species of butterfly fish.

Avapeihi Pass (Fitii Pass; Map p96) A long-standing favourite, just a five-minute boat ride from Fare. The highlight of the site is the dazzling aggregation of barracudas, snappers, trevallies and grey reef sharks. The best opportunity to spot predators is during an outgoing current, when they patrol the pass in search of drifting lagoon fish. The only drawback is the slightly reduced visibility.

Les Grottes (The Caves; Map p96) One of the most atmospheric sites in the Society Islands, Les Grottes features a series of deep, large overhangs and arches carved into the inner reef at about 30m. Dancing rays of sunlight flood through these openings and play with the blue hues. Don't expect swarms of fish – it's the scenery that makes this dive so rewarding.

Ra'iatea & Taha'a

Ra'iatea has the only real wreck dive in French Polynesia. Taha'a has a clutch of superb sites that are suitable for all levels, including lagoon dives and drift dives.

Nordby (Map p108; Ra'iatea) This 50m vessel that sank in August 1900 is easily accessible, right off the former hotel Raiatea Hawaiki Nui, lying on its side on a sandy bottom, between 18m and 29m. Look for the resident fish that hide in the darker parts, including groupers, soldierfish, Moorish idols, lionfish, a couple of moray eels and crustaceans. Visibility is not the strong point of this dive.

Teavapiti Pass (Map p108; Ra'iatea) As in all passes in French Polynesia, a strong tidal current runs through Teavapiti Pass, providing food for the little guys at the bottom of the food chain, who, in turn, attract middle- and upper-chain critters. Expect grey, blacktip and whitetip sharks, plus trevallies, red snappers, Napoleon wrasses and, if you're lucky, manta rays.

Miri Miri Pass (Map p108; Ra'iatea) This pass off the western coast has lots of fish action and delicate bunches of purple *Distichopora* coral.

Roses (Map p108; Ra'iatea) At about 45m, the seabed is blanketed with gorgeous *Montipora* coral formations. Off the northwestern coast, it's for advanced divers.

Octopus Hole (Map p108; Taha'a) A spectacular blue hole that penetrates well into the reef. It's in the lagoon, to the southeast of Taha'a. The entrance is at 27m. For seasoned divers.

Lagon Tau Tau (Map p108; Taha'a) A superb dive inside Taha'a's lagoon – perfect for beginners. Features coral gardens and a small drop-off.

Tau Tau (Map p108; Taha'a) Off Taha'a's west coast. A gently sloping reef with regular sightings of trevally, tuna, barracuda and Napoleon wrasses. Visibility is usually top-notch.

Ceran Pass (Map p108; Taha'a) Off Taha'a, this site is renowned for its spectacular topography and prolific fish life, including grey sharks, barracudas and trevallies.

Tiva Pass (Map p108; Taha'a) Off Taha'a, this site offers a superb underwater terrain and a fine cast of reef fish and pelagics.

DIVING IN TAHITI & FRENCH POLYNESIA – AN OVERVIEW

ISLAND	WRECK DIVES	FISH LIFE	SPECIAL FEATURES
Ahe	N/A	++	Off the beaten track, corals, fish life, great topography
Bora Bora	N/A	++	Shark dives, manta-ray cleaning station
Fakarava	N/A	+++	Shark dives, manta rays, drift dives, corals
Huahine	N/A	++	Shark dives, drift dives, corals
Makemo	N/A	++	Off the beaten track, corals, drift dives
Marquesas	N/A	+++	Hammerhead sharks, manta rays, plankton-filled waters
Mataiva	N/A	++	Great topography, easy dives
Maupiti	N/A	++	Manta-ray cleaning station, corals, drop-offs
Mo'orea	N/A	+	Water clarity, lemon sharks
Ra'iatea & Taha'a	++	+++	Pristine dives, shark & drift dives, corals
Rangiroa	N/A	+++	Shark dives, manta rays, drift dives
Tahiti	+	+	Drop-offs, corals
Tikehau	N/A	+++	Shark dives, manta-ray cleaning station

+ (average), ++ (good), +++ (very good)

PLAN YOUR TRIP DIVING

MICHAEL AW / GETTY IMAGES ©

IDREAMPHOTO / GETTY IMAGES ©

Top: Diving among butterflyfish, Rangiroa (p146)

Bottom: Snorkelling the shallows, Rangiroa (p146)

Bora Bora

Surprisingly, there are only four to five sites that are regularly offered on this magical island.

Anau (Map p124) In the lagoon off Anau, this spot features a manta-ray cleaning station in less than 20m. Visibility is average.

Tapu (Map p124) Tapu is known for its sightings of blacktip reef sharks and lemon sharks, usually found at around 25m. It's north of Motu Tapu.

Toopua & Toopua Iti (Map p124) South of Teavanui Pass in the west of Bora Bora. Enjoy the channel where you can spot eagle rays, or explore the area's varied topography, with numerous canyons, gullies, corridors and swim-throughs.

Haapiti (Map p124) A relaxed dive along a sloping reef, with regular sightings of blacktip reef sharks among very clear water.

Maupiti

Maupiti has some remarkable lagoon dives, and some superb reef and wall dives along the east side of the island.

Manta Point (Map p139) At this dive site to the south of the lagoon you can dive on a manta rays' cleaning station, where cleaner wrasses feed on parasites from the mantas' wings, in less than 8m of water. In theory they're here every morning between April and mid-September (but sightings can't be guaranteed).

Le Petit Bleu (Map p139) This is an easy lagoon dive, with coral pinnacles scattered over a sandy floor in less than 6m.

Faaapu (Map p139) A great reef dive; here the reef features a large circular basin at 12m and a succession of small sandy plateaus.

Coral Garden (Map p139) A superb lagoon dive, with copious fish life and pinnacles blanketed in corals. Great for beginners.

Rangiroa

Rangiroa is the stuff of legend, and one of the most charismatic dive areas in the South Pacific. It's brimming with adrenaline-pumping dive sites, and opportunities to approach big stuff just offshore. The weak points include the rather dull coral formations.

Avatoru Pass (Map p148) Although it doesn't have the aura of Tiputa Pass, this pass offers regular sightings of manta rays and, if you're lucky, a few intimidating silvertip sharks.

L'Éolienne (Map p148) By outgoing current, L'Eolienne, along the outer reef east of Tiputa Pass, is regularly scheduled.

Motu Nuhi Nuhi – The Aquarium (Map p148) Located at Motu Nuhi Nuhi – a coral islet that stretches across Tiputa Pass just inside the lagoon – the Aquarium is an ideal spot to take a first dive; it's shallow, protected and thick with neon-coloured fish. It also seems to be tailored to the expectations of snorkellers, with glassy turquoise waters and a smattering of healthy coral gardens around.

Tiputa Pass (Map p148) With its amazing drift dives and dense concentration of pelagics, Tiputa Pass is almost a spiritual experience. Incredible rides are guaranteed every time, as are great

RESPONSIBLE DIVING

The French Polynesian islands and atolls are ecologically vulnerable. By following these guidelines while diving, you can help preserve the ecology and beauty of the reefs.

➡ Encourage dive operators in their efforts to establish permanent moorings at appropriate dive sites.

➡ Practise and maintain proper buoyancy control.

➡ Avoid touching living marine organisms with your body and equipment.

➡ Take great care in underwater caves, as your air bubbles can damage fragile organisms.

➡ Minimise your disturbance of marine animals. Avoid shark dives when baiting (the practice of attracting animals with scraps of fish placed in a cage) is involved, as it disrupts natural behaviour and may carry an element of risk for divers.

➡ Take home all your rubbish and any litter you may find as well.

➡ Never stand on corals, even if they look solid and robust.

numbers of grey reef sharks at the entrance of the pass. Eagle rays, manta rays, dolphins, tuna, trevallies and hammerheads are also regularly seen.

Tikehau

Although it's less charismatic than neighbouring Rangiroa, Tikehau has its fair share of underwater delights and deserves attention for less-crowded dive sites.

Tuheiava Pass (Map p155) Most dives take place in or around Tikehau's only pass, about 30 minutes by boat from Tuherahera village. Depending on the current, at least three different dives can be done here, and they never disappoint. When the tide is incoming, grey sharks, silvertips, barracudas, trevallies and the usual reef species regularly cruise by. With an outgoing current, you can dive the southern exit of the pass at a place named La Bouée (The Buoy) or the northern exit at Teonai, which both feature prolific fish life and lovely coral formations.

La Ferme aux Mantas (Mantas' Farm; Map p155) The only site inside the lagoon features a cleaning station where manta rays (usually three to five individuals) come to get scoured of parasites by little cleaner wrasses in less than 10m.

Le Trou aux Requins (Map p155) A steep drop-off south of Tuheiava Pass. It features a tunnel that descends well into the reef; the entrance is at 57m, but you don't need to go that deep to see a congregation of sharks that usually hang around the entrance. Massive shoals of soldierfish can be seen at around 25m. The reef is peppered with fissures, ledges and overhangs.

Mataiva

Diving off Mataiva is a fairly recent affair – the first commercial dive outfit started on a small scale in 2014. This is a distinct advantage as it consequently retains its atmosphere of virgin beauty.

La Passe (Map p158) A five-minute boat ride from Pahua, La Passe is an easy, uncomplicated dive suitable for all levels. The highlight is the scenic topography, with large boulders, fissures, arches and canyons that form a lunar seascape in less than 25m.

Toa Tere (Map p158) A virgin tract of reef north of the pass. It's broken up by a series of fissures and overhangs. Plenty of healthy corals and fish life.

Fakarava

A 40-minute plane hop from Rangiroa, Fakarava is one of the most fascinating atolls in the Tuamotus, with a true sense of wilderness, despite its increasing popularity. There are only two dive areas, Garuae Pass at the northern end of the atoll and Tumakohua Pass at the southern end. Fakarava shares the same characteristics as Rangiroa, with the added appeal of much healthier coral formations.

Garuae Pass (Northern Pass; Map p160) Swimming through the intense cobalt blue water towards the entrance of this gigantic pass is an unsurpassable experience. Expect to come across hunting sharks, numerous reef fish and, if you're lucky, manta rays and dolphins. The dive usually finishes at **Ali Baba Cavern**, a large coral basin at 20m, replete with schooling fish. When the tide is

---

THE FIRST TIME

Always fancied venturing underwater on a scuba dive? Now's your chance. French Polynesia is a perfect starting point for new divers, as the warm, turquoise water in the shallow lagoons is a forgiving training environment. Most resorts offer courses for beginners and employ experienced instructors, most of them competent in English.

Just about anyone in reasonably good health can sign up for an introductory/discovery dive (baptême in French), including children aged eight and over. It typically takes place in shallow (3m to 5m) water and lasts about 30 minutes. You're escorted by a dive master.

If you choose to enrol in an open-water course while in French Polynesia, count on it taking about three to four days, including classroom lectures and open-water training. Once you're certified, your C-card is valid permanently and recognised all over the world.

going out, you dive along the outer reef at **Ohotu** or **Maiuru**, away from the current. Here you can find some really healthy coral gardens and scenic white-sand valleys.

Pufana (The Red Buoy; Map p160) This easy site inside the lagoon is great for brushing up your skills before tackling the atoll's passes.

Tumakohua Pass (Southern Pass; Map p160) This iconic pass at the southern end of the atoll is renowned for its shark population. When the tide is incoming, dozens of grey reef sharks (up to 300 individuals on one single dive!) can be seen along the right side of the pass, at 28m. At the entrance of the pass, you'll see a profusion of small and large reef fish, including bigeyes and marbled groupers (they breed here in June and July). Other attractions include white-sand gullies, where whitetip sharks usually lie, as well as healthy coral formations in the shallows at the end of the dive.

Toau

You've probably never heard about Toau, and for good reason: this is wilderness at its best. This atoll is almost uninhabited and absolutely pristine. There's no infrastructure but it's accessible from neighbouring Fakarava atoll. When the weather conditions are optimal, Fakarava's dive centres sometimes organise day trips there. Don't miss the opportunity to sample some sensational dives in the two spectacular passes.

Ahe

Yes, there's now diving on Ahe! This off-the-beaten track island is a true gem with a smattering of untouched sites for those willing to venture away from the tourist areas. Another draw is the atmosphere: there's a true sense of eeriness and you'll have the sites to yourself. Ahe has only one pass, with dive sites around it.

Tiarerloa Pass A 30-minute boat ride from the local dive centre, this pass is a stunner. The usual dive plan is a drift dive with the incoming current. You'll be captivated by the prolific fish life, including barracudas, leopard rays, spear-fish and emperor fish. The pass also features a big arch and numerous canyons. With an outgoing current, you can dive the northern or southern wall of the pass. Every year in around May–June, masses of marbled groupers come to breed here.

Makemo

Makemo is still a secret, word-of-mouth destination for divers. If you venture this far in the central Tuamotus, you'll be rewarded with pristine sites.

Arikitamiro Pass This pass is a mere five-minute boat ride from Pouheva. Sharks, Napoleon wrasses, barracuda, tuna, groupers and the whole gamut of tropicals can be spotted here. As if it wasn't enough, the reef is perforated with canyons and swim-throughs and the corals are in good condition. At least four different dives can be done here.

The Marquesas

A three-hour flight from Tahiti, the Marquesas open up a whole new world of diving. The main highlight is the dramatic seascape, with numerous drop-offs, caverns, arches and ledges, giving the sites a peculiarly sculpted look and an eerie atmosphere. To top it all off, the environment is still unspoiled. However, don't expect gin-clear waters. Since the Marquesas are devoid of any protective barrier reefs, the water is thick with plankton and visibility doesn't exceed 10m to 15m. You should also be prepared to cope with sometimes difficult conditions to get to the sites. Diving is available on a very small scale on Nuku Hiva only.

Sentinelle aux Marteaux (Map p169; Nuku Hiva) At the entrance of Taiohae Bay, this is a great spot to see hammerheads. Sadly, visibility usually doesn't exceed 10m.

Cap Martin (Tikapo Point; Map p169; Nuku Hiva) Cap Martin is a point that juts out into the ocean, to the southeast of the island. The dive takes place in a safe, protected area. The varied underwater terrain acts as a magnet for a host of species, including hammerheads, manta rays, leopard rays and stingrays.

Tikapo (Map p169; Nuku Hiva) Off Cap Martin (Tikapo Point), to the southeast of Nuku Hiva, this is a sensational site packed with fish action. Expect strong currents, though. For advanced divers.

Motumano Point (Map p169; Nuku Hiva) Off the southwestern coast of the island, this site is known for its concentration of manta rays, eagle rays and sharks.

Dive Centres

There are about 25 professional dive centres in French Polynesia. They are open year-round, most of them every day. All are land-based and many of them are attached to a hotel (but welcome nonguests). You can expect the following from the dive centres:

➜ They offer a whole range of services and products, such as introductory dives (for children aged eight years and over, and adults), Nitrox dives, night dives, exploratory dives and certification programs. They typically offer two to four dives a day.

➜ All are affiliated to one or more internationally recognised certifying agencies (PADI, CMAS, SSI).

➜ All require you to have a dive medical certificate if you enrol in a certification course, which they can arrange (about 3200 CFP).

➜ In general, equipment is well maintained, facilities are well equipped and staff are friendly, knowledgeable and can speak English.

➜ Most offer free pick-up from, and drop off to, your accommodation.

➜ Almost all accept credit cards.

Live-Aboards

Only two live-aboards operate on a regular basis in French Polynesia. Prices start at €2400 for a week.

Aqua Polynésie (www.aquatiki.com) This reliable operator runs excellent live-aboard dive trips aboard a luxurious 18m catamaran around the northern Tuamotus and, on occasion, the Marquesas. Trip lengths vary from nine to 18 days. The nine-day/eight-night voyages, which serve Fakarava, Toau and Kauehi, are among the most popular. Departures are from Fakarava, Makemo (Tuamotu) or Nuku Hiva (Marquesas).

Niyati Plongée (☑87 79 10 54; www. niyati-plongee.com) Based in Ra'iatea. Operates a live-aboard dive boat that specialises in the Society Islands. Small groups only (maximum four people).

Master Liveaboards (☑+66 0 76 367 444; www.masterliveaboards.com) This operator started launching live-aboard dive trips around the Tuamotus in 2016. Trip lengths vary from seven to 10 nights and cost from US$4300. Trips around the Marquesas are also an option.

Costs

Diving in French Polynesia is fairly expensive; expect to pay about 7000 CFP to 9000 CFP for a single dive. However, there are multidive packages, which become much cheaper per dive. Prices include equipment rental, so you don't need to bring all your gear. Count on between 8000 CFP and 10,000 CFP for an introductory/discovery dive and from 55,000 CFP for an open-water course.

Topdive (www.topdive.com) has its own interisland pass that can be used in Tahiti, Mo'orea, Bora Bora, Fakarava and Rangiroa. Another good-value pass is Te Moana Pass (www.temoanadiving.com), an inter-island dive pass that's accepted in 16 dive shops in French Polynesia and can be used by two divers. Purchase it at any of the participating dive shops.

Recompression Chamber

There's one recompression chamber in Pape'ete, Tahiti, at the Centre Hospitalier du Taaone (p240).

Plan Your Trip
Travel with Children

French Polynesia is tropical Disney Land. Warm weather, outdoor action – either on the ocean or in the jungle – and a smiling and child-adoring culture makes this the happiest family travel place on Earth. Get thee off thy electronic gadgets and head straight to the beach.

Activities

French Polynesia is a water playground for all ages. But beyond sun and swimming it's also a place of gentle culture and adventures to caves and waterfalls.

Diving, Snorkelling & Swimming

Babies and toddlers will be happy on a soft beach and perhaps with a hermit crab to hassle. For slightly older children, any place with a shallow sandy bottom is a great place to learn to swim. Seasoned swimmers can paddle around the lagoon in areas free of currents and boat traffic.

Once kids are comfortable in a mask and snorkel, it can be hard to get them out of the water. Just be sure that they don't touch or walk on coral, both for their safety and for the preservation of the underwater environment. If no one touches anything, there are few dangers beyond sunburn.

Many dive centres offer 'Bubble Maker' courses for children eight years and up, where kids take their first breaths under water. Good swimmers over nine years can enrol in junior PADI open-water courses, and in some cases even get school credit for it; see www.padi.com.

Best Regions for Kids

Mo'orea
The best beaches, dolphin- and whale-watching, horse riding, dive centres catering to kids and lots of amenities.

Huahine
A true Polynesian cultural experience, plus soft, white beaches and places to swim and snorkel. Enjoy a history lesson by taking an island tour and strolling the Maeva archaeology site.

Bora Bora
The lagoon is like a giant swimming pool and resorts will cater to your every need, including babysitting. Cycling around the island is a good family outing.

Tahiti
Great for teens, with lively beaches, dances and a surf scene. Hike, surf, horse ride and find dive centres with kids' programs.

Rangiroa
For water- and beach-loving families wanting to dive, snorkel and watch dolphins frolicking at sunset.

BEACH & SHALLOW-WATER CRITTERS

Wear plastic or protective sandals when playing in the water to guard against stonefish – fish that look exactly like a piece of rock or coral and have poisonous spines that can potentially ruin your trip. Another critter to look out for is the sea urchin, which often live on coral and in crevices. They are less present in the daytime but are another great reason to protect your feet in the water and never walk on coral.

What you're more likely to see are black or beige sea cucumbers in the shallows that can be picked up safely. Be gentle! Hermit crab races make for hours of fun. Then, most importantly, put the track star crabs, or whatever else you've found, back where you found them.

Whatever you do, never, ever pick up a cone-shaped shell. Not all are dangerous but there are a variety or two that are deadly. They sting from the bottom opening where the spine comes out, so are not dangerous unless you touch that one area of the shell.

Wildlife-Watching

Dolphin- and whale-watching will thrill kids, but if it's rough out, the unpleasantness of seasickness may outweigh the excitement of seeing marine mammals. Snorkelling with myriad fish can be tons of fun for all ages, from shallow sandy-bottom areas to coral reef passes filled with sharks – depending on the children's ages and swimming experience, of course.

Surfing & Boogie Boarding

It can be hard to find a board in French Polynesia, but some hotels and *pensions* have them for guests. Boogie boards are often sold in local shops; if you buy one, you'll make a local kid's year by leaving it with them when you leave. The best beach breaks are found on Tahiti and Mo'orea. Surf lessons are available on Tahiti.

Hiking

Kids aged over eight will love Tahiti's interior, which is chock-a-block with waterfalls, many with icy pools to swim in. There are also plenty of dark caves, though these can be scary so take it slow.

Archaeology

French Polynesian archaeological sites are fun for kids because there is tons of open space. You can climb on almost anything and the surrounding jungles often hold discoveries such as wild passionfruit. Remember the mosquito repellent.

Horse Riding & Cycling

There are several places for horse riding on Tahiti, Mo'orea, Huahine and in the Marquesas. In general, the routes go through hilly regions and plantations, and are geared to all ages.

Bicycles can be rented on most islands and, other than on Tahiti, traffic is light. Child-sized bicycles can be hard to find.

Eating Out

French Polynesian food is rarely spicy and most menus have kid-friendly dishes. Don't expect booster seats or high chairs, but do expect a welcoming atmosphere in most eateries. Kids will love digging into dishes such as *chevrettes* (freshwater shrimp), *brochettes* (shish kebabs of meat or fish) or *poisson cru* (fish in coconut milk). Western-style food is also widely available.

For babies, jarred baby food and infant formula can be found even in remote areas. Polynesians love children; don't be afraid to ask for assistance in finding certain foods or cooking facilities.

The water is safe to drink in Pape'ete, on Bora Bora and on Tubuai, but you may like to buy bottled water anyway. On other islands, you will all be dependent on bottled or filtered water.

Teen Nightlife

It's normal in French Polynesia for families to party together; teens are welcome, and usually show up in numbers at any sort of local dance performance or show.

In Pape'ete, discotheques such as Mana Rock Café are swarming with high-schoolers. Be warned that alcohol flows freely and it's a meat-market atmosphere.

Children's Highlights

Beach Yourself

➡ **Swimming & splashing** Temae Beach (Mo'orea) is like a giant swimming pool; Matira Beach (Bora Bora) has gorgeous white sand and shallow swimming; Fare (Huahine) is a mellow, white beach with swimming and snorkelling.

➡ **Surfing** Teahupoo (Tahiti) has a great beach break at the river mouth that's swarming with local kids; Papenoo (Tahiti) is where the island learns to surf thanks to the line-up of easy waves.

➡ **Snorkelling** Plop in almost anywhere in the lagoon in the Tuamotus, but be prepared to see sharks (attacks to swimmers are unheard of); Temae Beach and Hauru Point on Mo'orea offer easy, shallow snorkelling; plunge in from Fare Beach on Huahine for some beautiful underwater life; sandy Bora Bora is a good spot for beginners; the *motu* (small islands) of Maupiti are better for confident swimmers, with plenty of fish and corals.

A History Lesson

➡ **Archaeology** Taputapuatea (Ra'iatea) is big so it's great to run around while learning about it; the *tiki* (sacred statues) at Iipona (the Marquesas) will make older kids feel like Indiana Jones; look for wild passionfruit around Marae Titiroa (Mo'orea).

➡ **European & American contact** Pointe Vénus (Tahiti), where Captain Cook first landed, and Cook's Bay (Mo'orea); Bora Bora's WWII guns; the Gambier for European-style coral churches.

➡ **Museums** Musée de Tahiti et des Îles (Tahiti) has great history displays and is right on the beach; kids who know the *Mutiny on the Bounty* story may appreciate seeing how the author lived at the House of James Norman Hall (Tahiti); Espace Culturel Paul Gauguin (Hiva Oa) in the Marquesas, has a life-sized replica of Gauguin's house and Jacques Brel's airplane.

Budding Naturalists

➡ **Caves** Mara'a Grotto (Tahiti) is set in a lush, fairytale-like park; the brave can swim to the back of a pitch-black cave at Vaipoiri (Tahiti) and let their eyes adjust to the light; Hitiaa Lava Tubes (Tahiti) is best for older kids who can swim and hike well (guides often provide wetsuits for the cold water); Rurutu has tons of easy-access caves full of stalactites and stalagmites.

➡ **Gardens** Tahiti's botanical gardens is one of the best places for kids on the island with plenty

WHAT TO PACK

All ages need sunscreen, insect repellent and rain gear.

Babies & Toddlers
☐ a folding pushchair for most areas; a baby carrier for hiking or exploring archaeological sites

☐ changing mat, handwash gel etc (baby-changing facilities are a rarity)

☐ nappies (diapers) are available (about 2000 CFP for 38 nappies)

Six to 12 years
☐ binoculars for young explorers

☐ a camera to inject fun into 'boring' grown-up sights and walks

☐ field guides to local flora and fauna

Teens
☐ a French phrasebook

☐ mask, snorkel and flippers

☐ a copy of *Mutiny on the Bounty*

of space to run around, vines to swing on, and ducks and two Galapagos turtles to ogle.

➡ **Waterfalls** At Faarumai Waterfalls (Tahiti) look for star fruit along the way and crane your head to see the tops of these incredibly high falls; Vaipahi Spring Gardens (Tahiti) has a beautiful landscaped area around its waterfall.

➡ **Dolphin- & whale-watching** Mo'orea has heaps of boats available; Tahiti is less popular, so you can avoid the crowds; Rurutu is better for older kids who are confident on big adventures.

Planning
Where to Stay

Choosing the right place to stay is important. The majority of lodgings will cater to children, but some are geared more towards families than others. Some resorts offer kids' clubs and babysitting, while family *pensions* are usually a great place for your children to play with local youngsters!

Discounts

The **Carte Famille** (Family Card; 2000 CFP) entitles you to significant reductions on some flights. At hotels and guesthouses, children under 12 generally pay only 50%; very young children usually stay for free.

Regions at a Glance

French Polynesia is made up of five archipelagos, each with a different culture, language and topography. Linked by their history and European colonisation, the islands within these archipelagos hold even more variations between them – you could spend a lifetime exploring the nuances.

The Society Islands hold the places most of us have heard of – Tahiti, Mo'orea, Bora Bora – while we've narrowed down other lesser-known destinations by archipelago name.

Unless you have unlimited time and money, you'll only scratch the surface of this island territory. You'll get a much deeper appreciation for the place, however, by veering off the beaten path, even if it's just for a few days.

Tahiti

Hiking
Surfing
Culture

Waterfall Valleys

Tahiti is riddled with spring-fed rivers that, over hundreds of thousands of years, have carved mystical fern-carpeted valleys. Explore them on foot, preferably with a guide since trails are not maintained.

The Teahupoo Monster

Don't surf? Get in a taxi boat and watch the pros get gobbled into this wave's cavernous tube from so close you can see their facial expressions. Surf? Then you'd better have guts.

Dance Spectacular

Watch the locals wiggle at warp speed at traditional dance performances or local parties. Or get your own groove on at Pape'ete's raucous clubs.

p48

Mo'orea

Hiking
Diving
Surfing

Pineapples to Peaks

Hike or horse ride through jungle-encircled pineapple plantations to viewpoints of peaks carved so intricately by time that they look like they might break off in a strong wind.

Dolphins, Whales & Stingrays

Take a dolphin- or whale-watching tour to see giants breaching and frolicking. You can also get into the lagoon with rubbery stingrays and friendly, snack-seeking reef sharks.

Surfing & Kiteboarding

Surf one of the country's better beach breaks at Haapiti and meet friendly locals in the surf. Otherwise, let your kite be towed over stretches of blue lagoon by heady trade winds past white-sand beaches and palm-fringed shores.

p75

Huahine

Archaeology
Culture
Diving

Ancient Village

Stroll the remains of Maeva, a seaside village that was once the seat of royalty on Huahine. Explore the waterfront temples then scramble up the hillside to find crumbling stone vestiges in the bush.

Lost in Time

Slip into island time in Fare, the somniferous capital of Huahine. Fishing boats come in, fishing boats go out, women in flowered clothing buy groceries and, if you're lucky, the cargo ship may be unloading the island's supplies.

Relax Underwater

Low-key diving, snorkelling and beaches are a Huahine speciality. Expect lots of fish, stretches of sand and mellow conditions; great for novices.

p94

Ra'iatea & Taha'a

Archaeology
Hiking
Diving

The Big One

You'll feel a spiritual buzz at Marae Taputapuatea. Once a meeting place for Polynesians throughout the Pacific, this *marae* (traditional temple) is still one of the most important and well-preserved ancient temples of its kind.

Rare Flower

The *tiare apetahi* is a delicate five-petalled flower that only grows on the Temehani Plateau in Ra'iatea. To see it you'll have to make a challenging hike to the summit and hope for good luck – sightings aren't guaranteed.

What a Wreck

Ra'iatea is home to the *Nordby,* the only real diveable wreck in French Polynesia. Expect fish and corals but not great visibility.

p105

Bora Bora

Resorts
Diving
Hiking

Glamorous Life

Welcome to over-the-water bungalow heaven where drinks are served with a view and pampering is on your tab. Top dining, luxury lagoon tours and sparkling white sands complete the package.

Every Shade of Blue

Bora Bora's sandy-bottom lagoon reflects the sky in so many hues it changes the definition of the word blue. There's not much coral unless you head out to the fringing reef, but it's as safe as a swimming pool.

View from Above

Hike the interior with a guide through deserted forests. If you want to sweat, make the challenging climb up Mt Pahia, the island's signature square peak.

p120

Maupiti

Diving
Culture
Hiking

Gentle Mantas

Watch huge, graceful manta rays come in to have small fish come and nibble off their parasites, all in 6m of clear water. Snorkelling off the fringing islets is also fantastic.

Ia Ora Na

Maupiti is a place where everyone still waves hello as you stroll or pedal by. Islanders are busy tending their hibiscus bushes, gossiping or making crafts to sell from their homes or at the community craft shop.

Summits

There are two peaks to climb: Mt Hotu Paraoa and Mt Teurafaatiu. Both offer splendid views over the turquoise lagoon, and on clear days you'll spot Bora Bora.

p136

The Tuamotus

Diving
Culture
Pearls

Live Large

The current-filled passes are where you'll see the big stuff: sharks, manta rays, eels and giant tuna – and you don't even need a dive bottle to do it. Otherwise take it easy with plenty of fish (and some mellow reef sharks) inside the lagoon.

Desert-Island People

People of the Tuamotus, called Paumotu, are some of the hardiest people on earth: collecting rain water for drinking, farming sandy soil and mastering everything that has to do with coconuts.

Gems of the Lagoon

Tahitian pearls seem to capture the liquid reflections of the Tuamotus lagoons. Check out how they're farmed and buy something special.

p143

The Marquesas

Archaeology
Culture
Hiking

Land of the Lost

Stone *tikis*, temple platforms and the foundations for ancient homes fill the jungles. Often covered in moss and shaded by giant banyan trees, these sites feel like something out of Tomb Raider.

Wood & Tattoos

The most revered wood carvers and tattoo artists live here. Admire Virgin Mary statues in churches, visit carvers' workshops and, for the ultimate souvenir, get an authentic Marquesan tattoo from a master.

Crater Walks

Hike ridges to waterfall valleys and empty beaches or through lush jungles to archaeological sites. Horseback is a local mode of transport and you may find yourself riding with a wooden saddle.

p166

The Australs & the Gambier Archipelago

Culture
Kitesurfing
History

Polynesian Feast

On Raivavae, Rapa and Rimatara, most families eat traditional Polynesian food including lots of taro, tuna and pork. Tubuai is the primary fruit and vegetable producer in the country and you'll see bananas growing alongside peach trees.

Windy Lagoon

Kitesurfers rejoice! Tubuai gets an average of 300 days of wind per year on its cerulean lagoon.

Churches

A coral cathedral, plus several churches and vestiges dot this archipelago with an eerie splendour. The buildings were built in the 1800s. Today they sit near-empty and are scarcely able to be kept up by the residents of the islands.

p193

On the Road

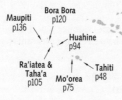

The Marquesas
p166

Maupiti
p136

Bora Bora
p120

Huahine
p94

Ra'iatea &
Taha'a
p105

Mo'orea
p75

Tahiti
p48

The Tuamotus
p143

The Australs
p193

The Gambier
Archipelago
p193

Tahiti

POP 186,909

Includes ➡

Pape'ete 51
Around Tahiti Nui 63
West Coast 63
East Coast 68
Taravao & Tahiti Iti 70

Best Places to Stay

➡ Vanira Lodge (p73)

➡ Mitirapa Villa (p73)

➡ Taaroa Lodge (p67)

➡ Reva (p73)

➡ Intercontinental Resort Tahiti (p56)

Best Places to Eat

➡ Place Vaiete Roulottes (p57)

➡ Le Lotus (p59)

➡ Blue Banana (p68)

➡ La Plage de Maui (p74)

Why Go?

What Tahiti lacks in wide white-sand beaches, it makes up for in waterfall-laden, shadowy mountains, unpretentiously beautiful black-sand beaches, sheltered blue lagoons and a distinctly Polynesian, modern buzz. This is the heart of the islands, where the cultures from all the archipelagos are mixed in the cacophonous, dusty, yet smiling and energetic capital of Pape'ete. Outside the city, explore the majestic, mountainous interior on a 4WD tour, learn to dive in the translucent lagoon, wander amid mystical archaeological sites, and from July to October go whale-watching. In July, catch the country's most spectacular festival; the percussion and dance-heavy Heiva. Stay at a resort or head to Tahiti Iti to experience a more traditional pace of life – all international air travel goes through Tahiti, and it would be a shame to miss such an essential part of this region's cultural puzzle.

When to Go

➡ Tahiti enjoys a year-round tropical climate, but you're most likely to get good weather in the dry season, from May to October. During this time the weather is cooler, and the drier west and north coasts in particular will likely have lots of sun and clear skies – but this is the tropics and rain is possible at any time of year.

➡ The rainy season begins in November and continues until the end of April, with frequent heavy showers and occasional storms, but you could also luck out and have clear skies.

➡ The island has a rather busy social calendar year-round, but in July Pape'ete is in full swing with the Heiva.

4 Tetiaroa Atoll
(40km)

0 ——— 10 km
0 ——— 5 miles

Ferries to
Mo'orea
(25km)

MAHINA
PAPENOO
Onohetia Pass

PIRA'E
ARUE
2 Pape'ete

FAA'A
Faa'a International Airport

PUNA'AUIA

Mt Marau
(1493m)

5 Mt Aorai (2066m)
Diadème ▲ Mt Orohena
(1321m) ▲ (2241m)

Tahiti
Nui

Lake Tahinu

Lake Vaihiria

PA'EA

6
Whale-
watching

TIAREI
3 Papenoo Valley

MAHAENA

HITIAA

FAAONE

TARAVAO

Phaeton Bay TOAHOTU PUEU

PAPARA ATIMAONO PAPEARI AFAAHITI TAUTIRA
Plage de Taharuu **7** 7 MATAIEA VAIRAO Tahiti Iti

Mt Teava
(1306m) ▲
Fenua Aihere 1

Mt Ronui
(1332m) ▲

TEAHUPOO

Te Pari Cliffs

SOUTH PACIFIC OCEAN

Tahiti Highlights

1 Embarking on a boat excursion past the road's end at Teahupoo to visit the remote **Fenua Aihere** (p72) and **Te Pari** (p72).

2 Perusing the colorful **Marche de Pape'ete** (p51) and dining at the very local-style waterfront **roulottes** (p57) in Pape'ete.

3 Taking a 4WD excursion to explore the lushness and archaeological sites of the **Papenoo Valley** (p69).

4 Sailing to the bird-filled paradise of **Tetiaroa Atoll** (p56) for the day.

5 Huffing to the top of **Mt Aorai** (p66) for the sensational views.

6 Witnessing 30-tonne humpbacks on a **whale-watching trip** (p65).

7 Spending the day sunning, surfing and strolling the magnificent black sands of **Plage de Taharuu** (p64).

History

Tahiti was not the first of the Society Islands to be populated in the great Polynesian migrations. Legends have the first settlers arriving in Tahiti from Ra'iatea, which was the most politically important island despite being much smaller than Tahiti.

Tahiti's importance increased as more and more European visitors made the island their preferred base, and it soon became a minor pawn in the European colonial game.

Today Tahiti's population constitutes more than 70% of French Polynesia's entire population. It's the economic, cultural and political centre of French Polynesia.

Geography & Geology

Tahiti is neatly divided into two circles connected by an isthmus: the larger and more populated Tahiti Nui (Big Tahiti) to the northwest and the smaller Tahiti Iti (Little Tahiti) to the southeast. The narrow coastal fringe of Tahiti Nui, where the vast majority of the population is concentrated, sweeps rapidly inwards and upwards to a jumble of soaring, green-clad mountain peaks.

A fringing reef encloses a narrow lagoon around much of the island, but parts of the coast, particularly along the north coast from Mahina through Papenoo to Tiarei, are unprotected.

The mountainous centre of Tahiti Nui is effectively one huge crater, with the highest peak being Mt Orohena (2241m). A number of valleys run down to the coast from the mountains, the most impressive being the wide Papenoo Valley to the north.

❶ Getting There & Away

AIR

Faa'a International Airport (www.tahiti-aeroport. pf) is the aviation centre of French Polynesia. All international flights arrive here, and Air Tahiti flights to the other islands leave from here. Flights within each archipelago hop from one island to the next, but most connections between archipelagos are via Faa'a (fa-ah-ah).

In Pape'ete, **Air Tahiti** (☑ 87 86 42 42, 40 47 44 00; www.airtahiti.pf; Rue du Maréchal Foch; ⊙ 8am-5pm Mon-Fri, 8-11am Sat) is at the intersection with Rue Edouard Ahnne. It also has an **office** (⊙ 6am-4.30pm Mon-Fri, 6am-4pm Sat & Sun) at the airport.

BOAT

All passenger boats to other islands moor at the **Gare Maritime** (Blvd Pomare) in Pape'ete. The numerous cargo ships to the different archipelagos work from the Motu Uta port zone, to the north of the city.

❶ Getting Around

BUS

French Polynesia's once-famous le trucks have now mostly gone to bus heaven. The 'real' air-con buses (still often referred to as le trucks) now, in theory, only stop at designated stops (with blue signs) and run to a timetable, but in reality the routes haven't changed and the drivers will usually stop if you wave them down.

Weekdays, buses around Pape'ete and along the west and north coasts operate roughly every 15 minutes from dawn until about 5.30pm except for the Pape'ete–Faa'a–Outumaoro line, which supposedly operates 24 hours but in reality gets very quiet after 10pm. Buses to Taravao run about every hour from around 5am to 5pm, and buses to/from Teahupoo or Tautira run hourly (and sometimes less frequently) between 5am and 10am, plus one or two services towards Teahupoo and Tautira only in the afternoon. At the weekend, particularly on Sunday, services are far less frequent. Fares for the shortest trips, say from Pape'ete to a little beyond the airport, start from 200 CFP (100 CFP for children and students). Outside this area, the prices are less clear. Out to about 20km from Pape'ete, the fare will go up in stages to around 400 CFP; getting to Tahiti Iti costs 600 CFP.

Tahiti's buses have their route number and the final destination clearly marked. There are basically three routes: greater Pape'ete, which is handy for the Pape'ete–Faa'a airport trip (catch this along Rue du Général de Gaulle); the east coast (catch this along Blvd Pomare); and the west coast (catch this along Rue du Maréchal Foch and Rue du Général de Gaulle). Both the east- and west-coast buses can be taken to reach Tahiti Iti.

CAR

Driving on Tahiti is quite straightforward, and although accident statistics are not encouraging, the traffic is fairly light once you get away from Pape'ete. Apart from on the Route de Dégagement Ouest (RDO) freeway out of Pape'ete to the west, the traffic saunters along at an island pace. As always, beware of children, dogs and chickens wandering on the road, and prepare yourself for a rather casual approach to overtaking. Don't leave anything in view in your car and always lock up; hire cars all have big orange stickers on them, which can act like a thief magnet.

For the price you'll be paying, you may be unpleasantly surprised by the standard of hire cars. Rates start at about 4000 CFP per day with local companies, but expect 8000 CFP per day or more from internationally run places. Prices drop after three days.

Most car-hire companies on Tahiti are based at Faa'a airport and stay open until the last departure. They can deliver vehicles to hotels and *pensions* on the west coast. Some companies also have desks at the bigger hotels.

Avis Pacificar (☑ 40 85 02 84; www.avis-tahiti.com; Faa'a International Airport) Also has a branch in Taravao.

Daniel Rent-a-Car (☑ 40 82 30 04, 40 81 96 32; www.daniel-location.com/en; Faa'a International Airport) Old standby with a desk at the airport and good rates.

Ecocar Tahiti (☑ 89 50 44 77; www.ecocar-tahiti.com) Had the least expensive cars at the time of writing, starting from 4000 CFP. Reserve in advance for the best deals. Also rents scooters. Located across from Faa'a International Airport.

Europcar (☑ 40 86 61 96; www.europcar-polynesie.com; Faa'a International Airport)

Hertz (☑ 40 82 55 86; Faa'a International Airport)

PAPE'ETE

Metropolis this is not. Pape'ete is really just a medium-sized town (by Western standards) of moulding architecture with a lively port, lots of traffic, plenty of smiling faces and maybe a guy or two playing ukulele on the curb. You'll either get its compact chaos and colourful clutter or you'll run quickly from its grimy edges and lack of gorgeous vistas. Sip an espresso at a Parisian-style sidewalk cafe, shop the vibrant market for everything and anything (from pearls to bright *pareu* – sarongs) or dine at a *roulotte* (mobile food van) in the balmy evening.

History

Translated from Tahitian, Pape'ete's name literally means 'basket of water'. Historians theorise that this name is probably a reference to the springs where people collected water.

In 1769, when James Cook anchored in Matavai Bay, there was no settlement in Pape'ete. Towards the end of the 18th century, European visitors realised the value of its sheltered bay and easy access through the reef. London Missionary Society (LMS) missionaries arrived in Pape'ete in 1824 and the young Queen Pomare became a regular visitor to the growing town, which gradually swelled to become a religious and political centre.

Visiting whaling ships made Pape'ete an increasingly important port, and it was

THE HEIVA

The Heiva is French Polynesia's premier festival and is held at various venues in and near Pape'ete. It lasts about four weeks from late June to late July and is so impressive that it's almost worth timing your trip around it. Expect a series of music, dance, cultural and sporting contests.

selected as the administrative headquarters for the new French protectorate in 1843. Chinese merchants and shopkeepers also started to trickle into Pape'ete, but at the beginning of the 20th century the population was still less than 5000. A disastrous cyclone in 1906 and a German naval bombardment in 1914 took a toll, but during WWII the population reached 10,000 and by the early 1960s it was more than 20,000. The last few decades have seen the almost total destruction of the charming old colonial heart of Pape'ete.

◎ Sights

★ **Marché de Pape'ete** MARKET
(Pape'ete Market; cnr Rue Colette & Rue du 22 Septembre; ⊙7am-5pm Mon-Fri, 4-9am Sun) A Pape'ete institution. If you see one site in town, make it this market, which fills an entire city block. Shop for colourful *pareu* (sarongs), shell necklaces, woven hats and local produce in the main hall. Dotted among the meat and fish sellers are lunchtime hawkers selling takeaway *Ma'a Tahiti* (traditional Tahitian food), fresh fruit juices and local ice cream.

Grab an ice-cold coconut before strolling upstairs to peruse pearl shops or sit in the cafe sipping an espresso or smoothie. The most fun time to visit is early Sunday morning when locals flock in as early as 4am.

Temple de Paofai CHURCH
(Blvd Pomare) Although the Catholic cathedral is placed squarely in the town centre, Tahiti remains predominantly Protestant, a lasting legacy of the LMS missionaries. The large pink Temple de Paofai makes an unforgettably colourful scene on Sunday morning, when it is bursting at the seams with a devout hat-wearing congregation dressed in white and belting out soul-stirring *himene* (hymns). The church is on the site of the first Protestant church in Pape'ete, which was built in 1818.

Tahiti

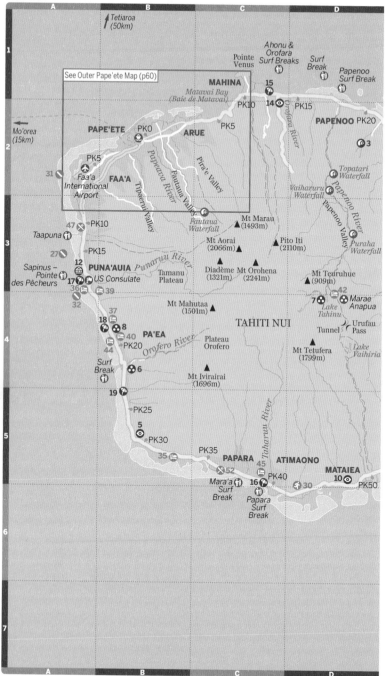

See Outer Pape'ete Map (p60)

Tetiaroa (50km)

Mo'orea (15km)

Pointe Venus

Ahonu & Orofara Surf Breaks

Surf Break

Papenoo Surf Break

MAHINA
Matavai Bay (Baie de Matavai)
PK10
15
14
PK15

PAPENOO PK20

3

PAPE'ETE PK0
ARUE
PK5

Papeava River

Fautaua Valley

Pirae Valley

Orofena River

Papenoo River

Papenoo Valley

Topatari Waterfall

Vaiharuru Waterfall

Puraha Waterfall

31

PK5

Faa'a International Airport

FAA'A

Tipaerui Valley

Fautaua Waterfall

Mt Marau (1493m)

47 PK10
Taapuna

27

PK15

Sapinus – Pointe des Pêcheurs

12
17
36
32

PUNA'AUIA
US Consulate

39

Punaruu River

Tamanu Plateau

Mt Aorai (2066m)

Diadème (1321m)

Mt Orohena (2241m)

Pito Iti (2110m)

Mt Teuruhue (909m)

42
7
Marae Anapua

Lake Tahinu

Tunnel

Urufau Pass

Lake Vaihiria

18
40
8

PA'EA

44
PK20

Orofero River

Mt Mahutaa (1501m)

Plateau Orofero

TAHITI NUI

Mt Tetufera (1799m)

Surf Break

6

19

Mt Ivirairai (1696m)

PK25

5
PK30

35

PK35

Taharuu River

PAPARA

ATIMAONO

45
52
16
PK40

30

MATAIEA
10
PK50

Mara'a Surf Break

Papara Surf Break

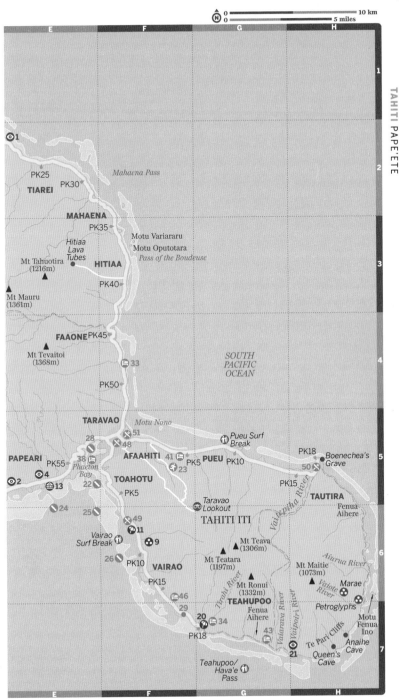

0 ———— 10 km
0 ———— 5 miles

E **F** **G** **H**

1

PK25
PK30
TIAREI

Mahaena Pass

MAHAENA
PK35

Motu Variararu
Hitiaa Lava Tubes
Motu Oputotara
Mt Tahuotira (1216m)
HITIAA
Pass of the Boudeuse

PK40

Mt Mauru (1361m)

FAAONE PK45

Mt Tevaitoi (1368m)

📠 33

SOUTH PACIFIC OCEAN

PK50

TARAVAO *Motu Nono*

28
🍴 51
🍴 48
Pueu Surf Break

PAPEARI PK55
38 🏠
41 🏠 PK5 **PUEU** PK10
AFAAHITI
🏠 23
PK18
Boenechea's Grave

Phaeton Bay
50

2 🎯 4 🎯
🏛 13
22 🛶
TOAHOTU
PK5
PK15
TAUTIRA

24 🛶
Taravao Lookout
Fenua Aihere

25 🛶
TAHITI ITI

49 🍴
11 🎯
Vairao Surf Break
9 ☢
Mt Teava (1306m)
Mt Maitie (1073m)

26 🛶 PK10
VAIRAO
Mt Teatara (1197m)
Marae

PK15
Mt Ronui (1332m)
Petroglyphs

🏠 46
29
TEAHUPOO
Motu Fenua Ino

20 🎯
🏠 34
Fenua Aihere
43 🏠
Te Pari Cliffs
Anaihe Cave

PK18
21 🎯
Queen's Cave

Teahupoo/ Hava'e Pass

Vaitepiha River
Aiurua River
Vaiote River
Vairaru River
Vaipori River
Teahu River

E **F** **G** **H**

Tahiti

◉ **Sights**
1	Arahoho Blowhole	E2
2	Bain de Vaima & Vaipahi Spring Gardens	E5
3	Faarumai Waterfalls	D2
4	Jardins Botaniques	E5
5	Mara'a Grotto	B5
6	Marae Arahurahu	B4
7	Marae Farehape	D4
8	Marae Marae Taata	B4
9	Marae Nuutere	F6
10	Mataiea	D5
11	Maui Beach	F6
12	Musée de Tahiti et des Îles	A3
13	Musée Gauguin	E5
14	Papenoo	C2
15	Plage de Hitimahana	C1
16	Plage de Taharuu	C5
17	Plage de Toaroto	A3
18	Plage de Vaiava	B4
	Plage du Mahana Park	(see 18)
19	Plage du PK23.5	B5
20	Teahupoo	G7
21	Vaipoiri Cave	H7

◉ **Activities, Courses & Tours**
22	Hole in the Lagoon	E5
23	L'Amour de la Nature à Cheval	F5
24	Le Tombant de Papeari	E6
25	Les Tables de Taravao	E6
26	Marado	F6
27	St Etienne Drop-Off	A3
28	Tahiti Iti Diving	E5

29	Teahupoo Tahiti Surfari	F7
30	Terrain de Golf Olivier Breaud	D5
31	The Aquarium	A2
32	The Spring	A4

◉ **Sleeping**
33	Fare Arearea	F4
34	Green Room Villa	G7
35	Hiti Moana Villa	B5
36	Le Méridien Tahiti	A3
37	Le Relais Fenua	B4
	Manava Suite Resort Tahiti	(see 47)
38	Mitirapa Villa	E5
39	Pension de la Plage	B3
40	Pension Te Miti	B4
41	Punatea Village	F5
42	Relais de la Maroto	D3
43	Reva	G7
44	Taaroa Lodge	B4
45	Taharuu Lodge	C5
46	Vanira Lodge	F6

◉ **Eating**
47	Blue Banana	A3
48	Chez Loula & Remy	F5
49	La Plage de Maui	F6
	Le Carré	(see 36)
	Le Club House	(see 30)
	Le Kaimoana Cafe Restaurant	(see 35)
50	Snack du Bout de Monde	H5
51	Taumatai	F5
52	Vahine Vata Beach	C5
	Vanira Lodge Restaurant	(see 46)

Cathédrale Notre-Dame
CATHEDRAL

(Ave du Général de Gaulle) Taking pride of place in the centre of town is the Cathédrale Notre-Dame. The cathedral's story began in 1856, when plans were hatched for it to be built of stone imported from Australia, with a doorway carved out of granite from Mangareva in the Gambier Archipelago. Construction on the cathedral began, but then the money ran out; the original edifice was demolished in 1867, and a smaller cathedral was finally completed in 1875.

Jardins de Paofai
GARDENS

(Blvd Pomare) This is the main walking area along the waterfront, where you'll find paved walking paths that meander past blooming planter boxes and the occasional tree. While the traffic still buzzes by, it's an almost relaxing place for a stroll. As you walk east there are racing *pirogues* (outrigger canoes) lined up on the pebbly shore. Local teams can be seen practising some afternoons and every Saturday morning.

Musée de la Perle
MUSEUM

(Pearl Museum; ☏ 40 46 15 54; www.robertwan.com; Blvd Pomare; ⊙ 9am-5pm Mon-Sat) **FREE** This pearl museum was created by pearl magnate Robert Wan with aims of luring visitors into his glamorous shop. It's a worthwhile, small and modern museum that covers all facets of the pearl-cultivating business. Explanations of the displays are in English, and ogling Monsieur Wan's gorgeous, albeit uncommonly pricey, jewellery collection is almost as fun as the museum.

Chinese Temple
TEMPLE

(cnr Ave Georges Clémenceau & Ave du Commandant Chessé) You'll be impressed by the massive proportions of the vividly colourful Chinese temple, also known as Kanti de Mamao. It's a 10-minute stroll east from the cathedral.

Place To'ata
SQUARE

(To'ata Sq) This square is an evolving multiuse development project on Pape'ete's western edge. The far end of the square is home to a 5000-seat pavilion, which is the scene of the July Heiva festivities; it also hosts rock concerts throughout the year.

Place Vaiete · SQUARE

(Vaiete Sq) Place Vaiete is home to multiple *roulottes* and occasional live-music performances at night, but is quite peaceful during the day. There are plenty of public benches where you can sit and watch the world go by.

Administrative District · AREA

The Territorial Assembly and other government buildings occupy Place Tarahoi, the former site of the Pomare palace. The termite-riddled 1883 palace was razed in 1960, but you can get an idea of what it looked like from the modern *mairie* (town hall), a few blocks east, which is built in a similar style.

On Rue du Général de Gaulle, the assembly building is fronted by a memorial to Pouvana'a a Oopa, the late pro-independence figure of heroic proportions. The High Commissioner's Residence that stands to one side of the assembly building replaced the 1843 Palace of the Governor (those pesky termites again). A more recent addition is the Presidential Palace, an imposing building used by the president.

Mairie de Pape'ete · BUILDING

(Town Hall; Rue Paul Gauguin) Pape'ete's *mairie* is two blocks back from Blvd Pomare and a block north of Marché de Pape'ete. It was completed in 1990, in vague imitation of the old queen's palace.

House of James Norman Hall · MUSEUM

(http://www.jamesnormanhallhome.pf; PK5.5; adult /child 600 CFP/free; ⊙9am-4pm Tue-Sat) Towards the outer edge of Pape'ete's urban sprawl in Arue is this lovely little replica of *Mutiny on the Bounty* co-author James Norman Hall's house. The house is in a shady garden and is decorated with Hall's original c 1920s furniture plus heaps of photos and memorabilia.

Pointe du Taharaa – One Tree Hill · VIEWPOINT

(PK8.1) At the top of the hill at around PK8, pull off to the lagoon side of the road and park in the lot that once belonged to Tahiti's very upmarket Hyatt Regency. From this crumbling site of the abandoned hotel you'll get sublime views of Matavai Bay all the way to Pape'ete, including the silhouette of Mo'orea in the distance.

One Tree Hill was named by Captain Cook who used a tree here (now gone) as a landmark. The hotel has been closed since 1998.

Plage Lafayette · BEACH

(PK7) On the edge of Matavai Bay, this wide curve of sparkling black sand is great for a dip. It never gets crowded. The eastern side is framed by steep sheltering cliffs. Public access is via a path just next to the Pearl Beach Resort (there's a sign).

Tombeau du Roi Pomare V · TOMB

(PK4.7) In Arue, on the water's edge, signposted and just a short detour off the coastal road, is the tomb of the last of the Pomare family. The Tomb of Pomare V looks like a stubby lighthouse made of coral boulders.

It was actually built in 1879 for Queen Pomare IV, who died in 1877 after 50 years in power. Her ungrateful son, Pomare V, had her remains exhumed a few years later and when he died in 1891 it became his tomb.

⚓ Activities

Scuba Tek Tahiti · DIVING, WHALE WATCHING

(☑40 42 23 55; www.scubatek-tahiti.com; Arue, PK4; single dive 5000 CFP) This small dive shop on the eastern outskirts of Pape'ete has the cheapest rates in French Polynesia. A five/10-dive package is 23,000/42,000 CFP. It specialises in dive sites between Arue and Faa'a and has whale-watching tours in season. It's part of the Te Moana Diving Pass.

🛏 Sleeping

Central Pape'ete is not the place to stay if you're looking for tranquillity or anything resembling a tourist brochure; the options on the outskirts of town offer more palmfringed, beachlike choices.

Fare Hau · PENSION $

(☑87 77 21 06, 49 90 05 89; www.farehau.pf; Faa'a; r without/with bathroom from 8500/11,500 CFP; ❄🤶) Close to the airport and to Pape'ete, this simple, welcoming place also has great views of Mo'orea from the terrace. The Moana room is the only room with its own bathroom and also has much more light, but the three other rooms are also good value. All prices include a delicious breakfast and airport transfers are free. Cash only.

Fare Suisse · GUESTHOUSE $

(☑40 42 00 30; www.fare-suisse.com; Rue des Poilus Tahitiens; d 9850 CFP; ❄🤶) This guesthouse is in a spotless and stylish cement home in a quiet area not far from the centre

TETIAROA

Leased by Marlon Brando in 1965 after he filmed *Mutiny on the Bounty* and fell in love with his Tahitian co-star Tarita Teriipia, the stunning atoll of Tetiaroa, 59km north of Tahiti, is now the home of the country's most luxurious 'eco' resort, the **Brando** (www.brando-hotel.com; villas incl meals & some activities s/d from 240,000/288,000 CFP; ❄ 🛜 ☒) 🗲, with its 35 outlandishly plush villas. While Brando was alive, the atoll remained a bird preserve and housed only one small *pension* where visitors could live like Robinson Crusoe in paradise. Brando, a pioneer of ecotourism, always made it clear that he wished the island to remain preserved and that any development would have to be ecologically sound and conform aesthetically to the atoll. Brando died in 2004, and by 2005 his estate executors had sold the rights to development to a major property developer in Tahiti.

The Brando has made a valiant attempt to be sustainable via renewable energy, a cooling system that uses sea water and use of only solar- or human-powered vehicles (among other things), but its critics (notably The Brando-Apocalypse Now, find them on Facebook) claim that the building of the resort was incredibly destructive to the atoll due to its extraction of sand and coral from the lagoon and cultural sites from the land.

There's an airstrip on the island available only to guests of the resort (flights cost around 53,000 CFP return). The only other way to get to the island is by charter yacht, a few of which line up along the Pape'ete waterfront advertising lovely day trips to the atoll. These trips visit several other spots around the atoll, but not the resort.

Chose from sailboats like **L'Escapade** (✆87 72 85 31; www.tahiti-charter-catamaran.com), which take around four hours to sail to the island, or the faster motorboat **Excursion Tetiaroa** (✆87 22 29 210; www.excursiontetiaroa.com; waterfront Pape'ete; day trips per person 15,000 CFP), which gets there in three hours and 15 minutes.

---

of town. The tiled rooms are simple but nicely decorated with bamboo furniture, and are bright and airy. But the best thing about this place is the owner Beni, who picks guests up free of charge at the airport, lets folks store their luggage and creates a super-pleasant atmosphere with his helpfulness.

Great for travellers who want to be close to the action or for island-hoppers on overnight layovers. Breakfast is an extra 1200 CFP.

Maison d'Hotes Tutehau　　GUESTHOUSE **$$**
(✆87 31 19 84; www.faredhotestutehau.com; Av du Chef Vairaatoa; s/d without bathroom from 8000/12,000 CFP, d/f with bathroom 15,000/18,000 CFP; ❄ 🛜) In Pape'ete, an 800m walk from the Gare Maritime, this friendly, clean and colourful little nest is a secure spot in an otherwise unprepossessing part of town (although it's fine in daylight hours). Hosts are helpful with finding you the best deals and there are plenty of hangout areas in the house proper and garden. Bikes and airport transfers are free.

Tiare Tahiti　　HOTEL **$$**
(✆40 50 01 00; hoteltiaretahiti@mail.pf; Blvd Pomare; d 14,000-16,500 CFP; ❄ 🛜) This clean hotel has an excellent location overlooking the water in the hub of Pape'ete, but sadly is afflicted by traffic noise. A somewhat kitschy

favourite with tour groups, it has 38 simply furnished, motel-like rooms that are expensive for what you get; the cheaper ones are at the back and lack views but are quieter. Breakfast costs 1000 CFP.

Intercontinental Resort Tahiti　　RESORT **$$$**
(✆40 86 51 10; www.tahitiresorts.intercontinental.com; Faa'a, PK8; r & bungalow d from 30,500 CFP; ❄ 🛜 ☒) Hands down, this is the best luxury resort on the island. The Intercontinental is as posh as Tahiti gets. Marble bathrooms, plush canopies and Mo'orea views from private balconies are standard both in the rooms and romantic overwater bungalows, which range from smallish to quite spacious.

The two swimming pools are fabulous (one features a slick, cascading horizon) and the water-sports centre is the best on the island. On the downside, the beach here is artificial (it's made from imported white sand) and the lagoon is not nearly as translucent or dreamy as ones that you'll find on other islands or even further away from Pape'ete.

Pearl Beach Resort Tahiti　　RESORT **$$$**
(✆40 48 88 00; www.tahitipearlbeach.pf; Arue, PK7; d from 33,000 CFP; ❄ 🛜 ☒) East of Pape'ete is this hotel on a stunning black-sand beach lined with almond trees and fronted with Mo'orea views. It was being

refurbished when we passed and was looking rundown, but we were assured this would soon change. Nearly all the dark but tastefully designed rooms have a sea view; angle for one on the upper floors for the most privacy.

✕ Eating

Whatever you think of the capital, you're sure to have memorable eating experiences here. You can skip from French to Polynesian to Chinese and back again via Italian and Vietnamese – you couldn't possibly tire of the cuisines in Pape'ete.

Ma'a Tahiti is often served as a special on Fridays at many budget and midrange places, and self-catering is a breeze. The market has fresh fish, fruit and vegies, and there's no shortage of supermarkets.

★ **Place Vaiete Roulottes**   TAHITIAN **$**
(Place Vaiete; mains from 900 CFP; ☺6pm-late)
The country's famous *roulottes* (literally 'caravans' in French, these are mobile food vans) are a cultural and gastronomic delight. These little stalls sizzle, fry and grill up a storm every evening from around sunset and things don't quiet down until well into the night.

There are dozens of *roulottes* to choose from. Get good thin-crust pizzas or everything and anything else from hamburgers to crêpes. Finish your meal with a Nutella-and-banana waffle. Live music enlivens the scene most weekend nights. Cash only.

Patachoux   SANDWICHES **$**
(☑87 83 72 82; Rue Lagarde; mains 600-1200 CFP; ☺6am-4pm Mon-Sat) Takeaway sandwiches here are the deluxe version – fresh wholemeal or French bread stuffed with gourmet meats, fish and/or salads. Otherwise sit at the outdoor patio (on a lively pedestrian-only street) and order from a menu of salads and fresh fish with international flair. Desserts such as fruit tarts, creamy French pastries and a divine chocolate fondant are not to be missed.

★ **Cafe Maeva**   TAHITIAN **$$**
(cnr Rue Colette & Rue du 22 Septembre; mains 1600-2700 CFP; ☺6am-5pm Mon-Fri, 8am-2pm Sat; ☎) An unexpectedly modern place on the 2nd floor of the Marche de Pape'ete that fills three needs: food, smoothies and coffee. For the first, chose from fresh Tahitian and French dishes; the smoothies and fresh juices are the best you'll find in

Pape'ete. Otherwise grab a stool at the table to take advantage of free wi-fi while sipping espresso.

Place To'ata Snacks   TAHITIAN **$$**
(Place To'ata; mains 1300-2700 CFP; ☺11.30am-1.30pm & 6-10pm) This cluster of open-air *snacks* (snack bars) with outdoor seating – Vaimiti, Chez Jimmy, Mado, Moeata, Toa Sushi – near Place To'ata are a great place to chill with regulars and savour the most authentic and best-value food in town (but no alcohol is served). From *poisson cru* (raw fish) and burgers to crêpes and sushi, each joint has its specialities.

Try the *poisson cru à la javanaise* (raw fish with a spicy sauce) served at Chez Jimmy or the crêpes at Vaimiti. The setting is simple; think plastic chairs under the shade of trees. Opening hours vary but there are usually at least two or three places serving during meal hours. Cash only.

L'Oasis   TAHITIAN, FRENCH **$$**
(☑40 45 45 01; cnr Rue Jeanne d'Arc & Rue du General de Gaulle; mains 1400-2600 CFP; ☺6am-3pm Mon-Sat) In a busy, central location good for people-watching, across from the cathedral, this place is always busy, but you won't have to wait long for a table on the breezy terrace. The range of daily specials on offer – mostly French dishes prepared with local ingredients – is well priced and filled with well-orchestrated flavours.

Le J'Am   VEGAN **$$**
(10 Rue Charles Viénot; sandwiches 700 CFP, mains 1900-2200 CFP; ☺11am-10pm Tue-Fri) This hip little spot serves sandwiches on gluten-free bread, and treats including fruit salads and vegan chocolate mousse. Also keep an eye out for daily specials such as tartare of tofu or Buddha bowls full of greens, grains and other good stuff. Wash it all down with fresh ginger juice, a smoothie or ice-cold coconut juice. There are often events in the evenings from music to meditation talks.

Lou Pescadou   ITALIAN **$$**
(☑40 43 74 26; Rue Anne-Marie Javouhey; mains 1200-2800 CFP; ☺11.30am-2pm & 6-9pm Tue-Sat) A Pape'ete institution, this cheery restaurant has hearty pasta and wood-fired pizza dishes. It's authentic Italian, right down to the red-and-white check tablecloths and carafes of red wine. Service is fast and there are lots of vegie options. Be sure to check out the quirky cartoons on the walls.

Central Pape'ete

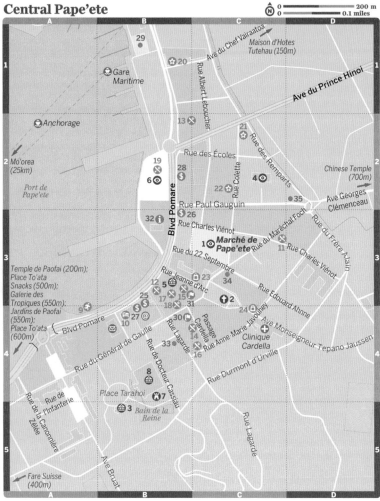

Les 3 Brasseurs BRASSERIE $$

(☑40 50 60 25; Blvd Pomare; mains 1800-2700 CFP; ⏰11am-late) You can't miss the inviting and open facade of this lively brasserie in front of the Gare Maritime. It might feel weird to sit down for *flammekueche* (an Alsatian pizza-like dish) and *choucroute* (sauerkraut) in the middle of the Pacific, but the fare is reasonably priced and quite good. Enjoy with one of the four house-made beers on tap.

You'll also find more mainstream dishes on the menu, which is laid out like a French newspaper. This place stays open late, which is not common in Pape'ete.

Le Rétro BISTRO $$

(☑40 50 60 25; Blvd Pomare; mains 1800-2500 CFP; ⏰11am-9pm) After an extensive renovation, this Pape'ete icon now features trendy furnishings and a hip outdoor terrace overlooking the busy boulevard. The wide-ranging menu covers enough territory to please most palates, from burgers and sandwiches to fish grills and salads. Sit as long as you want and watch traffic, pedestrians and Pape'ete life buzz by.

Le Royal Tahitien TAHITIAN $$

(☑40 50 40 40; Pira'e, PK3.1; mains 1500-3500 CFP; ⏰lunch & dinner) Le Royal Tahitien (af-

Central Pape'ete

◎ **Top Sights**
1 Marché de Pape'ete C3

◎ **Sights**
2 Cathédrale Notre-Dame C3
3 High Commissioner's
   Residence B5
4 Mairie de Pape'ete C2
5 Musée de la Perle B3
6 Place Vaiete B2
7 Presidential Palace B4
8 Territorial Assembly B4

◎ **Activities, Courses & Tours**
9 Excursion Boats to Tetiaroa A4

◎ **Sleeping**
10 Tiare Tahiti B4

◎ **Eating**
Cafe Maeva .... (see 1)
11 Le J'Am C3
12 Le Rétro B3
13 Les 3 Brasseurs B2
14 L'O à la Bouche C4
15 L'Oasis B3
16 Lou Pescadou C4
17 Morrison's Café B3
18 Patachoux B4
19 Place Vaiete Roulottes B2

◎ **Drinking & Nightlife**
Les 3 Brasseurs .... (see 13)

Morrison's Café .... (see 17)

◎ **Entertainment**
20 Le Paradise Night B1
Morrison's Café .... (see 17)
21 Royal Kikiriri C2
22 Ute Ute C2

◎ **Shopping**
Efraima & Simeon Huuti .... (see 1)
23 Galerie Winkler C3
Ganesha .... (see 17)
Marché de Pape'ete .... (see 1)
24 Odyssey C4

◎ **Information**
25 Banque de Polynésie B3
26 Banque de Tahiti B3
27 Banque Socredo B4
28 Banque Socredo & ATM B2
29 Bureau des Yachts B1
30 Chilean Consulate B4
31 New Zealand Consulate B3
32 Office du Tourisme de Tahiti
   et ses Îles B3

◎ **Transport**
33 Air France B4
Air New Zealand .... (see 31)
34 Air Tahiti C3
35 Air Tahiti Nui D2
Hawaiian Airlines .... (see 15)
LAN .... (see 17)

fectionately dubbed 'RT') is delightfully chilled-out – the vast, open-air dining room overlooks the lagoon and the decor is wonderfully c 1975 tiki-tacky. The food is simple and done without fanfare or flair, but the view is serene, and the staff and customers are convivial and relaxed. It's about 3km east of Pape'ete in Pira'e.

Morrison's Café FRENCH, TAHITIAN $$
(☑40 42 78 61; Vaima Centre; mains 1600-3200 CFP; ⊙6pm-5am Fri-Sun) Long-running yet still remarkably trendy, this casually elegant eatery on a rooftop with a view over the city is 'a delightful escape from the main drag. Savour well-prepared fish and meat dishes as well as salads and pastas. It stays open late and gets quite lively on Friday and Saturday nights. It was undergoing renovations at the time of research.

★**Le Lotus** FUSION $$$
(☑40 86 51 25; Faa'a, PK8; mains 2000-4700 CFP; ⊙noon-2.30pm & 6.30-9.30pm) Inside the Intercontinental Resort Tahiti, this uber-

romantic restaurant on the edge of the lagoon is perfect for a special night out; a good excuse to put on your best, but still casual, outfit. Flickering candles, a breezy terrace and the gentle lap of waves will rekindle the faintest romantic flame. The food is suitably refined; flavourful French and Polynesian favourites are whipped into eye-pleasing concoctions.

Make sure you arrive before sunset to watch Mo'orea bathed in a pink glow.

L'O à la Bouche FRENCH, TAHITIAN $$$
(☑40 45 29 76; Passage Cardella; mains 2500-4100 CFP; ⊙11.30am-1.30pm Mon-Fri & 7-9.30pm Mon-Sat) This handsome French restaurant is a perennial favourite with locals and tourists in the know. French-style dishes take inspiration from the tropics and are imaginatively prepared and beautifully presented. The wine cellar is good too.

O Belvédère FUSION $$$
(☑40 42 73 44; Pira'e, PK7; mains 2200-4800 CFP; ⊙11am-1.30pm & 6.30-9.30pm Wed-Mon) One of

Outer Pape'ete

TAHITI PAPE'ETE

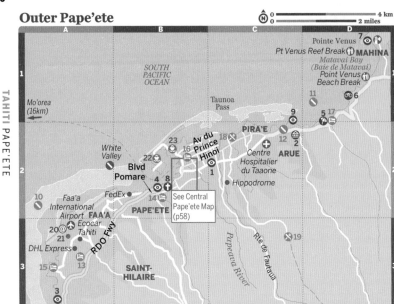

Outer Pape'ete

◉ **Sights**
1 Chinese Temple C2
2 House of James Norman Hall C2
 Jardins de Paofai .... (see 4)
3 Marina Taina A3
4 Place To'ata B2
5 Plage Lafayette D1
6 Pointe du Taharaa – One Tree
 Hill D1
7 Pointe Vénus & Matavai Bay D1
8 Temple de Paofai B2
9 Tombeau du Roi Pomare V C1

◉ **Activities, Courses & Tours**
10 Cargo Ship & Catalina A2
 Eleuthera Plongée............................(see 3)
11 Faults of Arue D1
 Fluid Dive Centre.............................(see 3)
12 Scuba Tek Tahiti C2
 Topdive.. (see 15)

◉ **Sleeping**
13 Fare Hau A3
14 Fare Suisse B2
15 Intercontinental Resort Tahiti.............. A3
16 Maison d'Hotes Tutehau...................... B2
17 Pearl Beach Resort Tahiti.................... D1

◉ **Eating**
 Le Lotus ....(see 15)
18 Le Royal Tahitien C2
19 O Belvédère C3
 Pink Coconut .... (see 3)
 Place To'ata Snacks .... (see 4)

◉ **Entertainment**
 Le Royal Tahitien ....(see 18)

◉ **Shopping**
 Galerie des Tropiques.................... (see 4)

◉ **Information**
20 Business Center A3
 Police aux Frontières .... (see 20)

◉ **Transport**
21 Air Calédonie International................... A3
22 Aranui.. B2
 Cobia III.. (see 22)
 Hawaiki Nui .... (see 22)
 Kura Ora II .... (see 22)
 Mareva Nui .... (see 22)
 Marina Taina .... (see 3)
 Nuku Hau .... (see 22)
 Saint-Xavier Maris-Stella ....(see 22)
23 Taporo VII... B2
 Tuhaa Pae IV .... (see 22)

Tahiti's most romantic dining destinations, with fantastic views over the city from 600m atop a hillside. It was being renovated and re-imagined as a 'concept restaurant' when we passed, but it promises to be as stylish as it is gourmet with fusion dishes in a romantic setting.

There will likely be a shuttle, but if you drive, take the first right after the Hamuta Total petrol station in Pira'e east of Pape'ete. The 7km road to the restaurant is steep, winding and rugged towards the top.

🍸 Drinking

After a stay on other islands, where nightlife is just about nonexistent, Pape'ete could almost pass itself off as a city of wild abandon.

Most restaurants at Marina Taina double as bars, so you can bar-hop on weekends for a low-key night out.

Top-end hotel bars are a focus of Pape'ete social life, especially on Friday and Saturday evenings. It's more fun than it might sound, pulling in a range of locals and tourists. Consider the bars at Pearl Beach Resort, Intercontinental Resort Tahiti, Manava Suite Resort and Le Méridien Tahiti.

Morrison's Café   BAR
(☑40 42 78 61; Vaima Centre; ⊙Tue-Sat) Upstairs in the Vaima Centre is this popular spot for a drink. There's a pleasant, loungey feel.

Les 3 Brasseurs   PUB
(Blvd Pomare; ⊙11am-late) This congenial brewpub has excellent microbrewed beer on tap and a constant stream of locals and tourists wanting to sample it. Cover bands perform here at the weekend and you can also chow on some good French-style pub grub for lunch and dinner.

☆ Entertainment

Dance Performances
Tahiti is a good island for tapping your toes along to some of the best Polynesian dance and music groups, many of which appear several times a week in the big hotels. Those worried about cheesy, touristy performances can rest assured; these groups are very professional and are enjoyed every bit as much by locals as by wide-eyed visitors. When held in the luxury hotels, these performances are often accompanied by a buffet (which usually costs around 9000 CFP), although parking yourself at the bar and ordering a drink will sometimes suffice. Check with the hotel reception desks at the Pearl Beach

Resort, Intercontinental Resort Tahiti and Le Méridien Tahiti about their programs and entrance policies.

Live Music
Ute Ute   LIVE MUSIC
(☑40 53 46 46; Rue Colette; ⊙Mon-Sat) Meaning 'red hot' in Tahitian, it's exactly what Ute Ute is right now. Decor is city lounge–style red and black, and the coolest DJs and live bands play here Friday and Saturday nights. Variable cover charge for music and events.

Morrison's Café   LIVE MUSIC
(☑40 42 78 61; Vaima Centre; ⊙Tue-Sat) Rock, electro, jazz and blues groups play several times a week, and occasionally foreign DJs stop by for a spin. Variable cover charge on music nights.

Le Royal Tahitien   LIVE MUSIC
(Pira'e, PK3.1; ⊙Fri & Sat) Local musicians perform on Friday and Saturday evenings and the place can really rock with locals.

Nightclubs
From the Tahitian waltz to electronic music, it's all here. Dress codes are enforced and men in shorts or flip-flops will be turned away; women can get away with wearing as little as they like. Admission for men is between 1500 CFP and 2000 CFP (usually including a drink), but women can usually get in for free. Clubs typically close around 3am or 4am.

Le Paradise Night   CLUB
(Blvd Pomare; ⊙Wed-Sat) This is the classic, slightly kitsch Pape'ete bar-disco. Playing international tunes, it attracts a mixed crowd of Polynesians and French.

Royal Kikiriri   NIGHTCLUB, BAR
(Rue Colette; ⊙Thu-Sat) A local favourite, the Royal Kikiriri showcases live music with its namesake band on weekends. Just about everyone gets asked to dance and you'll soon be swaying your hips in local foxtrot or *tamure* (Tahitian dance) style. It's at its liveliest on Friday.

ℹ WHAT'S ON?

For up-to-date listings of live-music gigs, DJ clubs, dance shows and cultural events, pick up a copy of *What's On* at the tourist office. Also check the website www.tahiti-agenda.com.

🛍 Shopping

The Marche de Pape'ete (p51) is the obvious place to start any shopping adventure, but there are plenty of great shops as well. Here you can buy products from all over French Polynesia, including clothes, pearls and more pearls.

Odyssey   MUSIC
(off Rue Edouard Ahnne; ⊘9am-5pm Mon-Sat) This music shop has a decent selection of CDs by local artists; you can listen before you buy.

Ganesha   HANDICRAFTS
(☑40 43 04 18; www.ganeshatahiti.com; Vaima Centre; ⊘9am-5.30pm Mon-Fri, 9am-noon & 2-5.30pm Sat) This high-end boutique sells all kinds of quality arts and crafts from French Polynesia and other Pacific islands.

Efraima & Simeon Huuti   TATTOO PARLOUR
(☑87 70 36 34; Marché de Pape'ete, cnr Rue Colette & Rue du 22 Septembre; ⊘by appointment) This popular studio in the Marché de Pape'ete (upstairs) is run by two brothers who are originally from the Marquesas. They create traditional-style black-ink tattoos and have good credentials.

Galerie des Tropiques   ARTS
(☑40 41 05 00; cnr Pomare Blvd & Rue Cook; ⊘9am-noon & 2-6pm Tue-Fri, 9am-noon Sat) This highly reputable gallery has works from established artists, such as Christian Deloffre and Gotz, as well as works from emerging painters or sculptors.

Galerie Winkler   ARTS
(☑40 42 81 77; Rue Jeanne d'Arc; ⊘9am-12.30pm & 1.30-5pm Tue-Fri, 8.30am-noon Sat) This gallery near the cathedral has an interesting mix of etchings, paintings and crockery. It's a great place to buy works from local artists, both well known and emerging.

HOW TO BUY A PEARL

There are so many jewellery shops and pearl specialists in Pape'ete that you have to be careful not to trip over them.

Depending on the quality, you can buy a single pearl for around 10,000 CFP (cheaper if you don't mind imperfections and much more expensive for something truly exceptional); for a decent-quality ring you are looking at anywhere from 60,000 CFP. Also bear in mind that there are numerous pearl shops and pearl farms on the outer islands, so don't rush into purchasing.

When shopping around look out for these qualities:

Shape Pearls come in various shapes, from perfectly round or teardrop shaped (the two most expensive) to misshapen globs. Some pearls have rings etched around them (called *circlé*) that increase their artistic value but decrease their price.

Size Tahitian pearls start at around 7mm and go up from there (the biggest Tahitian pearl ever recorded is 25mm). The bigger they are, the pricier they are.

Colour From black to white to everything in between. Look for greens, pinks, silvers, golds, blues and purples. What you like is up to you.

Surface quality Dimples, scrapes, cloudy spots and other imperfections decrease a pearl's value. A dull white spot anywhere means the pearl is of very low quality, so don't buy it.

Lustre How shiny is it? A high-quality pearl has a near liquid-looking surface with layers of colour.

Nacre thickness This refers to the thickness of the layer of mother-of-pearl on top of the nucleus inside. Nacre wears away eventually so if the layer is too thin you'll be left with dull patches on your pearl, especially if you wear it a lot. The only way to determine nacre thickness is with an x-ray, so in many cases you simply can't know. Use common sense: if you buy cheap pearls in the 1000 CFP bin of shops, you're probably getting a thin-skinned pearl.

But the most important factor is do you like the pearl? Many people try so hard to determine how much a pearl is worth that they forget to take into account their own tastes. If you love it, buy it.

ℹ Information

EMERGENCY
Ambulance (☎15)
Police (☎17)

INTERNET ACCESS
Business Center (Faa'a International Airport; per hr 500 CFP; ⊙8am-6pm & 8-10pm Mon-Fri, 8am-noon Sat & Sun) In the domestic area of the terminal. Also sells local SIM cards.
Cybernesia (Vaima Centre; per hr 1000 CFP; ⊙8.30am-5pm Mon-Fri, 9am-1pm Sat)

MEDICAL SERVICES
Centre Hospitalier du Taaone (☎40 48 62 62, 24hr emergencies 40 42 01 01; Pira'e) The biggest hospital in French Polynesia, with good facilities and a range of medical specialities.
Clinique Cardella (☎40 42 04 25; Rue Anne-Marie Javouhey; ⊙24hr) Private clinic behind the cathedral.

MONEY
There are banks (Banque Socredo, Banque de Tahiti and Banque de Polynésie) and ATMs scattered around Pape'ete and its suburbs. Banque Socredo has a branch at Faa'a airport, where there's also an ATM.

A few places in town will accept US dollars and euros but will give change in CFP.

POST
Post Office (OPT; www.opt.pf; Blvd Pomare; ⊙7.30am-5pm Mon-Fri, to 11am Sat) Pape'ete's main post office is next to Parc Bougainville.

TOURIST INFORMATION
Office du Tourisme de Tahiti et ses Îles (Tourist Office; ☎40 50 40 30; www.tahiti-tourisme.com; Fare Manihini, Blvd Pomare; ⊙7.30am-5.30pm Mon-Fri, 8am-4pm Sat, 8am-noon Sun) Has lots of information on all of French Polynesia. Although Mo'orea and Bora Bora have tourist offices, the more remote islands don't, so if you have any queries, ask here. Very friendly and helpful.

ℹ Getting Around

There aren't any city buses, but Pape'ete can easily be covered on foot.

TO/FROM THE AIRPORT
The taxi drive to central Pape'ete will set you back 1800 CFP during the day and 2500 CFP at night (8pm to 6am).

If you arrive at a reasonable time of the day, you'll be able to catch any bus going towards town from the airport (northeast bound or to your left as you leave the airport), which will take you straight to the centre of Pape'ete (15 minutes, 200 CFP) but services only run until about 6pm.

DON'T MISS

HANDICRAFTS FAIRS

Handicrafts fairs (Salons de l'Artisanat) featuring the work of artisans from across French Polynesia are held several times a year in Pape'ete. Check out the weeklong Salons de l'Artisanat in February and October that are hosted at the Territorial Assembly, as well as the Heiva des Artisans from late June to late July in Pira'e.

Walk straight across the car park outside the airport, up the steps to street level and across the road to hail a city-bound bus.

From Pape'ete to the airport, take a bus heading to Faa'a and Outumaoro – the destination will be clearly posted on the front – from along Rue du Général de Gaulle.

TAXI
All the big hotels have taxi ranks, and there are plenty of taxis in central Pape'ete. Any trip of a reasonable length will approximate a day's car hire, so if you want wheels you may as well hire them.

AROUND TAHITI NUI

It's another world outside of Pape'ete; the sea is a deep blue, the jagged, green mountains frame the sky, and cars putter along at 50km/h. While many people just zip around the 120km circuit of Tahiti Nui taking everything in from their car windows, it's better to do as the locals do by taking it slow, stopping often and soaking in the incredible lushness. And smile, because this is paradise.

West Coast

Tahiti Nui's west coast is busier and much more touristy than the island's eastern side. It has the greatest concentration of places to stay outside Pape'ete, plus many of the museums and major sights. The chic suburb of Puna'auia, which stretches from around PK10 to PK18, has an excellent restaurant scene and Tahiti's best beaches (though this is not saying a lot). The most expensive homes on Tahiti are found along this stretch of coast, along the beach and high above the coast to better enjoy the breathtaking views across to Mo'orea.

> **ⓘ THE PK**
>
> The *point kilométrique* (PK; kilometre point) markers start at zero in Pape'ete and increase in both a clockwise and an anticlockwise direction around Tahiti Nui until they meet at Taravao, the town at the isthmus that connects Tahiti Nui with Tahiti Iti. Taravao is 54km from Pape'ete (via the east coast) and 60km anticlockwise (via the west coast). The counting starts again on Tahiti Iti, where the markers only go as far as the sealed road – there's no road at all along the easternmost coast.

Moving further away from Pape'ete, the coastline from the village of Pa'ea to Taravao is much quieter. Here you'll find a few interesting sights as well as some decent places to sleep and eat.

◎ Sights

The following sights are listed in order counterclockwise from Pape'ete to Taravao.

Marina Taina   MARINA
(PK9) The elegant Marina Taina is a trendy spot featuring restaurants, bars, two diving centres and, of course, lots of yachts.

Plage de Toaroto   BEACH
(PK15.4) This narrow stretch of white coral sand is suitable for swimming and has public facilities.

Musée de Tahiti et des Îles   MUSEUM
(Museum of Tahiti & its Islands; ☑ 40 54 84 36; PK15.1; admission 600 CFP; ⊙ 9am-5pm Tue-Sun) Only 15km from Pape'ete along the west coast, this excellent museum, in Puna'auia, is divided into four sections: geography and natural history; pre-European culture; the European era; and outdoor exhibits. It's in a large garden and if you tire of the exhibits, you can wander out to the water's edge to watch the surfers at one of Tahiti's most popular breaks.

Plage de Vaiava   BEACH
(Plage du PK18; PK18) Beloved by locals, Plage du PK18 is a stunning beach to sun yourself on, but not that great for swimming or snorkelling due to the shallow water. The sands can get jammed on weekends, but that's part of the scene.

Plage du Mahana Park   BEACH
(PK18.5) Plage du Mahana Park has calm waters and a snorkelling reef close to shore. On weekends there are kayaks for hire.

Marae Marae Taata   ARCHAEOLOGICAL SITE
(PK19) This very well-maintained site holds three adjoined stone courtyards, each with its own *ahu* (alter). It was probably used for religious fishing rituals since Papara was, and still is, a major fishing district.

Marae Arahurahu   ARCHAEOLOGICAL SITE
(PK22.5) Whether or not you believe in the powers of the *tiki* (sacred statue), it's hard to deny there is an amazing energy radiating from Marae Arahurahu in the Pa'ea district. Tranquil, huge and beautifully maintained, the *marae* (traditional temple) is undoubtedly the best-looking one on the island and even rivals those on other islands.

Plage du PK23.5   BEACH
(PK23.5) This rather wide (by Tahiti standards) beach is popular with families and has public facilities. The sand is white-grey.

Mara'a Grotto   CAVE
(PK28.5) Lush gardens, overhung caverns, crystal-clear pools and ferny grottoes are all standard features at gorgeous Mara'a Grotto. The fairy-tale park is found along the coastal road, and a manicured path runs throughout.

Plage de Taharuu   BEACH
(Papara; PK39) Everybody loves Plage de Taharuu – locals taking the kids for a swim, tourists on day trips from Pape'ete and surfers catching some great waves. This gently curving black-sand beach is long, broad and fairly protected. It usually has some good swimming conditions. There's also a little *snack* eatery right on the beach if you get peckish.

Mataiea   VILLAGE
(PK48-PK45) Between 1891 and 1893, Paul Gauguin lived in Mataiea where he produced works including *Two Women on the Beach*, *Woman with a Mango* and *Ia Orana Maria – Hail Mary*. The village has two notable buildings – the Church of St John the Baptist (1857) and the quirky Protestant chapel, which looks vaguely like a Hindu temple.

Bain de Vaima &
Vaipahi Spring Gardens   GARDENS
(PK49) Bain de Vaima (Vaima Pool) is where locals come from all over to bathe in the

icy but exceptionally clear waters that are thought to have healing properties. Unfortunately there are so many visitors here on weekends and holidays that the 'clean' pools can get filled with rubbish.

The Vaipahi Spring Gardens further along is a beautifully landscaped garden with a magnificent natural waterfall.

There's a small network of hiking trails that lead from a signpost with a map up to more waterfalls and forests of mape (chestnut) and pine trees. The longest loop takes a little over two hours to walk if you're in reasonable shape – some parts are pretty steep!

Jardins Botaniques   GARDENS
(PK51; 600 CFP; ⊘9am-5pm) The 137-hectare Jardins Botaniques has walking paths that wind their way through the garden past ponds, palms, a massive banyan tree and a superb mape forest. The gardens were founded in 1919 by an American, Harrison Smith, who introduced many plants to Tahiti including the large southeast Asian pomelo known on Tahiti as *pamplemousse,* the French word for grapefruit.

Unfortunately, Smith also introduced one or two botanical disasters that Tahiti could well have done without, including the *Miconia calvescens*, which has caused serious damage to other plants. Mosquitoes in the gardens can be fierce.

Musée Gauguin   MUSEUM
(Gauguin Museum; ☑40 57 10 58; PK51; admission 300 CFP; ⊘9am-5pm) This museum has been closed for years but hopefully it will

reopen during the life of this book. The airy site surrounded by lush foliage is lovely, and although it's not expected to hold any original works by Gauguin, it's an interesting trip through his life and art.

The museum gardens are home to three superb *tiki* from Raivavae in the Australs. *Tiki* do not like to be moved, and there are colourful stories about what happened to the men who moved these *tiki* here (they apparently died 'mysteriously' within weeks).

🏃 Activities

Diving & Whale-Watching
There are some excellent diving opportunities to be had in Tahiti. Most dive shops lead whale-watching tours between July and October when humpbacks swim near the coasts. Half-day trips cost from 8000 CFP per person. Dolphin-watching tours run year-round and are slightly cheaper.

Eleuthera Plongée   WHALE WATCHING
(☑87 77 65 68, 40 42 49 29; www.dive-tahiti. com; Marina Taina, PK9; single/2-tank dive 7900/13,230 CFP) A big dive outfit that also leads whale-watching excursions. It charges 7200 CFP for an introductory dive and 31,500/58,500 CFP for a five-/10-dive package. Nitrox dives are also offered. It's part of the Te Moana Diving Pass.

Fluid Dive Centre   DIVING
(☑87 70 83 75, 40 85 41 46; www.fluidtahiti.com; Marina Taina, PK9; single/2-tank dive 7000/12,600 CFP) Fluid is known for friendly service and

---

SURFING ON TAHITI

Polynesia is the birthplace of surfing, and Tahiti offers some fabulous beginner breaks, particularly at Papenoo and other beach breaks along the east coast. More advanced surfers can head to the Papara shore break and the reef breaks at Sapinus and Taapuna along the west coast and the big and small Vairao passes at Tahiti Iti. Tahiti's most famous and radical wave is at Hava'e Pass on Tahiti Iti where there's a big international surf contest (p71) held each August. In general the west-coast waves break the biggest between May and October, while the east coast is best from November to April – waves are fickle, so this isn't set in stone.

To paddle out for your first time or hone your skills, contact the following outfits:

Aloha Surf School Tahiti (☑89 33 82 09; www.alohasurfschooltahiti.com; group lessons 4500 CFP) Beginner classes on the beaches of Mahina, Papenoo and more advanced sessions at Papara.

Tama He'e (☑87 79 06 91; www.tahitisurfschool.com) Private and group surfing or bodyboarding classes with Michel Demont, world longboard champion in 1994. Prices vary.

Tura'i Mataare Surf School (☑40 41 91 37; www.tahitisurfschool.info; half-day lessons 12,000 CFP) Courses are run by a qualified instructor and include equipment, transport to the different surfing spots and insurance.

DON'T MISS

HIKING ON TAHITI

Tahiti's interior is home to some of the most exquisite – and challenging – hikes in French Polynesia. Bring plenty of water.

Fautaua Valley Trail One of the most beautiful and accessible walks on Tahiti, on the east coast. The easy 4km walk to the Fachoda (Tearape) Bridge takes about an hour. Then there's a rather steep climb, and after about 45 minutes you reach a superb viewpoint over Fautaua Waterfall. Another half an hour takes you to the summit of the waterfall, a prime swimming spot. In theory, the Fautaua Valley trail doesn't require a guide, but we suggest hiring one. You'll need an access permit (adult/child 600/150 CFP), available from Pape'ete Town Hall.

Mt Aorai The third-highest peak on Tahiti (2066m), Mt Aorai's ascent is one of the island's classic climbs. The path, starting at O Belvédère restaurant, is clearly visible and well maintained, so you don't need a guide, but we suggest hiring one for safety reasons. It takes at least 4½ hours of steady walking to reach the top. It's possible to summit the peak and return in a day, but start at dawn because the summit tends to be covered in cloud after 11am. A better option is to spend the night in one of two simple shelters (free of charge) on the route. Each accommodates about 20 walkers, has electricity and is equipped with aluminium cisterns that are usually filled with drinkable rain water.

Lava tubes At Hitiaa on the east coast, these lava tubes are elongated tunnels formed by the cooling and rapid hardening of lava. A river runs through the giant, wormlike caves so that hiking through them actually means lots of swimming in cold water. The hike can only be attempted when there's little or no chance of rain (you wouldn't want to be here during a flash flood) and it's imperative to have a guide. You'll need a good torch (flashlight) and waterproof shoes for the three-hour hike/swim. Wetsuits are provided by guides. It's less than 15 minutes' walk from the parking area to the first tube, at 750m, which is around 100m long. The second tube is 300m long with two waterfalls. The third tube is the longest and darkest, and, at about 100m in, it divides: the left fork continues about 300m to an exit, while the right fork leads to a large cave, complete with lake and waterfall.

Hiking Guides

There are also plenty of other hikes on the island. Most trails require a guide as they aren't marked and it's easy to get lost. For a DIY hike, consider the trail from the Vaipahi Spring Gardens (p64). Guides charge around 6000 CFP per day for two to three hikers.

We recommend the following guides:

Aito Rando (☑87 76 20 25; https://www.facebook.com/aitorando987) Very dynamic guides who have made some new routes. Best contact is via Facebook.

Tahiti Reva Trek (☑87 74 77 20; www.tahitirevatrek.com; hikes from 5900 CFP) Run by a female guide who has lots of experience and offers a wide range of hikes for all levels.

Tahiti Evasion (☑40 56 48 77; www.tahitievasion.com; all-day hikes per person from 9000 CFP) Very reputable operators.

small groups. It also offers introductory dives (8000 CFP) as well as 10-dive packages (49,000 CFP).

Topdive   DIVING
(☑40 53 34 96; www.topdive.com; Intercontinental Tahiti Resort, PK8; single/2-tank dive 9800/19,000 CFP) This large and efficient operation offers a full range of dives, from Nitrox to introductory dives (10,000 CFP). Six- and 10-dive packages (which can be used at

their locations on other islands as well) are 50,000/80,000 CFP.

Golf

Terrain de Golf Olivier Breaud   GOLF
(☑40 57 43 41; Atimaono, PK42; 9/18 holes 2800/8000 CFP; ⊗8am-6pm) Located at Atimaono, this beautiful 18-hole, par 72 course, with some rather difficult par 3s, occupies a pleasant estate that was the site of the 1860s Terre Eugénie cotton plantation –

whose immigrant workers from China are the ancestors of many of today's Tahitian-Chinese islanders. There's a clubhouse here and a good restaurant (p68).

🛏 Sleeping

There are a number of places to stay along the west coast, particularly around Puna'auia. Compared with Pape'ete these places offer much more of a beach-holiday type of experience.

Taaroa Lodge   GUESTHOUSE **$**
(☑ 40 58 39 21; www.taaroalodge.com; PK18.2; dm/d/bungalow 2800/6400/10,600 CFP) Right on the waterfront, Taaroa Lodge has the most luxe location for the price tag on this coast. The dorm is basic and the one private en-suite room downstairs is dark but comfortable. The two individual bungalows in the garden are definitely the highlight here and have lovely views of Mo'orea. There are kitchen facilities and a friendly atmosphere.

Kayaks are free, and the nearest public beach is a two-minute walk away. The lodge is owned by Ralph Stanford, a former longboard surfing champion of Tahiti and France.

Le Relais Fenua   STUDIOS **$**
(☑ 87 77 25 45, 40 45 01 98; www.relaisfenua. fr; PK18.25; studios without/with kitchenette 8500/10,900 CFP; ❄ 🛜 🛆) A great, super-friendly option in Pa'ea, with seven immaculate, spacious and bright studios with TVs set around a little swimming pool. Each little unit has its own back patio. Plage de Mahana Park is stumbling distance away, and there are a few affordable eating options just around the corner, all making this an even better deal for the price. Breakfast is 1000 CFP per person.

Pension Te Miti   PENSION **$**
(☑ 40 58 48 61; www.pensiontemiti.com; PK18.6; dm with breakfast 2500 CFP, d with shared bathroom 6600-7600 CFP; @) Run by a young, friendly French couple, this fun place has a low-key backpacker vibe and is deservedly popular with budgeteers. It's on the mountain side of the main road in Pa'ea, about 200m from the beach. Digs are spread across two houses and include simple but clean four-bed dorms as well as fan-cooled rooms.

There's a computer with internet for guests' use but no wi-fi to ensure travellers talk to each other. Other perks include an equipped communal kitchen, a few bicycles

for guests' use and a laundry service; 24-hour airport transfers are available for 1500 CFP per person (1800 CFP at night).

Pension de la Plage   PENSION **$**
(☑ 40 45 56 12; www.pensiondelaplage.com; PK15.4; s/d from 8500/9500 CFP; 🛜 🛆) Just across the road from Plage de Toaroto, this impeccably maintained place offers comfortable motel-style rooms in several gardenside buildings around a swimming pool. Each has tile floors and giant windows; some have kitchenettes. There's a bit of street noise but nothing to lose sleep over. Breakfast is available for 1000 CFP, dinner for 2600 CFP. Snorkel gear is complimentary.

Taharuu Lodge   GUESTHOUSE **$**
(☑ 87 74 79 32; PK39; s/d with shared bathroom 7500/8500 CFP; 🛜) This surfer haven occupies a colorful, breezy building amid gorgeous tropical gardens. Location is ace – Plage de Taharuu is just across the road. The eight rooms are spartan and overpriced considering they share a bathroom, but the views and cleanliness make this an OK choice just the same. The outside ablution block is in good shape and has hot-water showers.

There are surfboards (5000 CFP per day) and boogie boards (3000 CFP per day), a fully equipped kitchen for self-catering and a vast lounge area. There's free fruit on offer and you'll find several shops nearby. Breakfast is 1000 CFP.

Hiti Moana Villa   BUNGALOW **$$**
(☑ 40 57 93 93; www.hitimoanavilla.com; PK32; bungalow d from 10,500 CFP; 🛜 🛆) Eight bungalows, including four with kitchenettes, set around a well-tended garden make this lagoonside complex in Papara a lovely option, despite the fact only two bungalows have direct sea views and it's all a bit isolated. There's no beach, but there's a pontoon and a small pool. The Le Kaimoana Cafe Restaurant (p68) here gets rave reviews. Free kayaks.

Le Méridien Tahiti   RESORT **$$$**
(☑ 40 47 07 07; www.lemeridien-tahiti.com; PK15; d from 25,000 CFP; ❄ @ 🛜 🛆) Le Méridien has truly lovely grounds dotted with lily ponds and fronted by a natural white-sand beach that has Mo'orea views – if you want a resort where you can swim in the lagoon, this is your best bet. The overwater bungalows are stylishly built with hard woods and natural materials, although parts of the resort are showing signs of wear.

Service is a bit hit or miss at the resort but the waterfront Le Carré restaurant is always a wonderful dining experience.

Manava Suite Resort Tahiti RESORT **$$$**
(☑40 47 31 00; www.spmhotels.com/resort/tahiti; PK10.8; studio/ste from 27,360/30,780 CFP; ✳☎⛱) This hotel is an odd mix of a resort and serviced apartments. Units are modern with clean lines and you won't have staff fawning over you during your stay, although the front desk is very helpful if you need them. The biggest draw is the fantastic infinity pool on a little white-sand beach, all overlooking the silhouette of Mo'orea.

With the apartment-like spaciousness and kitchen facilities in every unit, this is a great choice for longer stays or families. The on-site restaurant here also has an excellent reputation.

🍴 Eating & Drinking

There are plenty of tasty *roulottes* that open up along the roadside at night.

⭐**Blue Banana** FRENCH, POLYNESIAN **$$**
(☑40 41 22 24; http://bluebanana-tahiti.com; PK11.2; mains 1400-3500 CFP; ⊙11am-2pm Tue-Sun, 6.30-9.30pm Mon-Sat) Success has done nothing to dull the buzz at Blue Banana, a hip lagoonside restaurant in Puna'auia. The food is as good as the ambience – feast on innovative French and Polynesian dishes (small portions but artistically presented) and fine French vintages from the air-conditioned cellar. Pizzas also grace the menu.

Make sure you ask for a table out on the pontoon and arrive early enough to sip a drink and watch the sun set over Mo'orea. Reservations are recommended on weekends.

Vahine Vata Beach TAHITIAN, FRENCH **$$**
(☑40 45 50 10; PK36.8; pizzas 1300-2000 CFP, mains 1900-2800 CFP; ⊙11am-2pm & 6-9pm Tue-Sun) In a casual, yet beautiful and romantic setting on a verandah overlooking the black-sand beach of Papara, this place serves unique and tasty dishes. Expect fish with papaya sauce, cassoulet and especially good thin-crust pizzas, although the menu changes daily. There's occasional live music on weekends.

The *gendarmerie* is next door so don't be alarmed if the place is full of cops – they love the food too!

Pink Coconut FRENCH **$$**
(☑40 41 22 23; www.tahitipinkcoconut.com; Marina Taina, PK9; mains 1800-3600 CFP; ⊙11am-10pm Mon-Sat) We love this lively spot located right on Marina Taina with great views of stylish yachts at anchor. Dine on French-inspired fare with a contemporary twist. At night it's candlelit and there's live music and dancing on the weekends.

Le Kaimoana Cafe Restaurant TAHITIAN, INTERNATIONAL **$$**
(PK32; 1900-3200 CFP; ⊙11.30am-1.30pm & 6.30-9pm) Over the water in an out-of-the-way location outside of Papara, diners here can enjoy locally inspired specialties like *korori* (pearl oyster) carpaccio and creative fresh fish dishes. It's relatively new but already creating a buzz and becoming a destination dining favorite for locals who know good food and service when they get it. It's at the Hiti Moana Villa hotel.

Le Club House POLYNESIAN **$$**
(☑40 57 40 32; Atimaono, PK42; mains 1900-2200 CFP; ⊙8am-7pm) At the Atimaono golf course, this is a good find and you don't have to be a golfer to eat here. If you have a weakness for ultrafresh fish, Le Club House is the place to indulge. Tables overlook the golf course and a small lake. It also has a small swimming pool that diners can use.

Le Carré FRENCH, POLYNESIAN **$$$**
(☑40 47 07 23; Le Méridien Tahiti, PK15; lunch mains 2400-3500 CFP, dinner 2900-4600 CFP; ⊙noon-2.30pm & 7-9.30pm) Dining at this stylish eatery is a treat. At night it's a romantic spot to enjoy a gastronomic extravaganza of finely prepared and unique dishes: from breadfruit gnocchi to lobster in orange coulis. Lunch is more casual with treats like seared tuna steak, and even a kids' menu with burgers and the like. It overlooks a stunning beach and blue water.

East Coast

The east coast is the quietest and most isolated section of Tahiti Nui. From lava tubes to waterfalls and a blowhole, it has some seriously great natural attractions. The road winds between cliffs and sea, and the views – deep into valleys and out along the reefless, jagged coast – are simply stunning. Sleeping and eating options are limited on this coast, but it's a must-see for a day trip.

INLAND THRILLS

Archaeological remains, mossy, velvet-green mountains and sensational vistas await you in Tahiti Nui's lush (and uninhabited) interior.

Papenoo to the Relais de la Maroto

The very rough 18km 4WD route from **Papenoo** (p70) on the north coast to the Relais de la Maroto motel follows the wide Papenoo Valley, the only valley to cut right through the volcanic interior of Tahiti. In Papenoo, the turn-off is just past PK17. The Papenoo River is the largest on Tahiti. When Christianity began to spread along the coastal regions, the Papenoo Valley became a last refuge for those faithful to the ancient Polynesian religion, and until 1846 it was also a shelter for the Tahitian rebel forces that opposed the French takeover. There are several waterfalls along the valley, including the **Topatari Waterfall**, the **Vaiharuru Waterfall** and, further, the **Puraha Waterfall**. Between the Vaiharuru Waterfall and the Puraha Waterfall lies the **Marae Vaitoare**, a well-preserved sacred site. Then the track reaches the Relais de la Maroto.

Around the Relais de la Maroto

The **Relais de la Maroto** (☑ 40 57 90 29; www.relais-maroto.com; d 7000-10,000 CFP, bungalows d 13,000 CFP, mains 1400-2800 CFP) is the only place to stay and eat, smack in the lush heart of the island. It was originally built as accommodation quarters for workers on the hydroelectricity project that began in 1980. Under new ownership, there are plans to completely rebuild it over the next few years. However it turns out, it will be sure to offer sensational mountain views. The restaurant is a great spot to break the journey.

The restored **Marae Farehape** site is almost directly below the ridge line on which the Relais de la Maroto perches; you can see an archery platform from where arrows were shot up the valley. Another archaeological site, **Marae Anapua**, has also been beautifully restored and is worth a gander.

From Relais de la Maroto to Mataiea

From Relais de la Maroto, the track makes a very steep and winding climb to a pass and a 200m-long **tunnel**, at a height of about 800m, before plunging down to **Lake Vaihiria** (450m). Most tours stop here before returning via the same route; at the time of research the road was closed further down the valley due to a barricade built by the area's residents. Legal proceedings were under way to ensure that the road would remain accessible both to visitors and to Tahiti's hydroelectric company workers. Check when you're on Tahiti.

Tours

The best way to explore the area is to join a 4WD tour. Specialised 4WD operators do the Papenoo-to-Vaihiria route regularly. Full-day trips cost 6500 CFP; children under 10 are half-price and hotel pick-up is included. You'll stop at Relais de la Maroto for lunch (not included). The following are favourite operators:

Tahiti Safari Expeditions (☑ 40 42 14 15, 87 77 80 76; www.tahiti-safari.com) This is the biggest operator, with reliable standards.

Ciao Tahiti (☑ 87 73 73 97; www.ciaotahiti.com) Comfy 4WDs and good credentials.

⊙ Sights

Listings here follow the coastal road around from Pape'ete.

Pointe Vénus & Matavai Bay   HISTORIC SITE
(PK10) Part of Captain Cook's mission on his three-month sojourn in 1769 was to record the transit of Venus across the face of the sun in an attempt to calculate the distance between the sun and the Earth. Pointe Vénus, the promontory that marks the eastern end of Matavai Bay (Baie de Matavai), was the site of Cook's observatory.

Today Pointe Vénus is a popular beach stop. There are shady trees, a stretch of lawn, a black-sand beach, a couple of souvenir shops and an impressive lighthouse (1867).

The beach is crowded on weekends; however, midweek you'll have it all to yourself.

It's also a popular centre for local outrigger-canoe racing clubs – no doubt you'll see outrigger-canoe teams training for race events. There's a little sign for Pointe Vénus at the roundabout in central Mahina. The site is about 1.5km from the road to the car park near the end of the point.

Near the beach, there is also a memorial to the first LMS Protestant missionaries, who made their landfall at Pointe Vénus on 4 March 1797.

Plage de Hitimahana BEACH, ISLET
(PK11) The black-sand Plage de Hitimahana is exposed to the prevailing winds, which makes it an excellent kitesurfing and wind-surfing spot.

Papenoo VILLAGE
(PK17) There's a popular surf break just before the headland that signals the start of the small village of Papenoo. A long bridge crosses the Papenoo River at the far end of the village, and the 4WD route up the Papenoo Valley, cutting through the ancient crater rim to Relais de la Maroto, starts up the west side of the river.

Arahoho Blowhole NATURAL SITE
(PK22) When the swell is big enough, huge sprays of water shoot out from the *trou du souffleur* (blowhole) in a little park by the road just after the tunnel at PK22, coming from Pape'ete. The blowhole is at the end of the path and there's a small parking lot. Just past the blowhole is a fine sliver of black-sand beach, nice for a picnic.

Faarumai Waterfalls WATERFALL
(PK22.1) Through the village of Tiarei where the road swoops around a black-sand beach, you'll see a sign on the mountain side of the road for the exceedingly high Faarumai Waterfalls. Unfortunately you can't swim here anymore since a tourist was hit on the head by a falling rock, so bring mosquito repellent and just enjoy the view.

It's a couple of hundred metres through a forest of mape trees to Vaimahutu, the first of the waterfalls. Another 20-minute stroll leads to the other two falls, Haamarere Iti and Haamarere Rahi, which stand almost side by side. You technically aren't supposed to swim here either, but many people do.

Sleeping & Eating

There is almost nowhere to stay on the east coast. Heading east out of Pape'ete, there are not many restaurants until you reach Taravao, although there are a few little *snacks*.

Fare Arearea PENSION $
(☑ 87 78 19 20; www.farearearea.com; PK46.5; bungalows d with breakfast 9500 CFP; ☎) It's only a 6km drive from Taravao to reach this remote and wild-feeling spot. The three bungalows with faux coconut thatch sit back on a large green lawn, fronted by a black-sand beach pounded by surf and often laden with driftwood. Each bungalow has a kitchenette and there's a communal dining area steps from the beach. Cash only.

TARAVAO & TAHITI ITI

Traditional Polynesian villages, beaches, archaeological sites and caves are all part of the alluring charm of Tahiti Iti. Unpretentious and beautiful, the smaller loop of Tahiti's figure eight quietly attracts independent, outdoorsy folk looking for a more authentic glimpse of Polynesia. More commonly called the Presqu'île, Tahiti Iti has made a bit of a name for itself in recent years thanks to the promotion of its famous wave at Teahupoo. But despite its surfing fame, there's much more to do in Tahiti Iti than ride the waves. Exceptional walks, boat tours to the incredibly remote Fenua Aihere and Te Pari, and horseback riding are just a few of the options.

Taravao is this region's 'capital'. From this main hub, roads run along the north and south coasts of Tahiti Iti and to the interior, mountainous Tahiti Iti plateau.

◉ Sights

The best way to explore Tahiti Iti is to drive to the ends of both the north- and south-coast roads.

◉ Taravao

Strategically situated at the narrow isthmus connecting Tahiti Nui with Tahiti Iti, the town of Taravao has been a military base on and off since 1844, when the first French fort was established. Today the Faratea Port, on the northeastern side of the isthmus, is being built to shift commercial sea trade here from Pape'ete (which is getting gussied up for tourists). Although there is little of interest in the town, it is growing and has plenty of shops, banks, petrol stations and a number of small restaurants.

North-Coast Road

The north coastal road from Taravao runs through Afaahiti to Pueu, past steep hills and waterfalls, to the road's end at Tautira.

This stretch of coast is one of the least visited areas on the island, though historically things were different. In 1772 the Spanish Captain Boenechea, who was leading the first missionary expedition to French Polynesia, anchored his ship *Aguilla* about 10km beyond Tautira; Cook landed here in 1774; and many years later, in 1886, the writer Robert Louis Stevenson spent two months here. The landings of French Catholic missionaries at Tautira eventually led to the French takeover of Tahiti and the end of the Protestant monopoly.

The black-sand beach at PK6 in Pueu is good for boogie boarding or surfing but can be rough for swimming.

The sealed road ends at Tautira, but you can bump along for another kilometre or two before the road becomes impassable to vehicles. A walking track leads round the coast for another 10km or so before reaching the Te Pari Cliffs.

Tautira itself is a lovely village and unique on Tahiti as it's not clustered along one main road but has many small residential lanes that criss-cross the town in a near grid. There's a sweeping black-sand beach at the edge of town; it's often empty and offers good swimming. You can also visit Boenechea's grave in front of the Catholic church in the centre of town.

Offshore close to Afaahiti is the stunning white-sand Motu Nono, a popular picnic spot for locals and tourist excursions.

Inland

There are two routes that climb to an inland lookout and can be combined to make a loop.

In Afaahiti, at PK2.5, you'll find the turnoff by looking out for the equestrian-centre signpost. The 7km road climbs through green fields, some home to very un-Tahitianlooking herds of cows, to the little covered lookout.

The alternative route turns off the southcoast road at PK1.3 (turn inland at the grain factory, pass the high school and its football field then take a right at the stop sign). It meets the first route where the road forks, from where it's a short walk to the view-

TAHITI BILLABONG PRO

Held at Teahupoo every August, the famous Billabong Pro surfing contest attracts the industry's best riders and draws surf fans and media from around the world. Until the early 2000s, the Teahupoo wave was only known to local surfers. It now ranks as one of the most photographed and powerful waves on the planet – on a par with Pipeline in Hawaii. Teahupoo (tee-ah-hoo-poh-oh – please don't say 'poo') is a left that breaks over a very shallow reef, producing a perfect, awe-inspiring barrel.

This experts-only level wave breaks year-round on south swell. The contest in August is timed to coincide with the most likely period for very big waves. Beginner surfers can bring their surf or bodyboards to the beach break at PK18. It's swarming with kids when school is out, but is otherwise empty.

Otherwise, grab a taxi boat with Teahupoo Excursion (p72) or Teahupoo Tahiti Surfari (p72) to watch the pros ride the massive tubes. It's a spectacular sight.

point. There are superb vistas across the isthmus of Taravao to the towering bulk of Tahiti Nui.

South-Coast Road

The south-coast road runs by beaches and bays before abruptly stopping at the Tirahi River at PK18.

A picturesque strip of white sand, Maui Beach (Vairao, PK8) gets packed and noisy on weekends, but is peaceful during the week. It's right on the road but has shallow swimming, perfect for children, as well as deeper swimming and snorkelling off the reef.

A signposted turn-off at PK9.5 leads a short distance inland to the rarely visited remains of Marae Nuutere, restored in 1994. There are three paved yards known as *tohua* (meeting places) with *ahu* (altars) at the end of them.

Starting at PK15, Teahupoo is world famous among surfing circles for its monster wave – home to the Billabong Pro Tahiti. Park at Teahupoo's Tirahi River, then cross the footbridge. From here it's a lovely five-minute walk through a shaded residential

DON'T MISS

EXPLORING THE FENUA AIHERE & TE PARI

This coast from the end of the road at Teahupoo, which is accessible only by boat or on foot, is called the Fenua Aihere, which literally means 'the bush country'. Locals have asked walkers to stop walking this trail where there are houses, and the aggressive unchained dogs along the way will talk you out of it even more. Best is to take a boat excursion, which will often take in the dark, legend-rich **Vaipoiri Cave** and all the good snorkelling spots along the way before reaching the end of the reef at the **Te Pari Cliffs**.

Once the reef ends, the coastline becomes steep and gets pounded by waves when there's swell. It's possible to hike the entire 8km of this precarious coast dotted with archaeological treasures, wild passion fruit, waterfalls and caves, but no current human habitation. You can only do it in good weather and if the swell isn't too big. Near the Vaiote River are some interesting **petroglyphs** inscribed on coastal boulders and a series of **marae** inland in the valley.

On the northern half of Tahiti Iti towards Tautira, the coastline continues along from the Te Pari Cliffs another 10km or so through a second Fenua Aihere, till the paved road begins once again at Tautira village. You can walk past people's homes all the way to the village along this section without too many bad dogs.

A guide (p66) is highly recommended both for safety and to help you discover all the very hidden gems found mostly off the trail. It takes two days to hike from Teahupoo to Tautira and camp is usually made in an airy and open beachside cave. Most guides also offer one-day hikes on a section of the coast, in combination with a boat transfer. It's an unforgettable experience.

area and past lily ponds to a public **beach** with black sand and a few shady almond trees. It's safe for swimming and suitable for kids. There's also decent **snorkelling** and usually a nice local vibe. Do wear plastic sandals here though, since stonefish are plentiful.

Teahupoo is the obvious place to base yourself for boat tours into the **Fenua Aihere** (the 'bush country' after the road ends but within the confines of the barrier reef) and **Te Pari** (the sea-pounded cliffs that rise up after the Fenua Aihere and where there is no barrier reef).

🏃 Activities

Diving

Very few divers know that there's fantastic diving on Tahiti Iti. Most sites are scattered along the south coast, between Taravao and Teahupoo. You can expect pristine sites and fabulous drop-offs. There's only one centre that offers dives to the area.

Tahiti Iti Diving   DIVING
(📞40 42 25 33, 87 71 80 77; www.tahiti-iti-diving. com; PK58.1; single dive 5800 CFP; ⏰Tue-Sun) This well-run dive shop is based near Taravao on Tahiti Nui but runs dive trips to Tahiti Iti. It also charges 6800 CFP for an introductory dive and 52,000 CFP for a 10-dive package. Cash only.

Boat Excursions

Probably the most fun you can have in a day on Tahiti Iti is by taking a boat excursion, which invariably includes a picnic lunch, a visit to Vaipoiri Cave and, if the weather permits, Te Pari (which requires calm conditions). All *pensions* in the area can arrange excursions.

⭐**Teahupoo Tahiti Surfari**   BOAT TOUR
(📞87 77 72 26; www.facebook.com/Teahupoo-Tahiti-Surfari-Taxi-Boat-Excursions; PK17; half-/full-day tours 6500/8500 CFP) Captain Cindy and her family are surfing royalty and are the masters of this coast. The main tour involves a trip around the Fenua Aihere and Te Pari including lots of swimming, hiking the most scenic stretches, bathing in waterfalls and even diving off cliffs if you're up for it. Tours are flexible, tons of fun and include a picnic.

⭐**Teahupoo Excursion**   BOAT TOUR
(📞87 75 11 98; www.teahupooexcursion.com; half-/full day 6000/9000 CFP) Contagiously happy, skilled boatman Michael organises à la carte tours or will shuttle folks out to the Teahupoo wave to watch surfing or to surf for 2000 CFP per person. His day tours focus on water-based activities including snorkelling and surfing and can include a picnic, often with a charming local family in the Fenua Aihere.

Surfing

Tahiti Iti is chock full of surf breaks from the world-famous Teahupoo to lesser known spots like big and small passes in Vairao.

Tour operators Teahupoo Excursion and Teahupoo Tahiti Surfari can both arrange surf trips and are good sources of info.

Hiking

By far the best hike on Tahiti Iti is along the Te Pari between Teahupoo to Tautira. Another popular hike is the cross-island trek from Tautira to Teahupoo (or conversely), which requires two days.

Horse Riding

L'Amour de la Nature à Cheval   HORSE RIDING
(☑87 73 84 43; http://lamournatcheval.onlc.fr; Taravao, PK2.5; rides from 2500 CFP) This equestrian centre offers guided rides to rarely visited points on the plateau with stunning views. It's best to reserve a few days in advance; there are no set hours.

🛏 Sleeping

Punatea Village   BUNGALOW $
(☑87 77 20 31, 40 57 71 00; www.punatea.com; Afaahiti, PK4.7; d with shared bathroom 6000 CFP, bungalow d 12,000 CFP; ❄🛜🏊) Four stand-alone bungalows and five tiny rooms in their own building sit in a lovely, verdant property opening onto the lagoon and black-sand beach. The beach area has been landscaped into a little protected bay that's great for kids – or otherwise there's also an OK pool. The owner is super-friendly and helpful, and there's a communal kitchen to make your own meals.

★ Vanira Lodge   BUNGALOW $$
(☑40 57 70 18; www.vaniralodge.com; Teahupoo, PK15; bungalows 17,900-27,900 CFP; ❄🛜🏊) Our favourite *pension* in Tahiti, this place is up a steep driveway on a miniplateau with vast views of the lagoon, surf, village and myriad island colours. The bungalows are fabulously eclectic and are all built from some combination of bamboo, thatch, rustic planks of wood, glass, adobe, coral and rock. One of the bungalows has an earth roof that's bursting with flowers.

Cosy nooks, hand-carved furniture, airy mezzanines and al-fresco kitchens (in the family-size bungalows that sleep four) are nice touches. There's tons of open space for kids as well as a little lily pond, a pool and fruit trees. The on-site restaurant is fantastic. Bikes, kayaks and snorkel gear are available for rent. You'll definitely need a car if you stay here.

★ Mitirapa Villa   VILLA $$
(☑87 76 90 64; www.villamitirapa.com; PK3; villa 19,000-30,000 CFP; ❄🛜🏊) Five mini-villas are spread over two waterfront locations: the first on the lagoon, with views over aqua water; and the second on Phaeton Bay with its green waters backed by steep, high mountains. The Balinese-style masterpieces are some of the best value lodging on the island. Each unit has two bedrooms, kitchen, living space, private gardens and a dipping pool.

Reva   PENSION $$
(☑87 77 14 28, 40 57 92 16; www.reva-teahupoo.org; Fenua Aihere; bungalow per person incl full board 13,000 CFP) 🐾 Reva is in a beautifully isolated place that's only accessible by boat from Teahupoo. It takes full advantage of the waterfront property, with a long pontoon jutting out over the lagoon – great for swimming. There are four well-designed bungalows scattered amid lush gardens. Plenty of activities are on offer to keep you busy if that's what you're after.

The electricity is generated from solar power and prices include transfers from Teahupoo. Cash only.

Green Room Villa   RENTAL HOUSE $$$
(www.vrbo.com/411295; Teahupoo, PK18; house from 21,000 CFP; 🛜) Rent this exquisite three-bedroom, two-bathroom house for a romantic getaway or bring up to seven other people (eight total) for a family or surfing get-together. The house is octagonal-shaped with a huge covered wooden deck, tons of windows, teak flooring, brightly painted walls and a fully equipped kitchen. The quiet, private property is a five-minute walk to Teahupoo's beach.

The property is managed by a welcoming Tahitian family next door who often bring by free fruit. There's a three-day minimum stay.

🍴 Eating

Snack du Bout de Monde   TAHITIAN, CHINESE $
(Tautira Marina, PK18; mains 1000-1500 CFP; ⏱noon-3pm Tue-Sun) A wonderful little bright blue-painted cheaply with a serene view of the water. Get baguette sandwiches from 300 CFP or order simple but well-prepared mains including chow mein, Chinese-style *poisson cru* (raw fish marinated with pickled vegetables) or grilled locally caught fish, and let the world pass you by. Cash only.

★ **La Plage de Maui**   TAHITIAN **$$**
(☑87 74 71 74; Vairao, PK7.6; mains 1600-3200 CFP; ☺10am-5pm) Dine with your toes in the sand and a view just out the window of fish darting around in the clear blue water – this is by far the best setting for a meal on Tahiti Iti. Best go with the Polynesian plates that usually include steamed fish and local produce such as taro and breadfruit.

Steer clear of the raw fish dishes that are overpriced and not at all special. There are also cheaper burgers and such for the kids. Cash only.

Taumatai   FRENCH, TAHITIAN **$$**
(☑41 57 13 59; Taravao; mains 1700-3000 CFP; ☺11.30am-2pm & 6.30-9pm Tue-Sat, 11.30am-2.30pm Sun) This delightful little place in Taravao serves fantastic French and Tahitian food in an elegant garden – it's by far the most peaceful and beautiful setting in Taravao and is a great spot for a romantic lunch or dinner. The shellfish in particular (try the *varo* – mantis shrimp – if they have it) is fresh and always prepared to perfection.

The restaurant is hidden behind a stone wall so it's a little hard to find; it's on the road to Tautira just across from Chez Loula & Remy's.

★ **Chez Loula & Remy**   FRENCH **$$$**
(☑40 57 74 99; Taravao; mains 2100-4500 CFP; ☺11.30am-3pm daily, 6.30-9.30pm Mon, Tue & Thu-Sat) This family-run, very old-school French place in Taravao on the Tautira road has continuously served some of the best French-style grilled meats and fish in the country for donkey's years. Environs are boozy, congenial and often a bit smokey if you sit by the door (ye olde French smokers have been pushed outdoors but not without a fight!).

The duck breast in pineapple or honey sauce, veal's head (for real, it's a house speciality) and catch of the day in a pastry shell and vanilla sauce are always excellent.

Vanira Lodge Restaurant   TAHITIAN, FRENCH **$$$**
(☑40 57 70 18; Teahupoo, PK15; mains 2400-2900 CFP; ☺6-9pm daily, 11.30am-2pm Sat & Sun) There are only a handful of small tables at this gardenside and very intimate open-air restaurant so you'll definitely want to reserve in advance to nab one. The food is simply sublime with French twists on Polynesian fare done to perfection. Highlights include a fish roll on breadfruit cakes with lemon tomato sauce and duck breast in lychee sauce.

Mo'orea

POP 17,230

Includes ➡

History 76
Sights 77
Activities 80
Tours 84
Sleeping 84
Eating 90
Drinking & Nightlife 92
Shopping 92

Best Places to Stay

➡ Résidence Linareva (p89)

➡ Green Lodge (p89)

➡ Sofitel Moorea la Ora Moorea Beach Resort (p90)

➡ Tehuarupe (p89)

➡ Les Tipaniers (p87)

Best Places to Eat

➡ Coco Beach (p92)

➡ Le Mayflower (p92)

➡ Snack Mahana (p91)

➡ Crêperie Toatea (p90)

➡ Le Coco's Moorea (p92)

Why Go?

If you've been dreaming of holiday-brochure turquoise lagoons, white-sand beaches, vertical peaks and lush landscapes, you'd be hard-pressed to find better than this gem of an island. Hovering less than 20km across the 'Sea of the Moon' from its big sister, Tahiti, Mo'orea absorbs its many visitors so gracefully that its feels surprisingly nontouristy.

Mo'orea has a healthy selection of top-end resorts, but it is also host to a good choice of smaller hotels. There are pretty white-sand beaches, but nothing big and sweeping. The drawcard is the limpid, warm water of the vibrant lagoon. If you need some action, learn to kitesurf, take a hike, go on a whale- or dolphin-watching tour, hire a bike or a kayak, or go horse riding. Whatever the experience, there's only one word to describe Mo'orea: divine!

When to Go

➡ November to April are the wetter months.

➡ From May to October it's usually much drier – perfect for outdoor activities, especially hiking.

➡ July and August are fairly windy and may be chilly when the *mara'amu* (southeast trade wind) blows.

➡ Diving and surfing are popular year-round

➡ The whale-watching season runs from July or August to October.

History

The island's ancient name was Eimeo (sometimes spelled Aimeho). Some say that Mo'orea, which means 'yellow lizard', was the name of one of the island's ruling families, while others attribute this name to an image seen by a high priest while visiting the island.

Mo'orea was heavily populated before the Europeans arrived on its idyllic doorstep. Samuel Wallis was the first European to sight the island (1767); he was soon followed by Louis-Antoine de Bougainville (1768) and James Cook (1769). The missionaries arrived on the scene in the early 1800s and made themselves at home, soon establishing their headquarters on the island. As elsewhere, European diseases and the introduction of weapons and alcohol had a disastrous effect on the population of Mo'orea, which declined during the 19th century.

Copra and vanilla were important crops in the past, but these days Mo'orea is the

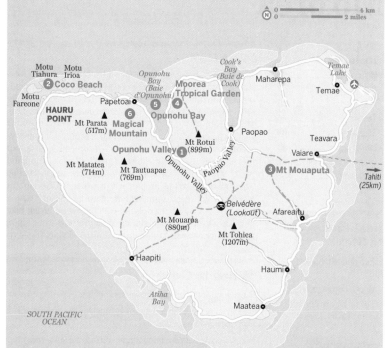

Mo'orea Highlights

1 Getting lost in **Opunohu Valley** (p81), with its ancient *marae* (traditional temples), breathtaking vistas and hidden walking paths.

2 Paddling to Motu Tiahura from Hauru Point for lunch at **Coco Beach** (p92).

3 Taking an unforgettable hike to **Mt Mouaputa** (p83).

4 Sampling tropical delights at **Moorea Tropical Garden** (p80).

5 Diving amid a concentration of lemon sharks in **Opunohu Bay** (p77).

6 Savouring fabulous lagoon vistas from the **Magical Mountain** (p77).

pineapple-growing centre of French Polynesia. Tourism is the other major industry, but Mo'orea saw its economic bottom begin to fall out in 2008. Today, the island is a weekend escape for many Pape'ete residents.

⊙ Sights

The following circuit starts near the airport and moves in an anticlockwise direction, following the northern PK markers.

Temae Beach BEACH
(Map p78; PK1) The best beach on the east coast, and the widest perhaps in all of French Polynesia, stretches from Teavaro round to the airport. The Sofitel Ia Ora Moorea Beach Resort occupies part of the beach, where there's superb snorkelling in the shallow water and out on the lagoon side of the fringing reef. The public section of Temae Beach, just north of the Sofitel, usually gets crowded on weekends. Do not leave valuables in your car.

Toatea Lookout VIEWPOINT
(Map p78; PK0.6) This spot really fits the picture-postcard ideal. Atop the hill north of the Sofitel la Ora Moorea Beach Resort, this lookout affords dazzling views of the hotel, the lagoon mottled with coral formations, the barrier reef and Tahiti in the background.

Maison Blanche HISTORIC BUILDING
(Map p85; PK5.2, Maharepa) In Maharepa, you can't miss this early 20th-century building on the mountain side of the road. It's a fine example of a *fare vanira*, a plantation house from Mo'orea's vanilla-boom era. The Maison Blanche is now a souvenir shop and has a fairly typical selection of *pareu* (sarongs), Balinese woodcarvings, T-shirts, jewellery and other souvenirs.

★ Cook's Bay BAY
(Map p85; PK6–PK11) The spectacular Cook's Bay is something of a misnomer as Cook actually anchored in Opunohu Bay. With Mt Rotui as a backdrop, Cook's Bay is a lovely stretch of water. There's no real centre to Cook's Bay; shops, restaurants and hotels are simply dotted along the road.

At the base of Cook's Bay is the sleepy village of Paopao. The road inland from Paopao and Cook's Bay is called Route des Ananas (Pineapple Road) and meets the Opunohu Valley road, just before the agricultural college. Note that only the first kilometres are asphalted – a 4WD is recommended.

ⓘ PK MARKERS

Adhering to French Polynesian practice, the *point kilométrique* (PK; kilometre point) markers start at PK0 at the airport and go around the coast in both clockwise and anticlockwise directions; they meet at Haapiti, which is at PK24 along the southern (clockwise) route and at PK37 along the northern (anticlockwise) route.

Distillerie et Usine de
Jus de Fruits de Moorea DISTILLERY
(Map p78; ☑ 40 55 20 00; www.manuteatahiti.com; PK11; ⊙ 8.30am-4.30pm Mon-Fri, 8.30am-12.30pm Sat) FREE About 300m inland from the coastal road, this juice-processing factory and distillery is well worth a stop. It produces various juices and alcoholic beverages, including yummy liqueurs and a devilish 'Tahitian punch'. The tasting of liqueurs and juices is free. Tours are available at 9am and 2pm from Monday to Thursday and last about 40 minutes. The gift shop sells drinks and souvenirs.

Ta'ahiamanu Beach BEACH
(Map p78; PK14.5) At last, a public beach! Ta'ahiamanu (Mareto) Beach is one of the few public access beaches on the island. This narrow stretch of white sand is a popular spot for both tourists and locals on weekends. Fear not, you'll find plenty of room to stretch out without bumping anyone else's beach towel. Despite the lack of facilities, it's ideal for splashing about, sunbathing or picnicking. Snorkellers will find plenty of coral and marine life right in front of the beach.

★ Opunohu Bay BAY
(Map p78) Magnificent Opunohu Bay feels wonderfully fresh and isolated. The coastal road rounds Mt Rotui, and at about PK14 turns inland along the eastern side of Opunohu Bay. There is less development along here than around Cook's Bay, and it's one of the more tranquil and eye-catching spots on the island. At PK18, a road turns off inland along the Opunohu Valley to the valley *marae* and the *belvédère* (lookout).

Magical Mountain VIEWPOINT
(Map p78; admission 300 CFP) At PK21, a cement road veers inland and makes a very steep climb to a lookout called 'Magical Mountain', at a height of 209m. It's an

Mo'orea

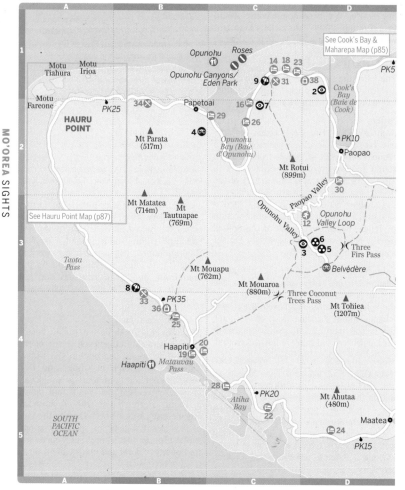

arduous, 45-minute walk, but the view over the northern part of the island and the lagoon is mesmerising. The access road is private, so permission must be obtained before entering the property; the owners live in the house across the road from the entrance of the property. Start early before it gets too hot.

Papetoai   VILLAGE

(PK22) A busy village with a few shops and services, Papetoai was established as the Pacific headquarters of the London Missionary Society (LMS) in 1811. In the 1870s,

the missionaries constructed an octagonal church at Papetoai; today this is the oldest standing European building in the South Pacific. As was often the case, missionaries deliberately built this church atop an old *marae*.

Hauru Point   POINT

(Map p87; PK25–PK30) The coastal road rounds Hauru Point, between PK25 and PK30. Hauru Point has one of the best beaches on the island, a narrow but sandy stretch that extends for a couple of kilometres, with turquoise water and good snorkelling. That

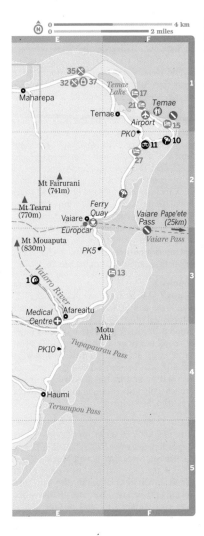

Mo'orea

◎ Sights
1 Afareaitu Waterfalls	E3
2 Distillerie et Usine de Jus de Fruits de Moorea	D1
3 Lycée Agricole	D3
4 Magical Mountain	B2
5 Marae Fare Aito	D3
6 Marae Titiroa & Marae Ahu-o-Mahine	D3
7 Moorea Tropical Garden	C2
8 Painapo Beach	B3
9 Ta'ahiamanu Beach	C1
10 Temae Beach	F2
11 Toatea Lookout	F2

⊕ Activities, Courses & Tours
la Ora Diving	(see 27)
12 Ranch Opunohu Valley	D3

🛏 Sleeping
13 Atuana Lodge	F3
14 Fare Junette	C1
15 Fare Maeva	F1
16 Fare Vaihere	C2
17 Green Lodge	F1
18 Hilton Moorea Lagoon Resort & Spa	C1
19 Kahekaro	B4
20 Mark's Place Moorea	B4
21 Moorea Golf Lodge	F1
22 Moorea Surf B&B	C5
23 Motu Iti	C1
24 Pension Aute	D5
25 Résidence Linareva	B4
26 Robinson's Cove Villas	C2
27 Sofitel la Ora Moorea Beach Resort	F2
28 Tehuarupe	C4
29 Tipaniers Iti	C2
30 Village Temanoha	D2

⊗ Eating
Chez Fifi	(see 16)
Crêperie Toatea	(see 18)
Le K	(see 27)
31 Lilikoi Garden Café	C1
32 Lollipop	E1
33 Pizza Daniel	B4
34 Snack Mahana	B2
35 Snack-Resto La Canadienne	E1

🛍 Shopping
36 Moorea Tattoo	B4
37 Opeta Tattoo	E1
38 Purotu Tattoo	D1

said, finding your way to the beach is not easy because there's no public access. Your best bet is to walk through the grounds of hotels and have a drink at their beachfront bar or restaurant.

Hauru Point is one of the island's major tourist enclaves, although it has seen better days – a number of shops, restaurants and hotels have closed since 2008. The area is often referred to as Haapiti, since it's in the Haapiti district, even though the village of Haapiti is well to the south.

Immediately offshore are two attractive little *motu* (islets) so close to the shore you can easily paddle out to them (beware of the current, though). Remember that the actual *motu* are private (although the littoral areas aren't).

DON'T MISS

MOOREA TROPICAL GARDEN

This delightfully peaceful **property** (Map p78; PK15.5; ⏱8am-5pm Mon-Sat, 8am-noon Sun) perched on a small plateau is heaven on earth for the sweet-toothed, who can sample (and buy) homemade organic jams, dried fruits, vanilla and delicious ice creams; there are lots of original flavours, such as *noni* and breadfruit (in season). Freshly squeezed juices are also on offer. If you happen to be there on Friday or Saturday, don't miss out on the Polynesian lunch menu (1500 CFP). Needless to say, the lagoon views are fantastic. Take the dirt road across the road from the *snack* Chez Fifi.

Painapo Beach   BEACH
(Map p78; PK33) You can't miss the huge (though falling apart) statue of a tattooed man holding a club at the entrance of this private property overlooking a lovely strip of white sand. There's an access fee to get to the beach – ask around.

Haapiti   VILLAGE
(PK24) The largest village on the west coast, Haapiti is home to the splendid twin-towered Catholic **Église de la Sainte Famille**, which is made of coral and lime. The **Protestant Temple** is another notable building; it's at PK23.5, on the lagoon side of the road.

Atiha Bay   BAY
(PK18) Mo'orea's lazy west-coast atmosphere continues right round to Atiha Bay (Baie d'Atiha), a quiet fishing village that also attracts surfers.

Afareaitu   VILLAGE
(PK10) Afareaitu is the island's administrative centre. There are two **waterfalls** (Afareaitu) that are worth a gander (although they are but trickles in winter). Ask for directions.

Vaiare   VILLAGE
(PK4) The constant toing and froing of ferry boats and high-speed catamarans at the ferry quay, the busy market scene and the cars, taxis and buses shuttling visitors around render the 100m or so near the dock area the busiest patch of real estate on Mo'orea.

🏃 Activities

It is wise to book activities as soon as you arrive on the island; contact organisers directly or check with your hotel or guesthouse.

Diving & Snorkelling

Mo'orea is one of French Polynesia's main underwater playgrounds (p34), which is no surprise considering its high visibility and clean waters. Although it can't rival with the Tuamotus, it offers safe, relaxed diving, and for beginners, it's a great place to learn to dive and get certified. The underwater scenery is every bit the equal of what's on land: you can dive sloping reefs and may go nose-to-nose with sharks – especially lemon sharks – rays and numerous reef species. Most dive operators are concentrated at the northwest of the island. Prominent sites include Tiki (p34), with a good shark population, Taotoi (p34) and Opunohu Canyons/Eden Park (p34).

For snorkelling, join a lagoon tour or DIY around Hauru Point and its *motu*, around the interior of the reef beyond Temae Beach or off Ta'ahiamanu (Mareto) Beach.

Topdive   DIVING
(Map p87; ☑40 56 31 44; www.topdive.com; PK25; intro/single dive 10,000/9800 CFP) This well-established dive shop at Intercontinental Moorea Resort & Spa offers the full range of scuba activities, with Nitrox dives at no extra cost. Six- and 10-dive packages go for 50,000 CFP and 80,000 CFP and can be used at any of the Topdive centres in French Polynesia. Snorkelling trips can be arranged. Free pick-up.

Ia Ora Diving   DIVING
(Map p78; ☑40 56 35 78; www.iaoradiving.com; introductory/single dive 8500/8000 CFP) Due to its location (at Sofitel Ia Ora Moorea Beach Resort) on the northeastern corner of the island, Ia Ora specialises in dive sites near Temae and Vaiare. Five- and 10-dive packages cost 32,000 CFP and 60,000 CFP. It also offers snorkelling trips to a site called Lagoonarium (6900 CFP). Free pick-up.

Moorea Blue Diving   DIVING
(Map p85; ☑40 55 17 04, 87 74 59 99; www.mooreabluediving.com; PK5; introductory/single dive 8000/7500 CFP) At Moorea Pearl Resort & Spa, this small dive shop gets good reviews. If you've never been diving before, these are the people to see. Six- and 10-dive packages are 42,000 CFP and 64,000 CFP. Moorea Blue Diving is a member of **Te Moana Pass** (www.temoanadiving.com), an inter-island dive pass that's accepted in 16 dive shops in French Polynesia. Free pick-up.

DON'T MISS

PAOPAO & OPUNOHU VALLEYS

From Mo'orea's two great bays, valleys sweep inland, meeting south of the coastal bulk of Mt Rotui. Both valleys are of great historical significance. In the pre-European era, they were densely populated and the Opunohu Valley was dotted with *marae* (traditional temples) as well as dwellings, archery platforms and other structures, some of which have been restored and maintained. It's believed the valley was continuously inhabited for six centuries, and the oldest surviving structures date from the 13th century.

If you're driving, note that only the Opunohu Valley road, also knows as Route du Belvédère, is entirely asphalted.

Lycée Agricole (Map p78; Agricultural College; ☑40 56 11 34; ⊙8.45am-4pm Mon-Sat) A small shop at the college sells jams in local flavours as well as honey, coffee, fruit juices and, on occasion, ice cream. If you've got itchy feet, there's a small network of walking trails that lead through the estate, in the basin of the caldera. These are detailed in leaflets that are available at the shop. The longest loop takes a little over two hours to walk. From the college, the road continues inland and up to various *marae* and finally to the *belvédère* (lookout).

Marae Titiroa & Marae Ahu-o-Mahine (Map p78) Past the agricultural college, the valley road comes to a parking area beside this vast complex, on the edge of a dense forest of magnificent chestnut trees. From the main *marae* a track leads to the *tohua* (council platform), and two smaller *marae*. Continue along this track until you reach the *marae* Ahu-o-Mahine, a more recent platform of round stones with an imposing three-stepped *ahu* (altar). There are explanatory panels in French and English.

Marae Fare Aito (Map p78) This large *marae* has a small, raised-terrace *ahu* (altar), and back rests that were used by the priests. It is flanked by two crescent-shaped archery platforms. Archery was an activity exclusively practised by noblemen in the pre-European era.

Belvédère (Map p78) Up the Opunohu valley road, this lookout is the island's highest point accessible by car. It offers superb views of Opunohu and Cook's bays, Mt Rotui (which splits the two bays), and back to the towering mountains that rise in the centre of the island and which once formed the southern rim of the ancient crater.

Moorea Fun Dive DIVING
(Map p87; ☑40 56 40 38; www.moorea-fundive. com; PK26.7; introductory/single dive 7500/6600 CFP) This small operation at Hauru Point, on the beach, is the only dive shop on Mo'orea that's not part of a hotel. Run by a friendly French couple, it offers knowledgeable and personal service. Two-tank dives (12,500 CFP) are excellent value. Add an extra 500 CFP per dive for Nitrox dives. Free pick-up. It's a member of Te Moana Pass.

Scubapiti DIVING
(Map p87; ☑87 78 03 52, 40 56 20 38; www. scubapiti.com; PK25; introductory/single dive 6800/6400 CFP) At hotel Les Tipaniers. Goes out with small groups. Online prepaid bookings attract a 10% discount. Four-/six-/10-dive packages cost 24,000/34,000/53,000 CFP. Add an extra 700 CFP per dive for Nitrox dives. It's a member of Te Moana Pass.

Undersea Walks

Aquablue WATER SPORTS
(Map p87; ☑87 73 24 40, 40 56 53 53; http:// contact.aquablue.free.fr; PK25; 8000 CFP; ⊙10am & 2pm Mon-Sat) If you want to experience diving but aren't quite sure it's for you, try this outfit at the Intercontinental Moorea Resort & Spa. It offers a 30-minute excursion in which you walk along the sea bed wearing a weighted helmet with air pumped into it. Since you actually walk on the bottom, you don't even need to be able to swim. Children over six are welcome.

Lagoon Excursions

The best way to discover Mo'orea's magnificent lagoon is by joining a lagoon excursion. Tours typically visit the Cook's and Opunohu bays, stop to swim with the rays at a spot off the Intercontinental Moorea Resort & Spa, and picnic and snorkel on a *motu*.

Note that Mo'orea has a long history of shark and ray feeding, but mentalities are

MO'OREA FOR CHILDREN

Don't hesitate to bring the whole family, as Mo'orea is particularly kid-friendly. Some highlights:

➡ approaching colourful fish on a lagoon tour

➡ splashing about on Temae Beach

➡ taking an introductory dive in the shallow waters of the lagoon

➡ enjoying an ice cream at Moorea Tropical Garden

➡ clip-clopping amid volcanic landscapes

➡ riding an ATV – in the passenger seat

changing. It's now illegal to feed the animals within the lagoon or near a pass. Some tour guides do 'bait', though, using tuna scraps they put in a box.

Moorea Eco Tour – Manu   BOAT TOUR
(Map p87; ☑87 35 79 16; PK25; half-day tour 8000 CFP) Uses a small motorised catamaran. Offers a full tour of Mo'orea, with swimming and snorkelling stops. It's based at the Intercontinental Moorea Resort & Spa.

Moorea Boat Tours   BOAT TOUR
(☑40 56 28 44, 87 78 68 86; www.mooreaboat-tours.com; half-day tour 8000 CFP) A popular operator that has good credentials. The tour includes dolphin-watching as well as swimming and snorkelling.

What To Do Moorea –
Hiro's Tours   BOAT TOUR
(☑87 78 70 10; www.hirotour.com; 7000 CFP; ⊙Tue, Wed, Fri & Sun) Tours that include dolphin-watching, a visit to Cook's and Opunohu bays as well as swimming and snorkelling stops. Prices include a picnic on an islet.

Moorea Loca Boat   BOATING
(Map p87; ☑87 78 13 39; www.moorealocaboat.com; PK25; 2/4hr incl fuel 7000/10,000 CFP; ⊙9am-5pm) This outfit right on the beach beside Les Tipaniers rents outboard-powered boats – an ideal way to explore the lagoon and small *motu*. A map of the lagoon is provided. No licence is required. Also has pedal boats.

Whale & Dolphin Watching

This activity has exploded in recent years. You can count on finding dolphins year-round, but it's the whales, who migrate to Mo'orea from July (or August) to October, who draw in the crowds. If you're lucky, you'll get to swim with the mammals, but just seeing them in the water is a real thrill. Most dive centres run whale-watching trips, or you can contact the following outfits, which have green credentials and employ well-trained guides.

Dr Michael Poole   WILDLIFE WATCHING
(☑40 56 23 22; www.drmichaelpoole.com; half-day trip 8000 CFP; ⊙morning Mon & Thu) A world specialist on South Pacific marine mammals and an advocate for their protection, Dr Poole began the first whale-watching tours and continues to lead the best ones available, although his boats can get crowded in season (up to 26 people). If you book a second tour, the price drops to 6000 CFP.

Moorea Deep Blue   WILDLIFE WATCHING
(☑87 76 37 27; www.moorea-deepblue.com; half-day trip 8000 CFP) A former dive instructor runs small-group whale- and dolphin-watching trips with environmental awareness and with minimal impact on the animals.

Polynesia Dream Boat   WILDLIFE WATCHING
(☑87 34 78 44; full-day trip 7500 CFP) A well-regarded outfit that adheres to strict procedures when it comes to approaching whales. Also runs lagoon tours and dolphin-watching tours. If you're coming from Tahiti, you can be picked up (and dropped off) at the Vaiare ferry quay. No website, but there's a Facebook page.

Kayaking & SUP

The translucent waters of the lagoon are as inviting for kayakers and paddlers as they are for divers and snorkellers. Many places to stay offer free kayaks for guests' use.

Tip Nautic   KAYAKING
(Map p87; ☑87 78 76 73; www.tipnautic.com; PK25; single/double kayak per hr 500/1000 CFP; ⊙8am-5pm) This reputable outfit based on the beach at Les Tipaniers rents out various kayaks that are in tip-top shape. The beach here is the optimal launching pad to get to the nearby islets. Also rents out stand-up paddleboards.

Kayak Nomad Polynesia   KAYAKING
(☑87 23 44 97; www.kayaknomadpolynesia.com; half-/full-day tours 5000/10,000 CFP) For something unique, contact this outfit, which organises kayak tours to various scenic spots on the lagoon.

Fenua Stand Up Paddle WATER SPORTS
(☏87 24 06 54; www.fenua-standuppaddle.com; 2/3hr tour 3800/5500 CFP) Stand-up paddleboarding is an ecofriendly way to commune with the natural environment. This outfit offers guided SUP tours up to various spots on the lagoon – there are eight different itineraries, which all include swimming and snorkelling stops.

Surfing

The island's excellent surfing waves are for experienced to advanced surfers.

Haapiti SURFING
Mo'orea's most popular surfing spot has the regularity and strength of reef waves with the security of a beach wave; plus it's pretty deep at the take-off point.

Temae SURFING
Temae is a difficult right-hander at a recess in the reef. It works year-round, depending on the winds.

Opunohu SURFING
This great surfing spot (November to April) enjoys a sensational setting.

Kitesurfing

With an easterly wind blowing much of the time, and its shallow waters protected by the barrier reef, kitesurfing has become very popular on Mo'orea and on windy days you'll see dozens of kites whipping across the lagoon in front of the Intercontinental Moorea Resort & Spa.

Lakana Fly KITESURFING
(☏87 70 96 71; introductory course 12,000 CFP) This outfit offers beginner to advanced kitesurfing lessons for ages nine and up. The introductory course lasts about two hours. It also rents out gear.

XPR - Expair Moorea KITESURFING
(Map p87; ☏89 50 42 32; www.expair-tahiti.com; PK25; introductory course 15,300 CFP) This well-regarded outfit based at Intercontinental Moorea Resort & Spa specialises in small groups, so you're guaranteed personalised attention. The introductory course lasts about two hours. Also rents gear.

Hiking

Exhilarating hikes of varying difficulty tackle the lush inland area. With the exception of the Three Coconut Trees Pass walk, most trails are infrequently used and poorly marked, so it's necessary to use a guide. For

---

MO'OREA'S TATTOO ARTISTS

If you think about getting tattooed during your stay in French Polynesia, you've come to the right place. Some of French Polynesia's best tattoo artists live on Mo'orea.

Moorea Tattoo (Map p78; ☏87 30 08 83; www.mooreatattoo.com; PK32) James Samuela is highly trained, young and professional, and speaks good English.

Purotu Tattoo (Map p78; ☏87 77 79 42, 40 56 49 00; PK13) A very experienced tattoo artist.

Taniera Tattoo (Map p87; ☏40 56 16 98; PK27.3) Charismatic Taniera produces high-quality work.

Opeta Tattoo (Map p78; ☏87 25 05 21; www.mooreaopetatattoo.blogspot. fr; PK2.5, Maharepa) Originally from the Marquesas, Opeta specialises in elaborate Marquesan designs.

---

an easy, DIY hike, consider the trails at the Lycée Agricole (p81).

Opunohu Valley Loop HIKING
This long walk (about six hours) starts at the Lycée Agricole (Agricultural College). Climb to the Three Coconut Trees Pass, which is accessed after about two hours. Then, descend to the turn-off for the *belvédère*, which you'll reach after about 1½ hours. From there, it's about 45 minutes to Three Firs Pass. The last stage is the return to the Lycée Agricole, about 1¾ hours.

The highlight of the hike is the unforgettable view of Cook's Bay and Opunohu Bay from Three Firs Pass.

Three Coconut Trees Pass HIKING
Mo'orea's most popular hike, this climb is hard work, but the pay-off is superb views from the ridge between Mt Mouaroa (880m) and Mt Tohiea (1207m). You can start from the agricultural college or the *belvédère*. Count on three hours return. The track is relatively well marked so you don't really need a guide. Don't look for three coconut trees at the pass – two were blown down in an early 1980s cyclone.

Mt Mouaputa HIKING
If you're really fit, you can try the arduous climb up to Mt Mouaputa (830m), one of Mo'orea's iconic summits. It's a seven- to

nine-hour hard-going return hike from Afareaitu, with some difficult uphill scrambles, but the 360-degree panorama at the summit is worth the effort.

Mt Rotui   HIKING

A strenuous but scenic hike, the Mt Rotui (899m) climb starts from near Moorea Pearl Resort & Spa. You walk almost all the way along a ridge (no shade). It's steep, but the reward is a tremendous view of the island. Allow roughly six hours there and back.

Moorea Hiking   HIKING

(☑87 79 41 54; hirohiking@gmail.com) Hiro Damide is a reputable guide who's very knowledgeable about local flora and geology. He charges 5300 CFP per person for the Three Coconut Trees Pass and 7400 CFP for the Opunohu Valley Loop. A minimum of two people is required.

Tahiti Evasion   HIKING

(☑87 70 56 18; www.tahitievasion.com) Run by a professional guide who offers a wide range of hikes for all levels. He charges 10,500 CFP for Mt Rotui, Mt Mouaputa or Opunohu Valley Loop. Half-day walks, including Three Coconut Trees Pass and Three Firs Pass, are 5200 CFP (minimum two people). This outfit can also organise canyoning outings. Prices include transfers.

Horse Riding

Ranch Opunohu Valley   HORSE RIDING

(Map p78; ☑87 78 42 47; Paopao Valley; 2hr rides 5500 CFP) Two-hour guided rides into the island's interior are available mornings and afternoons. The ranch is up in the Paopao Valley (it's signposted).

ATV

ATV Moorea Tours   ADVENTURE TOUR

(Map p87; ☑87 70 73 45; www.atvmoorea.com; PK24.6; tours per ATV 14,000-21,000 CFP) Double-seater ATV 4WD buggies are a fun but expensive way to see some rugged interior areas near the Lycée Agricole and the Magical Mountain; 2½-hour and 3½-hour guided tours are available and include several stops. A driving licence is required.

Skydiving

Tahiti Parachutisme   SKYDIVING

(☑87 33 97 23; www.tahiti-parachutisme.com; 51,000 CFP) This adventure outfit offers a whole new way to check out the island – from 3200m in the air as you zoom towards the earth after jumping from a plane.

🎯 Tours

Several operators organise island tours on open 4WDs. They usually last three hours and are good value if you don't want to hire a car.

FranckyFranck
Moorea Tours   CULTURAL TOUR

(☑87 76 40 28; www.franckyfranck-mooreatours. com; half-day tour 4500 CFP) Runs a complete tour of the island with visits to the archaeological sites in the Opunohu Valley, stops at the *belvédère* and visits to pineapple plantations and the fruit-juice factory. Free pick-up.

🛏 Sleeping

Most accommodation is on the eastern side of Cook's Bay and around Hauru Point.

🏠 Cook's Bay

Magnificent Cook's Bay does not have any beach, and so it's the quieter, less touristy sister of Hauru Point.

Village Temanoha   BUNGALOW **$$**

(☑87 21 65 59; www.villagetemanoha.com; Paopao; bungalows d 11,000-13,000 CFP) If stepping out of your room and digging your toes in the sand isn't a must, this venture is a great option, with five spacious wood and stone bungalows surrounding an inviting pool. Best of all, it enjoys a spectacular mountain-side setting beneath Mt Rotui in a 2-hectare tropical garden. Breakfast is an extra 1500 CFP and dinner is 2000 CFP.

It's about 1.5km from the coastal road; it's best to have your own wheels.

Kaveka   RESORT **$$**

(☑40 56 50 50; www.hotel-kaveka-moorea.com; PK7.3; bungalows d 10,000-19,000 CFP; ❄🛜) Popular with English-speaking visitors (the owner is from New Zealand), this few-frills complex on the eastern shore of Cook's Bay has been around for years; although its 30 bungalows are showing their age a tad, they are serviceable and well organised. Note that the cheaper units are fan-cooled.

Amenities include a restaurant and bar on stilts over the water, which offer prime sunset-watching. The beach is minimal (a breakwater fronts most of the property), but you can swim or snorkel off a wooden pier that extends over the lagoon to a magnificent drop-off. Bikes, kayaks and wi-fi cost extra.

Club Bali Hai   RESORT **$$**

(☑40 56 13 68; www.clubbalihai.com; PK8; d 12,000 CFP, bungalows d 14,000-16,500 CFP;

✳ 🛜 🏊) One of Mo'orea's few midprice accommodation options, Club Bali Hai has a range of anonymous rooms in a two-storey, motel-like building as well as an assortment of local-style bungalows, including a handful of overwater units that are among the least expensive in French Polynesia. A tiny swimming pool and a restaurant (breakfast and lunch only) over the water round off the offerings.

The decor is nothing special, but the setting – it sits on the eastern shore of Cook's Bay with a picture-postcard view of Mt Rotui – and the relaxed feel more than make up for the slightly dated sense of style. White sand has been brought in to form a sunbathing patch along the shore, and there's superb snorkelling a few fin-strokes away. Frequent online promotional deals provide real value.

Moorea Pearl Resort & Spa   RESORT **$$$**
(📋40 55 17 50; www.spmhotels.com; PK5; bungalows d 35,000-75,000 CFP; ✳ 🛜 🏊) The infinity pool here is the island's best. There's a wide range of accommodation options, including duplex units for families as well as less expensive rooms in a two-storey building at the rear of the property. Pick of the bunch are the deluxe garden bungalows, which come with a private pool. Facilities include a restaurant, a spa and a dive centre.

If you opt for an over-the-water bungalow, take a premium one as these are over deeper, clearer water. The artificial, white-sand beach is smaller than those at other resorts, but the Pearl's vibe is more intimate and relaxed.

🛏 Cook's Bay to Hauru Point

Tipaniers Iti   BUNGALOW **$**
(📋40 56 12 67; www.lestipaniers.com; PK21; bungalows d/q 9800/10,700 CFP; 🛜) Depending on your perspective, you'll find Tipaniers Iti either quiet or isolated. Looking out over spectacular Opunohu Bay, it consists of a handful of bungalows that are identical in a verdant property on the water's edge. Try for one of the two bungalows that face the lagoon. There's an over-the-water dock for lounging, but no beach. Snorkelling is good, but the water is deep.

Tipaniers Iti is an annex of Les Tipaniers, which is at Hauru Point, about 4km to the west. A free shuttle runs between the two properties in the evening, and guests can participate in Les Tipaniers' activities. Snorkelling gear and bikes are complimentary.

Cook's Bay & Maharepa

Cook's Bay & Maharepa

◎ Sights
1 Maison Blanche.............................. B1
2 Old Fish Market............................A3

◉ Activities, Courses & Tours
  Moorea Blue Diving .... (see 5)

🛏 Sleeping
3 Club Bali Hai A2
4 Kaveka A2
5 Moorea Pearl Resort & Spa................B1

🍴 Eating
6 Allo Pizza.....................................A2
7 Caraméline B1
  L'Ananas Bleu – The Blue
    Pineapple .... (see 3)
8 Le Rudy's......................................B1
9 Moorea Beach Café B1
10 Moz Café B1

ⓘ Information
11 Banque de Polynésie.....................B1
12 Banque de Tahiti...........................B1
13 Banque Socredo B1

Fare Vaihere   BUNGALOW **$$**
(📋40 56 19 19; www.farevaihere.com; PK15.5; bungalows d incl breakfast 18,000 CFP; 🛜) On the eastern shore of Opunohu Bay, Faire Vaihere consists of four bungalows resting in a leafy plot. They're nothing special (and for the

price, you'd expect air-conditioning), but are well kitted out; book in to the 'Badamier', which is right on the water. There's no beach, but snorkelling is excellent off the pontoon and Ta'ahiamanu (Mareto) Beach is a 15-minute walk away.

The owner is a dive instructor who readily dispenses expert opinions about local snorkel and dive trips. Evening meals are prepared to order (3950 CFP). Bikes, kayaks and snorkelling gear are complimentary. Rack rates are a tad overpriced, but specials are available between November and May for longer stays.

Fare Junette   BUNGALOW $$
(☎87 71 61 91; www.farejunettemoorea.com; PK14; bungalows q 12,000-14,000 CFP; 🖧) Two self-contained bungalows open onto a small patch of white sand. Both have private outside bathrooms. Nothing is fancy, but it all feels very proper. The setting is chilled out, and there's a child-friendly beach, with safe swimming. Free kayaks.

Motu Iti   BUNGALOW, DORM $$
(☎87 74 43 38, 40 55 05 20; www.pensionmotuiti. com; PK13.2; dm 1700 CFP, bungalows d 10,500-12,000 CFP; 🖧) This modest place is an acceptable standby for unfussy travellers. The five bungalows are tightly packed together on a small property overlooking the lagoon. Be sure to book one of the three sea-facing bungalows (the garden units have blocked views). The 10-bed dorm is a blessing for those watching their francs, but the crude bathrooms downstairs lack maintenance.

There's a bit of road noise but nothing to lose sleep over. There's no communal kitchen, but the waterfront restaurant serves acceptable food. Swimming is not that tempting, with very shallow waters and a profusion of algae, but guests can make use of kayaks to get to more appealing spots on the lagoon. As it's far from most tourist hot spots, you'll need your own transport to get around.

Hilton Moorea Lagoon
Resort & Spa   RESORT $$$
(☎40 55 11 11; www.moorea.hilton.com; PK14; bungalows d from 58,000 CFP; ❄🖧🏊) Magnificently laid out with real style and class, the Hilton is one of Mo'orea's best resorts. Of the 103 guest units, 54 are built over the water and come with the requisite glass floor panels for fish-viewing and decks with steps down into the clear, waist-deep water. The garden bungalows have their own (small) plunge pool but are quite squeezed together.

Try for Deluxe Garden bungalows 46, 47, 48, 50 and 51, which have great lagoon views. Amenities include a water-sports centre, a dive shop, a pool, a spa, a gym, two bars and two restaurants, including a great *crêperie* on a pontoon. The beach here is particularly attractive (with top snorkelling) and the activities desk is great – both of these aspects are important since the hotel is quite isolated from the main areas of the island.

🛏 Hauru Point

Fare Tokoau   BUNGALOW $
(☎87 35 21 98, 87 35 21 97; www.facebook.com/ tokoau; PK28.3; bungalows d 9500 CFP; 🖧) Run by a friendly young couple, this great-value abode features a clutch of self-contained bungalows that are scattered on a neat property. The beach here is disappointingly thin, but you can paddle free kayaks out to the white-sand *motu* across the lagoon. It's within walking distance of shops and restaurants, and bikes are available for hire. Cash only.

Camping Nelson   CAMPGROUND, BUNGALOW $
(☎40 56 15 18, 87 78 71 53; www.camping-nelson. pf; PK27; camp sites per person 1700-1800 CFP, dm 2400 CFP, d without bathroom 5200-5600 CFP, bungalows d from 6800-10,000 CFP; 🖧) A long-time budget favourite – an easy distinction given the lack of competitors – Camping Nelson boasts a spiffing lagoon frontage (but no shade to speak of). Pitch your tent on the grassy plot within earshot of the gentle surf, or choose one of the claustrophobic cabins in a barrackslike building. For more privacy, consider one of the pricier, more comfortable bungalows.

The spartan three-bed dorms, devoid of electrical sockets, fans and mosquito nets, are best avoided. Perks include hot water in the (salubrious) shared bathrooms and wi-fi access at the reception (open from 8.30am to noon and 1.30pm to 5pm). There's no communal kitchen, but there are cheap eateries nearby. Cash only.

Fare Miti   BUNGALOW $$
(☎87 21 65 59, 40 56 57 42; www.mooreafaremiti. com; PK27.5; bungalows q 13,000-15,000 CFP; 🖧) Deservedly popular and occupying a thin but picturesque stretch of sand (with a small *motu* as a backdrop), Fare Miti has only eight functional bungalows with few frills and a friendly relaxed atmosphere. They were modernised in 2015 and can sleep up to four (at a pinch). Kayaks and snorkel gear

Hauru Point

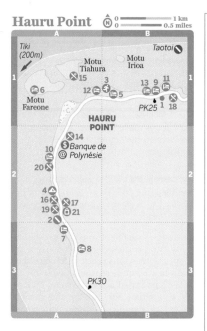

Hauru Point

Activities, Courses & Tours
	Aquablue ....(see 11)
1	ATV Moorea Tours................................ B1
	Moorea Eco Tour – Manu ....(see 11)
2	Moorea Fun Dive A2
3	Moorea Loca Boat B1
	Scubapiti......................................(see 12)
	Tip Nautic.....................................(see 12)
	Topdive...(see 11)
	XPR - Expair Moorea ....(see 11)

Sleeping
4	Camping Nelson....................................A2
5	Domloc B1
6	Dream Island A1
7	Fare Miti A3
8	Fare Tokoau...A3
9	Fenua Mata'i'oa B1
10	Hotel Hibiscus A2
11	Intercontinental Moorea Resort & Spa B1
12	Les Tipaniers A1
13	Taoa Here Beach House B1

Eating
14	A L'Heure du Sud A2
	Beach Café ....(see 12)
15	Coco Beach A1
16	Coco d'Isle A2
17	La Paillotte A2
18	Le Coco's Moorea B1
19	Le Lézard Jaune Café...........................A2
20	Le Mayflower A2
	Le Sunset ....(see 10)
	Les Tipaniers ....(see 12)

Shopping
21	Taniera Tattoo......................................A2

are complimentary. It's all within walking distance of shops and restaurants.

You can also order a meal and have it delivered to your bungalow. The best choice and most expensive unit, bungalow 5, is right on the beach; bungalows 4 and 6 offer great lagoon views.

Les Tipaniers　　　　　　　　　RESORT **$$**
(☑40 56 12 67; www.lestipaniers.com; PK25; d 9200 CFP, bungalows d 17,000-19,500 CFP; ☜) It's a bustling hub of activity on this lovely knuckle of beach jutting out towards a coral-laden stretch of lagoon. Scattered amid a flowery garden, the 22 bungalows aren't going to win any architectural awards but are big, clean and practical (most have kitchens and one to two bedrooms). It also has four cheaper, smaller rooms (book well ahead). One quibble: there's no air-con.

Les Tipaniers is a great spot for families and friends, but not private enough for a honeymoon. The resort also features two restaurants, a bar, a dive shop and a small water-sports centre. Free bikes.

Domloc　　　　　　　　　　　　VILLA **$$**
(☑87 72 75 80; www.domlocpolynesie.com; PK25; bungalows from 18,000 CFP; ☀☜) Domloc is actually a time-share vacation club, but it's run like a hotel – a cool hotel indeed, with eight well-appointed, fully equipped villas.

They're closely packed but are buffered by lush gardens, and the beach is just a few steps away from the property. Prices fluctuate wildly according to seasons and school holidays. Free kayaks. Cash only.

It's perfect for families as most villas can sleep between four and six people.

Hotel Hibiscus　　　　　　　　HOTEL **$$**
(☑40 56 12 20; www.hotel-hibiscus.pf; PK27; d 16,500 CFP, bungalows 16,500-30,000 CFP; ☀☜☷) The best part of this venture is the grounds, covered in swaying palms and expansive lawns and highlighted by a svelte ribbon of white sand. The 29 functional thatched-roof bungalows, although they won't knock your socks off, are tidy enough. Next to the pool there's also an undistinguished motel-like building with 12 rooms. They're bland but may be an option if air-conditioning is important to you. Hint: bungalows 1–3, 7–8

ⓘ VILLA RENTALS

For groups, families or long-term stays, renting a villa or house is a good bet, and this is a growing business on Mo'orea. Villas are great because you have room to stretch out, do your own cooking and enjoy plenty of privacy. These properties range from affordable units to lavish villas. A minimum stay of three nights is usually required. Check the following:

Abritel (www.abritel.fr) Offers villa rentals on Mo'orea.

Dream Island (☑87 77 84 79; www.dream-island.com; Motu Fareone; bungalow q 29,000 CFP; 🐕) A three-minute boat ride from Hauru Point brings you to this superbly located, exclusive island paradise. The two houses/bungalows were built using local materials in authentic Polynesian style and are equipped with kitchens. There is a four-night minimum and credit cards are accepted.

Robinson's Cove Villas (www.robinsoncove.com; Opunohu Bay; ❄🐕) Luxurious, fully equipped villas overlooking the water in Opunohu Bay.

Tahiti in Style (www.tahitiinstyle.com) Has a good selection of fully serviced villas.

---

and 11–13 have lagoon views. The on-site restaurant overlooks the beach.

Taoa Here Beach House   BUNGALOW $$$
(☑40 56 13 30; www.taoaheremoorea.com; Village Tiahura, PK25; bungalows d 22,000-25,000 CFP; ❄🐕) This upscale option offers four smartly finished bungalows built from quality materials, including local hardwoods and volcanic stones. Hint: try for the 'Painapo', which is partly built on stilts and offers unimpeded lagoon views. They're all self-contained and geared for families looking for a quiet spot that overlooks the sea, although there is not really a beach here. Kayaks are free.

Fenua Mata'i'oa   VILLA $$$
(☑40 55 00 25; www.fenua-mataioa.com; PK25, Village Tiahura; ste 28,000-60,000 CFP; ❄🐕) After something extra-special? Make a bee-line for this tropical cocoon with spiffing water frontage. Here you'll go giddy over the exuberant, slightly over-the-top interior. Resting in leafy grounds, the five suites are dripping with colourful paintings, silks and antiques. A good choice for honeymooners who are after some serious cosseting and privacy but don't want to stay in a resort.

Half-board is an extra 11,000 CFP per person. The only downside is that although it has lagoon access, there's no beach.

Intercontinental Moorea Resort & Spa   RESORT $$$
(☑40 55 19 19; www.moorea.intercontinental.com; PK25; r & bungalows d from 42,000 CFP; ❄🐕🛶) Spread over more than 10 hectares along the seashore, Mo'orea's biggest resort boasts 147 units and features a host of facilities and amenities, including two pools, two restaurants, two bars, a well-respected spa, a gift shop, a water-sports centre, a full dive shop and a marine-turtle rehabilitation centre.

With its varied accommodation options, it's appropriate for couples and families alike. Pick a garden bungalow with plunge pool or a unit that sits on a small artificial island with a terrace over the water. The cheaper units occupy a curving two-storey motel-style wing. One proviso: some guests have found the service a bit lackadaisical.

🛏 Haapiti to Vaiare

Mark's Place Moorea   BUNGALOW $
(☑87 78 93 65, 40 56 43 02; www.marksplacemoorea.com; PK23.5; bungalows d/q from 8000/12,000 CFP; 🐕) The vast, lush garden and creative, smartly finished bungalows – it helps that the American owner is a carpenter – make this a good option on Mo'orea, but we've heard the odd grumble about variable service. No two units are alike, but they are all equipped to a high standard and competitively priced. The amply sized Manu and Opuhi units are ideal for families.

It's away from the beach and just about everything else besides the Haapiti surf break, but bike and kayak hire (1000 CFP per day) make getting around less of a chore. There's a minimum stay of two nights.

Moorea Surf B&B   GUESTHOUSE $
(☑87 70 80 29; http://mooreasurfbnb.wix.com/moorea-surf-bnb; PK20.3; d/q without bathroom & incl breakfast 10,500/13,000 CFP; 🐕) More a guesthouse than a B&B, this venture is popular with unfussy travellers and surfers lured by the proximity of the Haapiti surf

break. Owner Tama speaks English and can guide you to the spot for 4000 CFP (two hours). Accommodation-wise, it consists of four pokey, wood-panelled rooms in a chalet-like building. There's a communal kitchen, or you can order a meal (2500 CFP).

The property opens onto a lovely bay, but don't get too excited – there's no beach and the waters are murky at low tide. You'll need to rent a scooter or a car to get around the island from here. Cash only.

★ **Résidence Linareva**   BUNGALOW **$$**
(☑40 55 05 65; www.linareva.com; PK34.5; studios & bungalows d 16,700-23,100 CFP; ✉☎) Résidence Linareva has a great reputation and features a cluster of well-furnished, self-contained bungalows in a lush garden by the lagoon. What's missing is a swimmable beach, but there's great snorkelling off the long pontoon jutting out over the lagoon. If you don't mind the isolated location (a vehicle is essential), it's a great place to stay.

No meals are served except breakfast (1650 CFP). Bicycles, kayaks and snorkelling equipment are provided free of charge. The on-site dive shop is an added bonus.

Tehuarupe   BUNGALOW **$$**
(☑40 56 57 33; www.moorea-paradise.com; PK22.2; bungalows d 12,000 CFP; ☎✉) On the mountain side of the road, these four seaview units are a home away from home, with lovingly finished interiors, wooden decks, vast beds and tastefully chosen furniture (but no air-con). They're spacious and self-contained. Expect a bit of road noise during the day. The catch? They're not on the lagoon (though within hopping distance of the sea). Cash only.

There's no beach nearby, but guests are provided with free kayaks to paddle to coral gardens, or you can chill by the small pool. As it's isolated, you'll definitely need your own wheels if you want to explore the island.

Kahekaro   BUNGALOW **$$**
(☑87 37 95 78, 87 75 76 58; www.kahekaro.com; PK23.5; bungalows d/q 12,000/15,000 CFP; ☎) This venture is a particularly great find for families as the kitchen-equipped bungalows comfortably sleep four and they're well spaced out. They face a small 'beach', which is just adequate for a waist-high dip at high tide, although free kayaks offer compensation. The nearest store is just a 10-minute walk away. Note that sheets and towels cost extra (3000 CFP). Two-night minimum.

Pension Aute   BUNGALOW **$$**
(☑87 78 23 34; www.pensionaute.com; PK16.4; bungalows d 11,200-13,200 CFP; ☎) This family-run abode is a bit isolated, but that's part of its appeal. Three bungalows are ideally positioned on a skinny stretch of white sand and offer killer views over the turquoise water. There are also five garden bungalows with no views. They're tightly packed in exotic garden areas, but they're all tidy and well equipped, and the larger ones are suitable for families.

Here the lagoon is shallow, which makes it safe for young children. Adults can kayak to superb coral gardens closer to the barrier reef. It's quite far from the 'action', but car hire makes it easier to get around. Rates are discounted for longer stays (except during school holidays).

Atuana Lodge   B&B **$$**
(☑40 56 36 03; www.atuanalodge.com; PK6.3; bungalow d 13,000 CFP, r incl half-board per person 12,500 CFP; ✉☎) Concealed behind a rather dull wall is this welcoming place run by a French-Tahitian couple. The two rooms in the owners' house are immaculate; try for the one upstairs, which has a better lagoon view. For do-it-yourself types, there's also a self-contained bungalow with a tiny bedroom and outside toilets. Kayaks are free. What's missing? A 'real' beach.

There are no eateries nearby, but you can order a meal if you don't fancy cooking. Transfers to/from the ferry quay are free. There's a two-night minimum stay. Cash only.

🏖 Temae

Fare Maeva   BUNGALOW **$**
(☑87 74 10 14; www.maeva-i-moorea.com; bungalows d 10,000 CFP; ☎) A good deal for chill-seekers. This low-key, isolated place is dominated by coconut trees and coral gravel. The three bungalows are no-frills but tidy and have a kitchen. The property is just 100m from the (rocky) shore; for swimming, you'll need to head to Temae Beach, which is 500m away. No meal service, but there's a grocery store nearby. Cash only.

Green Lodge   BUNGALOW **$$**
(☑87 77 62 26, 40 56 31 00; www.greenlodge.pf; d incl breakfast 16,000-20,000 CFP, bungalows d incl breakfast 20,000-33,000 CFP; ✉☎✉) This relaxing cocoon with a boutique feel offers all the luxuries of the fancy resorts, but with enough intimacy and local flavour to remind you that you're still in Polynesia. The sensitively

furnished bungalows come with all mod cons and orbit around an alluring pool and a nicely laid-out tropical garden. Evening meals are available on request (4500 CFP).

The beach here is nice for sunbathing, less so for swimming; Temae Beach is a five-minute walk away. Bikes are available for hire. Overall, it's a good option for couples looking to get away from the resort scene.

Moorea Golf Lodge   BUNGALOW **$$**
(🖉40 55 08 55; www.mooreagolflodge.pf; bungalows d from 12,000-16,000 CFP; ❄🕿) This peaceful haven sits on a quiet strip of beach (walk five minutes to the better main beach). The four pine bungalows resemble Swiss chalets and are very large (sleeping up to six people) and airy. All have equipped kitchens. Hint: try for the 'Bora Bora' or the 'Mangareva', which are more expensive but offer unimpeded ocean views. Prices drop for stays longer than two nights.

Sofitel la Ora
Moorea Beach Resort   RESORT **$$$**
(🖉40 55 12 12; www.sofitel-moorea-iaora.com; bungalows d from 40,000 CFP; ❄🕿☀) No, you're not hallucinating, the lagoon here is *that* turquoise. This excellent, modern Polynesian resort sports 114 units, including 39 opulent overwater bungalows and luxuriously appointed beach and garden units. It's on the best beach on the island. The list of facilities is prolific, with two restaurants, a wonderful spa, a small pool and a diving centre.

It's the only resort facing Tahiti, whose cloud-capped summits form a picture-postcard backdrop. This also means that it gets less sunshine in the afternoon.

✖ Eating

There's a good range of independent restaurants on Mo'orea, with Maharepa, Cook's Bay and Hauru Point the island's dining epicentres. Many hotels and resorts have in-house restaurants also open to nonguests.

There are quite a few supermarkets and smaller shops around the island where you can buy fresh baguettes and basic supplies.

✖ Maharepa to Hauru Point

Moz Café   CAFETERIA **$**
(🖉40 56 38 12; Maharepa; mains 500-1100 CFP; ☻7am-2.30pm Mon-Fri; 🕿) You wouldn't guess it from the outside (it's next to a bank, upstairs), but this zinging joint is a great place to enjoy a satisfying breakfast or a light meal

at lunchtime. There's everything from palate-pleasing salads to well-made sandwiches (from 300 CFP) and devilish desserts (hmmm the crème brûlée). No outdoor seating.

Lollipop   ICE CREAM **$**
(🖉87 20 76 56; PK2.5, Maharepa; 1/2 scoops 250/450 CFP; ☻10am-5.30pm Mon-Sat, 1-5.30pm Sun) Generous scoops and about 30 flavours are the trademarks of this drool-inducing ice-cream parlour on the eastern outskirts of Maharepa. As if that wasn't enough, it also tempts the weak-willed with homemade doughnuts, muffins and pancakes. Sweet!

Caraméline   CAFETERIA **$**
(🖉40 56 15 88; Maharepa; mains 900-2300 CFP; ☻7am-4pm Mon-Sat, 7am-2pm Sun; 🕿) Get all-day American, French or Tahitian breakfasts (from 600 CFP), burgers, pizzas, salads, ice-cream treats and daily specials at this affordable and popular cafeteria right in the centre of Maharepa. Local gourmands rave about the French-style pastries and crêpes.

★**Crêperie Toatea**   CREPERIE **$$**
(🖉40 55 11 11; Hilton Moorea Lagoon Resort & Spa, PK14; mains 1300-3100 CFP; ☻6.30-10pm) Not your average *crêperie*, this venture is renowned for its gourmet crêpes prepared to order by an Alsatian chef. Where else could you savour a crêpe stuffed with fresh fish in white-wine sauce? Another draw is the setting – it's inside the Hilton Moorea, on the pontoon that leads to the overwater bungalows (nonguests are welcome).

At night the water is lit up so you can watch rays and blacktip sharks swim below. Pricey, but well worth it for the experience. It's such a shame that service is so slow.

Snack-Resto
La Canadienne   INTERNATIONAL, BURGERS **$$**
(🖉87 73 45 78; PK2.5, Maharepa; mains 1300-2600 CFP; ☻11.30am-2pm Mon & Wed-Sun, plus 6-9pm Wed-Sun) Run by two Quebecers, this eatery gets rave reviews for its lusty burgers, which come in many variations – the *mahimahi* option is tops. It also serves up grills, crêpes and salads as well as desserts with – you guessed it – maple syrup.

Chez Fifi   CAFETERIA **$$**
(🖉40 56 14 23; PK15.5; snacks 300-600 CFP, mains 1500-1900 CFP; ☻11am-4pm Tue-Sun; 🕿) If you're decadent, you'll bypass the mains and go straight for the crêpes, waffles or ice creams at this friendly cafeteria on the coastal road. If you're hungry, you may begin with an excellent grilled fish. And for the sensible?

Tuck into frondy salads or well-prepared paninis. The décor is plain and no-nonsense, but the effort goes into the food.

Lilikoi Garden Café INTERNATIONAL $$
(☑87 29 61 41; PK14; mains 1500-2000 CFP; ◷11am-3pm daily, plus 6-9pm Fri; ☎) Not your average *roulotte* (food van operating as a snack bar), Lilikoi is painted in vivid colours and positioned in lush tropical gardens. Foodwise, it serves light meals made with locally sourced ingredients, including sandwiches, salads and lunch specials. Great smoothies, too. It's about 300m west of the Hilton Moorea Lagoon Resort & Spa, on the mountain side of the road.

Allo Pizza PIZZA $$
(☑40 56 18 22; PK7.8, Cook's Bay; mains 1400-1800 CFP; ◷11am-2pm & 5-8.30pm; ☎) Despite its unpromising location across the road from the *gendarmerie* (police station), this is a great place to taste wood-fired pizzas. There's a huge variety of toppings, including fresh tuna. There's also a small selection of salads and steaks as well as a limited dessert menu – titillate your tastebuds with the unusual 'banana pizza' or a homemade chocolate mousse. Takeaway is available.

**L'Ananas Bleu –
The Blue Pineapple** TAHITIAN $$
(☑40 56 13 68; Club Bali Hai, PK8, Cook's Bay; mains 600-2300 CFP; ◷7am-2pm Wed-Mon, 6-9pm Fri) On the water in the Club Bali Hai, this hotel restaurant serves snacks and light lunches, but it's the setting that's the pull here, more than the food – the views of Cook's Bay are divine. Catch the dance show and seafood barbecue on Friday nights at 6.30pm.

Moorea Beach Café TAHITIAN, FRENCH $$$
(☑40 56 29 29; www.mooreabeachcafe.com; PK6.7, Maharepa; mains 1600-3200 CFP; ◷11am-9pm; ☎) This hip lagoon-front resto-bar is as adept at serving up light bites as it is heartier meals. The menu is eclectic and inventive, and the breezy, sunset-friendly deck overlooking the water is super-atmospheric. In-house cocktails are very nice, too. Free pick-up.

Le Rudy's FRENCH, TAHITIAN $$$
(☑40 56 58 00; www.rudysmoorea.com; PK6.8, Maharepa; mains 2700-3800 CFP; ◷5.30-10pm) This white hacienda-style building on the mountain side of the road is quite popular with American visitors staying at nearby resorts and looking for a special night out. Dig into well-executed meat and fish dishes and wash it down with a glass of wine. Free pick-up.

Try the fillet of parrotfish stuffed with crab or the lamb curry in coconut milk, the house's signature offerings.

Hauru Point

A L'Heure du Sud SANDWICHES $
(☑87 70 03 12; PK25; sandwiches 450-1000 CFP; ◷10.30am-3pm Thu-Tue) Bargain! A great variety of well-stuffed sandwiches (think steak or fish and barbecue sauce stuffed in a baguette) are served at this blue *roulotte* in front of Le Petit Village shopping centre. It also dishes up generous burgers and voluminous salads that are best enjoyed at the tables behind the van. Cash only.

La Paillotte FAST FOOD $
(☑40 56 48 49; PK27.3; mains 700-1500 CFP; ◷10.30am-2.30pm & 6-8.30pm Thu-Mon) This popular *roulotte* is worth visiting for its cheap snacks and generous mains, including burgers, salads, grilled chicken, raw fish in coconut milk, crêpes and generous sandwiches. Take your plunder to the beach or grab a (plastic) table in the garden beside the *roulotte*. For an energy bolt, slug down a freshly squeezed pineapple juice (500 CFP).

★**Snack Mahana** TAHITIAN $$
(☑40 56 41 70; PK23.2; mains 1600-2300 CFP; ◷11.30am-2.30pm Tue-Sat) In a sublime location overlooking the turquoise lagoon, breezy Mahana is a heart-stealing open-air *snack*. Linger over burgers, a plate of grilled *mahimahi* (dorado) or tuna sashimi while savouring the lagoon views. Light years away from the glitz usually associated with French Polynesia, it can't get more mellow than this. So Mo'orea. Cash only. Tip: arrive before 1pm and reserve a table by the sea.

Le Lézard Jaune Café FUSION $$
(☑40 56 35 00; PK27.3; mains 2200-3100 CFP; ◷6.30-9.30pm Wed-Sun; ☎) A surprisingly hip restaurant inside a house complete with dark-wood interior, this cool culinary outpost opened in 2015 specialises in creative fish and meat dishes seared *a la plancha*. For dessert, don't miss the impressive caramelised (or flambéed) banana or pineapple. Free pick-up.

Les Tipaniers FRENCH, ITALIAN $$
(☑40 56 12 67; PK25; mains 1500-2900 CFP; ◷6.30-9.30pm) Part of the eponymous hotel, this elegant roadside restaurant serves up wholesome Italian and French-inspired dishes, including pizzas, pastas, salads, fish and meat dishes. Dim lighting contributes to romantic dining under a natural thatched roof.

Beach Café INTERNATIONAL $$

(☑40 56 12 67; Les Tipaniers, PK25; mains 1400-2500 CFP; ⊙11.30am-2.15pm) As the name suggests, this eatery has a fabulous beach frontage. After a morning spent paddling across the lagoon, re-energise with a copious salad, a juicy burger or a plate of spag. Good sandwiches (500 CFP), too. It's part of Les Tipaniers hotel, but nonguests are welcome.

Le Sunset INTERNATIONAL $$

(☑40 56 26 00; Hotel Hibiscus, PK27; mains 1000-3500 CFP; ⊙11.30am-2pm & 6-9pm) This eatery in the Hotel Hibiscus has a great beachside setting; the terrace offers front-row seats for the sunset. From pizzas and salads to burgers and satisfying grilled meats, the menu covers enough territory to please most palates.

Coco d'Isle INTERNATIONAL $$

(☑40 56 59 07; PK27.3; mains 1400-3000 CFP; ⊙6.30-9.30pm Mon-Sat) Don't be discouraged by the modest exterior and the unspectacular location on the main road. The cool sand floor – delicious between your toes – is a nice touch, although the plastic chairs mar the experience a bit. The food is a crowd-pleasing mix of steaks, fish dishes, seafood, salads and pizzas. Free pick-up.

★ Le Coco's Moorea FUSION $$$

(☑40 55 15 14; PK24.8; lunch mains 2200 CFP; menus 6000-14,000 CFP; ⊙6-9.30pm Mon-Thu, 11.30am-9.30pm Fri-Sun; 🛜) This posh restaurant was designed with couples in mind – the widely spaced tables, attentive service, dim lighting and strong design-led interior create a suitably romantic atmosphere. The menu drips with panache, with an inventive mix of local ingredients and European flair. Lunch specials are a bargain. Needless to say, the wine list is top-notch. Alas, there are no direct lagoon views.

Le Mayflower FRENCH $$$

(☑40 56 53 59; PK27; mains 2300-3600 CFP; ⊙11.30am-1.45pm Wed-Fri, 6.30-9.30pm Tue-Sun) The G-spot for local gourmands. A neo-classical French menu puts the emphasis on fish and meat dishes with the addition of locally grown (or caught) ingredients. The signature dish? Lobster ravioli. Thanks to subdued lighting and elegant furnishings, it manages to be atmospheric and snug despite its location on the main road. Free pick-up.

✕ Motu Tiahura

★ Coco Beach INTERNATIONAL $$

(☑87 72 57 26; mains 1300-2700 CFP; ⊙11.30am-2.30pm Wed-Sun, Tue-Sun during school holidays) This friendly eatery with a casual atmosphere has an idyllic setting on Motu Tiahura that is guaranteed to help you switch to 're-lax' mode. The choice is limited and prices are a bit inflated, but the food is fresh and tasty – the octopus salad will certainly win your heart. Bookings are essential on weekends. Cash only.

You can get a boat to the *motu* from the mainland (700 CFP per person return).

✕ Haapiti to Temae

Pizza Daniel PIZZA $

(☑40 56 39 95; PK34; mains 1300-1500 CFP; ⊙11am-9pm Fri-Wed) Locals swear this little shack, which has been around for more than 20 years, serves the best pizza on Mo'orea. Pull up a stool, order the thin-crust tuna pizza (with fresh tuna – delicious!), chat with the owner, and then check out the eels in the adjacent stream.

Le K INTERNATIONAL $$$

(☑40 55 12 25; Sofitel Moorea la Ora Beach Resort, Temae; menu 15,000 CFP; ⊙6-9.30pm Mon-Wed, Fri & Sat) One of Mo'orea's most prestigious venues, Le K offers the intoxicating mix of fine dining, romantic atmosphere and the feel of sand between your toes. Flickering candles, soft music, carved wooden tables and chairs, a soaring thatched-roof ceiling and an attentive service make it a real date-pleaser. The seven-course menu changes daily. Reservations are essential.

🍷 Drinking & Nightlife

Mo'orea is more the place to pay off a sleep debt than to kick up your heels. The big hotels have bars where all are welcome to whet their palates with a predinner drink, and some restaurants host occasional live music.

A couple of times a week the bigger hotels organise Polynesian music and dance performances. Call hotels for dates and times.

🔒 Shopping

There are two small shopping centres on the island. The shopping centre in Maharepa has a few shops and stores.

The coastal road is littered with places selling *pareu* (sarongs; some of them hand-painted), T-shirts and other curios. There are also a number of places dotted around the island where artists display their work.

Although no pearl farms are located on Mo'orea, a number of places around the island specialise in black pearls. Prices are generally the same as on Tahiti, but you'll have to shop around.

ℹ Information

Most hotels and *pensions* have wi-fi access. There's a medical centre in Afareaitu, and several private doctors and three pharmacies.

Banque de Polynésie (Le Petit Village, Hauru Point) Has one ATM.

Banque de Polynésie (Maharepa; ⏱ 8-11.30am & 1-4pm Mon-Fri) Changes major currencies and has an ATM.

Banque de Tahiti (Maharepa; ⏱ 8-11.30am & 1-4pm Mon-Fri) Changes major currencies and has an ATM.

Banque Socredo (Maharepa; ⏱ 8-11.30am & 1-4pm Mon-Fri) Changes major currencies and has an ATM.

Magic Photo Electroménager (☑ 40 56 59 59; PK26.5, Hauru Point; per hr 450 CFP; ⏱ 8am-noon & 1.30-5pm Mon-Fri, 8am-noon Sat; 🛜) Internet and wi-fi access.

ℹ Getting There & Away

There's less than 20km of blue Pacific between Tahiti and Mo'orea, and getting from one island to the other is simplicity itself.

AIR

Air Tahiti (☑ 40 86 42 42; www.airtahiti.pf) flies between Mo'orea and Pape'ete (4900 CFP one way, one to three daily), Huahine (14,000 CFP one way, three weekly), Ra'iatea (16,000 CFP one way, five weekly) and Bora Bora (22,000 CFP one way, daily).

BOAT

It's a breezy ride between Tahiti and Mo'orea. At the **Gare Maritime** (p50) in Pape'ete, you can hop on one of the high-speed ferries and be on Mo'orea in about half an hour. First departures in the morning are usually around 6am; the last trips are around 4.30pm or 5.30pm. You can buy tickets at the ticket counter on the quay just a few minutes before departure. If you are bringing a car, it's best to book in advance.

Aremiti 5 (☑ 40 56 31 10, 40 50 57 57; www.aremiti.pf; adult/child 1500/950 CFP) This catamaran jets to and from Mo'orea in about 35 minutes, three times daily from Monday to Friday. For a bike/car, it costs 250/5000 CFP.

Aremiti Ferry 2 (☑ 40 56 31 10, 40 56 57 57; www.aremiti.pf; adult/child 1500/950 CFP) Runs three to five times daily between Pape'ete and Mo'orea and takes about 45 minutes to cross. For a bike/car, it costs 250/5000 CFP.

Terevau (☑ 40 50 03 59, 40 50 03 56; www.terevau.pf; adult/child 1200/600 CFP) Runs four to six times daily between Pape'ete and Mo'orea and takes about 35 minutes. It costs 240/4200 CFP for a bike/car.

ℹ Getting Around

The coastal road is about 60km. Getting around Mo'orea without a car or scooter is not that easy. Distances aren't great but are often too far to walk. Bear in mind that many restaurants will pick you up for free or for a nominal fee if you call them.

TO/FROM THE AIRPORT & QUAY

All ferries dock at the quay in Vaiare. In principle, buses (300 CFP) meet all *Aremiti 5* catamaran arrivals and departures but not the *Aremiti* ferry. From the quay, one bus heads south and the other north, completing the island circuit and dropping you off wherever you need to be. Mo'orea's taxis are notoriously expensive: from the airport to the Intercontinental Moorea Resort & Spa will cost about 4500 CFP.

The airport is in the island's northeastern corner. Most hotels offer airport transfers.

BICYCLE & SCOOTER

Bikes can be hired. Some hotels and *pensions* supply them free to guests, or the following can deliver then to your hotel:

Albert Location (☑ 40 56 19 28, 40 56 33 75; www.albert-transport.net) Has three outlets around the island. Scooters are 6000 CFP for 24 hours. Also rents bikes (2000 CFP a day).

Moorea Fun Bike (☑ 87 70 96 95) Offers scooters/bikes for 5500/1900 CFP for 24 hours.

Rent a Bike – Rent a Scooter (☑ 87 71 11 09; www.rent-a-bike-moorea.e-monsite.com) Scooters cost 5500 CFP per 24 hours.

CAR

Having your own wheels is useful but expensive. Car-hire operators can be found at the Vaiare ferry quay and at some of the major hotels. Generally, you'll pay from around 9500 CFP per day including liability insurance and unlimited kilometres. Try booking online for cheaper rates. Reserve in advance on weekends.

There are petrol stations near the Vaiare ferry quay, close to the airport, beside Cook's Bay and at Le Petit Village on Hauru Point.

The following can deliver to your hotel:

Albert Location (☑ 40 56 33 75, 40 56 19 28; www.albert-transport.net) Has three outlets on the island. Rates start at 9000 CFP but discounts are available.

Avis (☑ 40 56 32 61, 40 56 32 68; www.avis-tahiti.com) At the ferry quay at Vaiare, Intercontinental Moorea Resort & Spa and Club Bali Hai. Negotiate, but figure on 8800 CFP per day for a small car.

Europcar (☑ 87 73 32 40, 40 56 28 64; www.europcar-tahiti.com; Vaiare) Prices from 7700 CFP.

Huahine

POP 6430

Includes ➡

History 95
Sights........................... 95
Activities 98
Tours 100
Sleeping 100
Eating 103

Best Places to Stay

➡ Maitai Lapita Village (p101)

➡ Tifaifai Motu Mahare (p101)

➡ Tupuna (p102)

➡ Moana Lodge (p102)

➡ Meherio (p101)

Best Places to Eat

➡ Chez Tara (p103)

➡ Huahine Yacht Club (p103)

➡ Tenahe – Relais Mahana (p103)

➡ Omai Restaurant (p103)

Why Go?

Huahine is immaculately tropical and effortlessly Polynesian. Lush and scarcely developed, this is an island to visit for extreme calm, communing with nature and a genuine taste of culture. There are plenty of opportunities for diving, surfing, snorkelling, exploring top-notch archaeological sites and horse riding, but the beauty of this place is just how easy it is to relax and do very little at all. The days go by, your skin gets a little darker and your smile a little wider.

Huahine feels like one island, but in fact it's two, connected by a short bridge. Huahine Nui (Big Huahine), to the north, is home to the bustling little village of Fare and most of the main tourist and administrative facilities. Rugged and isolated Huahine Iti (Little Huahine), to the south, offers the islands' best beaches, azure lagoons and a serene, get-away-from-it-all atmosphere.

When to Go

➡ July through to September is the dry and sunny high season – perfect for outdoor activities, especially hiking.

➡ In July, the Heiva cultural festival is a prime time to be on the island for some spontaneous fun.

➡ May, June, October and November are good shoulder-season months for decent weather. French Polynesia's biggest sporting event, Hawaiki Nui canoe race, starts on Huahine in early November.

➡ Diving and surfing are popular year-round.

History

Europeans first arrived here in 1769, when James Cook and company landed on Huahine's shores. Polynesians inhabited the island for thousands of years before Europeans arrived: archaeological excavations to the north of Fare reveal some of the earliest traces of settlement in the Society Islands. Despite a hostile reception from the native inhabitants, Cook returned to Huahine twice, in 1774 and 1777. In 1808 a group of London Missionary Society (LMS) missionaries moved to Huahine to escape the turmoil on Tahiti. They remained for only a year but returned in 1818 to further the spread of Christianity in the region. Huahine supported the Pomare royal family in the struggle against the French, and there were several clashes between 1846 and 1888 before French rule was eventually accepted. Although the French kicked the English Protestant missionaries out, the island remains predominantly Protestant.

◉ Sights

◎ Huahine Nui

A convenient way to see the sights is to start in Fare and complete a 60km circuit around the larger island in a clockwise direction.

Fare TOWN, BEACH

A visit to tiny Fare almost feels like stepping back in time, so perfectly does it capture the image of a sleepy South Seas port. There's not a lot to do, but that's part of Fare's appeal. Check out the colourful waterside market or a few creative boutiques, or hire a bicycle and just pedal around a bit.

You'll find a good stretch of white-sand beach on the northern outskirts of town (follow the coastline from New Te Marara restaurant). It's great for sunbathing and swimming, and offers excellent sunset vistas. The wide, super-clear lagoon here drops off quickly, providing some truly great snorkelling amid stunning coral and dense fish populations.

Fare looks out over Haamene Bay, which has two passes to the sea: the northern Avamoa Pass is the main entry point for inter-island shipping, while the Avapeihi (Fitii) Pass to the south is a great diving site.

Lake Fauna Nui LAKE

About 2km north of Fare, the main sealed road runs along the inland side of Lake

Huahine Highlights

❶ Snorkelling over colourful fish and coral at **Le Jardin de Corail** (p98).

❷ Taking the uphill *marae* walk at **Maeva** (p97).

❸ Hiking **Mt Tapu** (p100) for panoramic views over the island and lagoon.

❹ Diving in the **Avapeihi (Fitii) Pass** (p35).

❺ Feasting on Tahitian specialities at **Chez Tara** (p103).

❻ Horse riding around **Lake Fauna Nui** (p100).

❼ Hiring a dinghy and finding your own slice of paradise at **Hana Iti Beach** (p98).

Fauna Nui. It's also possible to turn off to the airport and take the road on the ocean side of the lake and then return to the main part of the island by the bridge at Maeva village.

The shallow expanse of Lake Fauna Nui (also known as Lake Maeva) is in fact an inlet from the sea. The land to the north of this is known as Motu Ovarei.

Huahine

Motu Tresor MUSEUM
(☎87 23 03 23; www.motutresor.com; ⊙9.30am-5.30pm Mon-Fri, Sat & Sun by appointment) **FREE**
On the airport road, what's even more impressive than this collection of more than 500 French Polynesian shells is the fasci-nating tour (in English or French) about the behaviour, ecology and history of each species. Count on one hour for the tour then don't forget to peruse the pearl shop – the owner is the only professionally trained jeweller on Huahine.

Huahine

⊙ Sights
1 Avea Bay C6
2 Fare Potee.................................... C2
3 Fish Traps.................................... C2
4 Gallery Umatatea.......................... C2
5 Hana Iti Beach B5
6 Huahine Nui Pearls & Pottery C3
7 Lake Fauna Nui.............................. B1
8 Le Jardin de Corail........................ C2
9 Maeva... C2
10 Marae Anini................................. C6
11 Marae Manunu C2
12 Matairea Hill Archaeological Sites........ C2
13 Motu Tresor................................. B1

⊙ Activities, Courses & Tours
14 Distillery Huahine Passion.................... A2
   Huahine Randonnée......................(see 22)
   La Jardin de Corail..........................(see 8)
15 La Petite Ferme.............................. B2
16 Les Grottes (The Caves)...................... A3
17 Mahana Dive................................... A6
18 Motu Topati D3
19 Pacific Blue Adventure....................... A6

🛏 Sleeping
20 Chez Guynette A6
   Chez Tara.................................. (see 34)
21 Fare Maeva B1

22 Hiva Plage.................................... C6
23 Huahine Vacances........................... B3
24 Maitai Lapita Village...................... A5
25 Meherio...................................... A5
26 Moana Lodge C6
27 Pension Fare Ara B2
28 Rande's Shack A1
29 Relais Mahana.............................. C6
30 Tifaifai & Café............................. C2
31 Tifaifai Motu Mahare...................... C2
32 Tupuna....................................... B4
33 Villas Bougainville......................... B3

🍴 Eating
   Chez Guynette ....(see 20)
34 Chez Tara C6
35 Huahine Yacht Club A6
36 Market....................................... B6
   Omai Restaurant ....(see 24)
37 Pizzeria Roulotte Italia..................... B2
38 Roulottes.................................... B6
39 Super Fare Nui – Super U B6
   Tenahe – Relais Mahana.............(see 29)

ℹ Transport
40 Air Tahiti A6
41 Avis... B6
42 Europcar A5
   Fare Maeva.................................(see 21)

HUAHINE SIGHTS

Gallery Umatatea

ART GALLERY

(☑40 68 70 79; www.polynesiapaintings.com)
FREE On an isolated property by the road on Motu Ovarei, you'll find this art gallery, where the exotic paintings of the highly respected artist Melanie Dupre are on display and prints are on sale. The gallery is open when the artist is home.

Maeva

VILLAGE

Prior to European influence, Maeva village, about 7km east of Fare, was the seat of royal power on the island. It's mostly famous for its concentration of pre-European archaeological sites, including a host of *marae* (traditional temples) scattered along the shoreline and also up the slopes of Matairea Hill.

Excavations and restoration of the site commenced in 1923; nearly 30 *marae* have since been located, more than half of which have been restored. The exceptional density of *marae* on the hillside has led to a theory that it was entirely inhabited by nobility and the families of the chiefs.

Situated on the water's edge on the Fare side of Maeva, the **Fare Potee** (donation; ⊙8.30am-3.30pm Mon-Fri, 9-11am Sat & Sun) is a replica of an open traditional house, which now holds a lovely little museum and is tended by the lovely Maui, who can answer questions and explain more about the site. Around the site are 10 or more *marae*, some of which may date back to the 16th century. Flagstones cover a wide expanse of land along the shoreline.

In the village, look for the **Maison de la Vanille** (☑28 96 43; ⊙8am-4pm Mon-Sat), a family-run outfit that sells sweet-scented vanilla pods.

Beside the bridge coming off Motu Ovarei are a number of V-shaped fish traps, made from rocks. They have been here for centuries and some are still in use. The tips of the Vs point towards the ocean, the long stone arms emerging above the water level. As the fish are pulled towards the sea by the ebb tide they become trapped in the circular basin at the point of the V, where they are easily caught, usually by net or harpoon.

Marae Manunu

ARCHAEOLOGICAL SITE

Marae Manunu stands on the *motu,* across the bridge from the main Maeva complex. The massive structure is 2m high, 40m long and nearly 7m wide. It features a two-stepped *ahu* (altar) platform. (The only other such

WORTH A TRIP

HANA ITI BEACH

Here's a secret spot (shhh; map p96): the beach of the former Hana Iti Hotel. This dreamlike cove lapped by lapis-lazuli waters offers a nice patch of sand backed by lush hills, with a row of palm trees leaning over the shore. There's no access road; get there by kayak or hire a dinghy.

platform in the Leeward Islands is at Marae Anini, the community *marae* of Huahine Iti.) This *marae* was primarily dedicated to Tane, Huahine's own god of war and fishing.

Le Jardin de Corail   BEACH
If solitude is what you're seeking, head for this secluded beach at the southern tip of Motu Ovarei, just off the now defunct Sofitel. It features shade trees, white sand, calm waters and healthy coral gardens a few finstrokes away.

Huahine Nui Pearls & Pottery   PEARL FARM
(☑87 78 30 20; www.huahine-pearlfarm.com; ⏲10am-4pm Mon-Sat, 10am-noon Sun) FREE
This little pearl shop is located on a pearl farm in the middle of the lagoon and also features the work of the founder, renowned potter Peter Owen. From Faie a ferry departs for the studio every 15 minutes from 10am to 4pm. You'll be given a demonstration of pearl farming and have an opportunity to browse the pearl jewellery collection.

Faie   VILLAGE
The coast road turns inland beside narrow Faie Bay to the village of Faie. Huahine's famous blue-eyed eels can be seen in the river just over the bridge – buy a can of sardines from the stand here and handfeed them if you're brave enough. Inland from Faie it's a steep climb to the *belvédère*, or lookout, on the slopes of Mt Turi. From this high point, the road drops even more steeply to the shores of Maroe Bay.

Fitii   VILLAGE
Just before completing the Huahine Nui circuit, the road passes through the Fitii district. This is an important agricultural area in the shadow of Mt Paeo (440m), where taro, vanilla and other crops are grown.

Distillery Huahine Passion   DISTILLERY
(bottles from 1800 CFP; ⏲9am-4pm Mon-Sat) Delicious liquors and *l'eau de vie* (fruit

spirit) made from Huahine's exotic fruit. Taste as many as you can, but we recommend the dried banana and kaffir lime. The coconut and vanilla are great for mixing. It's located just south of Fare.

◉ Huahine Iti

Maroe   VILLAGE
Dotted with the reminders of the god Hiro's splitting of the island in two, the village of Maroe sits on the southern side of **Maroe Bay**. You can spot the marks left by Hiro's paddle, the imprint of his finger, and even his rocky phallus.

Tefarerii   VILLAGE
From Maroe, the coast road skirts across the mouths of a number of shallow inlets, looking across to Motu Murimahora, before coming to Tefarerii (House of the Kings). A century ago this small village was the home of Huahine's most powerful family. Today the inhabitants devote their time to fishing and growing watermelons and other produce on the nearby *motu*.

Marae Anini   ARCHAEOLOGICAL SITE
Right on the southern tip of Huahine Iti, Marae Anini was a community *marae* made of massive coral blocks. The comparatively recent construction was dedicated to 'Oro (the god of war) and Hiro (the god of thieves and sailors). There's a signpost from the coast road.

Beside Marae Anini, **Anini Beach** is a lovely spot for a picnic. It's also great for sunbathing and swimming – a shallow reef close to shore makes for calm, protected waters.

Avea Bay   BEACH
Find some of the island's best beaches around this bay. The lagoon is wide and good for swimming. The best beach is at Relais Mahana. Further on, the road comes to a junction. To the left is the little village of Haapu; to the right the road leads to a bridge from where you can continue the island tour.

🏃 Activities

Diving & Snorkelling
Huahine has two scuba centres offering magnificent dives for all experience levels. Just offshore from Fare, the Avapeihi Pass (p35) is the most sought-after site, with dense fish action at all times. Snorkelling is no less impressive. On the east coast, near the visitor car park at the now defunct Sofitel, you'll

MARAE WALK

This walk up **Matairea Hill** is a high point for anyone interested in archaeology. A signpost on the Fare side of Maeva, about 200m west from the Fare Potee, points to the start of the hiking trail. You'll go past a **fortification wall**, which was built during the pre-European era, probably as protection against the warlike Bora Bora tribes, before reaching **Marae Tefano**, draped upon the hillside. There's a massive banyan tree overwhelming one end of the *ahu* (altar).

Further on, a trail branches off to the left and runs slightly downhill to **Marae Matairea Rahi**. Once the principal *marae* at Maeva, where the most important island chief sat on his throne at major ceremonies, it was superseded by Marae Manunu, on the *motu* below. Also surviving are the foundations of a *fare atua* (god house), where images of gods were guarded day and night. Retrace your steps to the main trail and continue to the turn-off to **Marae Paepae Ofata**, a steep climb above the main trail but worth the effort. The *marae* is like a large platform perched on the edge of the hill, with fine views down the hillside and across Motu Papiti to the outer lagoon, and down to the mouth of Lake Fauna Nui. Return to the main path, which drops steeply down to the road.

Given the lack of signboards and proper waymarks, it makes sense to hire a guide. Contact American anthropologist Paul Atallah, from **Island Ecotours** (p100) – a more knowledgeable person you'd be hard-pressed to find. Count on 5000 CFP for the tour (about three hours). Take some drinking water as well as strong insect repellent.

HUAHINE ACTIVITIES

find Le Jardin de Corail, which offers superb snorkelling among coral pinnacles and rich marine life only a few metres offshore. **Motu Topati**, at the entrance to Maroe Bay, and **Motu Vaiorea**, at the entrance to Bourayne Bay, are magnificent sites for snorkelling that are accessible by boat.

Mahana Dive　　　　　　DIVING
(☑87 73 07 17; www.mahanadive.com; single dive 6200 CFP) This outfit in Fare is run by English-speaking Annie and offers hands-on beginner dives as well as a slew of personalised trips for experienced divers. It also charges 7000 CFP for an introductory dive and 23,200 CFP for a four-dive package. It's part of the Te Moana Diving Pass (p80).

Pacific Blue Adventure　　　　DIVING
(☑40 68 87 21; www.divehuahine.com; single dive 6200 CFP; ☉Mon-Sat) A friendly centre on the quay at Fare. It's part of the Te Moana Diving Pass (p80).

Lagoon Excursions

The best way to experience Huahine's picture-perfect azure lagoon and brooding green sillhouette is to get out on the water and visit the uninhabited *motu* – the beaches are isolated and fantastic.

Various lagoon tours are offered on Huahine, with stops for snorkelling, swimming, fish or shark feeding, a pearl-farm visit and a *motu* picnic. Departures are at around 9am or 10am, returning towards 4pm. A minimum number of participants is required, so book ahead.

Huahine Nautique　　　　BOAT TOUR
(☑40 68 83 15; www.huahine-nautique.com; tours from 9000 CFP) Offers outrigger-canoe trips that include a picnic on the lagoon, stops for snorkelling and also the chance to learn about the island's history. Also offers sports fishing from 30,000 CFP per day.

Poetaina Cruises　　　　BOAT TOUR
(☑40 60 60 06; www.poetaina.com; tours from 9500 CFP) This family-run company offers lagoon tours that include a *motu* picnic, a visit to a pearl farm, and French Polynesian song and dance performances.

Huahine Lagoon　　　　BOATING
(☑40 68 70 00; boat rental per day from 10,000 CFP) Rents out boats with outboard motors (no license required) for DIY lagoon exploration. They will pick up and drop off from most hotels and *pensions* or from the Fare pier.

Saling Huahine Voile　　　　SAILING
(☑87 23 23 79, 40 68 72 49; www.tahitisailingcharter .com; full-day tours from 12,500 CFP) Offers half-/full-day trips aboard a monohull along Huahine's west coast. The itinerary is flexible.

Water Sports

Huahine provides opportunities to dip a paddle around the quiet lagoon. You can steer to Hana Iti Beach, Motu Araara or any

HUAHINE'S TOP SURF SPOTS

Huahine has some of the best and most consistent surf in French Polynesia, with left and right reef breaks best tackled by experienced surfers. Local surfers can be possessive, however, so be sure to be courteous in the waves, smile and say 'hi', don't show up in a big group and, especially, don't bring a camera. If you're cool and friendly, that's how you'll be treated too. The following spots have good surf year round:

Fare Reef break Northwest of Huahine Nui. The left here attracts the big names of world surfing. The right is also pretty good. Best with a southwest swell.

Fitii Reef break Northwest of Huahine Nui. Best when a southwest swell is running.

Parea Reef break South of Huahine Iti. Beautiful waves as long as the trade winds aren't blowing.

other *motu,* but bear in mind that many of the *motu* belong to local families: don't treat the land as yours to explore without permission. Most places to stay either hire out or offer free sea kayaks for guests' use.

Guillaume Chastagnol   WATER SPORTS
(☑ 87 25 62 62; kite rental per day 9000 CFP; guide service from 4000 CFP) Those seeking kitesurfing instruction or gear hire can contact Guillaume. Make reservations a few days in advance for lessons.

Horse Riding

La Petite Ferme   HORSE RIDING
(☑ 40 68 82 98; lapetiteferme@mail.pf; 2hr trips from 7500 CFP) To see the island from the back of a horse, head to this equestrian centre between Fare and the airport. The two-hour ride through coconut plantations and around the shore of Lake Fauna Nui is truly enchanting. Longer excursions include an all-day ride (18,000 CFP), which includes a visit to a vanilla plantation, and a stop for a picnic and snorkelling.

The horses are suitable for all levels as well as for children. Transfers are free.

Hiking

There are no clearly marked trails on Huahine and the occasional paths in the interior grow over quickly if they're not maintained

(which is usually the case), so DIY hikes are limited. The *marae* walk at Maeva is the most interesting option (although we suggest hiring a guide who can explain the cultural significance of the archaeological sites). Other walks require a guide.

Mt Pohue Rahi   HIKING
Mt Pohue Rahi (462m) on Huahine Iti offers sublime views of rolling mountains and the nearby lagoon. About four hours, moderate.

Mt Tapu   HIKING
Walk to the top of Mt Tapu (429m) on Huahine Nui for seriously breathtaking views of the island. About four hours, moderate.

Huahine Randonnée   HIKING
(☑ 87 73 53 45; teriitetumu@mail.pf; Camping Hiva Plage; half-day hikes per person 4500 CFP) 🌿 Professional guide Terii Tetumu has limited English skills but is extremely friendly and competent. He offers hikes to the tops of either Mt Tapu on Huahine Nui or Mt Pohue Rahi on Huahine Iti, as well as a walk on Matairea Hill and around Avea Bay.

🖝 Tours

A few 4WD tours offer a good overview of the island. They typically start in the morning or early afternoon and take three hours, and a minimum number of participants (usually two) may be required. The tours cover the principal places of interest, including villages, archaeological sites, viewpoints, plantations, fish parks and handicraft outlets.

Island Ecotours   TOUR
(☑ 87 71 30 83; www.islandecotours.net; tours from 5000 CFP) Owner Paul Atallah is an American anthropology enthusiast who specialises in highly interesting guided walks on Matairea Hills, with a focus on history and archaeology. Doesn't have an office, but does hotel pick-up.

Huahine Land   DRIVING TOUR
(☑ 40 68 89 21; tours from 5000 CFP) 🌿 This American-run outfit has an excellent reputation and offers a bit of everything. Picks you up from your hotel.

🛏 Sleeping

🛏 Fare & Around

The places listed here are either right in town or a few kilometres to the north or south.

Chez Guynette GUESTHOUSE **$**
(✍ 40 68 83 75; www.pension-guynette-huahine.
com; dm 2000 CFP, r from 4900 CFP;) This
excellent-value place right in the centre of
Fare – it's in front of the quay – offers seven
simple but comfortable rooms with fans and
bathrooms (with hot water). The eight-bed
dorm is spacious and clean (though not at
all private), there's a big communal kitchen
and the reasonably priced terrace restaurant has the best people-watching this side
of Pape'ete.

The French owner is friendly and helpful.
Airport transfers are 500 CFP per person
(one way), and wi-fi is a flat fee of 500 CFP
for your whole stay. Minimum stay of two
nights.

Meherio PENSION **$**
(✍ 40 68 80 52; meherio.huahine@mail.pf; s/d incl
breakfast 8400/10,500 CFP;) Situated about
150m from a stunning beach with great
snorkelling, and only a short stroll from
Fare, the rooms here surround a convivial
little dining area and flowery garden. Room
exteriors are woven bamboo, interiors have
lots of colourful local fabrics, and two units
are wheelchair accessible. Local-style three-
course meals (dinner is 2650 CFP) are available on request. Bikes, kayaks and airport
transfers are free.

Pension Fare Ara PENSION **$**
(✍ 87 74 96 09; www.fare-ara.blog.fr; s/d
6000/7000 CFP, 2-bedroom apartment 8500-
12,500 CFP;) One kilometre south of Fare,
this hidden block of large, clean apartments
and studios, all with kitchens, offers a great
deal for self-caterers who want to be close
to town. The units and flowery garden are
impeccably kept by host Tinau, who takes
many extra steps to ensure his guests are
happy and comfortable.

Airport transfers are free, bikes/kayaks
are 1000/2000 CFP per day, and car and
boat rentals are available.

Fare Maeva BUNGALOW **$**
(✍ 40 68 75 53; www.fare-maeva.com; d/bunga-
lows 7500/13,000 CFP;) On a coral-rock
beach (not good for swimming), this place
has elementary bungalows sleeping two to
four people, all with kitchens. Five room
units are smaller versions of the bungalows.
The on-site restaurant won't win any dining
awards, but expect a great time when a band
shows up (along with many local revellers)
for dinner and dancing nights.

There's a room-plus-car deal from 14,600
CFP per day for two people.

Rande's Shack BUNGALOW **$$**
(✍ 40 68 86 27; randesshack@mail.pf; bungalows
12,500-16,500 CFP;) Great for families and a
long-time surfer favourite. American Rande
and his lovely Tahitian wife give a character-
filled welcome and offer two great-value
self-catering houses, one which sleeps up
to six people. While the houses aren't fancy,
they're spotless, have mosquito screens, are
well maintained and are located on a small
beach perfect for swimming and snorkelling,
a short walk from Fare. Bikes and kayaks are
complimentary. Airport transfers are 600
CFP (one way).

★**Maitai Lapita Village** RESORT **$$$**
(✍ 40 68 80 80; www.hotelmaitai.com; bungalows
d from 29,000 CFP;) The Maitai
isn't just another luxury resort. No overwater units here, but an array of creatively
designed bungalows around a small lake
complete with water lilies. All units mimic
fare va'a (outrigger-canoe huts). They're
not just posh and huge, they also blend into
the environment. The beachfront restaurant serves fine food at reasonable prices
and there's fantastic swimming mere steps
away.

It's ecofriendly: there's a solar-powered
energy system, some of the food is grown
organically and green waste is composted.

Around Huahine Nui

★**Tifaifai Motu Mahare** BUNGALOW **$**
(✍ 87 77 07 74; www.tifaifai-et-cafe.com; bungalows
d/tr 8000/9900 CFP) This retreat on a dreamy,
coconut-clad, surf-lapped *motu* has two
authentic Polynesian (rustic), sand-floored,
thatched bungalows with bathrooms
(cold-water showers). Solar panels provide
electricity. There are lovely swimming and
snorkelling spots just offshore and the *motu*
is edged with lovely white-sand beaches.
Dinner is often available if you order in advance (2000 CFP) and there's an impeccable
communal kitchen.

The friendly caretaker will happily drive
you to the market in Fare. Dine with your
feet in the water at a shaded table in the
lagoon or lounge in a mosquito-screened
common area – which is a godsend since
mosquitoes are a problem. Free kayaks and
free airport transfers. Cash only.

HUAHINE SLEEPING

HUAHINE NUI OR HUAHINE ITI?

Staying near Fare means easy access to facilities. Huahine Iti's beaches do put Huahine Nui's to shame, but if you choose to stay on this side of the island and don't have a car, you'll have to rely on hitchhiking or your legs to get around. That said, most lodging options on Huahine Iti have on-site restaurants or guest kitchens and offer free bikes and kayaks to their clients.

Tifaifai & Café
B&B $

(☑ 87 77 07 74; www.tifaifai-et-cafe.com; s/d incl breakfast 5900/7900 CFP; ☎) Isolated out on Motu Ovarei, this is a place for a back-to-nature escape. Run by the affable Flora, it exudes low-key vibes and features two comfy rooms in the owner's house. The house overlooks a stretch of coral-and-sand beach that isn't swimmable, but La Jardin de Corail is a short walk away. You can order dinner (2000 CFP). Cash only. Free airport transfers.

Tupuna
BUNGALOW $$

(☑ 40 68 70 36, 87 79 07 94; www.pensiontupuna.com; bungalows d incl breakfast 9000-13,000 CFP; ☺ closed Dec; ☎) 🏄 In a remote, lush tropical garden bursting with all sorts of exotic trees, the four rustic Polynesian-style bungalows here all have a private hot-water bathroom. Mostly organic meals (dinner 3900 CFP) are served family-style by the charming nature-enthusiast and creative and talented chef owner; kayaks and snorkelling equipment are free.

Note that there's no beach and the waters are murky at low tide; for a dip, you'll need to paddle to the beautiful and usually empty Hana Iti Beach. Airport transfers are 1500 CFP. Cash only.

Villas Bougainville
VILLA $$

(☑ 40 60 60 30; www.villas-bougainville.com; villas from 21,000 CFP; ❄☎) The four villas here are great for self-caterers and are set in well-tended tropical gardens. You're near the water (but not a beach), and the tariff includes car and boat hire. There's a minimum stay of three nights and airport transfers are free.

Huahine Vacances
VILLA $$

(☑ 40 68 73 63; www.huahinevacances.pf; villas from 21,000 CFP; ☎) This is an incredibly tranquil spot with three spacious villas in a flowery garden. The price includes full use of a car and a boat, which is great since there are no restaurants or beaches nearby (although the property is across from a scenic bay). Airport transfers are free.

Huahine Iti

The (marginally) smaller island has several ideally situated places.

Hiva Plage
CAMPGROUND, GUESTHOUSE $

(☑ 87 78 19 10, 40 68 89 50; teriitetumu@mail.pf; camp sites s/d 1300/1800 CFP, s/d with shared bathrooms 2800/5000 CFP; ☎) Run by friendly Terii Tetumu (a licensed hiking guide) and his French wife, the green location here bordering a white coral seashore is the kind of place where you lose track of the days. Pitch your tent on the grass or choose one of the small, very basic rooms; wherever you choose, you'll be lulled by trade winds and lapping waves.

Precious perks include a rusty but clean kitchen for guests' use, surfboard, scooter and tent hire, wi-fi access, laundry service and complimentary bikes and kayaks. If you don't fancy cooking, meals are available on request (from 1500 CFP). Airport transfers are 1500 CFP per person return. Cash only.

Moana Lodge
PENSION $$

(☑ 87 35 60 98; www.moanalodge.jimdo.com; bungalows incl breakfast 12,500-14,500 CFP; ☎) This new place has three dark wooden bungalows that are spacious and sparsely elegant and only steps from an arc of white sand and blue lagoon. The whole place sits on a large lawn of soft Japanese grass – perfect for kids. Tailor-made boat tours are available (from 5000/9500 CFP for a half/full day), as are fresh and healthy lunches and dinners (2500 CFP) on request. Transfers, bikes, kayaks and snorkelling equipment are all free.

Chez Tara
BUNGALOW $$

(☑ 40 68 78 45; bungalow d/f incl breakfast 12,000/16,000 CFP) Next to the eponymous restaurant, this place has two wonderfully rustic units that hover over the beach like almost-over-the-water bungalows. It may not be the best deal on the island, but it's a great location, the welcome is wonderfully Polynesian and good eats are steps away. Free kayaks.

Relais Mahana
RESORT $$$

(☑ 40 68 81 54; www.relaismahana.com; bungalows d 22,200-34,900 CFP; @☎☒) This hotel is on what's arguably the best beach on Huahine, and there's a sensational coral garden just offshore. Bungalow interiors are tastefully decorated with local art in soothing muted colours, and most bathrooms have indoor-outdoor showers in private minigardens. Not all units have sea views, but there's a sense of luxury, especially with the pricier choices.

Prices are very high for what you get, but this is an indisputably lovely spot. The food at the on-site restaurant was recently revamped; it's a great place to try raw fish dishes. Airport transfers are 4200 CFP per person return.

✖ Eating

Fare & Around

Once you've left Fare there aren't too many places to eat, apart from the hotels and a few scattered, inexpensive *snack* (snack bars).

Chez Guynette TAHITIAN $
(☑40 68 83 75; mains 800-1900 CFP; ⊙7.30am-2.30pm Mon-Sat, to 1.30pm Sun) Fare's best coffee plus fresh fruit juices, breakfast dishes and light meals are served on a lively open-air terrace. The tuna steak and the skewered *mahimahi* (dorado) certainly won our hearts. Brilliant value.

Pizzeria Roulotte Italia PIZZA $
(☑87 31 41 89; pizzas around 1400 CFP; ⊙10am-9pm Tue-Sun) Follow the sign from the main road about 1.5km north of Fare to find this Italian-run mobile food van serving Huahine's best pizzas plus a few extras such as *saccotini* (small fried pizzas) lasagne and tiramisu. Try the 'Huahine' pizza with fresh tuna and Roquefort cheese or the 'lobster', which as the name suggests, is topped with fresh, local crustacean.

Roulottes TAHITIAN, INTERNATIONAL $
(mains 1000-1500 CFP; ⊙11am-2pm & 6-9pm) The quayside *roulottes* (food vans) are Huahine's best bargain for cheap eats. Huge portions of fish, chicken, burgers, steaks and chips are the order of the day, but there are also pizzas, crêpes and ice cream. During the day, walk a little further south and look for the vendor selling delicious *uru* (breadfruit) chips.

Super Fare Nùi – Super U SUPERMARKET $
(⊙6am-6.30pm Mon-Sat, 6-11.30am Sun) If you're self-catering, head to this well-stocked supermarket opposite the waterfront.

Market MARKET $
(⊙Mon-Sat) For fruits and vegetables, as well as fresh fish, nothing can beat the market on the waterfront.

★**Huahine Yacht Club** TAHITIAN $$
(☑40 68 70 81; mains 1600-2400 CFP; ⊙11am-2pm & 6-9pm) In a great location right on the lagoon, this lively restaurant is a favourite local watering hole and the best place to eat around Fare. With polished oyster shells nailed to the walls and lights strewn from the thatched ceiling, it has a beach-bar vibe and cooks a mean shrimp curry.

The menu is meat- and seafood-based, portions are generous. Linger over a fruity cocktail as the sun sinks low on the horizon or get rowdy over a few pitchers with friends old and new after the dinner crowd heads home.

Omai Restaurant FUSION $$
(☑40 68 80 80; mains 1700-3000 CFP; ⊙11.45am-2pm & 6.45-9pm) With a view over the Maitai Lapita Village hotel's pool and out to sea, this is Huahine's swankiest dining option and the food – from roast swordfish to Marquesan goat curry, grilled beef tenderloin and even burgers – fits perfectly with the elegant yet relaxed atmosphere. Finish the meal with a rich chocolate mousse or tropical crème brûlée.

Huahine Iti

★**Chez Tara** TRADITIONAL TAHITIAN $$$
(☑40 68 78 45; mains 1300-3500 CFP; ⊙11.30am-9pm) One of Huahine's unexpected gems, Chez Tara is easily the best place on the island to sample Tahitian specialities. Head here on Sundays for its legendary *ma'a Tahiti* (traditional Tahitian food, served buffet-style at noon; 3500 CFP), which should satisfy all but the hungriest of visitors. It's in a great location, right on the lagoon. Bookings essential.

Tenahe – Relais Mahana FUSION $$
(☑40 68 81 54; mains 1600-2400 CFP; ⊙11.30am-9pm) In a lovely setting right on the beach, this classy yet barefoot-appropriate restaurant specialises in raw fish dishes created with fusion flair, from Mediterranean style with olives and feta cheese to spicy and curried versions. There's also a smaller menu of basics such as burgers and fish and chips, and the cocktails are also recommended.

ℹ Information

The following are all in Fare, where you'll also find private doctors and a pharmacy. Visiting yachties can obtain water from Pacific Blue Adventure, on the quay.

Ao Api New World (📋 40 68 70 99; per hr 1000 CFP; ⊘ 8.30am-7pm Mon-Fri) Internet access with a view of Fare's port. It's upstairs.

Banque de Tahiti (⊘ 8.15am-noon & 1-3.30pm Mon-Fri) Currency exchange and ATM.

Banque Socredo (⊘ 7.30-11am & 1.30-4pm Mon-Fri) Currency exchange and ATM.

Comité du Tourisme (Tourist Office; 📋 40 68 78 81; ⊘ 8.30am-3.30pm Mon-Fri, 9-11am Sat & Sun) On Fare's main street. There's also a small but fun craft market next door with lots of jewellery and decent souvenirs.

Post Office (OPT; ⊘ 7.15am-3.15pm Mon-Thu, 7.15am-2.15pm Fri; 🛜) Internet and wi-fi access (with the Manaspot network).

ℹ Getting There & Away

Huahine, the first of the Leeward Islands, is 170km west of Tahiti and 35km east of Ra'iatea and Taha'a.

AIR

Air Tahiti (📋 40 86 42 42, 40 68 77 02; www.airtahiti.pf; ⊘ 7.30-11.30am & 1.30-4.30pm Mon-Fri, 8-11.30am Sat) has an office on the main street in Fare. Destinations include Pape'ete (14,000 CFP, 35 minutes, daily), Ra'iatea (8200 CFP, 15 minutes, daily), Bora Bora (10,500 CFP, 20 minutes, daily) and Mo'orea (16,300 CFP, 30 minutes, daily).

BOAT

Two cargo ships, the **Hawaiki Nui** (p236) and the **Taporo VII** (p236), make two trips a week between Pape'ete and Bora Bora (via Huahine, Ra'iatea and Taha'a), leaving Pape'ete on Tuesday and Thursday around 4pm. Note that it's pretty difficult for tourists to get passage aboard the *Taporo* as it's usually booked out by locals.

ℹ Getting Around

TO/FROM THE AIRPORT

Huahine's **airport** is 2.5km north of Fare. *Pensions* and hotels will arrange taxi transfers (sometimes included in the tariff – usually meaning that they will pick you up). It costs from 500 CFP to go to Fare and up to 2000 CFP to get to Huahine Iti.

BICYCLE & SCOOTER

You can hire bicycles from Europcar or **Huahine Lagoon** (p99) for about 2000 CFP a day. For scooters, check with Europcar, which charges 6200 CFP for 24 hours.

CAR

A sealed road follows the coast all the way around both islands. Huahine's car-hire operators will deliver directly to the airport or to your hotel. Public rates are exorbitant – from 9200 CFP per day – but discounts are available if you book through your hotel or *pension*. There are two petrol stations in Fare.

Avis (📋 40 68 73 34) Next to the Mobil petrol station in Fare, it also has a counter at the airport.

Europcar (📋 40 68 82 59) The main agent is north of the centre of Fare near the post office; there are also counters at the airport and **Relais Mahana** (p102).

Fare Maeva (📋 40 68 75 53; www.fare-maeva.com) At the Fare Maeva *pension*.

Ra'iatea & Taha'a

Includes ➡

Ra'iatea 106
Sights 106
Activities 109
Sleeping 111
Eating & Drinking 113
Taha'a 115
Sights 115
Activities 116
Sleeping 116
Eating & Drinking 118

Best Places to Stay

➡ Sunset Beach Motel (p112)

➡ Raiatea Lodge (p112)

➡ Opoa Beach Hotel (p112)

➡ Fare Pea Iti (p117)

➡ La Pirogue Api (p117)

➡ Villa Tonoi (p112)

Best Places to Eat

➡ Opoa Beach Hotel (p113)

➡ Tahaa Maitai (p118)

➡ La Plage (p118)

➡ Raiatea Lodge (p113)

➡ Le Ficus (p118)

Why Go?

Ra'iatea and Taha'a are encircled by a common lagoon, but the two islands couldn't be more different. Ra'iatea is high, imposing and fiercely independent, has the second biggest town in French Polynesia after Pape'ete and is considered by many to be the spiritual seat of the Polynesian Triangle. Taha'a, on the other hand, has graceful low hills, is famous for its sweet-scented vanilla and is arguably the quietest of the Society Islands. Both islands are ideal places to explore a mysterious and wild-feeling Polynesia.

The islands have few beaches but the reef is dotted with *motu,* secluded white-sand, palm-fringed, blue-lagoon islets. Within the vast lagoon itself is a never-ending aquarium perfect for diving, snorkelling, kayaking or just splashing around. On land, the mountains, particularly on Ra'iatea, make you want to hike off in search of breezy vistas, waterfalls and one of the world's rarest flowers, the *tiare apetahi.*

When to Go

➡ The dry winter period from May to October is the best time to go; the weather is cooler and there is much less rainfall – perfect for outdoor activities, especially hiking, but note that in this tropical climate it can rain or shine at any time of year.

➡ In July both islands are in full swing with the Heiva cultural festivities, including dancing contests.

➡ The Hawaiki Nui canoe race in early November is another highly colourful event, with the boats stopping en route from Huahine.

➡ Diving is popular year-round.

RA'IATEA

POP 12,832

Ra'iatea is the second largest of the Society Islands after Tahiti and also the second most important economic centre, but its lack of beaches has left it relatively off the tourist radar. What dominates here are the high, steep mountains and the vast, reef-fringed lagoon – the combination of the two are quite awe-striking and tend to override any disappointment that there's no beach. The capital, Uturoa, is the only real town; explore the rest of the island and you'll find an intensely calm, back-to-nature reality.

Ra'iatea is home to Marae Taputapuatea, once the most important traditional temple in Polynesia, which many believe still exudes power today. What is undeniable is that the island emanates a hard-to-pinpoint, mysterious energy that you won't feel anywhere else in French Polynesia.

History

Ra'iatea, known as Havai'iki Nui in ancient times, is the cultural, religious and historic centre of the Society Islands. According to legend, Ra'iatea and Taha'a were the first islands far to the northwest to be settled, probably by people from Samoa.

Cook first came to the island on the *Endeavour* in 1769, when he anchored off Opoa. He returned in 1774 during his second Pacific voyage, and in 1777 he made a prolonged visit before sailing to Hawaii on his last voyage.

Protestant missionaries came to Ra'iatea in 1818 and from here continued to Rarotonga in the Cook Islands in 1823 and to Samoa in 1830. Following the French takeover of Tahiti in 1842 there was a long period of instability and fierce Ra'iatean resistance. It was not until 1888 that the French attempted a real takeover of the island, and in 1897, troops were sent to put down the final Polynesian rebellion.

◉ Sights

We recommend hiring a vehicle and driving the 98km sealed-road circuit around Ra'iatea. Exploring the island this way gives you the opportunity to experience not only its wild natural beauty, but also its relaxed atmosphere.

◎ Uturoa

At first glance you'd never guess this little place is French Polynesia's second largest town (after Pape'ete), but wander around and you'll catch its feisty buzz, especially on weekday mornings, when you'll experience the only traffic jams outside of Tahiti. For a peek at local life, nothing beats the **covered market** (◷6am-4pm Mon-Fri, 6am-noon Sat), right in the centre. The town's name means 'long mouth' in English and many islanders believe that the name comes from the locals' propensity for gossip.

The town is dominated by the bulky 294m **Mt Tapioi**.

DON'T MISS

MARAE TAPUTAPUATEA

The most important *marae* (traditional temple) in French Polynesia, sprawling Marae Taputapuatea dates from the 17th century. It's dedicated to 'Oro, the god of war, who dominated 18th-century Polynesian religious beliefs.

Despite its relatively short history, this *marae* assumed great importance in the Polynesian religion. Any *marae* constructed on other islands had to incorporate one of Taputapuatea's stones as a symbol of allegiance and spiritual lineage. This was the centre of spiritual power in Polynesia when the first Europeans arrived, and its influence was international: *ari'i* (chiefs) from all over the Maohi (Polynesian) world, including the Australs, the Cook Islands and New Zealand, came here for important ceremonies.

The main part of the site is a large paved platform with a long *ahu* (altar) stretching down one side. At the very end of the cape is the smaller **Marae Tauraa**, a *tapu* (taboo) enclosure with a tall 'stone of investiture', where young *ari'i* were enthroned. The lagoonside **Marae Hauviri** also has an upright stone, and the whole site is made of pieces of coral.

The well-restored *marae* complex is an imposing sight, but unfortunately there is little information for visitors beyond some signboards that explain what a *marae* is, with nothing specific about Taputapuatea.

Uturoa to Marae Taputapuatea

Bustling Uturoa blends seamlessly into **Avera**. From here the road follows the contours of the narrow and magnificent **Faaroa Bay**. The islet that lies offshore is **Motu Iriru**. After going round the base of the bay and crossing Faaroa River, you reach the inland turn-off to the south coast.

From the turn-off, the road runs to a *belvédère* (lookout), with great views of Faaroa Bay, the coast and the surrounding mountains, before dropping down to the south-coast road.

If you don't take the turn-off to the south coast, the road winds around the lush south coast of Faaroa Bay and through the village of **Opoa** to Marae Taputapuatea. Next to the *marae* (traditional temple) there's a small artificial beach that makes for a great picnic spot.

Motu Oatara

The glassy waters around Motu Oatara, just across from Opoa village, are excellent for snorkelling. This idyllic, deserted islet also harbours a small colony of sea birds. It can be visited on tours or reached by kayak from Opoa Beach Hotel or Hotel Atiapiti.

Marae Taputapuatea to Tevaitoa

The stretch of road from Marae Taputapuatea to Tevaitoa is the most remote part of Ra'iatea and it's here you'll really get a glimpse of the old spirit of the island. The road wriggles along the coast past agriculture and mucky beaches backed by blue lagoon. Between PK42 and PK44, there's a long stretch where the steep green mountainsides are streaked with waterfalls during the wetter months of the year. Past the village of **Puohine**, the majestic **Faatemu Bay** comes into view. The road follows the coast before reaching the village of **Fetuna**. During WWII, when the US military occupied Bora Bora, a landing strip was constructed here.

The sparsely inhabited coast continues all the way along to **Tevaitoa**, with vistas over the lagoon and some particularly large *motu* quite close to shore. In the middle of Tevaitoa you'll find the island's oldest Protestant church, an architectural curiosity built smack on top of the magnificent **Marae Tainuu**. Behind the church, the walls of the

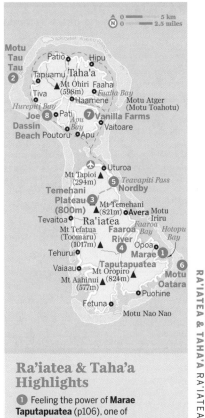

Ra'iatea & Taha'a Highlights

1 Feeling the power of **Marae Taputapuatea** (p106), one of Polynesia's greatest spiritual centres.

2 Spending a day on Taha'a with an island tour, stopping at **Motu Tau Tau** (p116) for a bout of snorkelling.

3 Taking an unforgettable hike to **Temehani Plateau** (p110) and looking for the *tiare apetahi*, one of the world's rarest flowers.

4 Kayaking to *motu* in either lagoon or up **Faaroa River** (p110), the country's only navigable waterway.

5 Diving the **Nordby** (p35), a superb wreck very close to shore.

6 Absorbing the silence on the deserted **Motu Oatara** (p107) and snorkelling in crystal-clear waters.

7 Learning how vanilla is prepared and purchasing a sweet-scented vanilla pod at a **vanilla farm** (p119).

8 Unwinding on blissful **Joe Dassin Beach** (p116), Taha'a's hidden gem.

RA'IATEA & TAHA'A RA'IATEA

Ra'iatea & Taha'a

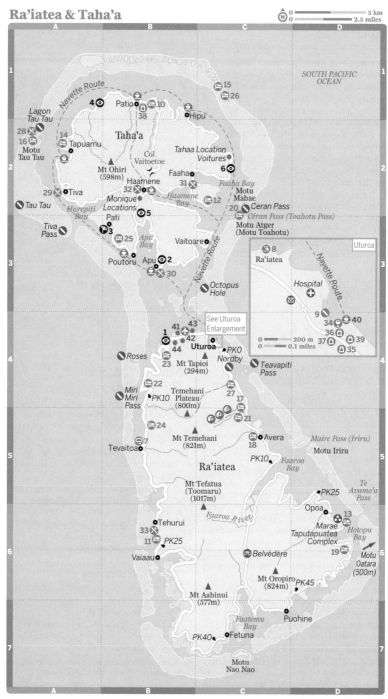

Ra'iatea & Taha'a

SOUTH PACIFIC OCEAN

Navette Route

Lagon Tau Tau
28
16
Motu Tau Tau

4 Patio
38

15
26

10

Hipu

14 Tapuamu

Taha'a

Col Vaitoetoe

Tahaa Location Voitures

6

Mt Ohiri (598m)

Haamene
32
5
Monique Locations
Pati

Faaha
31

Haamene Bay

12

20

Faaha Bay
Motu Mahae

Ceran Pass

Céran Pass (Toahotu Pass)
Motu Atger (Motu Toahotu)

29 Tiva

Tau Tau

Tiva Pass

Hurepiti Bay

3
25
Poutoru

Apu Bay

2 Apu
30

Vaitoare

Octopus Hole

Navette Route

Uturoa

8
Ra'iatea

Hospital

Navette Route

9
34
37
40
36
39
35

See Uturoa Enlargement

0   200 m
0   0.1 miles

1
41 43
42
44
Uturoa

PK0
Nordby

Roses
23
Mt Tapioi (294m)

Teavapiti Pass

Miri Miri Pass
22
PK10
Temehani Plateau (800m)

27
17

24
21
Mt Temehani (821m)

Tevaitoa
7

18
Avera

Maire Pass (Iriru)
Motu Iriru

PK10
Faaroa Bay

Te Avamo'a Pass

Ra'iatea

Mt Tefatua (Toomaru) (1017m)

PK25

Opoa
13

Faaroa River

Marae Taputapuatea Complex

Hotopu Bay

33 Tehurui
11
PK25

19

Motu Oatara (500m)

Vaiaau

Belvédère

Mt Oropiro (824m)
PK45

Mt Aahinui (577m)

Puohine

Faatemu Bay

PK40 Fetuna

Motu Nao Nao

Ra'iatea & Taha'a

⊙ Sights
1 Apooiti Marina B4
2 Ferme Perlière Champon B3
3 Joe Dassin Beach................................... B3
4 Love Here... A1
5 Maison de la Vanille B2
6 Vallée de la Vanille C2

⊕ Activities, Courses & Tours
7 Anapa Perles B5
  Hemisphere Sub .... (see 1)
8 Lagon Aventure..................................... C3
  Moorings .... (see 1)
  Sunsail.. (see 1)
  Tahaa Diving.................................. (see 16)
  Tahiti Yacht Charter .... (see 1)
9 Te Mara Nui D4

⊜ Sleeping
  Chez Louise .... (see 29)
10 Fare Pea Iti..B1
11 Fare Vai Nui B6
12 Hibiscus.. C2
13 Hotel Atiapiti.. D6
14 La Perle de Taha'a A2
15 La Pirogue Api C1
16 Le Taha'a Private Island & Spa A2
17 Les 3 Cascades C4
18 Opeha... C5
19 Opoa Beach Hotel................................ D6
20 Pension Atger....................................... C2
21 Pension Manava.................................... C5
22 Raiatea Lodge B4
23 Sunset Beach Motel B4
24 Temehani B5
25 Titaina... B3
26 Vahine Island Private Island
  Resort..C1

27 Villa Tonoi...C4

⊗ Eating
  Atiapiti Restaurant ....(see 13)
28 Chez Annette & Norbert....................... A2
29 Chez Louise... A2
  La Plage ....(see 16)
30 Le Ficus..B3
  Opoa Beach Hotel ....(see 19)
  Raiatea Lodge .... (see 22)
31 Snack Bellevue B2
32 Tahaa Maitai..B2
33 Vai Nui Restaurant................................B6

⊙ Drinking & Nightlife
34 La Cubana D4

⊜ Shopping
35 Arii Creation D4
36 Central Market.......................................D4
37 Galerie Anuanua....................................D4
38 Tavita B1
39 Te Fare D4

ⓘ Information
  ITS ....(see 40)
  Raiatea Visitors
    Information Centre ....(see 40)

ⓘ Transport
40 Ferry...D4
41 Hertz...B4
42 Moana Rent a Car...................................B4
43 Raiatea Location....................................B4
44 Renault Rent B4
  Taxi Stand ....(see 36)

RAIATEA & TAHA'A RA'IATEA

---

marae stretch for just over 50m, with some of the massive upright stones standing more than 4m high.

⊙ Tevaitoa to Uturoa

You'll find the megabucks **Apooiti Marina** between Tevaitoa and Uturoa. With a few shops, yacht charter companies, a restaurant, a bar and a diving centre, it's a pleasant place to stop for a sunset cocktail or early dinner – although the food isn't great. From the marina, the road passes by the airport before circling back to Uturoa.

🏃 Activities

Diving & Snorkelling

There are around 15 dive sites along the east and west coasts and around Taha'a. Highlights include the superb Teavapiti Pass and the *Nordby,* the only real wreck dive in French Polynesia.

The Nordby (p35) is a 50m vessel that sank in August 1900, is easily accessible, right off the former hotel Raiatea Hawaiki Nui, lying on its side on a sandy bottom, between 18m and 29m. Look for the resident fish that hide in the darker parts, including groupers, soldierfish, Moorish idols, lionfish, a couple of moray eels and crustaceans. Visibility is not the strong point of this dive.

Ra'iatea has two diving centres, although a few of the charter boat services also offer scuba to clients. Both of these companies provide transport from your hotel.

Hemisphere Sub   DIVING
(☑40 66 12 49, 87 72 19 52; www.hemispheresub. com; single/2-tank dive 6500/12,300 CFP) This operation based at the Apooiti Marina has

TIARE APETAHI: A RARE FLOWER ON A STRANGE ISLAND

Ra'iatea is home to one of the world's rarest flowers, the *tiare apetahi*. The endemic species is only found on the Temehani Plateau – although attempts have been made, it simply won't grow elsewhere. The delicate, five-petaled white flower is thought to resemble a woman's hand. The petals close at night then open at dawn with a whisper of a crackle. You should be able to see the flower on a guided hike. Note that it is strictly protected, so no picking.

excellent gear and a well-trained staff. It offers dives on the east and west coasts as well as around Taha'a. It also charges 7500 CFP for an introductory dive and 36,000 CFP for a six-dive package and is included on the Te Moana Pass (p80).

Te Mara Nui   DIVING
(✆40 66 11 88, 78 72 60 19; www.temaranui.pf; Uturoa Marina; single dive 6200 CFP) This small outfit offers personalised service. It charges 6800 CFP for an introductory dive and 37,500 CFP for a certification course.

Sailing
Ra'iatea's central position in the Society Islands, and its fine lagoon, have helped make it the yacht-charter centre of French Polynesia. Most operations will offer whatever a customer demands and prepare fully stocked and equipped boats. Bare-boat charter rates vary seasonally (July to August is the high season). A few of the better known operations:

Dream Yacht Charter   SAILING
(✆40 66 18 80; www.dreamyachtcharter.com) Offers catamaran and monohull cruises in all of French Polynesia's archipelagos.

Moorings   SAILING
(✆40 66 35 93; www.moorings.com; Apooiti Marina) This international outfitter has about 16 monohulls and 12 catamarans on offer for custom-crewed or bare-boat cruises in the Leeward Islands.

Sunsail   SAILING
(✆40 60 04 85; www.sunsailtahiti.com; Apooiti Marina) Operates a variety of bare-boat charters and crewed cruises in the Leeward Islands

and the Tuamotu Islands. Offers monohulls and catamarans.

Tahiti Yacht Charter   SAILING
(✆40 66 28 80; www.tahitiyachtcharter.com; Apooiti Marina) Has catamarans and monohulls.

Water Sports
Many hotels and *pensions* offer free kayaks – paddling out over the fantastically blue lagoon to an empty white-sand beach on a *motu* can be a highlight of a visit to Ra'iatea. Half- and full-day tours with an operator will add even more adventure and can take you way up the jungle-clad Faaroa River, an experience unique to Ra'iatea in French Polynesia. The trip brings you up the cool, rocky banks into the complete serenity of this wild region where you can paddle, swim and enjoy another side of paradise.

Lagon Aventure   KAYAKING, SUP
(✆87 79 26 27; www.raiatea-activities.com; Uturoa) For something unique, sign on with this company, which leads a bevy of water-based activities from kayak tours (half/full day around 5000/8000 CFP) to kitesurfing lessons (introductory course 15,000 CFP). Kayak and stand-up paddleboard rentals are also available (2500/1500 CFP per hour).

Lagoon Excursions
Boat tours are one of the most fun things you can do with your time. Full-day lagoon tours usually spend all of their time on the island of Taha'a, but most companies are based on Ra'iatea and pick up from the pier in Uturoa.

Anapa Perles   SNORKELLING
(✆40 66 34 52; www.anapapearls.com) Take an excursion to this little grafting house and pearl boutique to learn about how pearls are made, and then take a dip with mask and snorkel to check out what goes on underwater. The setting is spectacular both above and below the surface. Hopes are, of course, that you'll buy some pearl jewellery while you're here.

☞ Tours
Book early as a minimum of two to four people is required for these tours.

★ Trucky Tour   BUS TOUR
(✆87 78 23 36, 87 75 66 02; full-day tour per person 5000 CFP) A really great overview of the island with a visit to a pearl farm, a vanilla plantation, the Marae Taputapuatea and much more. Includes lunch.

🛏 Sleeping

🛏 East Coast

Pension Manava PENSION $
(📞40 66 28 26; www.manavapension.com; PK6; bungalows d 9500 CFP; 📶) This is a friendly, well-managed place with four spacious bungalows, all with kitchens and private bathrooms (hot water), dotting a tropical garden. There's a bit of road noise, but nothing to lose sleep over. For swimming and snorkelling, ask to be dropped off on nearby Motu Iriru (1500 CFP, minimum four people).

Excursions to Marae Taputapuatea and Faaroa River are also available. No meals are made at the *pension* except breakfast (1000 CFP), but the owners can order a catering service direct to your bungalow or drive you to other *snacks* and restaurants for 500 to 1000 CFP per person. Airport transfers are free.

Les 3 Cascades PENSION $
(📞40 66 10 90; www.pensionles3cascades.com; PK6; r without bathroom 7000 CFP, bungalows d 8000-12,000 CFP; 📶) Laid-back Les 3 Cascades has four spartan but clean rooms opening onto an airy communal area with a guest kitchen. The three free-standing bungalows offer more comfort and privacy. Meals can be prepared on request (breakfast 1200 CFP, dinner 3000 CFP) – a definite plus, especially given the lack of restaurants nearby.

No beach, but the owner can drop you off on Motu Iriru (2500 CFP per person return) and he also runs reputable boat tours to Taha'a (L'Excursion Bleue). Airport transfers are free for a minimum stay of two nights.

Opeha PENSION $
(📞40 66 19 48; www.pensionopeha.pf; PK10.5; bungalows d incl breakfast 10,000 CFP; ❄📶) A crisp and compact waterfront abode, Opeha has a handful of very white, very clean, kitchen-equipped bungalows, lined up in a row on a tiny, immaculate property. They're charmless but perfectly serviceable, and prices include a copious breakfast, kayaks and bikes. There's a pontoon, but the area is not good for swimming; for a dip, paddle to Motu Iriru.

The owners run their own lagoon tours, which come recommended. Airport transfers are 1000 CFP per person return. Cash only.

RAʻIATEA & TAHAʻA RAʻIATEA

DON'T MISS

HIKING ON RA'IATEA

Ra'iatea has the usual assortment of water-based activities, but it also offers plenty of great hiking opportunities in its mountainous interior.

Temehani Plateau A very scenic hike. Starting from the coastal road south of Uturoa (near PK6) a dirt track leads through a pine forest to the 800m-high Temehani Plateau, which affords fantastic island views. The highlight of the hike is the rare *tiare apetahi,* a white gardenia endemic to Ra'iatea. About seven hours return. Moderate.

Les Trois Cascades (Three Waterfalls) This hike takes you past three waterfalls. It's an easy stroll to the first (the smallest), which has a great swimming hole, but the trail climbs steeply from here, with some tricky scrambles. After passing the second waterfall, the trail follows the riverbed through a bamboo forest. The third waterfall is the most splendid – a 40m beauty with a fabulous swimming hole at its basin. About four hours return. Moderate.

Sentier de Faaroa An easy loop in a vast forest near Faaroa Bay. About three hours return. Suitable for families.

Mt Tapioi Bulky Mt Tapioi (294m) affords sensational views of the lagoon between Ra'iatea and Taha'a. You don't need a guide to climb up it – just follow the dirt track that starts between the post office and the *gendarmerie* (police station) in Uturoa. Count on two hours return. Beware of dogs.

With the exception of the walk to Mt Tapioi, a guide is required. Thierry Laroche at **Raiatea Randonee** (📞40 66 20 32, 87 77 91 23; raiatearando@mail.pf) is a reputable guide who's very knowledgeable about local flora. He charges 6000 CFP per person. Prices include transfers and snacks.

ℹ️ SWIMMING & SNORKELLING

Ra'iatea has no beaches besides rare, skinny strips of sand – a hotel or guesthouse pontoon is your best bet for chilling or snorkelling. The reef *motu*, however, have splendid beaches and even more snorkelling. The most scenic include **Motu Iriru** to the east, **Motu Miri Miri** to the west, and **Motu Oatara** to the southeast. Ask at your accommodation about joining a lagoon tour or arranging boat transfers to a *motu*.

Villa Tonoi   PENSION $$
(📋87 29 21 79; www.villatonoi.com; PK 1.5; bungalow for up to 4 people 12,000 CFP; 🛜🏊) It's well worth the short but steep drive up to these spotless, modern and comfortable kitchen-equipped bungalows with magnificent views over the Teavapiti Pass to Huahine (look for whales from your terrace from October to November). But what really stands out here are friendly hosts Laura and Kevin, who go above and beyond to ensure their guests have a great time.

There's a small bar (with excellent prices), and for meals besides breakfast (1500 CFP) a catering service can deliver to your door. You're also only 1.5km from Uturoa, which is a hot and sticky, but doable, walk from the *pension*. There's a two-night minimum stay.

Hotel Atiapiti   RESORT $$
(📋40 66 16 65; www.atiapiti.com; PK 31; bungalows d 15,900 CFP, bungalow for up to 7 people 29,800 CFP; 🛜) This mellow beachside spot has a beautiful but remote location next to Marae Taputapuatea and has a great pontoon to jump off for snorkelling (a manta ray swam by when we passed). The kitchen-equipped bungalows seem expensive for how basic they are, but the site and service make up for this – host Marie is also knowledgeable about Maraie Taputapuatea.

Breakfast and lunch are served at the homey and popular restaurant, and there are a few basic nearby dinner options if you have a car. Airport transfers are 4500 CFP. The beach and spaciousness makes this a good choice for families.

★Opoa Beach Hotel   RESORT $$$
(📋40 60 05 10; www.hotel-raiatea.com; PK37; bungalows 26,600-30,750 CFP; 🛜🏊) This small resort with a boutique feel is one of Ra'iatea's top hotels, and it's easy to understand why. An effortless tropical charm pervades the collection of cottages set amid beautifully landscaped gardens. From the outside, the white facades and blue tin roofs lack the wow factor, but each one is artistically decorated with local materials and teak furnishings.

The pool is small and the beach is skinny, but there's great swimming off the long pontoon jutting out over the lagoon; or ask for a boat transfer to Motu Oatara just offshore. The restaurant is also highly respected, so you'll eat very well. The resort is isolated, which gives it an intimate, secluded feel, but you'll definitely need your own wheels if you plan to explore the island.

🏨 West Coast

★Sunset Beach Motel   BUNGALOWS, CAMPGROUND $$
(📋40 66 33 47; www.sunset-raiatea.pf; PK5; campsites per person 1500 CFP, bungalows d 12,000 CFP, additional people 1500 CFP; 🛜) The location (on an expansive coconut plantation fronting the lagoon) alone would make this one of Ra'iatea's best options, but the 22 bungalows – which are perhaps better described as small homes – make this one of the best deals on the islands. It's a particularly great find for families, as the kitchen-equipped bungalows comfortably sleep four and they're well spaced out.

Bikes, snorkelling equipment and airport transfers are free. A grassy, shady plot is set aside for campers, who have their own ablution block and kitchen. The name is a bit misleading as there is no beach, but you can swim in the lagoon from the fantastic pontoon. No meals are served except breakfast (1200 CFP), but you'll find a few *snacks* and grocery stores down the road, and the friendly owners will happily drive you to Uturoa to stock up on essentials. Brilliant value.

Raiatea Lodge   HOTEL $$
(📋40 66 20 00; www.raiateahotel.com; PK8.8; s/d from 19,500/23,500 CFP; ❄️🛜🏊) Raiatea Lodge pays elegant homage to colonial architecture, with a two-storey plantation-style building sitting quietly at the back of a coconut plantation. It's a good, choice for those looking for comfortable rooms and amenities, including a restaurant and a pool, but with a boutique, intimate vibe. All rooms feature tropically inspired con-

temporary furnishings and are bright and inviting.

Add 5000 CFP (up to four people) for return airport transfers. Bikes, snorkelling gear and kayaks are free and English is spoken. No beach, but you can paddle to Motu Miri Miri.

Temehani   B&B **$$**
(☑ 87 77 54 87, 40 66 12 88; www.vacances-tahiti.com; PK11.3; d incl breakfast 10,500-13,500 CFP; ☎) This mellow B&B is just a 10-minute drive from Uturoa, but feels a million miles away. In the owner's waterfront home, it has three guest rooms in total – two with shared bathrooms, and one with private bathroom and lagoon views. They are all decorated with handmade bedspreads and plenty of wood. Excellent French-Polynesian dinners (3400 CFP) are served family-style.

There's not really a beach, but you can paddle free kayaks out to a scenic sandbar offshore or to Motu Miri Miri. The owners also organise reputable lagoon tours aboard a monohull and you can borrow the free bicycles to get to and from Uturoa. Airport transfers are free. Cash only.

Fare Vai Nui   BOUTIQUE HOTEL **$$**
(☑ 40 66 30 96; www.farevainui.com; PK 22.5, Vaiaau; d 15,000 CFP; ☎ ☒) A row of small yet very comfortable and polished wooden bungalows line a gorgeous stretch of blue water with Bora Bora in the distance. Even though the road sits close by, this part of the island is so peaceful that few cars drive by. Locals drive all the way here in decent numbers to dine at the respected restaurant.

The beach isn't great for swimming, but you can jump off the pontoon, grab a free kayak to explore the nearby *motu* or take a dip in the tiny pool. It's run by a French family and the welcome isn't going to knock your socks off, but it's completely reasonable.

🍴 Eating & Drinking

All the best restaurants on Ra'iatea are at the hotels and *pensions*. If you're not staying somewhere with a great restaurant, there are independent eateries at which you can reserve a table – you can also do as the locals do and make a day of it by hanging out on the beach or using the pool after your meal, which is considered perfectly acceptable.

Uturoa has several well-stocked supermarkets, open Monday to Saturday and some on Sunday morning. For fruit and vegies, head to the Covered Market (p106).

Vai Nui Restaurant   TAHITIAN **$$**
(☑ 40 66 30 96; Vaiaau; mains 1600-2900 CFP; ☺ 11.30am-1.30pm & 6.30-9pm Wed-Sun) This lovely little restaurant with views over the water (there's not much of a beach) is worth the drive. Choose from an upscale, tasty menu of French Polynesian dishes, such as grilled meat or fish in Roquefort or vanilla sauce (among many other choices), or simple dishes, such as chow mein and *poisson cru* (raw fish dish). Portions are huge.

Atiapiti Restaurant   TAHITIAN **$$**
(☑ 40 66 16 65; Opoa; mains 1500-2800 CFP; ☺ noon-2pm Sun-Fri; 🚗) This is a great place at which to eat, then chill out on the beach, dive off the pontoon or check out Marae Taputapuatea next door. The food is good and copious, but is definitely more home-style than haute cuisine. Wash down your fish brochettes or coconut curry with an ice-cold coconut. There's also a good kids' menu.

La Cubana   BAR
(Uturoa; mains 1200-2200 CFP; ☺ noon-late) More of a watering hole than anything else, this big, open place has the best location in downtown Uturoa, overlooking the water from the port. There's live music, DJs and karaoke some nights, but the food is mediocre, mostly pizza and simple fare. Still, it's the only logical place to eat or go for a drink in town.

★ Opoa Beach Hotel   HOTEL RESTAURANT **$$$**
(☑ 40 60 05 10; PK37; set menu 5000 CFP; ☺ dinner by reservation) At the Opoa Beach Hotel, this is Ra'iatea's most glamorous dining spot. The chef earns raves for her high-flying creative dishes combining fresh produce (fish and shellfish in particular) and spices. The menu changes daily. The decor is elegant and the tables are candlelit, which is perfect for a tête-à-tête. Hotel guests have priority, so reserve early.

Raiatea Lodge   HOTEL RESTAURANT **$$$**
(☑ 40 66 20 00; PK8.8; mains 2200-3200 CFP; ☺ 11.30am-2pm & 6.30-9pm) For refined dining, opt for the Raiatea Lodge's on-site restaurant. The semi-outdoor Zen-style setting is superb and is a great place for a drink as well as a meal. There's sure to be a dish on the extensive menu that suits your palate, but be sure to leave room for dessert.

🔒 Shopping

Central Market   SOUVENIRS
(Uturoa; ⊙ 5.30am-5pm Mon-Sat, 5-9am Sun)
Fruit, vegies and souvenirs. Also a good
place to find local vanilla pods.

Galerie Anuanua   ARTS & CRAFTS
(www.galerie-anuanua.com; Uturoa; ⊙ 8am-5pm
Mon-Fri) This is a lovely gallery featuring
works by island craftspeople, including
sculptures, pottery, paintings and mother-
of-pearl objects.

Te Fare   SOUVENIRS
(📋 40 66 17 17; Uturoa; ⊙ 8am-noon & 1-5pm
Mon-Fri, 8.30am-noon Sat) Has decently priced
clothes, paintings, jewellery, wooden handicrafts and decorative trinkets. The friendly
and helpful owner will help you find what
you're looking for.

Arii Creation   CLOTHING
(Uturoa; ⊙ 7.30-11.30am & 1.30-5pm Mon-Fri,
8-11am Sat) Sells a wide variety of clothes and
T-shirts all made with local-style floral or
patterned fabrics.

ℹ Information

Uturoa has three banks, all with ATMs.
Hospital (📋 40 60 08 01; Uturoa) Opposite the
post office; offers emergency services.
ITS (Uturoa; per 30min 500 CFP; ⊙ 8am-noon &
1-5pm Mon-Fri, 8-11.30am Sat) Internet access.
Inside the *gare maritime* (boat terminal).
Post Office (OPT; ⊙ 8am-12.30pm & 2-4pm
Mon-Fri, 8-10am Sat; 🖥) North of the centre,
towards the airport. Internet and wi-fi access
(with the Manaspot network). Has an ATM.
There's another branch upstairs at the port in
Uturoa with erratic hours.
Raiatea Visitors Information Centre (📋 40
60 07 77; ⊙ 8am-4pm Mon-Fri) In the *gare
maritime* and open longer hours when visiting
cruise ships are in port. We were bluntly told
'we have no information here'. Insist and you
may get something out of them. Hopefully
there will be improvements in the future.

ℹ Getting There & Away

Ra'iatea is 220km northwest of Tahiti and 40km
southeast of Bora Bora.

AIR

Air Tahiti (📋 40 86 42 42, 40 60 04 44; www.
airtahiti.pf; ⊙ 7.30-11.30am & 1.30-3.30pm
Mon-Fri, 7.30-11.30am Sat) has an airport
office. The airline operates direct flights from
Tahiti (17,200 CFP, 40 minutes, seven to eight
daily) with connections onwards to Mo'orea

(18,360 CFP). There are also direct flights
to Bora Bora (8700 CFP, 20 minutes, daily),
Huahine (8400 CFP, 20 minutes, daily) and
Maupiti (9400 CFP, 20 minutes, two weekly).

BOAT

Ra'iatea is separated from Taha'a by a 3km-wide
channel.

The *navette* (shuttle boat) services on the
Te Haere Maru (📋 40 65 61 33) run between
Uturoa and various stops on Taha'a – Apu,
Poutoru, Tiva, Tapuamu, Patio, Hipu and
Haamene – twice a day, at 5.30am and 11.30am.
From Taha'a, they leave at 9.30am and 3.30pm.
There is no service on Saturday afternoon or
Sunday. It takes less than 15 minutes to get from
Uturoa to Apu, the closest stop on Taha'a (but
almost one hour to Patio); the one-way fare is
780 CFP. You can buy tickets onboard.

There is also a **taxi-boat service** (📋 87 74 72
22) between the two islands, which operates
daily. It costs 7000 CFP to go to southern Taha'a
and 13,700 CFP to get to the north of the island
(prices are for two people). You can be picked up
at the airport or any of the accessible pontoons.
Advance booking (24 hours) is required.

The **Maupiti Express** (📋 40 67 66 69) travels
between Bora Bora, Taha'a and Ra'iatea. On
Monday and Friday it departs from Vaitape (Bora
Bora) at 7am, arriving at Taha'a (Poutoru) at
8.30am and at Uturoa around 8.45am. It leaves
Uturoa on the same days at 4pm, stopping at
Taha'a (Poutoru) and arriving back at Bora Bora
at 6pm. On Sundays the same route runs, but
starts from Bora Bora at 2pm. Fares are 5400
CFP one way between Ra'iatea and Bora Bora
and 800 CFP to go from Ra'iatea to Taha'a.

The cargo ships *Taporo* and *Hawaiki Nui* also
make a stop at Ra'iatea.

ℹ Getting Around

A sealed road hugs the coast all the way around
the island. *Point kilométrique* (PK; kilometre
point) distances start in Uturoa near the
gendarmerie (police station) and then run south
to Faatemu Bay. The options for getting around
are to hire a car or hitchhike. Hitchhiking is fairly
accepted here because of the low-key tourism
and lack of public transport. However, remember
that there are always dangers associated with
hitching.

TO/FROM THE AIRPORT

The airport, which also serves Taha'a, is on the
northern tip of the island. There are taxis at the
airport; the 3km trip into Uturoa costs 1000 CFP.
Most island accommodation will pick you up if you
have booked (although there may be a charge).

BOAT

Raiatea Location hires out small boats with
outboard motors for 10,300 per day; they're

the perfect way to explore the lagoon, and no boat licence is required.

CAR & SCOOTER

Hertz (☑ 40 66 35 35; www.herz-raiatea.com) Has a desk just outside the airport and charges 6600 CFP per day for an economy car.

Moana Rent a Car (☑ 87 75 08 30; www. moanarentacar.com) This very friendly island-style (our car's bumper was held on by duct tape) venture near the airport charges a pocket-friendly 5000 CFP per day for an economy car.

Raiatea Location (☑ 40 66 34 06; www. raiatealocation.com) One-day economy car rentals start at 6500 CFP. Also has scooters for around 5000 CFP.

Renault Rent (☑ 40 66 34 35; www.renault-rentraiatea.com) One of the less expensive choices, car rentals start at 5800 CFP per day.

TAXI

There's a **taxi stand** (☑ 40 66 20 60) by the market. Taxis can also be found at the airport, but even the shortest trips don't cost less than 1000 CFP.

TAHA'A

POP 5301

Larger than you'd think (it's bigger than Mo'orea) and roughly orchid-shaped, this island specialises in two of the most pleasant things French Polynesia has to offer: vanilla and pearls. This befits the subtle and sweet personality of Taha'a, where smiles are as common as hibiscus flowers and the scent of vanilla wafts through the air. There's not much going on, but that's what's so wonderful about this island. Forget the world while soaking in the incredible quiet and natural beauty. From the string of sandy *motu* to the north of the island, the silhouette of Bora Bora sits so close you could almost believe you were in the high-rolling neighbour's lagoon.

A sealed coast road encircles most of the island, but traffic is very light and there is no public transport. Taha'a's easily navigable lagoon and safe anchorages make it a favourite for visiting yachties and day-trippers from Ra'iatea.

◉ Sights

A 70km sealed road winds around the island and the population is concentrated in eight villages on the coast. Tapuamu has the main quay, Patio is the main town, and Haamene

is where the roads around the southern and northern parts of the island meet, forming a figure eight. Apu Bay to the south, Haamene Bay to the east and Hurepiti Bay to the west offer sheltered anchorages. Every sight is not listed here. There are also a few more pearl farms and a few local craft shops that are well worth a visit. All have easy-to-spot signage.

◉ From Vaitoare to Haamene

Starting from the village of Vaitoare, the road follows the coast around Apu Bay. At the top of the bay there's a turn-off south to **Poutoru** and **Pati**, a delightful hamlet that really feels like the end of the line; then the main road leaves the coast and climbs up and over to the larger village of **Haamene**.

Ferme Perlière Champon   PEARL FARM
(☑ 40 65 66 26; www.champonperles.com; ◷ 8am-4pm) This well-run pearl farm/shop is known for its high-quality mounted and loose pearls. It's at the southeastern end of Apu Bay.

Maison de la Vanille   VANILLA FARM
(☑ 65 67 27; ◷ by reservation) **FREE** On the right of the road into Haamene is this small family-run operation where you can see vanilla preparation and drying processes and also purchase vanilla pods. If you haven't reserved, stop by and see if it's open anyway.

◉ From Haamene to Patio

A little further on, the road climbs again, making a long sweeping ascent and descent westwards to beautiful **Hurepiti Bay** and the village of **Tiva**. As you round the end of the bay, keep an eye out for the stunning silhouette of Bora Bora.

The island's main quay is located at **Tapuamu**, but **Patio**, further north, is the administrative centre of the island, with offices, a post office, a bank and shops.

Love Here   PEARL FARM
(☑ 40 65 62 62; ◷ 8am-2pm Mon-Fri) **FREE** An exceptionally friendly, family-run pearl farm right on the seashore, approximately halfway between Tapuamu and Patio. Visitors learn about the technique of grafting to create cultured pearls, as well as the varieties and their characteristics. It has a gift shop that sells mounted and loose pearls as well as jewellery. Prices are great.

WORTH A TRIP

JOE DASSIN BEACH

On Taha'a, if you're willing to take a bit of a walk you can get to deserted Joe Dassin Beach, on the southwest side of the island, a 15-minute walk along the coast north of Pati. The beach was once owned by and is now named after a famous, classic French singer – sort of the Bing Crosby of France. Ask a local in Pati to show you the trailhead, pack a lunch and get lost in paradise for the day. Oh, and bring snorkel gear: there's fantastic snorkelling just offshore.

From Patio to Vaitoare

Continuing around the coast, the road passes copra plantations before reaching Faaha and the eponymous bay. From the bay the road climbs over a headland and drops down to Haamene Bay. Where the coast road meets Haamene Bay, you can turn east to get to Hôtel Hibiscus. From Hôtel Hibiscus, the coast road goes around the northern side of the bay to the village of Haamene.

Vallée de la Vanille   VANILLA FARM
(☑40 65 74 89; ⊙10am-6pm) FREE This small operation, on the east coast between Faaha and Hipu, is known for its quality vanilla pods at economical prices. Visitors will get the low-down on vanilla cultivation.

🏃 Activities

Walking
Taha'a's interior is dense and caters to bushwalkers. The only real hiking trail into the interior follows a little-used 7km track across the centre of the island from Patio to Haamene over Vaitoetoe Ridge. From Vaitoetoe Ridge, you'll get dazzling views of Haamene Bay.

Diving & Snorkelling
Taha'a has one dive centre, but dive centres on Ra'iatea regularly use the sites to the east of the island and will collect you from lodgings in the south of Taha'a. As on Ra'iatea, you have to go to the *motu* for swimming and snorkelling. Some guesthouses will drop you on a *motu* for the day or you can join an organised *pirogue* (outrigger canoe) tour. The healthiest coral gardens are off Motu Tau Tau. The channel off Motu Tau

Tau is peppered with lots of coral formations in shallow waters.

Tahaa Diving   DIVING, SNORKELLING
(☑87 24 80 69, 40 65 78 37; www.tahaa-diving. com; single/2-tank dive 8750/15,600 CFP) This low-key operation is located at Le Taha'a Private Island & Spa. Most dive sites involve a 20- to 45-minute boat trip across the lagoon. Snorkelling trips are also on offer. It's part of the Te Moana Pass (p80).

👉 Tours

Tours allow you to get out to those sandy *motu* for swimming and snorkelling and/or visit local pearl farms, vanilla plantations and the interior via 4WD. Many tour operators are based in Ra'iatea and offer pick-up services from Ra'iatea if you just want to visit Taha'a for the day. If you're based on Taha'a or Ra'iatea, your *pension* may run tours, and if not, it'll have reliable operators it works with – most have similar itineraries. Full-day tours range from 8500 CFP to 10,500 CFP. Book ahead as a minimum number of people (usually four) is required.

🛏 Sleeping

🛏 The Island

Chez Louise   CAMPGROUND $
(Tiva; 1000 CFP) Mamie Louise offers campsites on the waterfront next to her restaurant (p118). The views of Bora Bora are sublime. Showers are rudimentary, toilets are inside the restaurant and you can use the kitchen for an extra 500 CFP per day. Louise has no phone or internet access, but she says to just show up, there's always room for everyone.

Titaina   PENSION $$
(☑87 29 17 13, 40 65 69 58; www.pension-titaina. com; Poutoru; bungalows d 12,500 CFP; ☏) Near the end of the road north of Poutoru, this delightfully secluded retreat has three bungalows spread out on grassy grounds surrounded by blooming tropical gardens. The bungalows are far from fancy but are prettily decorated and kept scrupulously clean. Your courteous hosts speak English and goes above and beyond to ensure you enjoy your stay.

Meals are so good they are worth it, although half-board is a steep 5400 CFP per person. There are (free) bikes and kayaks to keep you busy, and great snorkelling in a sheltered bay a short hop from the *pension*. Joe Dassin Beach is a leisurely 3km bike ride away along the seashore. No pick-up at Ra'iatea's airport, but the quay at Poutoru (for the Maupiti Express 2; p119) is just 200m down the road. Cash only.

La Perle de Taha'a   PENSION $$
(40 65 78 56, 87 70 62 07; www.perledetahaa. com; Tapuamu; r 8000 CFP, bungalows 12,000-22,000 CFP;) There's a mix here of small but bright backpacker rooms out back with shared bathrooms, a midpriced block of OK rooms in the middle, and bigger but dark and cramped bungalows with kitchens closest to the water and main road at the front. All are decorated with beautiful Asian furnishings, but are considerably overpriced.

Across the street is a little pontoon for swimming, with stunning views of Bora Bora. Meals are extra (1800 CFP for breakfast and 5000 CFP for dinner), and a pool is planned.

Hibiscus   HOTEL $$
(40 65 61 06; www.hibiscustahaa.com; Haamene Bay; bungalows d from 10,600 CFP;) The haphazardly run Hibiscus gets mixed reviews, but its promo deals (stay three nights, pay for two) make it a bargain. Seven simply built bungalows of varying sizes and shapes are clustered in an Edenlike garden on a hillside overlooking Haamene Bay. They all have bathroom, terrace and fan, and there are eight free boat moorings with dock access.

There's an on-site restaurant and a bar across the road, on the waterfront. Transfers from Ra'iatea cost 6000 CFP per person return.

★ **Fare Pea Iti**   PENSION $$$
(87 76 98 55; www.farepeaiti.pf; Patio; bungalows d 20,000-40,000 CFP;) This option offers lots of comfort and a beautiful, quiet, white-sand-beach setting with tons of individual attention and a low-key atmosphere. Bungalows are large and dotted with plenty of wood and bamboo touches, but won't win any decoration awards. Lap up on-demand tours (3000 CFP) to the *pension*'s own private, idyllic *motu* and plenty of other activity bargains.

With a total capacity of 10 guests at a time, everything is wonderfully intimate. The homemade meals are delectable with dinners at 7800 CFP for three courses. It's all a bit over-priced, but the mix of excel-

lent service and the location leaves few disappointed. Other features include a small pool and complimentary kayaks and bikes. If you're lucky, you may share your holiday with Independentist leader and sometimes president of French Polynesia, Oscar Temaru, who likes to stay here.

The Motu

Some *motu* digs are set in private paradises that rival (and some would say exceed) the settings of Bora Bora's better resorts.

Pension Atger   PENSION $
(87 28 26 81; atgertheodore@mail.pf; Motu Atger; bungalows incl full board per person s/d 10,000/9000 CFP;) Hooray for *motu* digs without the hefty price tag. This warm, family-run Polynesian retreat on Motu Toahotu has five clean, comfortable and large tiled en-suite (cold water) bungalows that open onto the swishing blue Toahotu Pass with views that continue to the lagoon. The atmosphere is delightfully chilled out, swimming and snorkelling are excellent, and kayaks are complimentary.

Many boat tours stop here at lunchtime to sample the well-prepared local specialities including a corori (pearl oyster meat) *poisson cru*. There's a fish trap out front that may catch your dinner, but the rays that are kept captive in a fenced-in underwater area next to it are surely not to everybody's taste. The whole place is solar powered and transfers to Ra'iatea are 5000 CFP. Cash only.

La Pirogue Api   RESORT $$$
(87 27 56 00; www.hotellapirogueapi.com; bungalows d from 55,000 CFP;) Recently relocated to a small and very private *motu*, the handful of massive bungalows here built from polished wood and thatch all have steps that lead directly into a swimming-pool-blue lagoon; views from the tiny islet take in the four high islands along with massive stretches of shimmering blue water. It's intimate, friendly and quite luxurious.

No air-con here – but who needs it with the sea breezes puffing in? That said, the *motu* is very unprotected from the weather and will probably have to be evacuated during storms or high swells. The restaurant has a varied menu and very good reputation, and half-board is 9500 CFP per person. Airport transfers are 8000 CFP per person return.

RA'IATEA & TAHA'A TAHA'A

Vahine Island
Private Island Resort   RESORT $$$
(☑40 65 67 38; www.vahine-island.com; Motu Tuuva-hine; bungalows d 51,000-74,000 CFP; ❄☎) The setting here, on a white-beach-clad *motu* with a stretch of manicured coconut palms and views of blue in all directions, can't be matched. This boutique resort hosts an odd mix of a near-elegant style of shells and adornments that feels very Polynesian, with the detached, professional management approach of a chain resort – which many guests love.

There was a large villa under construction on an adjoining part of the *motu* when we passed by that will offer an even higher level of luxury. Kayaks and snorkelling equipment are available for free; lagoon tours and fishing trips are organised. Half-board is an extra 10,800 CFP per person and airport transfers cost 8000 CFP per person return. Look out for internet deals.

Le Taha'a
Private Island & Spa   RESORT $$$
(☑40 60 84 00; www.letahaa.com; Motu Tau Tau; bungalows d from 88,000 CFP; ❄@☎☒) One of the country's most exclusive resorts, the exceptional Motu Tau Tau setting has views of Taha'a on one side and Bora Bora on the other (a short walk around the islet), plus outrageous snorkelling (wait till high tide to avoid injury). And if you don't have an overwater bungalow over spectacular blue water, you'll at least have your own pool.

There's plenty of space and a supreme level of privacy. Le Taha'a is definitely a destination resort (it's very isolated), but the place offers enough activities to keep most guests entertained for days.

✖ Eating & Drinking

There are shops in each village and a few *roulottes* (food vans) open around the island at night, but the dining options are very limited. The *motu* resorts all have their own bars, but otherwise your drinking options are also limited.

Snack Bellevue   TAHITIAN $
(Faaha; mains 1200 CFP; ☺7am-5pm Tue-Sun) High up on the Faaha crossing road, this rustic but agreeable little eatery has a fantastic view over Faaha Bay. Grab a crêpe, sandwich or homemade cake to go, or stay awhile with a heaping portion of the fish of the day.

★**Tahaa Maitai**   TAHITIAN $$
(☑40 65 70 85; Haamene; mains 1750-3500 CFP; ☺noon-10pm Tue-Sat, noon-3pm Sun) Everyone recommends this restaurant right on Haamene Bay, not only for its fabulous views but also for its delicious cuisine. The menu features lots of fresh seafood, local fruits and vegetables and delicious French desserts. There's also a long cocktail list, making this a popular local watering hole.

Chez Louise   TAHITIAN $$
(Tiva; mains 1400-1900 CFP, set menu 5500 CFP; ☺8am-10pm) Right beside the lagoon, this very local-style (perhaps a little too local for some people) open-air terrace offers mesmerising views of Bora Bora to the west – a photographer's dream at sunset. Louise cooks simple but good Polynesian specialities, or you can splurge on the amazing 'marina menu', which includes an array of fresh, locally caught shellfish and fish. Cash only.

Le Ficus   TAHITIAN $$
(☑87 34 98 38; Apu; incl dinner & punch 7000 CFP; ☺Fri & Sat) Dine with your toes in the sand while watching Tahitian dancers and a fire show followed by a band or DJ and dancing. The feast is cooked in a traditional Tahitian oven. It's not on all the time, but Fridays are your best bet. Call to find out if the show is on.

Chez Annette & Norbert   TAHITIAN $$$
(☑87 23 97 10; Motu Tau Tau; dinner 3000 CFP) You gotta love a shack decked out in thatch and Polynesian fabrics that sets up camp right behind a chichi resort. Guests at Le Taha'a looking for the authentic can dine here for a fraction of the cost of the resort's restaurants. It's also adjacent to the Motu Tau Tau coral gardens. Not at the resort? A shuttle costs 1000 CFP return.

The adventurous can also camp here for 3000 CFP per night. No English is spoken, but there are showers, toilets and cooking facilities.

★**La Plage**   RESORT RESTAURANT $$$
(☑60 84 00; Motu Tau Tau; mains 2000-3400 CFP; ☺lunch by reservation) At Le Taha'a Private Island & Spa, 'The Beach' is open to nonguests if it's not full (call ahead). Enjoy the incredible beach setting while savouring a local smoked fish salad or grilled delicacies – which cost the same as the very expensive burgers and sandwiches. Take the 11.30am shuttle at Tapuamu then spend the rest of the afternoon snorkelling.

🔒 Shopping

Vanilla and pearl farms sell their products to visitors.

Tavita TATTOOS
(☑87 70 37 32, 40 65 72 09; Patio) Tavita is one of the best tattoo artists in the country and is famous for his entirely tattooed face. He creates traditional-style black-ink tattoos and comes to your lodging upon request.

ℹ Information

There's internet and wi-fi access at the post offices in Patio and Haamene (with the Manaspot network).

The post offices in Patio and Haamene have an ATM, as do the Banque Socredo in Patio and the Bank of Tahiti in Haamene.

ℹ Getting There & Away

There is no airport on Taha'a. From the southern tip of Taha'a, the airport on Ra'iatea is only 15 minutes across the lagoon and some hotels will pick up guests from the airport or from the ferry quay at Uturoa on Ra'iatea.

There is a *navette* service between Ra'iatea and Taha'a.

The **Maupiti Express 2** (☑40 67 66 99) ferry operates on Wednesday, Friday and Sunday between Bora Bora, Taha'a (Poutoru) and Ra'iatea.

Inter-island ships stop at Tapuamu on Taha'a en route from Ra'iatea to Bora Bora, but not on every voyage.

ℹ Getting Around

There is no public transport on Taha'a. If you are contemplating hitching, remember that traffic is very light. Hiring a car or bike are the only ways

VANILLA, VANILLA, VANILLA

Taha'a is accurately nicknamed 'the vanilla island', since 80% of French Polynesian vanilla is produced here. Several vanilla farms are open to the public, and at these family-run operations you can buy vanilla pods at reasonable prices – about 3500 CFP per 100g. You can also find out about the technique of 'marrying' the vanilla, a delicate operation in which the flowers are fertilised by hand because the insects that do the job in other regions are not found in French Polynesia. Nine months later, the pods are put out to dry, and they turn brown over four to five months. They are then sorted and packed before being sold locally or exported.

to see the island independently. The coast road is mostly sealed and in good condition. If you do decide to tackle it by bicycle, keep in mind that there are some steep stretches on the south of the island that can be heavy going.

There are petrol stations in Patio and Tapuamu, which are open Monday to Saturday. You can save money on Taha'a's ridiculously expensive car costs by hiring a scooter on Ra'iatea and bringing it across on the *navette*.

Monique Locations (☑40 65 62 48; Haamene) Near the church in Haamene, hires out cars for 10,300 to 14,000 CFP for 24 hours.

Tahaa Location Voitures (☑40 65 66 75, 87 72 07 71; www.hotel-tahaa.com) Has cars for 8000/10,000 CFP for eight/24 hours. It's north of Faaha Bay.

RA'IATEA & TAHA'A TAHA'A

Bora Bora

POP 9600

Includes ➡

Sights..........................122
Activities....................122
Festivals & Events.......126
Sleeping.....................127
Eating.........................131
Drinking & Nightlife....134
Entertainment...........134
Shopping.....................134

Best Places to Stay

➡ Sunset Hill Lodge (p127)

➡ Intercontinental Bora Bora Resort & Thalasso Spa (p130)

➡ Sofitel Bora Bora Private Island (p130)

➡ St Régis Resort (p130)

Best Places to Eat

➡ Maikai Bora Bora (p132)

➡ Villa Mahana (p133)

➡ Restaurant Matira Beach (p133)

➡ Le St James (p132)

Why Go?

Ah, Bora Bora. The stuff of dreams. As you arrive by plane, the view says it all. How not to be mesmerised by this stunning palette of sapphire, indigo and turquoise, all mixed together in modern-art abstractions? And these sand-edged *motu* (islets) and soaring rainforest-covered basaltic peaks? With such a dreamlike setting, Bora Bora is, unsurprisingly, a honeymooners' choice. But there's much more to do than clink glasses with your loved one in a luxurious hotel. The good thing is that you can mix slow-paced sun-and-sand holidays with action-packed adventures. Diving, snorkelling, lagoon tours, hiking and parasailing are readily available. What you shouldn't expect, though, is a thriving nightlife. Bora Bora is a quiet island. And this dream destination is much more accessible than you think. As well as five-star resorts, a handful of low-key midrange hotels beckon.

When to Go

➡ June to October, the island's coolest months, are the most popular, but keep in mind that the lagoon doesn't *always* look like a turquoise-backed mirror, especially from June to August, when the *maraamu* (southeast trade wind) blows and may bring rain and dark clouds.

➡ The hottest and rainiest months are from December to April.

➡ Try to make your trip coincide with the Heiva i Bora Bora in July or the Hawaiki Nui canoe race in November – two highly engaging events.

History

James Cook sighted Bora Bora in 1769 on his first voyage to French Polynesia, and a London Missionary Society (LMS) base was established on the island in 1820. Bora Bora supported Pomare in his push for supreme power over Tahiti, but resisted becoming a French protectorate (established over Tahiti in 1842) until the island was annexed in 1888.

During WWII a US supply base was established here, prompted by the bombing of Pearl Harbor in 1941. From early 1942 to mid-1946, Operation Bobcat transformed the island, and at its peak up to 6000 men were stationed on Bora Bora. Today the runway on Motu Mute is the clearest reminder of those frenetic days. Eight massive 18cm naval cannons were installed around the island during the war; all but one are still in place.

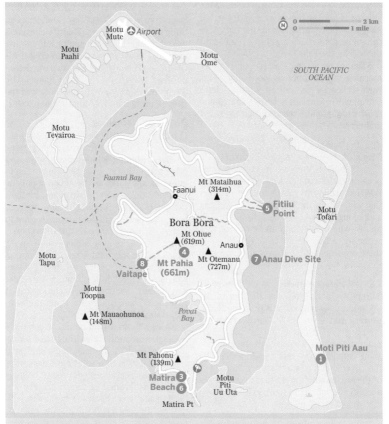

Bora Bora Highlights

1 Discovering all the perks of a world-class resort on **Motu Piti Aau** (p131).

2 Ogling the stunning cerulean-blue lagoon on a **boat tour** (p123) and enjoying a picnic on a *motu*.

3 Lazing on idyllic **Matira Beach**. (p122)

4 Huffing to the top of **Mt Pahia** (p125) to admire the sensational views.

5 Taking a 4WD tour to spot ancient ceremonial sites and WWII relics on **Fitiiu Point** (p122).

6 Enjoying a romantic dinner at Restaurant Matira

Beach, a gourmet restaurant on **Matira Beach** (p133).

7 Diving with manta rays at **Anau** (p37) dive site.

8 Getting a bird's-eye view of the surreal lagoon on a helicopter tour from **Vaitape** (p122).

◎ Sights

Matira Beach   BEACH
(Map p129) Bora Bora's only real beach, this stunning stretch of snow-white sand and pinch-me-I'm-dreaming turquoise sea is perfect for sunbathing and swimming (but less so for snorkelling). Matira Beach graces both sides of **Matira Point**, a narrow peninsula that extends south into the lagoon.

Vaitape   VILLAGE
(Map p124) The island's main settlement, Vaitape is not the most evocative town, but it's a great place to do a bit of shopping, take care of banking needs and just get a feel for the way locals really live.

Vaitape is at its liveliest on Sunday morning, when numerous food stalls selling such delicacies as *pahua taioro* (clams marinated in coconut seawater sauce) and *firifiri* (doughnuts) take position along the main road.

Coastal Defence Guns   HISTORIC SITE
(Map p124; Fitiiu Point; admission 500 CFP) Up a small hill on the eastern coast, a track peels off to the east and leads to two massive WWII coastal guns and a concrete bunker that were left by the US troops. The walking trail along the ridge starts behind the first house (where you'll pay the entrance fee), at the sharp bend in the road. From the site there are fine views out over the lagoon to the *motu*.

Coastal Defence Guns   HISTORIC SITE
(Map p124) Faanui Bay was the site of the US military base during WWII. At the south-western end of the bay, a steep and often muddy track climbs up to an old WWII radar station atop a ridge complete with two giant defence guns that were installed by the US troops. There are stupendous views of the lagoon and the *motu*. These vestiges are difficult to find (no sign), so it's not a bad idea to join an island tour.

Coastal Defence Guns   HISTORIC SITE
(Map p124) Coming from Faanui Bay, continue until you reach the quay of the Bora Bora Pearl Beach Resort & Spa on your left. Walk for another 50m and you'll see a steep track on your right. It climbs up to two WWII coastal defence guns, one of which is very well preserved.

Marae Fare-Opu   ARCHAEOLOGICAL SITE
(Map p124; Faanui Bay) There are only a handful of *marae* (traditional temple) ruins

on Bora Bora, including Marae Fare-Opu, which is squeezed between the roadside and the water's edge. Two of the slabs are clearly marked with the turtle petroglyphs seen incised in stones at numerous other sites in the Society Islands.

🏃 Activities

Scenic Flights

Tahiti Helicopters   SCENIC FLIGHTS
(Map p124; ☑40 67 54 90; www.tahiti-helicopters. com; Vaitape; 15/30min flight 20,000/40,000 CFP) Seen from above, Bora Bora's grandeur can bring tears to the eyes. Tahiti Helicopters has two scenic flights, including a 15-minute loop that takes you over Matira Point, Mt Otemanu, Faanui Bay, the airport, Teava-nui Pass, Motu Tapu and Motu Toopua. The 30-minute flight takes in Bora Bora and the neighbouring island of Tupai. Unforgettable!

Diving & Snorkelling

Diving in the bath-warm waters of Bora Bora is amazing and features sloping reefs. Sharks, including lemon sharks, rays and other marine life abound, and can be seen in quite shallow waters in the lagoon or outside the reef. Don't expect thriving coral gardens, though. If you're a beginner, you've come to the right place – Bora Bora is a great place to learn to dive or to take a certification course. A hot fave is Toopua & Toopua Iti (p37), which offer a memorable seascape and regular sightings of eagle rays. Shark lovers will make a beeline for Tapu (p37), where lemon sharks are common. At the site called Anau (p37), you'll have the opportunity to observe majestic manta rays.

No visit to Bora Bora would be complete without some snorkelling. The lagoon seems to be tailored to the expectations of avid snorkellers, with clear waters and a smatter-ing of healthy coral gardens around. Schools of glittering fish and perhaps a stingray or a blacktip shark are just a few of the regulars.

Alas, the best snorkelling spots can't be reached from the shore – you will have to rent a boat or opt for a lagoon tour.

Topdive   DIVING
(Map p124; ☑40 60 50 50; www.topdive.com; Va-itape; introductory/single dive 10,000/9800 CFP) This well-oiled diving machine offers the full range of scuba activities and prides itself on offering Nitrox dives at no extra charge. Two-tank dives are 19,000 CFP. It charges 50,000/80,000 CFP for a six-/10-dive pack-age that can be used at any of the Topdive

centres in French Polynesia (Tahiti, Mo'orea, Rangiroa and Fakarava). Free pick-up.

Eleuthera Bora Diving Centre   DIVING
(Map p124; ☑87 77 67 46; www.boradivingcenter. com; Matira; introductory or single dive 9500 CFP) Right on Matira beach, this midsized operation (not too big, not too small) gets props for fostering a sociable vibe while maintaining a high standard of service. Two-tank dives (mornings only) cost 17,500 CFP. Various packages starting from 48,000 CFP for six dives (valid for two divers) are also offered. Free pick-up.

Eleuthera is a member of Te Moana Pass (www.temoanadiving.com), an inter-island dive pass that's accepted in 16 dive shops in French Polynesia.

Dive'n Smile Bora Bora   DIVING
(☑87 24 48 02; www.divensmile.com; introductory/ single dive 9000/8000 CFP) This small diving outfit (one instructor) offers a wealth of experience in Bora Bora waters and specialises in small groups. Two-tank dives cost 15,000 CFP and six-/10-dive packages are 42,000/60,000 CFP. Nitrox dives are offered at no extra cost. Free pick-up.

Lagoon Excursions
Taking a cruise around Bora Bora's idyllic lagoon will be one of the highlights of your trip to French Polynesia. You'll get the chance to swim and snorkel in otherwise inaccessible places.

Competition is fierce among the various operators who provide trips on the lagoon and its surrounding *motu,* so don't hesitate to shop around. Ask what's included in a cruise and check the ethos of the operator, especially regarding interactions with sharks – a growing number of operators abstain from creating inappropriate interactions with animals. Most boats have snorkelling gear, but it's not a bad idea to bring your own.

Lagoon Service   BOAT TOUR
(☑87 75 69 57; www.lagoonservice.com; half-/full-day trips 6000/9000 CFP) Comfortable boats with a maximum of 12 people. It includes four swimming and snorkel stops. Half-day tours include fruit tasting in the warm waters of the lagoon, while full-day tours include an excellent picnic on a secluded *motu* near the airport.

Reef Discovery   BOAT TOUR
(☑87 76 43 43; www.reefdiscovery.pf; half-day trips 10,000 CFP) Run by a dive instructor

BORA BORA FOR...

Children
➡ Approach rays and colourful fish on a lagoon tour.

➡ Splash about on Matira Beach.

➡ Learn to dive in the calm, shallow waters of the lagoon.

➡ Walk along the seabed.

➡ Parasail over the turquoise lagoon.

Couples
➡ Luxuriate in a beachfront couples massage at a resort's spa.

➡ Explore the lagoon on a private boat tour.

➡ Book an overwater bungalow at a plush resort.

➡ Enjoy a candlelit dinner at one of Bora Bora's intimate restaurants.

➡ Sip a cocktail at a lagoonside bar.

who specialises in small groups and offers half-day tours aboard a luxurious boat (maximum eight people). Includes a snorkel stop at Anau for the manta rays.

Manu Tours   BOAT TOUR
(☑87 79 11 62; half-/full-day trips 6500/9000 CFP) Lagoon tour aboard a large outrigger canoe. Half-day tours include fruit tasting on Motu Fanfan, while full-day tours include a picnic.

Teremoana Nono Tours   BOAT TOUR
(☑87 78 27 61; www.cheznonobora.com; day trips 9500 CFP) A long-time operator famous for its superb barbecue lunch.

Undersea Walks
Aqua Safari   UNDERSEA WALKS
(☑87 28 87 77; www.aquasafaribora.com; trips 9500 CFP) This company provides the unique experience of walking underwater, wearing a diver's helmet and weight belt. Pumps on the boat above feed air to you during the 30-minute 'walk on the wet side', in less than 4m. Walks are available to everyone over the age of six. It's very reassuring that a dive instructor accompanies you on your walk.

Parasailing
Bora Bora Parasail   PARASAILING
(Map p129; ☑87 70 56 62; parasail@mail.pf; Matira; 15-25min trips 29,000-44,000 CFP; Mon-Wed, Fri & Sat, closed Jan & Feb) Picture yourself

BORA BORA ACTIVITIES

Bora Bora

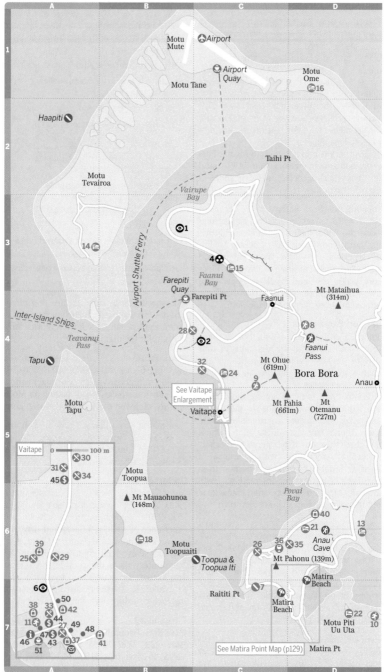

Motu Mute

✈ *Airport*

✈ *Airport Quay*

Motu Ome

📇 16

Motu Tane

Haapiti 🔘

Motu Tevairoa

Taihi Pt

Vairupe Bay

14 📇

🔘1

4 ✪

📇 15

Airport Shuttle Ferry

Farepiti Quay

Faanui Bay

Farepiti Pt

Faanui

Mt Mataihua (314m) ▲

🏃 8

Faanui Pass

28 🔘2

Inter-Island Ships

Teavanui Pass

32 ✪

📇 24

9 🏃

Mt Ohue (619m) ▲

Bora Bora

Anau ⊙

Tapu 🔘

See Vaitape Enlargement

Vaitape 🔘

Mt Pahia (661m) ▲

Mt Otemanu (727m) ▲

Motu Tapu

Vaitape

0 _____ 100 m

✪30

31 ✪34

45 💲

Motu Toopua

▲ Mt Mauaohunoa (148m)

Povai Bay

📇40

🛏 21

🏃

13 📇

39 📇

25 💲 ✪29

📇 18

Motu Toopuaiti

26 ✪

36 ✪35

Anau Cave

6 👁

Toopua & Toopua Iti 🔘

Mt Pahonu (139m) ▲

38 📇 33 ✪ 50 ●

11 💲 44 42 📇

46 47💲 27 ● 49 ● 48 ●

43 37🖂 41 📇

51

Raititi Pt

7 🔘

Matira Beach

Matira Beach

🔘

Matira Beach

📇 22

10 🏃

Motu Piti Uu Uta

See Matira Point Map (p129)

Matira Pt

comfortably seated, gracefully drifting above the multihued lagoon at Matira, feeling the caress of the trade winds on your face... You don't even get wet! Based at Matira Beach, this outfit offers 15-minute trips at 50m above the lagoon and 25-minute trips at 130m above the lagoon. Kids over four are welcome. Free pick-up.

Kitesurfing

Kitesurf School KITESURFING
(Map p129; ☑87 29 14 15; www.kitesurf-school-polynesie.com; Matira) At Matira Point steady winds and the reef-sheltered lagoon are the perfect combination for kitesurfing. Alban is a qualified instructor who offers beginner to advanced kitesurfing lessons and charges 15,000 CFP for a 90-minute course (for one person) or 25,000 CFP for a two-hour course (for two people).

Hiking

Not all the action is in the water on Bora Bora, and you could do worse than take the time to explore the island's spectacularly mountainous interior. A guide is essential, as the paths are notoriously difficult to find and follow.

Mt Ohue & Mt Pahia HIKING
(Map p124) If you're really fit, you can try the arduous climb up to Mt Ohue (619m) and Mt Pahia (661m), two of Bora Bora's iconic summits. It's a six-hour hard-going return hike from Vaitape, with some difficult uphill scrambles and a few treacherous sections, but the panoramic views will be etched in your memory forever.

Never attempt to do this hike on your own because there have been instances of walkers getting lost and injured along the way.

Kings' Valley & the Ancestors' Path HIKING
(Map p124) A half-day walk with a focus on flora, local legends and archaeology. It also includes the (easy) climb to Faanui Pass (views!). Moderate.

Anau Cave HIKING
(Map p124) From Anau village, you'll climb to a spectacular cave in a cliff at a height of about 400m. No shade along the way. About six hours return. Moderate.

Bora Bora Mountain Trek HIKING
(☑87 72 98 45; borabora.mountaintrek@gmail.com; half-/full-day hikes 6500/13,500 CFP) This professional guide speaks passable English and specialises in Kings' Valley, Mt Pahia and Anau Cave hikes. Transfers are included.

BORA BORA ACTIVITIES

Bora Bora

⊙ Sights

1 Coastal Defence Guns............................ B3
2 Coastal Defence Guns............................ C4
3 Coastal Defence Guns............................ E4
4 Marae Fare-Opu...................................... C3
5 Motu Fanfan E7
6 Vaitape A7

⊕ Activities, Courses & Tours

7 Eleuthera Bora Diving Centre C7
  Topdive...(see 32)
8 Kings' Valley & the Ancestors' Path D4
9 Mt Ohue & Mt Pahia C4
10 Rohivai Tours.. D7
11 Tahiti Helicopters A7

🛏 Sleeping

12 Bora Bora Camping E7
13 Bora Bora Ecolodge............................... D6
14 Bora Bora Pearl Beach Resort & Spa... A3
15 Bora Bungalove C3
16 Chez Alice & Raphael D1
17 Four Seasons Resort Bora Bora E2
18 Hilton Bora Bora Nui Resort & Spa B6
19 Intercontinental Bora Bora Resort &
  Thalasso Spa.. F5
20 Le Méridien Bora Bora F4
21 Rohotu Fare.. D6
22 Sofitel Bora Bora Private Island............ D7
23 St Régis Resort F4
24 Sunset Hill Lodge C4

🍽 Eating

25 Aloe Cafe.. A6
26 Bloody Mary's C6
27 Bora Bora Burger A7
28 Bora Bora Yacht Club B4
29 Chin Lee A6
30 Le Panda d'Or A5
31 Le St James.. A5
32 Maikai Bora Bora C4
33 Roulottes A7
34 Super U To'a Amok A5
35 Villa Mahana.. D6

🍸 Drinking & Nightlife

36 Tiki Bar C6

🛍 Shopping

37 Bora Art Upstairs.................................. A7
38 Bora i Te Fanau Tahi – Artisanat.......... A7
39 Deep Sea Pearls A6
40 Galerie Alain et Linda D6
41 La Perle de Maimiti................................ B7
42 Saltwater A7

ℹ Information

43 Banque de Polynésie A7
44 Banque de Tahiti A7
45 Banque Socredo.................................... A5
46 Bora Bora Tourist Office A7

ℹ Transport

47 Air Tahiti A7
48 Albert Store.. A7
49 Bora Bora Rent a Car – Avis A7
50 Europcar A7
51 Maupiti Express 2.................................. A7

Polynesia Island Tours HIKING
(☎87 29 66 60; polynesiaislandtours@mail.pf; half-/full-day hikes 6500/14,000 CFP) A professional walking guide who specialises in Mt Pahia and Anau Cave hikes as well as the Anau-Faanui crossing. Transfers are included.

☞ Tours

A couple of operators organise island tours aboard open 4WDs. Tours include visits to American coastal defence guns. Guides are informative, providing interesting titbits on the island's flora and fauna. These tours are good value if you don't want to hire a car.

Tupuna Mountain Safari CULTURAL TOUR
(☎40 67 75 06; www.tupunasafari.com; 7600 CFP) Runs half-day trips that visit American WWII sites along with a few stops at lookouts.

Vavau Adventures CULTURAL TOUR
(☎87 72 01 21; www.vavau4x4adventures.com; 7500 CFP) Offers half-day trips that take in American WWII sites and various lookouts. Also includes fruit tasting.

Natura Discovery CULTURAL TOUR
(☎87 25 72 00; www.naturadiscovery.com) Natura Discovery runs a tour of the island's main attractions, including a couple of inland roads (for lookouts) and American WWII sites. The three-hour tour includes fruit tasting and transfers.

✵ Festivals & Events

Heiva i Bora Bora CULTURAL
(☉Jul) This annual festival takes place in Vaitape, on a big stage set up near the quay. It features a program of parades, dance, singing and sports contests, as well as beauty pageants and floral floats. It's said to be the best Heiva after the one held in Pape'ete.

Hawaiki Nui SPORTS
(www.hawaikinuivaa.pf; ☉early Nov) The arrival of the Hawaiki Nui canoe race on Matira Beach is an indescribably cheerful event,

with dozens of colourful *pirogues* (outrigger canoes) congregating on the beach.

🛏 Sleeping

Glossy brochures and promotional literature focus on Bora Bora's ultraswish resorts, but a smattering of affordable establishments have sprung up over the last two decades.

Although places to stay can be found all around the island, as well as on the *motu,* the majority are concentrated along the southern coast.

Vaitape & West Coast

⭐**Sunset Hill Lodge**   BUNGALOW **$$**
(Map p124; ✆87 79 26 48; www.sunsethilllodge. com; Vaitape; bungalows d 8000-15,500 CFP; ❄🖥) Although the location, on the northern outskirts of Vaitape, about 8km away from Matira Beach, doesn't exactly scream 'vacation', this is a real find if you're working to a tight budget. It's a convenient base – banks, supermarkets and restaurants are within walking distance – and accommodation options include four fully equipped apartments with air-con, and two cheaper, simpler fan-cooled units. They're all spotlessly clean.

Of the four apartments, two units enjoy a spiffing water frontage (no beach, but swimming is possible). The two other studios are above the owner's house in a separate building that's a bit inland, and offer great views of Vaitape Bay. The cheaper units sit in the garden, with no views to speak of. Bonuses: complimentary kayaks and bikes. Cash only.

Bora Bungalove   BUNGALOW **$$**
(Map p124; ✆40 67 73 58, 87 74 18 82; www.bora boralove.com; Faanui; d/bungalow 11,000/21,000 CFP; 🖥) You've got two options here: a comfy, spacious and kitchen-equipped bungalow with a terrace right on the water's edge and a rather cramped room with outside shower and toilets. OK, there's no air-con and you need wheels to stay here – Vaitape is 6km away and Matira Beach a further 8km away – but it's friendly, homey and well run. Bikes and kayaks are free.

The room also has its own terrace overlooking the bay. There's no beach, and the (deep) water is more blue-ish than turquoise, but snorkelling is good. No meals are served but there's a communal kitchen. Transfers to Vaitape quay cost 3000 CFP return per carload. Cash only.

Rohotu Fare   BUNGALOW **$$$**
(Map p124; ✆87 70 77 99; www.rohotufarelodge. com; Povai Bay; bungalows d 26,000-30,000 CFP; ❄🖥) This upscale venture is a more intimate alternative to a resort, with three all-wood, fully equipped bungalows cocooned in exotic gardens on the mountainside overlooking Povai Bay. No beach nearby, but Matira Point is an easy bike ride away, or you can arrange transfer with Nir, your Israeli host, who speaks excellent English. Free transfers to Vaitape quay and free bikes.

The two lagoon-view bungalows are the best, with stunning views and air-con, while the cheaper unit has garden views and a ceiling fan. They are all furnished in an elegant style with plenty of wooden furniture and appealing outdoor bathrooms. If you don't fancy cooking, there are several restaurants nearby.

Matira Point & Around

Much of the island's accommodation is clustered around Matira Point, at the southern toe of Bora Bora. This area also features the island's best beach.

Chez Robert & Tina   PENSION **$**
(Map p129; ✆40 67 63 55, 87 73 53 89; pension robertettina@mail.pf; Matira; d 10,100 CFP, without bathrooms 8100-9100 CFP) This place is a heartbreaker. Right at the tip of Matira Point, it enjoys a sensational setting, with unobstructed views of the turquoise lagoon, and it's competitively priced (by Bora Bora standards) and within walking distance of various shops and restaurants. Sadly, we've heard reports of variable service and a lack of maintenance.

If you can bear that, it's an acceptable plan B. Rooms are in bare, fan-cooled homes, all with shared kitchen. A few rooms have private facilities (cold-water bathrooms). Due to erosion, the shore is more rocky than sandy, but Matira Beach is just a coconut's throw away. No wi-fi when we visited.

ℹ **DIRECT BOOKINGS**

If you're staying at a fancy hotel, avoid booking a tour or an activity through the activity desk, as these places can tack on as much as 40% extra. Make direct arrangements with the tour companies. Most operators organise free pick-ups and drop-offs from hotels.

Intercontinental Bora Bora
Le Moana Resort RESORT $$$
(Map p129; ☎40 60 49 00; www.lemoana.inter-
continental.com; bungalows d from 70,000 CFP;
❄🛜🏊) If you're looking to do Bora Bora in
style but don't want to feel cut off from the
island, the Moana is your answer. It spreads
along the eastern side of Matira Point (good
for watching the sun rise), a thin stretch of
beach is right out the front and there's sen-
sational snorkelling offshore. It comprises
beach bungalows and overwater bungalows
that feature Polynesian designs.

It comprises beach bungalows and over-
water bungalows that feature Polynesian
designs. Most units were renovated a few
years ago; the most sought-after ones are
bungalows 11 to 18, with magnificent lagoon
views from the bedroom. Precious perks
include free kayaks, paddle boards and
snorkelling gear. It's also renowned for its
twice-weekly island night and buffet.

Le Maitai Bora Bora RESORT $$$
(Map p129; ☎40 60 30 00; www.hotelmaitai.
com; Matira; r/bungalows d incl breakfast from
20,000/35,000 CFP; ❄🛜) This midrange
resort prides itself on offering the cheapest
overwater bungalows in French Polynesia.
While much less exclusive and glam than

INTERACTIONS WITH SHARKS & RAYS

Many lagoon tours bill themselves
as 'safaris' because they include ray
'baiting' (the tour guides keep sardine
or tuna scraps in their hands to attract
the rays). The tuna scraps also attract a
number of blacktip sharks. This practice
is legal in French Polynesia; what's illegal
is shark feeding within the lagoon and
near the pass.

Although some say that 'playing'
with sharks and rays is a good way to
educate tourists, it's increasingly recognised that it disrupts natural behaviour
patterns. The worst scenario occurs
when a tour guide makes a stop outside
the lagoon, throws tuna scraps into
the ocean and starts to pet a 3m-long
lemon shark for the sake of impressing
camera-toting tourists. Stay clear of
these operators, as this practice is not
environmentally friendly and carries an
element of risk.

---

the ones found at other hotels, they get the
job done. Across the road from the beach, in
the hills amid lush jungle foliage, the rooms
are impersonal but well-tended and some
upper-floor rooms have stunning lagoon
views.

The overwater and beach bungalows
lack privacy (the coastal road passes just
behind) but their unbeatable location offers
adequate compensation. Amenities include
two restaurants and a bar. Free kayaks and
snorkelling gear. Wi-fi costs extra.

Hotel Matira BUNGALOW $$$
(Map p129; ☎40 67 70 51, 40 60 58 40; www.
hotel-matira.com; bungalows d 21,000-35,000 CFP;
🛜) Right on Matira Beach, this is surely
one of the most divinely situated hotels in
Bora Bora, especially if you score one of the
dearer bungalows (nos 1 and 11), which are
just steps from the turquoise water. That
said, the 14 units are in need of a lick of
paint (and varnish) and don't have air-con.
All told, it's about the location. It's handy to
restaurants, shops and supermarkets.

The bungalows are dotted around mani-
cured lawns and have dark-wood furniture,
cleanish bathrooms (with no doors, just a
curtain) and the essential sun deck. Wi-fi is
extra.

Village Temanuata BUNGALOW $$$
(Map p129; ☎40 67 75 61; www.temanuata.
com; bungalows d 20,000-24,000 CFP; 🛜) This
longstanding institution is starting to show
its age, especially the tired bathrooms. But
overall it's not bad value given the irresist-
ible location on Matira Beach and the promotional rates ('stay three nights, pay for
two') when it's slack. The 14 bungalows are
tightly packed together on a grassy property
overlooking a narrow stretch of beach.

Only two units (nos 1 and 6) have full
lagoon views. It's within walking distance
of various shops and restaurants. Breakfast
costs 1400 CFP, wi-fi is extra and there are
kayaks for hire.

Sofitel Bora Bora
Marara Beach Resort RESORT $$$
(Map p129; ☎40 60 55 00; www.sofitel-french-
polynesia.com; Matira; bungalows d from 42,000
CFP; ❄🛜🏊) Perhaps the least self-conscious
resort on Bora Bora, laid-back Sofitel
Marara is sandwiched between the coastal
road and the lagoon, which doesn't exactly
make it ideal for peace or privacy. It features
various accommodation options, including

Matira Point

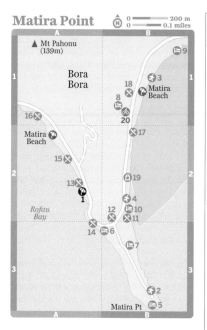

Matira Point

⊙ Sights
1 Matira Beach A2

⊕ Activities, Courses & Tours
   Bora Bora Parasail......................(see 3)
2 Kitesurf School....................................B3
3 La Plage..B1
4 Manu Taxi Boat B2

⊜ Sleeping
5 Chez Robert & Tina B3
6 Hotel Matira..B3
7 Intercontinental Bora Bora Le
   Moana Resort....................................B3
8 Le Maitai Bora Bora............................ B1
9 Sofitel Bora Bora Marara Beach
   Resort... B1
10 Village Temanuata..............................B2

⊗ Eating
11 Fare Manuia..B2
12 Magasin Matira B2
13 Matira Beach Burger A2
14 Moi Here..A3
15 Restaurant Matira Beach....................A2
16 Snack Matira A1
17 Tama'a Maitai..B2
18 Tiare Market B1

⊜ Drinking & Nightlife
   Hurricane ....(see 9)

⊜ Shopping
19 Marama Tattoo B2

⊕ Transport
20 Totara Loca B1

beach units, garden units, overwater bungalows and the odd 'half overwater, half on the beach' bungalow.

Most units need a freshen-up and the public areas are getting tired, but the beachfront location is the saving grace and there's a great coral garden. Facilities include an infinity pool, a bar and two restaurants.

East Coast

Bora Bora Ecolodge   PENSION **$$**
(Map p124; ☎87 33 80 52; www.bora-bora-ecolodge.com; Anau; bungalows d incl breakfast 12,000-14,000 CFP; �⏚) The name is misleading: there's nothing vaguely 'eco' or 'lodge' in this modest *pension* featuring six self-contained bungalows in Anau village. You won't be extolling to friends the bungalows or the location (the lagoon is muddy, there's no beach and it's isolated), but it's an acceptable port of call provided you keep your expectations in check.

Perks include free transfers from the Vaitape quay and free kayaks. If you don't rent a vehicle, the owners will happily drive you to Matira Beach, about 3km away. Dinners (3500 CFP) are available on request.

The Motu

Bora Bora Camping   CAMPGROUND **$**
(Map p124; ☎87 70 22 08; Motu Piti Aau; campsites per person 2000 CFP) Camping in Bora Bora? Yes, it's possible, but don't hold your breath. This is a very modest place with limited amenities (cold showers, basic self-catering facilities), but its location on the southern tip of Motu Piti Aau is idyllic, with swaying palm trees, gin-clear waters and mesmerising views of the mountainous mainland. Transfers to Matira are 2000 CFP per person return.

It's not permanently staffed; contact the owner a day before to organise transfers. Bring your own supplies as no meals are provided.

★**Intercontinental Bora Bora**
Resort & Thalasso Spa RESORT $$$
(Map p124; ☎40 60 76 00; www.tahiti.inter-
continental.com; Motu Piti Aau; bungalows d from
90,000 CFP; ❋☎☲) ✎ The Intercontinental
has one of the best resort reputations on the
island, and the accolades are well deserved.
Seen from above, the layout of the 80 over-
water bungalows resembles two giant crab
claws. The wow factor continues inside, with
floor-to-ceiling windows and Starck-inspired
decor. Two highlights: the lavish spa and the
overwater wedding chapel, complete with a
glass-floor aisle.

The seawater air-conditioning system,
which is the pride of the hotel, saves 90% of
the electricity consumed by a conventional
cooling system of similar capacity. One weak
point? Snorkelling is just average (the sea
floor is sandy).

Sofitel Bora Bora
Private Island RESORT $$$
(Map p124; ☎40 60 56 00; www.sofitel.com;
Motu Piti Uu Uta; bungalows d incl breakfast from
67,000 CFP; ❋☎) One of Bora Bora's most
popular honeymoon spots, this Sofitel
strikes a perfect balance between luxury,
seclusion, privacy (there are only 31 units)
and convenience – on hilly Motu Piti Uu
Uta, it's just five glorious minutes by shuttle
boat from the main island.

Due to its unbeatable position, it gets
plenty of sunshine, even in late afternoon,
and the views of the lagoon from the top of
the hill are sensational. Another draw is the
proximity of one of Bora Bora's best coral
gardens.

The three sunset-friendly 'lagoon view'
units are the brighter choices, but the
well-appointed overwater bungalows and
the tropically delicious villas positioned on
a greenery-shrouded hillside are also very
popular.

St Régis Resort RESORT $$$
(Map p124; ☎40 60 78 88; www.stregis.com/
borabora; Motu Ome; bungalows d from 105,000
CFP; ❋☎☲) This top-notch resort is a real
treat for honeymooners or couples looking
for a perfect high-style escape. Its super-
stylish public areas and gorgeous overwater
bungalows and beach villas make it per-
fectly suited to romantic beach holidays.
Though you would never guess it, the *motu*
is landscaped for optimum beach space and
features a series of turquoise channels and
inner lagoons.

Another highlight is the food. The St
Régis was one of the original pioneers of
fine à la carte dining on Bora Bora, and it's
safe to say you'll eat excellently in its two
restaurants. You can also book in for a beau-
ty treatment in the lavish Miri Miri spa. The
resort operates free shuttles to Vaitape.

Chez Alice & Raphael BUNGALOW $$$
(Map p124; ☎87 70 37 10; www.pensionaliceet-
raphaelborabora.com; Motu Ome; bungalow d incl
breakfast 22,000 CFP) Simple hedonists will
be hard-pressed to find a mellower spot
to maroon themselves for a languid holiday. On Motu Ome, two well-proportioned
bungalows are dotted around a vast coconut
grove by the lagoon. They were built using
local materials in authentic Polynesian style,
but the walls in the bathrooms don't make
it to the ceilings and there's no air-con (only
fans). Cash only.

It feels wonderfully secluded and relaxing, but take note this is not a resort; aside
from swimming, snorkelling and kayaking,
there are no activities – some guests may
feel a bit captive. That said, boat transfers
to the mainland can be arranged (from
500 CFP per person return, depending on
distance). Evening meals cost 3500 CFP. No
wi-fi access on the *motu*.

Four Seasons Resort
Bora Bora RESORT $$$
(Map p124; ☎40 60 31 30; www.fourseasons.
com/borabora; Motu Ome; bungalows d from
130,000 CFP; ❋☎☲) This wonderful place
is unique among the Polynesian resorts,
and since its opening in 2008, it has consist-
ently impressed. Indeed, this is one of the
few resorts that manages to get everything
so right with such little fuss: a combination
of splendid overwater bungalows, fantastic
setting, wonderful food and superb staff.

Each bungalow comes with its own size-
able pool on an enclosed deck overlooking
the sea, with direct access to the lagoon. The
international clientele is made up main-
ly of celebs, honeymooners and couples
who spend the day by the pool and being
treated at the sumptuous spa, but it's also
welcoming to families (young children and
teenagers have their own entertainment
program).

Bora Bora Pearl Beach
Resort & Spa RESORT $$$
(Map p124; ☎40 60 52 00; www.spmhotels.
com; Motu Tevairoa; bungalows d from 65,000 CFP;
❋☎☲) Of all Bora Bora's top-end options,

EXPLORING THE MOTU

Ah, the tantalising *motu* (lagoon or reef islets) on Bora Bora. Although they're not far from the mainland, it's not that easy to enjoy their paradisiacal setting unless you're a guest at one of the luxurious resorts. Keep in mind that all *motu* are private, so don't treat the land as yours to explore without permission. There are a few options, though.

La Plage (Map p129; ☑ 87 70 16 27, 87 28 48 66; www.laplage-borabora.com; Matira Beach; half-/full-day 14,000/21,000 CFP; ⊙ 8am-5pm) If you prefer setting your own pace and fancy tootling around the lagoon yourself, La Plage rents small four-seater motor boats that are easy to drive; no licence is required. A detailed map featuring the lagoon is provided, as well as life jackets, and petrol is included. It's based on the beach near hotel Maitai Polynesia Bora Bora. Call for transfers from your hotel. Bring a picnic and your snorkelling gear.

Manu Taxi Boat (Map p129; ☑ 87 79 11 62; per person 3000 CFP; ⊙ 9am-4.30pm) Can arrange transfers to Motu Fanfan, at the southernmost tip of Motu Piti Aau, for 3000 CFP. It's an idyllic spot, with sun-loungers, hammocks, an ablution block and a sensational coral garden just offshore. Meals (3000 CFP, by reservation) and drinks are available. Bring your snorkel gear.

Rohivai Tours (Map p124; ☑ 87 32 60 46; ⊙ 1-3.30pm) Can drop you off on private Motu Ringo (Motu Piti Uu Tai) for 3000 CFP. It usually departs at 1pm and returns at 3.30pm. The *motu* has sun-loungers and an ablution block.

the Pearl has the strongest Polynesian feel. The 50 overwater bungalows are lovely, but the 20 garden suites, which come complete with their own swimming pool, and the 10 beach suites, equipped with an outdoor Jacuzzi, will really win your heart over. They all blend perfectly into the landscaped property.

Other highlights include the dazzling infinity pool and the tropical spa, where only Polynesian treatments are offered. Two grumbles: it's exposed to the prevailing winds and wi-fi costs extra.

Hilton Bora Bora Nui
Resort & Spa   RESORT $$$
(Map p124; ☑ 40 60 33 00; www.hiltonhotels.com; Motu Toopua; bungalows d from 55,000 CFP; ❋ ☎ ☲) This splendid resort extends along a ravishing stretch of porcelain sand, on a hilly *motu*. With 120 units, including 84 overwater bungalows and hillside villas, the Hilton is certainly not a hideaway, but it's in harmony with its surroundings.

It boasts top-notch amenities, including an infinity pool, five restaurants and the obligatory glass-floor viewing panels in the overwater bungalows. Nestled in a grove overlooking the resort, the spa will make you go 'ahh'. One quibble: facing west towards the sea, it lacks the iconic view of Bora Bora.

Le Méridien Bora Bora   RESORT $$$
(Map p124; ☑ 40 60 51 51; www.lemeridien.com/borabora; Motu Piti Aau; bungalows d from 65,000 CFP; ❋ ☎ ☲) While lavish, the Méridien offers affordable luxury in its 98 units, including 14 beach villas and 82 overwater bungalows. The *motu* is a stunner, with a vast infinity-edge pool, a lovely inner lagoon fringed with chalk-white (artificial) beaches and an architecturally interesting space with timber and thatch for reception, restaurant and bar areas. Everything is luxurious, but nothing is over the top.

The 50-sq-metre overwater bungalows are not huge by Bora Bora standards but they boast vast glass floors and fabulous views of Mt Otemanu. A highlight is the Turtle Centre, which is a rehabilitation centre. Guests can swim with the turtles in a protected lagoon and watch babies being cared for under the guidance of a conservationist.

✖ Eating

There's a good choice of restaurants on Bora Bora, ranging from European gourmet dining to *roulottes* (food vans) and *snacks* (a small snack-bar-cum-cafe serving Tahitian staples and sandwiches). Some top-end hotels have an in-house restaurant that is also open to nonguests. Other than the *snacks,* nearly all of the restaurants accept credit cards.

All the luxury hotels have dance performances with buffet dinners several times a week (around 8000 CFP to 10,000 CFP).

Vaitape

A string of stalls along the main road sell fruit and cold drinks.

Bora Bora Burger   TAHITIAN, SANDWICHES **$**
(Map p124; mains 1200-1600 CFP; ⊙9am-4.30pm Mon-Fri) Located right on the main street, this simple but sweet cafeteria-cum-fast-food outlet is a handy spot for a cheap, uncomplicated, walk-in bite. Tuck into well-made sandwiches (from 300 CFP), paninis or burgers. The concise menu also includes salads and daily specials.

Roulottes   TAHITIAN **$**
(Map p124; mains 1000-1600 CFP; ⊙6.30-9.30pm) If money matters, these cheap and cheerful food vans that take up position on the main square near the quay are the ideal pit stop. Fork out about 1200 CFP for a plate of grilled fish or a voluminous chow mein and you'll leave patting your tummy contentedly.

Super U To'a Amok   SUPERMARKET **$**
(Map p124; ⊙5.30am-7pm Mon-Thu, 5.30am-8pm Fri & Sat) This is the best supermarket on the island. It sells almost everything self-caterers could want. It's at the northern end of Vaitape.

Chin Lee   SUPERMARKET **$**
(Map p124; ⊙5am-8pm) This well-stocked supermarket is north of the centre of Vaitape.

Le Panda d'Or   CHINESE **$$**
(Map p124; ☑40 67 62 70; mains 1500-2800 CFP; ⊙11am-1pm & 6-9pm Mon-Sat) This well-established venture serves up a wide assortment of Chinese staples at reasonable prices. If the rather charmless interior (think a vast, tiled room in a modernish building) doesn't inspire you, there's a takeaway counter outside, to the right. North of the centre of Vaitape.

Aloe Cafe   CAFETERIA **$$**
(Map p124; ☑40 67 78 88; mains 1200-2300 CFP; ⊙7.30am-6pm Mon-Sat; 🛜) This busy place right in the centre of Vaitape has the most eclectic menu in town and is a good place for a light meal any time of the day (last order is at 4.30pm). Get things going with palate-pleasing salads, well-prepared fish and meat dishes, pasta or pizza. Good

breakfasts (served until 10.30am) too and free wi-fi.

It's also famous for its to-die-for *pains au chocolat* (chocolate croissants). Come early; by 10am they are sold out.

★**Maikai Bora Bora**   FRENCH, TAHITIAN **$$$**
(Map p124; ☑40 60 38 00; www.maikaimarina.com; mains 1800-2900 CFP; ⊙noon-2pm & 6-9pm Mon-Sat; 🛜) This highly rated eatery offers excellent Polynesian cuisine with a refined twist, savoured in a vast and stylish dining room overlooking the lagoon (but only a few tables have lagoon views). Prices are surprisingly reasonable for the quality of the fare. On the northern outskirts of Vaitape. Free shuttle at dinner.

Everything's pretty good, but if you want a recommendation, go for the outstanding beef fillet with homemade mashed potatoes. Something sweet to finish? Try the luscious chocolate mousse.

Le St James   FRENCH **$$$**
(Map p124; ☑40 67 64 62; www.boraborastjames.com; mains 2800-3000 CFP, lunch menu 2900 CFP, dinner menu 7000-9500 CFP; ⊙11.30am-2.30pm Tue, Wed, Fri & Sat, 6.30-9.30pm Mon-Sat; 🛜) Don't be deterred by the odd location – it's hidden in the back of a small shopping centre in Vaitape – for, once inside, you'll find a convivial space that combines style with informality and an enticing deck affording lovely bay views. Foodwise, the emphasis is on French specialities with a bow to local ingredients. Free shuttle at dinner.

The lunch menu is excellent value by Bora Bora standards. Top selections: lamb shank with spices and *tournedos Rossini avec purée aux truffes* (a choice piece of steak with truffle-flavoured purée). There's an equally impressive wine list, and the desserts are a treat. It's also a great place for a sundowner.

Bora Bora Yacht Club   FRENCH, TAHITIAN **$$$**
(Map p124; ☑40 67 60 47; www.boraborayachtclub.net; mains 1700-3500 CFP; ⊙noon-2pm & 6-9.30pm; 🛜) Yes, the food is pretty good, but the real draw here is the stunning wooden deck overlooking the lagoon – very romantic at sunset. The menu runs the gamut from grilled fish to meat dishes and salads to pasta. The tartares and the finely sliced carpaccios come recommended. For dessert, try the belt-bustingly good passionfruit cheesecake. It's about 3km north of Vaitape. Free shuttle at dinner.

✕ Povai Bay

Villa Mahana GASTRONOMY **$$$**
(Map p124; ☎40 67 50 63; www.villamahana.com;
set menu 12,000-15,000 CFP; ⏱6-8pm Mon-Sat)
A true alchemist, the Corsican chef Damien
Rinaldi has got the magic formula right,
fusing Mediterranean with Polynesian to cre-
ate stunning cuisine, perfectly matched with
French wines. Exquisite execution extends
to the small dessert selection. It's housed in
a stylish villa reminiscent of Provence, with
lots of ochre and yellow tones. It's perfect for
a romantic *tête-à-tête*, but be sure to book
well in advance – there are only nine tables.

Bloody Mary's RESTAURANT **$$$**
(Map p124; ☎40 67 72 86; lunch mains 1200-
1800 CFP, dinner mains 3000-3700 CFP; ⏱11am-
3pm & 6-9pm Mon-Sat; 🐾) Bloody Mary's isn't
just a restaurant, it's an experience, especially at dinner (light meals only at lunchtime).
You walk on sand floors, sit on coconut stools
under a thatched roof and are surrounded
by exotic plants. You choose your meal from
an extensive display at the entrance, with a
presentation in English.

Very touristy, but it's a concept that has
been a cult since 1979, so go with the flow.
Call for a free shuttle.

✕ Matira Point & Around

Snack Matira TAHITIAN **$**
(Map p129; ☎40 67 77 32; mains 500-2200 CFP;
⏱10am-8pm Tue-Sat, to 4pm Sun) This unfussy
little eatery could hardly be better situated:
it's right on the beach at Matira (think terrific lagoon views). The menu concentrates
on simply prepared fish and meat dishes as
well as burgers, sandwiches and omelettes.
Eat alfresco or grab your victuals and find
your picnic spot on the beach.

Moi Here FAST FOOD **$**
(Map p129; ☎40 67 56 46; mains 1300-1500
CFP; ⏱8.30am-5.30pm) It's the location that's
the pull here, rather than the food. Greasy
burgers and sandwiches, omelettes, beef
steak and raw fish in coconut milk won't
knock your socks off, but you're literally
hanging over the beach, with dizzying views
of the turquoise lagoon.

Magasin Matira SUPERMARKET
(Map p129; ⏱6am-7.30pm Mon-Sat, 6-10am Sun)
This supermarket near Matira Beach sells
sandwiches and various ready-made meals.

Tiare Market SUPERMARKET **$**
(Map p129; ⏱6am-7pm Mon-Sat, 5.30am-1pm
& 3-6pm Sun) Self-caterers can stock up the
kitchenette at this local supermarket. It's
well stocked with all the necessities, from
wine and fresh bread to sunscreen and
toothpaste.

Fare Manuia FRENCH, TAHITIAN **$$**
(Map p129; ☎40 67 68 08; mains 1200-3500
CFP; ⏱11.30am-3pm & 6-9.30pm) The hardest
thing about eating at this local favourite is
deciding between the excellent meat or fish
dishes, crunchy salads and delicious pasta.
Skip the pizzas, though. Big appetite? Opt
for the huge wood-fired prime rib. Alas, no
sea view – it's in an enclosed area beside the
coastal road – but there's a small lounge sec-
tion with a tiny pool at the back. Free shuttle
at dinner.

Matira Beach Burger BURGERS **$$**
(Map p129; ☎40 67 59 99; mains 900-2000 CFP;
⏱11am-4pm Mon, 11am-7pm Tue-Sun) A seduc-
tive setting complete with an atmospheric
terrace right on Matira Beach is the draw
at this well-regarded joint. How about the
food? It serves up a colourful assortment of
palate pleasers, such as burgers, salads and
a few grills.

Tama'a Maitai INTERNATIONAL **$$**
(Map p129; ☎40 60 30 00; mains 1300-2800
CFP; ⏱11.30am-9pm) Part of Le Maitai Bora
Bora hotel, Tama'a Maitai overlooks the
lagoon and catches lots of breeze. All the
usual suspects are featured on the menu
including salads, pizza, fish and meat dishes,
as well as a few vegetarian options.

★ Restaurant
Matira Beach FRENCH, JAPANESE **$$$**
(Map p129; ☎40 67 79 09; www.restaurantmatira
beach.com; mains 1500-3900 CFP, dinner menu
5400-6000 CFP; ⏱11.30am-2pm & 6.30-9pm
Wed-Sun) This breezy, open-air restaurant
provides an enchanting dining experience
with delectable food. It's well known for its
Japanese cuisine (sushi, nigiri, *teppanyaki*)
as well as well-executed French and Polynesian dishes. Salads and burgers are also
available at lunchtime. Another clincher
is the gorgeous setting, with an agreeable
deck overlooking the beach. Free shuttle at
dinner.

Lunch has a casual atmosphere, but
dinner is a more romantic affair.

BORA BORA EATING

🍷 Drinking & Nightlife

For such a famous island, the bar scene is very tame on Bora Bora. However, there are a few cool spots where you can cut loose over some sunset cocktails in pleasant surrounds. If it's just the setting you want to absorb, check out the bars in the big hotels. Many restaurants also have a bar section: check out Maikai Bora Bora (p132), which has great tapas and occasional live music, Bora Bora Yacht Club (p132) and Le St James (p132).

Tiki Bar   BAR
(Map p124; ☎ 40 67 57 36; Povai Bay; ☺ 3pm-1am; 🐕) Opened in 2015, Tiki Bar is by far the most happening venue on Bora Bora. There's an interesting mix of people here, from hotel staff to tourists and locals, all drawn by the well-priced beer, cocktails, tapas and great atmosphere. It's usually packed on Friday and Saturday after 8pm. It hosts live bands certain evenings. Food is also served.

Hurricane   BAR
(Map p129; ☎ 40 60 55 00; Matira Beach; ☺ 10.30am-9pm; 🐕) The in-house bar at Sofitel Bora Bora Marara Beach Resort is friendly and sociable, with a pleasant outdoor deck.

⭐ Entertainment

If there's one thing you absolutely have to check out while you're on Bora Bora, it's a traditional dance show held in one of the luxury hotels. You can usually get in for the price of a drink at the bar, or for between 8000 CFP and 10,000 CFP, you can also feast on a buffet dinner. There are performances once or twice a week; ask at the reception desks about the schedule.

Other than that, nightlife is as restrained as it is on the other islands of French Polynesia.

🛍️ Shopping

Black-pearl jewellery is sold in many places around Bora Bora, at prices that are often higher than in Tahiti. Apart from pearls, shopping on Bora Bora tends to mean hopping between the few galleries and boutiques that are scattered around the island.

★ Marama Tattoo   TATTOO PARLOUR
(Map p129; ☎ 87 76 35 34; Matira) For traditionally designed tattoos head to this highly rated tattoo studio. Popular, sterile and reliable. Book well ahead as Marama is something of a legend in French Polynesia.

Saltwater   CLOTHING
(Map p124; ☎ 87 37 27 15; www.saltwater-family. com; Vaitape; ☺ 9am-5pm Mon-Fri, 9am-noon Sat) This trendsetting boutique has island-made shirts, T-shirts, caps, swimsuits and accessories. They're inspired by traditional island designs and transformed into contemporary looks. For men, women and kids.

Deep Sea Pearls   JEWELLERY
(Map p124; ☎ 40 67 61 76; Vaitape; ☺ 9am-6pm Mon-Sat) This store in the centre of Vaitape has a wide choice of mounted and loose pearls as well as jewellery pieces. Free transfers are available.

La Perle de Maimiti   JEWELLERY
(Map p124; ☎ 87 78 30 58, 87 75 60 29; www. maimiti.com; Vaitape; ☺ by appointment) Not your average pearl shop – it's in a private home – La Perle de Maimiti is run by an experienced salesman who has worked for various pearl companies on the island. He has a limited but interesting selection of loose and mounted pearls at reasonable prices (for Bora Bora). Most pearls come from the Gambier Archipelago. Free pick-up.

Bora Art Upstairs   ARTS
(Map p124; ☎ 40 67 71 82; Vaitape; ☺ 9.30am-5.30pm Mon-Sat) Loads of Polynesian works of art, including paintings and carvings by local artists and artisans, are sold at this pretty special gallery just next to the post office.

**Bora i Te Fanau Tahi –
Artisanat**   HANDICRAFTS
(Map p124; ☺ 8am-3.30pm) By the Vaitape quay, this crafts centre has lots of stalls selling *pareu,* basketwork, shell necklaces and bracelets and other crafts produced by island women.

Galerie Alain et Linda   ARTS
(Map p124; ☎ 40 67 70 32; www.borabora-art. com; Povai Bay; ☺ 8.30am-6pm Mon-Sat) About halfway between Vaitape and Matira Point, this gallery has a little bit of everything – including a mix of art, books, etchings and pottery.

ⓘ Information

Most of Bora Bora's services are found in Vaitape. There's a medical centre, several private doctors and a pharmacy.

Banque de Polynésie (Map p124; ⊙7.45-11.45am & 12.45-4.15pm Mon-Thu, to 3.30pm Fri) Currency exchange and ATM (Visa only). Near the quay at Vaitape.

Banque de Tahiti (Map p124; ⊙8am-noon & 1-4pm Mon-Fri) Currency exchange and ATM. Near the quay at Vaitape.

Banque Socredo (Map p124; ⊙7.30-11.30am & 1-3pm Mon-Fri) Currency exchange and ATM. At the northern end of Vaitape.

Bora Bora Tourist Office (Map p124; ☑40 67 76 36; www.borabora-tourisme. com; ⊙8.30am-noon & 1.30-4.30pm Mon-Fri, 8.30am-noon Sat) The office is on the quay at Vaitape and has pamphlets and other info.

Post Office (OPT; Map p124; Vaitape; internet per hr 500 CFP; ⊙7.15am-3.15pm Mon-Thu, to 2.15pm Fri; 🛜) Internet and wi-fi access (with the Manaspot network). Has an ATM.

ⓘ Getting There & Away

Bora Bora is 270km northwest of Tahiti.

AIR

Air Tahiti (Map p124; ☑40 86 42 42; www.airtahiti.pf; Vaitape; ⊙7.30-11.30am & 1.30-4.30pm Mon-Fri, 8-11.30am Sat) flies between Bora Bora and Tahiti (24,000 CFP, 50 minutes, eight to 10 flights daily), Huahine (11,800 CFP, 20 minutes, one to two flights daily), Maupiti (8500 CFP, one to two flights weekly), Mo'orea (25,400 CFP, one hour, one to three flights daily) and Ra'iatea (9100 CFP, 15 minutes, one to three flights daily). Air Tahiti also has direct flights from Bora Bora to the Tuamotus, with a very handy flight to Rangiroa (31,500 CFP, 1¼ hours, three to four flights weekly) and onward connections to other atolls, including Tikehau and Fakarava. If you're island-hopping, you can buy an Air Tahiti Pass (p234).

BOAT

The **Maupiti Express 2** (Map p124; ☑40 67 66 69) serves Ra'iatea/Taha'a on Wednesday, Friday and Sunday (5400 CFP one way, two hours), departing for Ra'iatea and Taha'a at 7am on Wednesday and Friday and at 2pm on Sunday. Tickets can be bought onboard or at the office on the Vaitape quay.

Two cargo ships, the **Hawaiki Nui** (p236) and the **Taporo VII** (p236), make two trips a week

between Pape'ete and Bora Bora (via Huahine, Ra'iatea and Taha'a). They leave Pape'ete on Tuesday and Thursday around 4pm, and leave Bora Bora on Wednesday and Friday. Note that it's pretty difficult for tourists to get passage aboard the *Taporo* as it's usually booked out by locals. Both dock at the **Farepiti Quay** (Map p124), 3km north of Vaitape.

ⓘ Getting Around

Bora Bora's 32km coast road hugs the shoreline almost all the way around the island.

TO/FROM THE AIRPORT

The airport is on Motu Mute, at the northern edge of the lagoon; transfers are offered to and from the Vaitape quay on two large catamaran ferries (included in the cost of your ticket). There's a shuttle bus from the quay to the hotels and *pensions* at Matira Point (500 CFP), but it has to be booked in advance by the place where you're staying.

When leaving by air, you need to be at the quay at least 1¼ hours before the flight. The top hotels transfer their visitors directly to and from the airport; all other passengers are picked up at the quay by the catamaran ferries (the cost of this is included in the ticket).

BICYCLE & CAR

There are two petrol stations in Vaitape.

Albert Store (Map p124; ☑87 78 46 60, 40 67 75 55; ⊙9am-5pm Mon-Sat) Rents cars (12,000 CFP per 24 hours), scooters (8000 CFP per 24 hours) and bikes (2000 CFP per 24 hours). In the centre of Vaitape.

Bora Bora Rent a Car – Avis (Map p124; ☑40 67 70 15; www.avis-borabora.com; ⊙7.30am-5.30pm Mon-Sat) Has its main office in the centre of Vaitape, as well as a desk near Matira Point. Cars cost from a whopping 11,900 CFP per 24 hours. It also has bikes (2100 CFP per 24 hours) and scooters (6800 CFP per 24 hours).

Europcar (Map p124; ☑87 71 73 31, 40 67 69 60; www.europcarpolynesie.com; ⊙7.30am-5pm Mon-Fri, to 2pm Sat) Rents cars for 12,500 CFP per 24 hours. In the centre of Vaitape.

Totara Loca (Map p129; ☑87 72 74 33; ⊙8.30-11am) This small outfit in front of Le Maitai Bora Bora rents bikes from 1800 CFP per day. It also has scooters for 6900 CFP per day. Prices drop to 4500 CFP per day for three days. It can also deliver the scooter to your hotel or *pension*. Outside hours, head to Le Maitai Bora Bora's reception.

Maupiti

POP 1230

Includes ➡

History 137
Sights..........................137
Activities 138
Sleeping 140
Eating.........................142

Best Places to Stay

➡ Maupiti Résidence (p141)

➡ Maupiti Paradise (p141)

➡ Kuriri Village (p142)

Best Outdoor Activities

➡ Diving (p138)

➡ Snorkelling (p139)

➡ Kayaking (p140)

➡ Walking (p141)

Why Go?

Bora Bora's discreet little sister, Maupiti is one of the most ravishing islands in French Polynesia. There's a shimmering lagoon with every hue from lapis lazuli to turquoise, a perfect ring of islets girdled with sand bars, palm trees leaning over the shore and large coral gardens. Although this little charmer is no longer a secret, it still remains a hideaway where visitors come to absorb the lazy lifestyle. There's only one road and virtually no cars, just bikes; there are no showy resorts, just a smattering of family-run *pensions* where visitors can sample delicious local-style meals and genuinely interact with their hosts. And when you want to play, there's just the right amount of activities to keep you buzzing, from walking and lagoon excursions to diving and kayaking.

When to Go

➡ As with most Society Islands the drier season (June to October) is the most popular time to visit Maupiti.

➡ In July, the island is in full swing with the Heiva cultural festivities.

➡ Divers and snorkellers might like April to June and September to November best, when the water is calmest.

➡ The manta-ray season runs from April to September.

History

Dutch explorer Jacob Roggeveen is credited with the European 'discovery' of Maupiti in 1722, nearly 50 years before Wallis, Bougainville and Cook made their important landfalls on Tahiti. European missionaries were quick to follow, eventually succeeding in installing Protestantism as the major religion.

Bora Bora began to assert influence over Maupiti in the early 19th century; the power struggles continued throughout the century. French influence also reached the island dur-

ing this period; missionaries and local chiefs continued to wield the most power until after WWII, when the French took over.

Maupiti has changed little over the last century; fruit crops on the *motu* (islets) are still major sources of income for the islanders.

⊙ Sights

From the air, Maupiti resembles a miniature Bora Bora: the mountainous island mass is surrounded by a wide but shallow lagoon fringed with five *motu*. There's only

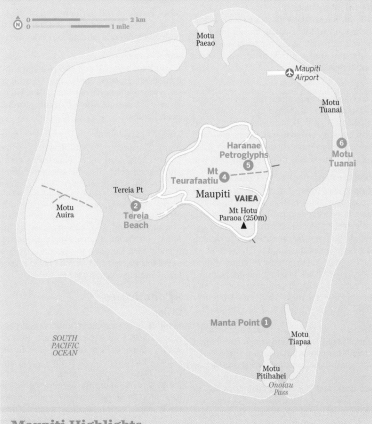

Maupiti Highlights

❶ Exploring Maupiti's gin-clear lagoon while snorkelling with manta rays at **Manta Point** (p37).

❷ Taking it real easy, basking lizardlike on heavenly **Tereia Beach** (p138).

❸ Paddling a **kayak** (p140) across the azure lagoon.

❹ Scaling **Mt Teurafaatiu** (p141) and feasting your eyes on 360-degree views of the translucent lagoon.

❺ Reflecting on Maupiti's bizarre past while spotting the well-preserved **Haranae petroglyphs** (p138).

❻ Finding your own paradise in a delightful *pension* on **Motu Tuanai** (p138).

one pass, between the lagoon and the ocean, Onoiau, to the south.

👁 The Main Island

★ Tereia Beach   BEACH
A more scenic spot you'd be hard pressed to find. Here the lagoon is crystal clear and the bone-white beach is nearly all sand (no smashed coral or broken rock). This beach is a stunning place to sun yourself and the east side is deep enough for swimming. There are no facilities except two small beach restaurants. At sunset, the spot becomes downright romantic.

From Tereia Beach it's easy to wade across the lagoon to Motu Auira during low tide. Or you can walk along the coastline to the south and find a string of secluded coves past Tereia Varua point.

Vaiea   VILLAGE
The village spreads along the east coast and is dominated by a sharp ridge running from north to south. Neat houses, brightened with hibiscus, are strung along the road and they often have *uru* (breadfruit) trees shading the family tombs fronting many of them.

Haranae Petroglyphs   ARCHAEOLOGICAL SITE
Maupiti has some interesting petroglyphs etched into boulders in a rocky riverbed. The most impressive is a turtle image. To reach the petroglyphs, head north out of Vaiea and round the point before passing the basketball court near the church. You're now in the Haranae Valley; on the mountainside is a signposted track heading inland. Follow it for 200m to a small pumping station, and then follow the rocky riverbed. After only 100m, on the left, you'll find the petroglyphs.

Marae Vaiahu   ARCHAEOLOGICAL SITE
Maupiti's most important *marae* (traditional temple) features a large coastal site covered with coral slabs and a fish box. Made of four coral blocks set edgewise in a rectangle, the box was used for ceremonial purposes to ensure successful fishing. Four fish kings are represented on the sides of the box. It's signposted, northwest of the main quay.

👁 The Motu

Maupiti's star attractions are its five idyllic *motu*, spits of sand and crushed coral dotted with swaying palms, floating in the jade lagoon that surrounds the main island. Many travellers choose to stay on these fabulous islets, but the mainland *pensions* will happily organise day trips for around 3000 CFP per person if you're staying on the island. Besides acting as quiet retreats, the *motu* also offer good beaches.

Motu Auira   ISLAND
There's an important melon-production plantation on Motu Auira, as well as a lovely coral sand beach. At low tide you can reach it from the mainland by wading across the lagoon – the water is warm and only waist high, but keep an eye out for rays.

Motu Paeao   ISLAND
Motu Paeao, at the northern end of the lagoon, is ideal for swimming and snorkelling, with fabulous coral gardens and jade waters.

Motu Pitihahei   ISLAND
If you have a kayak, you can paddle to this completely isolated *motu*, but be sure to steer way to the north of Onoiau Pass, which is very dangerous due to strong currents near the pass.

Motu Tiapaa   ISLAND
Motu Tiapaa has beautiful, sandy, white beaches and good snorkelling on its ocean and lagoon sides. It's also the most developed *motu*, with several *pensions*, so it can seem crowded by Maupiti standards.

Motu Tuanai   ISLAND
The airport and a couple of *pensions* are found on Motu Tuanai, another picture-friendly islet. However, the lagoon is shallow along this *motu*, which doesn't make it good for swimming except for young children.

🏃 Activities

Diving
Maupiti is an excellent underwater playground and a good place to learn to dive, with a couple of very safe dive sites in the lagoon, including Le Petit Bleu (p37) and Coral Garden (p37), which are perfect for beginners. Maupiti's signature dive site is Manta Point (p37), where you can observe manta rays in shallow waters. There are also outstanding dive sites outside the lagoon, but they aren't easily accessible due to the strong currents and swell in the pass.

Maupiti Diving   DIVING
(📋40 67 83 80; www.maupitidiving.com; single dive 7000 CFP) 🏊 This low-key diving venture specialises in small groups (maximum four divers) and offers an intimate feel on its aquatic adventures. A 10-dive package

Maupiti

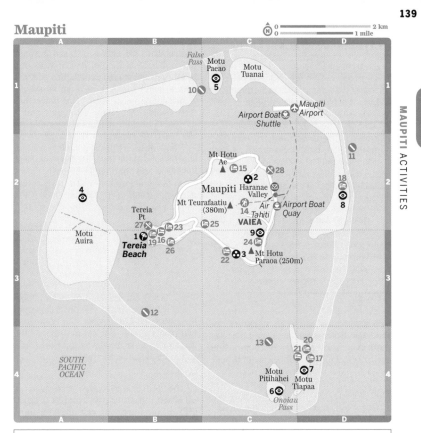

Maupiti

⊙ Top Sights
1 Tereia Beach.. B3

⊙ Sights
2 Haranae Petroglyphs C2
3 Marae Vaiahu C3
4 Motu Auira A2
5 Motu Paeao C1
6 Motu Pitihahei C4
7 Motu Tiapaa D4
8 Motu Tuanai D2
9 Vaiea C3

⊙ Activities, Courses & Tours
10 Coral Garden B1
11 Faaapu D2
12 Le Petit Bleu B4
13 Manta Point C4
14 Mt Teurafaatiu C2

⊙ Sleeping
15 Chez Ludo et Moyra C2
16 Espace Beach B3
17 Kuriri Village D4
18 Maupiti Paradise D2
19 Maupiti Résidence B3
20 Maupiti Village D4
21 Papahani – Chez Vilna D4
22 Pension Orovaru – Chez Rose et
   Firmin C3
23 Pension Tereia B2
24 Taputea C3
25 Tautiare Village C2
26 Teheimana B3

⊙ Eating
27 Chez Mimi B2
   Espace Beach ....(see 16)
28 Tarona C2

(valid for two divers) is 60,000 CFP. Book well ahead. Cash only. Free pick-up. From April to September, it offers diving trips to Manta Point.

Snorkelling & Lagoon Excursions

Maupiti's magnificent lagoon is crystal clear, bath-warm and filled with all manner of tropical marine life, from schools of

DON'T MISS

CLIMBING MT TEURAFAATIU

The ascent of Mt Teurafaatiu (380m) is vigorous, but the 360-degree panorama at the summit is worth the effort. Ribbons of blue water flecked with turquoise and sapphire, islets fringed with brilliant scimitars of white sand, lagoons mottled with coral formations, and Bora Bora in the background... hallucinogenic. The track starts virtually opposite Tarona *snack* and the climb is shaded for most of the way. Allow three hours for the return trip and be sure to bring plenty of drinking water.

The most difficult part is towards the end, with a climb up steep rock to reach the ridge. The track is relatively well marked, so you don't really need a guide. If you want to go with a guide, contact your *pension* to organise one (about 3000 CFP).

butterflyfish and parrotfish to manta rays and banks of flame-coloured coral. The best snorkelling sites are the reefs stretching north of Onoiau Pass (but beware of the currents) and Motu Paeao to the north.

Pensions run lagoon tours; figure between 5000 CFP and 6000 CFP for a full-day trip in a *pirogue* (outrigger canoe), gliding through the blue and stopping periodically to snorkel and free dive. In season, the *pensions* also offer snorkelling trips to the manta rays' cleaning station (about 2500 CFP).

Sammy Tours   ADVENTURE TOUR
(☑87 76 99 28; www.sammy-maupiti.com; half-/full-day trips 3500/6000 CFP) This independent operator offers well-run lagoon tours that include snorkelling and swimming stops. Another draw is the excellent beach barbecue at lunchtime. The boat is equipped with a roof. Free pick-up.

Kayaking

Sea kayaking is a popular activity of the DIY variety. Paddling around the quiet lagoon is very safe. Most accommodation places either rent or offer free sea kayaks for guests' use.

🛏 Sleeping

🛏 The Main Island

Guesthouses are all either right on the lagoon or very close to it.

Teheimana   PENSION **$**
(☑87 71 29 97, 40 67 81 45; www.pensionteheimana.blogspot.com; s/d without bathroom incl half-board 7500/15,000 CFP; 🛜) Tucked away in a beautifully landscaped garden, this *pension* with a family-run feel offers an affordable lagoonside tropical oasis. The house has three rooms that share bathrooms and a nice communal kitchen. It's very simple but clean, and the atmosphere is relaxed.

What's missing is a swimmable beach; instead of sand at the front, it's sharp coral and limestone rock, but Tereia Beach is only a 10- to 15-minute walk away. The owners also rent kitesurfing gear (half-day 9000 CFP) and will happily take you to the best spots.

Pension Tereia   PENSION **$**
(☑40 67 82 02, 87 70 50 78; www.pensiontereia.sitew.com; s/d without bathroom incl half-board 7500/15,000 CFP; 🛜) Everything is ultra-laid-back at this homey *pension* with an ace location, a mere two-minute walk from Tereia Beach. Sandra and Kete, your affable hosts, will treat you like family. Digs are in three tiny, no-frills rooms that share two bathrooms. Spend your day frolicking in the lagoon if you like, but be back for the excellent dinners that Sandra whips up.

Chez Ludo et Moyra   PENSION **$**
(☑40 67 84 07, 87 22 66 43; www.pensionludo.com; s/d without bathroom incl half-board 7500/15,000 CFP) An unpretentious *pension* with three modest guest rooms, which share bathrooms in the owners' house. Set in a verdant property 50m back from the coastal road, it offers few frills, just a genuine Polynesian welcome and hearty meals. It has no view to speak of, no direct lagoon access and no proper swimming area nearby, but Tereia Beach is a 10-minute bicycle ride away.

Tautiare Village   PENSION **$**
(☑87 32 42 67, 40 60 15 90; www.pension-tautiare-village.sitew.com; s/d incl breakfast 8000/12,000 CFP, incl half-board 10,000/16,000 CFP; 🛜) An unfussy *pension* with unpretentious appeal. The four adjoining rooms are spotless and come equipped with big hot-water bathrooms. They are set on grassy garden areas and face the lagoon, but don't get too excited: swimming is not *that* tempting here due to shallow (and sometimes murky) waters. Tereia beach is a 30-minute walk away.

**Pension Orovaru –
Chez Rose et Firmin**   PENSION **$**
(☑40 67 82 13, 87 70 74 81; s/d without bathroom incl half-board 7500/12,000 CFP; 🛜) This congenial

pension is a popular spot for unfussy travellers. Nobody's going to be writing about the four cramped rooms with shared bathrooms, but the rootsy Polynesian style and family atmosphere give this place a ramshackle charm. The shore is rocky – forget about swimming – but you can make arrangements to be dropped off on Motu Tiapaa (500 CFP).

Taputea PENSION $
(☑40 67 82 78; s/d 5000/10,000 CFP, without bathroom 4500/5000 CFP; ☎) There's nothing memorable about the three bare rooms in this concrete house in Vaiea, but you're not paying a lot, and there's a vast, shared living room that opens onto an inviting terrace. There's no swimming area near the *pension*, but guests can make use of the kayaks to explore the lagoon. Prices include breakfast. Evening meals (2000 CFP) can be arranged.

⭐**Maupiti Résidence** BUNGALOW $$
(☑40 67 82 61; www.maupitiresidence.info; bungalow d 11,000-13,000 CFP, q 15,000-17,000 CFP; ❄☎) The location, right on Tereia Beach, is to die for. While hardly glitzy, the two bungalows are spacious and serviceable, with a living room, two bedrooms, a terrace that delivers full-frontal lagoon views and a kitchen. Perks include free bicycles and kayaks, daily cleaning service, air-con (add 500 CFP) and washing machine, making this one of the best-value stays you'll have.

No meals are provided, but there are two beach restaurants nearby. The secret is out, so book early. Three-night minimum stays are preferred. Credit cards are accepted.

Espace Beach PENSION $$
(☑40 67 81 54, 87 71 46 11; www.pensionespacebeachmaupiti.com; s/d without bathroom incl half-board 11,500/18,000 CFP, bungalow d incl half-board 22,500 CFP; ☎) What a delightful spot! Here the setting is the clear winner: the property edges onto fabulous jade waters, right on Tereia Beach. Choose between a room in a three-room house with shared bathroom (and very limited privacy) or a pleasingly rustic beachside bungalow (with private facilities) made from woven palm fronds. Bikes and kayaks are free. Airport transfers are included and credit cards are accepted.

🛏 The Motu

Maupiti Village PENSION $
(☑40 67 80 08, 87 21 98 51; dm incl half-board 6000 CFP, bungalows s/d incl half-board 8000/16,000 CFP; ☎) This place is hit and miss. Some travellers like its casual atmosphere, some don't. On the plus side, the food is copious and flavoursome, and the location on the ocean side of Motu Tiapaa is good for snorkelling. Accommodation-wise, it's clean but spartan, with a bare-bones six-bed dorm and three basic bungalows (ask for the one facing the beach). If you can live with that, it's not a bad deal, especially given that kayaks are free. The lagoon side of the *motu*, blessed with an appealing swimming area, can also be easily accessed. Wi-fi costs 500 CFP per hour.

⭐**Maupiti Paradise** BUNGALOW $$
(☑40 67 83 83, 87 71 09 70; www.maupiti-paradise-lodge.com; Motu Tuanai; bungalows s/d incl half-board 11,000/22,000 CFP) Here the setting is magical – the property opens onto the lagoon and the ocean, with both Bora Bora and the majestic silhouette of the main island in the background. The five bungalows are well proportioned, comfortable and inviting. Sunbathing is top notch, but swimming is not that enthralling, with very shallow waters; paddling to more idyllic swimming spots expands your possibilities.

Papahani – Chez Vilna PENSION $$
(☑40 60 15 35; pensionpapahani@hotmail.fr; Motu Tiapaa; bungalows incl half-board s 11,000-12,000 CFP, d 22,000-24,000 CFP; ☎) An atmosphere of dreamlike tranquillity characterises this well-run *pension* with a fab lagoon frontage. Your biggest quandary here: go snorkelling (or kayaking) or snooze on the white-sand beach under the swaying palms? The four bungalows blend perfectly into the tropical gardens; the one that's right on the beach is well worth the few extra bucks.

Transfers to Vaiea cost 1500 CFP per person return and airport transfers are free. Wi-fi is extra (1500 CFP for the duration of your stay).

ℹ TO MOTU OR NOT TO MOTU?

Your biggest decision: staying on a *motu* (islet) or on the main island? For the full Robinson Crusoe experience, places on the *motu* are hard to beat, as they offer plenty of remote and tropical tranquillity. Be prepared to feel a bit of a captive, though, except if you're ready to paddle to the Vaiea or pay anything from 500 CFP to 1500 CFP for a transfer by boat to the mainland. If island life is your top priority, stay on the main island. Better yet: combine the two options!

Kuriri Village BUNGALOW $$
(☑87 74 54 54, 40 67 82 23; www.maupiti-kuriri. com; Motu Tiapaa; bungalows s/d incl half-board 15,300/26,300 CFP; 🛜) Watch dolphins frolicking in the waves from a little wooden deck (with Bora Bora as a backdrop), take a dip in the lagoon, relax in an attractive tropical garden – it can't get more laid-back than this. Digs are in four simply designed bungalows with a ramshackle charm. The property opens onto the lagoon and the ocean – two different settings, two different atmospheres.

As befits a French-run outfit, food is a highlight. Kayaks and snorkelling gear are free. Airport transfers are included and credit cards are accepted.

🍴 Eating

Most visitors opt for half-board options with their accommodation. In Vaiea, several small shops sell basic supplies and soft drinks.

Espace Beach TAHITIAN $
(☑40 67 81 54; Tereia Beach; mains 1200-1500 CFP) Opening onto the lagoon, this is the best place on Maupiti for a lagoonside lunch or dinner (by reservation only). The emphasis is on simply prepared fish dishes, including tuna sashimi.

Chez Mimi TAHITIAN $
(Tereia Beach; mains 400-1000 CFP; ⊙9am-3pm) Feel the sand in your toes at this casual spot soothingly positioned right on Tereia Beach. Make sure you get there on the early side (ideally before 1pm) – only one round of food, usually grilled fish, raw fish and beef steak, is made for the day. Generous sandwiches are also available.

Tarona TAHITIAN, CHINESE $
(☑40 67 82 46; mains 1300-1500 CFP; ⊙11.30am-1.30pm & 6-8pm Mon-Sat) Just north of Vaiea, this humble budget bite dishes up hearty portions of French Polynesian and Chinese staples at blessedly low prices. House specials include raw fish, grilled fish, tuna sashimi and chow mein. If you're really hungry after a day's Maupiti adventuring, the pork with taro will definitely fill you up.

🛈 Information

There's no bank and no ATM, so bring a wad of cash. There's wi-fi near the post office.

🛈 Getting There & Away

Maupiti is 320km west of Tahiti and 40km west of Bora Bora.

AIR

Air Tahiti (☑40 86 42 42, 40 67 81 24; www. airtahiti.pf; ⊙8-11am Mon, Wed & Thu, 8.45am-1pm Tue & Fri) flies from Maupiti to Tahiti (18,500 CFP, 1½ hours, three to five flights weekly), Ra'iatea (9800 CFP, 25 minutes, two flights weekly) and Bora Bora (8500 CFP, 20 minutes, one or two flights weekly). Flights to/from Maupiti are in high demand, so be sure to book well in advance.

BICYCLE

Maupiti is small (and flat) enough to be explored by bike, which is by far the best – and most enjoyable – way to get around the island. A 10km coast road hugs the shoreline almost all the way around the island and rarely rises above sea level. Most pensions can arrange bike hire for about 1000 CFP per day.

BOAT

Because of strong currents and a tricky sand bar in the Onoiau Pass, the lagoon can only be navigated by smaller ships, which are occasionally forced to wait for appropriate tidal conditions. The **Maupiti Express 2** (☑40 67 66 69, 87 78 27 22) ferry used to run between Maupiti and Bora Bora twice weekly, but this service was indefinitely suspended at the time of writing – check while you're there.

🛈 Getting Around

If you've booked accommodation, you'll be met at the airport, although some places charge for the trip (from 1000 CFP per person return).

It's simple to arrange a boat out to the *motu* from the village and vice versa. It costs 500 CFP to 1500 CFP to go from the main island to the *motu*. All the *pensions* on the mainland or *motu* can arrange these transfers.

The Tuamotus

Includes →

Rangiroa.....................145
Tikehau 154
Mataiva 157
Fakarava....................159
Ahe 164

Best Places to Stay

→ Ninamu (p156)

→ Kia Ora Resort & Spa (p151)

→ Ariiheevai (p158)

→ Havaiki Pearl Lodge (p162)

→ Tevahine Dream (p151)

Best Places to Eat

→ Raira Lagon – Beach Raira (p152)

→ Mitivai (p152)

→ Tikehau Village (p157)

→ Snack Kori Kori (p164)

Why Go?

The Tuamotus? It's the dream South Seas snapshot: the 77 atolls – narrow coral rings encircling turquoise lagoons – that make up this stunning archipelago are flung over an immense stretch of indigo-blue ocean.

Life in the atolls is equal parts harsh and paradisiacal: hardly anything grows, so there's little fruit and vegetables, and the only drinking water is collected from the rain. Yet the silence, starry skies, coral beaches, blue lagoons, idyllic *motu* (coral islets) and languid pace of life captivate nearly everyone who makes it here. Most tourists visit Rangiroa, Tikehau and Fakarava, which have the bulk of the tourist infrastructure, but it's also possible to explore lesser-known beauties such as Ahe, Mataiva and Makemo.

Anyone who loves the water will adore the Tuamotus. The vast, pristine marine area offers unparalleled opportunities to encounter the menagerie of marine life. For nondivers, fantastic lagoon excursions beckon.

When to Go

→ The Tuamotus get more sunshine than any other archipelago in French Polynesia.

→ The shoulder seasons (April to May and October to November) are the best times to visit.

→ From December to March is the period when storms and rain are more likely.

→ Between June and September, the prevailing trade winds produce pleasantly mild weather but rough seas – not ideal for boat excursions.

→ Diving is excellent year-round, but the seas are calmer from October to May.

The Tuamotus Highlights

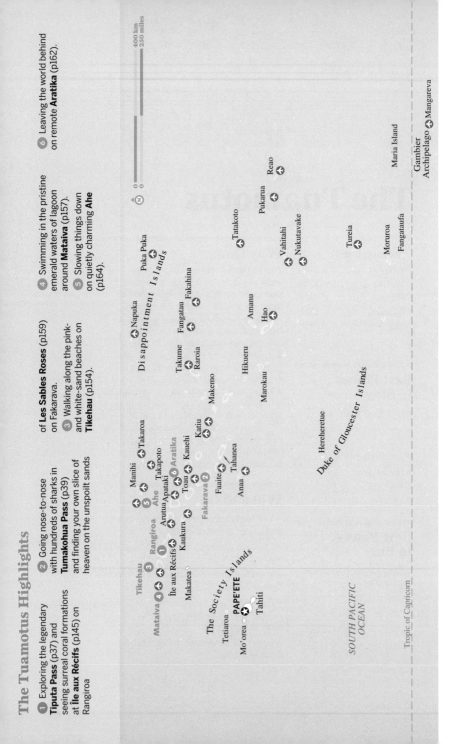

1 Exploring the legendary **Tiputa Pass** (p37) and seeing surreal coral formations at **Île aux Récifs** (p145) on Rangiroa

2 Going nose-to-nose with hundreds of sharks in **Tumakohua Pass** (p39) and finding your own slice of heaven on the unspoilt sands

of **Les Sables Roses** (p159) on Fakarava.

3 Walking along the pink- and white-sand beaches on **Tikehau** (p154).

4 Swimming in the pristine emerald waters of lagoon around **Mataiva** (p157).

5 Slowing things down on quietly charming **Ahe** (p164).

6 Leaving the world behind on remote **Aratika** (p162).

History

Early Tuamotu history is a mystery. One theory is that the Paumotu (people of the Tuamotus) fled from the Leeward and Marquesas Islands following conflicts during the 14th, 15th and 16th centuries. Another theory is that the eastern Tuamotus were populated at the same time as the major Polynesian diaspora moved on from the Marquesas to the Gambier Archipelago and Easter Island, around AD 1000.

European explorers were less than complimentary about the group – in 1616, Jacques Le Maire and Willem Schouten spoke of the 'Islands of Dogs', the 'Islands without End' and the 'Islands of Flies'. In 1722, Jacob Roggeveen called them the 'Pernicious Islands' and in 1768, French explorer Louis-Antoine de Bougainville dubbed them the 'Dangerous Archipelago'.

Thus the reputation of the group as an uninviting place was sealed and the Europeans turned their attention towards the more welcoming Society Islands.

When Tahiti was annexed by France in 1842, the Tuamotus, considered dependencies of the Pomares (the royal family of Tahiti), also came under French control.

Christian missionaries established copra production in the 1870s, and by 1900 copra represented 40% of the total exports of the colony. Pearl diving and mother-of-pearl production both enjoyed a golden age around 1850.

From 1911 until 1966, phosphate mining on Makatea was the principal export activity not only for the Tuamotus but for all of French Polynesia. The population of other islands began to decline dramatically in the 1960s as copra production fell away and plastic buttons killed off the mother-of-pearl button business.

In the 1970s, when airstrips were built on many of the islands, the population decline was slowed and the group's economic prospects began to brighten. The flights back to Tahiti carried not only suntanned tourists but loads of fresh reef fish for the busy markets of Pape'ete.

The 1970s brought another less congenial employment prospect when France's Centre d'Expérimentation du Pacifique (CEP) took over the central atoll of Hao and began to test nuclear weapons on the western atolls of Moruroa and Fangataufa.

Pearl cultivation began in the 1980s and the atolls flourished with wealth and

DON'T MISS

WATCHING DOLPHINS FOR FREE

Dolphin-watching has never been so straightforward. At the eastern end of the atoll, a small site overlooking Tiputa Pass has been cleared so that visitors can watch the daily performances of dolphins that dance in the waves created by the outgoing current. It's also a great place for a sundowner.

reverse migration from the late 1990s till around 2003 when pearl prices began to plummet. Today, on atolls such as Manihi and Tikehau, abandoned pearl farms dot the lagoon. Tourism and fishing are now the main sources of income.

RANGIROA

POP 2567

Rangiroa (rung-ee-roh-ah) is one of the biggest atolls in the world, with a lagoon so vast that it could fit the entire island of Tahiti inside of it. While visitors coming directly from Bora Bora or Tahiti will probably find Rangi (as it's known to its friends) to be a low-key, middle-of-nowhere sort of a place, this is the big city for folks coming from anywhere else in the archipelago. With paved roads, a few stores, a couple of resorts, plentiful internet and gourmet restaurants, there's really everything here you need – and in the Tuamotus, that's a really big deal!

But it's only the beginning: Rangiroa's richest resource lies below the surface. It's a diving mecca, with world-renowned dive sites blessed with prolific marine life just minutes from your bungalow.

For landlubbers, the never-ending string of remote *motu* is the real draw and boat trips across the lagoon to the stunning Île aux Récifs and Lagon Bleu are not to be missed. Do be warned, however, that beaches are scarce.

◉ Sights

★ Île aux Récifs   NATURAL SITE
(Island of Reefs; Map p146) South of the atoll, an hour by boat from Avatoru, Île aux Récifs is an area dotted with raised *feo* (coral outcrops), weathered shapes chiselled by erosion into silhouettes on the exterior reef. They stretch for several hundred metres,

Rangiroa

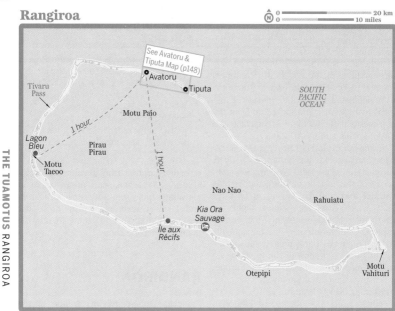

with basins that make superb natural swimming pools. There's a good *hoa* (shallow channel) for swimming and a coconut grove by the beach. You'll need to take a boat tour from Avatoru to get to Île aux Récifs.

★ Lagon Bleu
NATURAL SITE

(Blue Lagoon) This is what many people visualise when imagining a Polynesian paradise: a string of *motu* and coral reefs has formed a natural pool on the edge of the main reef, a lagoon within a lagoon. You can walk knee-deep across a (mostly dead) coral seabed to visit a bird island and laze on incredibly photogenic spits of white-and-pink coral sands. This intimate paradise is reached only on lagoon-excursion boats from Avatoru, about an hour away.

Tiputa
VILLAGE

(Map p146) Very few visitors venture to this charmingly quiet village edging the eastern side of Tiputa Pass. Although it doesn't have tourist facilities (all accommodation options are on Avatoru), it's well worth the trip for its wonderfully relaxed atmosphere and to get a sense of atoll life; getting a boat across the Tiputa Pass adds to the whole experience. A track continues east from the the village through coconut plantations until it's halted by the next *hoa*.

Avatoru
VILLAGE

(Map p146) Avatoru won't leap to the top of your list of preferred villages in French Polynesia, but its location, right by Avatoru Pass and the lagoon, is stunning. The two churches – one Catholic and one Mormon – are about the only buildings of interest.

Gauguin's Pearl
PEARL FARM

(Map p148; ☑ 40 93 11 30; www.gauguinspearl. com; ☺ guided tours 8.30am, 10.30am & 2pm Mon-Fri) FREE There are free tours (in English) of the pearl farm next to the boutique. They include a pearl-grafting demonstration. Call for free pick-up.

🏃 Activities

Diving & Snorkelling

The number-one activity on Rangiroa is diving (p37), and it's no wonder. The Tiputa Pass (p37) has achieved cult status in the diving community and offers some of the best drift dives in the world. Sharks, manta rays, eagle rays and dolphins are the big attractions, but you'll also encounter countless reef species as well as shoals of barracuda and trevallies.

Most dives are suitable for both experienced and novice divers, but novices would be advised to start with easier sites, such as Motu Nuhi Nuhi – The Aquarium (p37) or L'Éolienne (p37), before tackling more intimidating drift dives.

Snorkelling is another great way to visit the lagoon. You can just grab a snorkel and splash around near your hotel or guesthouse, but to really experience life under the sea it's necessary to sign up with a dive centre or a boat-tour operator and go out to further marine wonderlands.

Y'aka Plongée DIVING
(Map p148; ☑87 20 68 98; www.yakaplongeerangiroa.com; introductory/single dive 8000/7600 CFP) This welcoming outfit is run by Marco and Cathy, two of Rangiroa's long-standing dive instructors. They have plenty of experience, an excellent reputation for service and instruction, and offer great-value certification courses (from 42,000 CFP). Six- and 10-dive packages are 42,000/65,000 CFP. Add an extra 1000 CFP per dive for Nitrox dives. Also runs snorkelling trips through the Tiputa Pass. Free pick-up.

Rangiroa Plongée DIVING, SNORKELLING
(Map p148; ☑40 96 03 32, 87 77 65 86; www.rangiroaplongee.pf; introductory/single dive 7500/7000 CFP) This small dive outfit provides personalised service at affordable prices and specialises in small groups. The dedicated two-hour snorkelling trip through the Tiputa Pass (5000 CFP) and at Motu Nuhi Nuhi comes highly recommended (no experience is required). Free pick-up.

Prices drop by about 5% for more than four dives, and there's a slight discount for divers who have their own gear.

Eleuthera DIVING, SNORKELLING
(Map p148; ☑40 96 05 55; www.eleuthera-rangiroa.com; introductory/single dive 8500/7600 CFP) At the eastern end of Avatoru, this well-regarded dive shop runs the full gamut of beginner courses as well as diving trips. Also has a snorkelling trip that takes in the Tiputa Pass and Motu Nuhi Nuhi; depending on the weather, it includes dolphin-watching near the pass. Free pick-up.

Eleuthera is a member of Te Moana Pass (www.temoanadiving.com), an inter-island dive pass that's accepted in 16 dive shops in French Polynesia.

Topdive DIVING
(Map p148; ☑40 96 05 60; www.topdive.com; introductory/single dive 10,000/9800 CFP) Topdive is a fully fledged, well-organised dive shop that offers the full range of scuba activities. Prices are steep but Nitrox dives are

WHERE ARE THE BEACHES?

High hopes of sweeping expanses of silky sand might be dashed upon arrival on Rangiroa. Although the atoll boasts clear water and a brochure-esque appeal, it's not a beach destination. While most accommodation options are right on the lagoon, nearly none have sandy beaches. That said, they usually do have plenty of coral and good snorkelling, which is some compensation. You can also sign up for an excursion to Lagon Bleu or Île aux Récifs, which are blessed with superb sandy areas. Tikehau or Fakarava also have great strips of coral sand edging the lagoon.

offered at no extra charge. Six- and 10-dive packages go for 50,000/80,000 CFP and can be used at any of the Topdive centres in French Polynesia (Tahiti, Mo'orea, Bora Bora and Fakarava). Snorkelling trips can be arranged. Free pick-up.

Lagoon Excursions

Organised tours are really the only way of exploring the most scenic spots on the lagoon and, if you happen upon a nice group, make for a wonderful day. The most popular excursions – the Lagon Bleu and Île aux Récifs (p145) – are to the opposite side of the lagoon from Avatoru, which takes at least an hour to cross and can be uncomfortable if the sea is rough. Usually a minimum of four to six people is required.

Snorkelling gear is provided, although it's not a bad idea to bring your own equipment as not all sizes are available. When the weather's bad or the winds are too high, excursions are cancelled.

All bookings can be made through your hotel or *pension*, but you can also make direct arrangements with the boat-tour companies. Transfers are provided.

Pa'ati Excursion – Léon BOAT TOUR
(☑87 79 24 63, 40 96 02 57; 7500 CFP) Offers well-run tours to Île aux Récifs that include swimming, snorkelling and a short guided walk to the raised coral outcrops. On the way back, a snorkel stop is made near Motu Nuhi Nuhi followed by dolphin-watching in Tiputa Pass.

Another draw is the excellent beach barbecue at lunchtime; leftovers are discarded into the sea, which attracts a gang of (harmless) blacktip sharks near the shore.

Avatoru & Tiputa

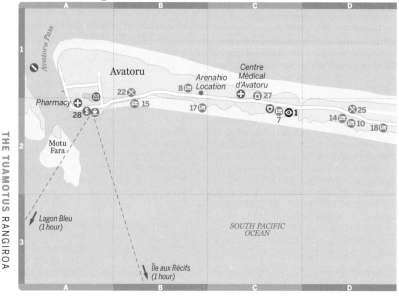

Tereva Excursions – Jean Pierre BOAT TOUR
(☑87 70 71 38, 40 96 82 51; 7500 CFP) Has the most popular tours to the Lagon Bleu. Snorkelling with (harmless) blacktip sharks, playing ukulele, wading across the lagoon to a bird island and feasting on barbecued fish are on the itinerary. Leftovers are discarded into the lagoon, which attracts plenty of seagulls and small blacktip sharks. On the way back, a snorkel stop is usually made near Avatoru Pass.

Tane Excursion BOAT TOUR
(☑40 96 84 68; 7500 CFP) Offers tours to Île aux Récifs and the Lagon Bleu. Prices include a barbecue lunch on an idyllic *motu.*

🛏 Sleeping

Most places to stay and eat are dotted along the string of islets east of Avatoru village.

Turiroa Village –
Chez Olga BUNGALOW, DORM $
(Map p148; ☑87 70 59 21, 40 96 04 27; pension.turiroa@mail.pf; dm 3500 CFP, d with shared bathroom 7000 CFP, bungalows 10,500 CFP; 🤟) Chez Olga may not have the Polynesian character of some of the other *pensions*, but it's a freakishly good deal for the Tuamotus, with three types of accommodation to suit all budgets. There's no beach, but a pontoon gives you access to a decent swimming area. No meals are provided except breakfast (500 CFP), but there's a well-equipped guest kitchen.

The six-bed dorm was refurbished in 2015 and easily wins the hearts of backpackers, while the four sea-facing bungalows are quite modern and well appointed. Two adjoining rooms were also added in 2015; both are plain, functional and fan-cooled, and share well-scrubbed bathrooms. Hot tip: try for the room with lagoon views.

Rangiroa Plage GUESTHOUSE, CAMPGROUND $
(Map p148; ☑87 75 43 40, 40 96 82 13; www. rangiroaplage.com; campsites per person 1400 CFP, dm 3000 CFP, d with shared bathroom 6500 CFP, d 8000-8500 CFP; 🤟) The 'Plage' (beach) bit is a gross misnomer, but this no-frills backpackers housed in a ramshackle building in Avatoru village has a spiffing lagoonside location. Pitch your tent on a coral gravel plot just 10m from the lagoon, or choose one of the four shoebox-sized rooms with or without bathrooms. The two- and four-bed dorms are cramped but serviceable.

The ablution block (cold-water showers) is in good nick, as is the communal kitchen. Perks include bike and scooter hire, laundry service (600 CFP), breakfast (500 CFP), free wi-fi, a lounge area, complimentary kayaks and an on-site eatery. Towels are extra (500 CFP). Cash only.

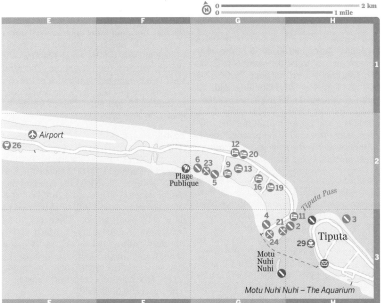

Avatoru & Tiputa

◎ Sights
1 Gauguin's Pearl C2

✪ Activities, Courses & Tours
2 Eleuthera H3
3 L'Éolienne H3
4 Rangiroa Plongée G3
5 Topdive G2
6 Y'aka Plongée G2

⬡ Sleeping
7 Chez Cécile C2
8 Chez Loyna B1
9 Kia Ora Resort & Spa G2
10 Le Maitai Rangiroa D2
11 Les Relais de Josephine H3
12 Miki Miki Lodge G2
13 Pension Bounty G2
14 Raira Lagon D2
15 Rangiroa Plage B2
16 Tamatuamai G2
17 Tevahine Dream B2
18 Turiroa Village – Chez Olga D2
19 Va'aitemoana G2
20 Vahaui Paradis G2

✕ Eating
21 Chez Lili G3

Chez Obelix .... (see 18)
Kia Ora Resort & Spa – Te
   Rairoa .... (see 9)
22 La Roulotte B1
Le Maitai Rangiroa – Le
   Lagon Bleu .... (see 10)
23 Mitivai G2
24 Puna G3
Raira Lagon – Beach Raira .... (see 14)
25 Snack Rio D2

◉ Drinking & Nightlife
26 Te Mao E2

⬡ Shopping
Gauguin's Pearl .... (see 1)
27 Ikimasho C1
Rairoa Création .... (see 6)

ⓘ Information
28 Banque de Tahiti A2
Eleuthera .... (see 2)

ⓘ Transport
Eleuthera .... (see 2)
29 Nova Transport H3

Tamatuamai BUNGALOW **$**
(Map p148; ☑ 40 96 03 07, 87 33 17 41; maruata.
mariteragi@yahoo.fr; bungalows q 12,500 CFP; ☜)
There's no view to speak of and the three

bungalows aren't on the water's edge, but
they're functional and kept spotlessly clean,
and there's lagoon access at the back of the

property. Half-board is available on request. A good deal for a group of divers or a family.

Chez Loyna
PENSION $

(Map p148; ☑87 29 90 30, 40 96 82 09; info@pensionloyna.com; s/d incl half-board 6600/13,200 CFP, bungalows s/d incl half-board 7600/15,200 CFP; ☎) Forget about swimming and sea views – this property doesn't have lagoon access. Despite its unassuming position, Chez Loyna is a safe bet for budget-minded travellers, with three modest yet practical rooms with hot-water bathrooms and a handful of larger bungalows out the back.

★ Chez Cécile
PENSION $$

(Map p148; ☑40 93 12 65, 87 77 55 72; www.rangiroa-cecile.com; bungalows s incl half-board 8000-11,000 CFP, d incl half-board 16,000-22,000 CFP; ☎) This solid-value option is run by a charming Paumotu family who will go the extra mile to help travellers. It features nine spacious wood bungalows in a flowery garden. Most units line the 'beach', which is actually a breakwater filled in with coral gravel, but you can swim off a pier extending over the lagoon. The cheaper bungalows are set in the garden. Food here is a definite plus, with generous meals using local ingredients. Prices include bikes and kayaks.

Raira Lagon
HOTEL $$

(Map p148; ☑40 93 12 30; www.raira-lagon.pf; bungalows s incl half-board 16,000-17,500 CFP, bungalows d incl half-board 29,000-32,000; ✳☎) A cross between a family-run place and a hotel, this is a reassuring choice with no surprises (good or bad) up its sleeves. It features 10 bungalows that meet modern standards, including air-con. They're spread throughout a garden fringed by a satisfying swimming area (but no beach), and the more expensive ones come with a lagoon view. Bonuses: free kayaks, bikes and snorkelling gear.

Tip: try for bungalow Raira, which has the best setting, right on the shore. The on-site restaurant is on a spacious outdoor deck.

Vahaui Paradis
BUNGALOW $$

(Map p148; ☑87 74 29 56, 40 96 02 40; www.rangiroapensionvahaui.com; bungalows d 17,000 CFP; ☎) Hats off to the owners: they dared build this venture directly on the ocean side of the atoll – a rarity in the Tuamotus. Pros: crashing waves, exposed reef, prevailing winds. Cons: crashing waves, exposed reef, prevailing winds. The two units are both large, comfy and cheery. Cash only.

The fully equipped Fare Arenui has a floor of crushed coral and is just steps from the reef, thus proffering unobstructed ocean views, while the Fare Tinihau – a refurbished bungalow from hotel Kia Ora – is slightly set back from the shore. The coral shelf is very high here and much of the reef is exposed at low tide; for a dip, you'll need to walk to a small public 'beach' on the lagoon side. Free bikes.

Va'aitemoana
BUNGALOW, DORM $$

(Map p148; ☑87 32 36 16; www.vaaitemoana.com; dm 5000 CFP, d without bathroom 12,000 CFP, bungalows d 16,000-19,000 CFP) Opened in late 2015, Va'aitemoana follows the standard recipe for success: offer clean, light-filled, spacious accommodation with prim bathrooms in a chilled-out setting. There are three bungalows in total (one of which comes equipped with a kitchenette), as well as a modern room and a four-bed dorm in the owners' house. The catch? There's no lagoon access. Free bikes and breakfast. No wi-fi.

Dinners cost 3000 CFP.

Les Relais de Josephine
BUNGALOW $$

(Map p148; ☑40 96 02 00; www.relais-josephine-rangiroa.com; bungalows s/d incl half-board 16,800/33,600 CFP; ☎) The setting of this very French interpretation of the Polynesian *pension*, right on the mythical Tiputa Pass, is arguably the prettiest on the atoll. The seven bungalows are decked out in minimalist colonial-style elegance but are not luxurious. Lounging on the deck here is a truly decadent experience, as is dining on the elegant French-style food made from local ingredients.

That said, there's no beach, no pool and no swimming access. Some guests opt for a pass-facing bungalow, while others prefer a garden unit (same price) because it's less exposed to the noise of the surf. This venture is a favourite with honeymooners, but take note that some front walls don't make it to the ceilings (good for natural ventilation, less so for privacy). Free bikes. Wi-fi is extra (800 CFP, flat fee).

Pension Bounty
BUNGALOW $$

(Map p148; ☑40 96 05 22; www.pension-bounty.com; s/d incl breakfast 12,500/17,000 CFP; ☎) Lodging here is in four identical adjoining rooms. They're bland and slightly claustrophobic, but they have kitchenettes and the whole place is kept shipshape. It's not directly beside the lagoon and there's no view to speak of, but there's a swimming

MAKEMO

Spectacular undersea landscapes, pristine *motu* and an unhurried pace of life make Makemo an ideal destination for anyone looking for an authentic Paumotu experience. **Pouheva** village is an administrative and school centre for the central Tuamotus. The church and the lighthouse near the pass are the only sights of significance.

Makemo is the place to go for unspoilt scuba diving. **Scuba Makemo** (✆40 98 03 19, 87 78 49 13; makemodive@mail.pf; Pouheva; introductory or single dive 5500 CFP) is run by a French instructor who's been conducting dives in the Tuamotus for more than 20 years. The main dive site is **Arikitamiro Pass** (p39), a mere five-minute boat ride from the village.

Above the water, Makemo will also take your breath away. At the eastern tip of the atoll, **Pohue** is an impossibly scenic natural site that looks like a huge glinting turquoise swimming pool. Another idyllic place is **Motu Napahere**, a deserted, white-beach clad islet that seems to be floating in the turquoise lagoon, a 30-minute boat ride away from the village. Oh, and there's **Tiketike**, a stunning beach lapped by topaz waters and backed by arching coconut trees. This magical spot is a mere 15-minute boat ride from Pouheva.

You can stay at **Relais Scuba Makemo** (✆87 78 49 13, 40 98 03 19; makemodive@ mail.pf; Pouveha; bungalow s/d incl half-board 7500/13,000 CFP; 🛜), which is run by dive instructor Ludovic. Digs are in four lagoon-facing, en-suite (cold water) bungalows on the outskirts of the village. They are simply laid out but clean and inviting. You'll eat with the family; meals are local-style and tasty. Lagoon tours cost about 5000 CFP per person. Airport transfers are included and kayaks are complimentary.

Tempted? Contact **Air Tahiti** (✆40 86 42 42; www.airtahiti.pf), which has three weekly flights to Makemo (53,000 CFP return), or if you're adventurous, embark on the **Kura Ora II** (p236) cargo ship.

THE TUAMOTUS RANGIROA

area a two-minute walk away. Dinner (3500 CFP per person) is available on request. Children are not accepted. English, Spanish and Italian are spoken. Free bikes.

Miki Miki Lodge   BUNGALOW **$$**
(Map p148; ✆87 70 96 55; www.rangiroa-mikimiki-lodge.com; bungalows d incl breakfast 18,500-19,500 CFP; ❄🛜) On the ocean side of the atoll, this unfussy 'lodge' consists of two refurbished bungalows from hotel Kia Ora, one of which offers superb ocean views. Air-con is extra (2000 CFP) and meals are available on request (3000 CFP). Good English is spoken.

Kia Ora Resort & Spa   RESORT **$$$**
(Map p148; ✆40 93 11 11; www.eu.hotelkiaora. com; villas d from 60,000 CFP; ❄🛜⛱) Welcome to one of the swankiest options in French Polynesia, with 50 plush bungalows, including 10 enormous overwater units on a perfect turquoise lagoon. The ravishing garden villas come with their own pool and are dotted around a magnificent coconut plantation situated on a fine little stretch of white sand. It incorporates restaurant, bar, spa and swimming pool.

For the ultimate escape, book a couple of days at **Kia Ora Sauvage** (Map p146; ✆40 96 03 84; www.hotelkiaora.com; bungalows incl full-board per person 47,000 CFP), on a deserted *motu* about an hour away by boat. The beach setting is stunning and there's a maximum of 10 guests at any time (minimum stay of two nights).

Tevahine Dream   PENSION **$$$**
(Map p148; ✆40 93 12 75; www.tevahinedream-rangiroa.com; bungalows s incl half-board 20,000-21,000 CFP, bungalows d incl half-board 31,000-33,000 CFP; 🛜) Tevahine Dream gets rave reviews from honeymooners who want something more personal and intimate than a hotel. Five rustic chic bungalows, three of which face the lagoon, are designed in a Zen-meets-Polynesia style. That said, the odd layout of the bathrooms – no doors and no walls, only a curtain – may not be to everybody's taste. Prices include kayaks and snorkelling gear. Cash only.

The two garden units, built of pine planks, have their own tiny pool. No beach, but the place is fringed with a good swimming area. Norbert, the owner, will treat you to excellent Polynesian and Chinese dishes served in an appealing dining room overlooking the lagoon. Minimum stay of two nights.

CORAL WINE

A vineyard? On an atoll? Strange but true. Vin de Tahiti has a 6-hectare vineyard planted on a palm-fringed *motu* about 10 minutes by boat from Avatoru village. This is the only atoll vineyard in the world, making the only wines produced from coral soil. It produces coral white wine, dry white, sweet white and rosé. Since October 2010 the wine has been made using the principles of biodynamic agriculture. Wanna sample a glass (or two)? Most restaurants on the atoll have it, and it's also sold at the supermarkets. For more on Vin de Tahiti's history, go to www.vindetahiti.com.

Le Maitai Rangiroa   RESORT $$$

(Map p148; ☑40 93 13 50; www.hotelmaitai.com; bungalows d incl breakfast 29,000-42,000 CFP; ❋🛜🖥) Privacy is not Le Maitai's forte – the 34 few-frills, functional bungalows are tightly packed on a small property – but otherwise this low-key resort is well run and serviceable. The six units that are right on the shore and, at a pinch, the first row of Premium Garden bungalows, which offer good lagoon views, are well worth the extra bucks.

The others are back in the garden. Amenities include a restaurant and a bar. No beach (the shoreline is craggy), but there's a small swimming-pool and a pontoon with lagoon access. Beware of extras that can quickly add up: wi-fi (500 CFP per hour), bikes (500 CFP for two hours) and airport transfers (1900 CFP return for a mere two-minute ride). What's free? Kayaks and snorkelling gear.

🍴 Eating

Most visitors opt for half-board at their hotel or *pension*, but there are also a few good independent eating options. Be sure to notify your *pension* that morning if you plan to eat elsewhere for dinner. Avatoru has also a few supermarkets.

★ Mitivai   TAHITIAN, BURGERS $

(Map p148; ☑87 20 08 77; mains 1000-1950 CFP; ⊙11.30am-2.30pm) A favourite haunt of hungry divers – it's conveniently located between two busy dive shops – this trusty joint is one of Rangiroa's hottest spots for lunch and serves fine food to accompany the wonderful lagoon views. Gorge on yummy burgers,

sandwiches, copious salads and tasty grilled fish. Leave room for the dangerously addictive desserts – *mmm*, the *profiteroles au chocolat*! Also rents paddleboards.

Puna   TAHITIAN $

(Map p148; ☑87 73 76 10; mains 1300-1500 CFP; ⊙11.30am-2pm Mon-Sat) Talk about location! The dining deck of this buzzing *snack* (snack bar) at the eastern tip of Avatoru is on the lagoon, literally. It features all the Polynesian classics as well as grills, sandwiches (550 CFP) and burgers. Mouthwatering crêpes and waffles will finish you off sweetly. It's a good place to catch local vibes and enjoy plenty of local colour at lunchtime.

La Roulotte   FRENCH, SANDWICHES $

(Map p148; ☑40 96 82 13; mains 1000-1700 CFP; ⊙11am-1.30pm & 5.30-8.30pm Mon-Sat, 5.30-8.30pm Sun) Simple meals are the order of the day at this no-frills eatery at the eastern end of Avatoru village. The food's not fantastically exciting – fish, steaks and sandwiches (from 400 CFP) are the mainstays – but portions are large enough to satisfy the most voracious diver.

Raira Lagoon –
Beach Raira   FRENCH, TAHITIAN $$

(Map p148; ☑40 93 12 30; mains 1600-3500 CFP; ⊙11.30am-2pm & 6-9pm) Located inside Raira Lagoon hotel (but open to nonguests), the well-respected Beach Raira is a terrific spot for a lagoonside meal, with alfresco tables overlooking the water. Prices are reasonable considering the location and the fresh ingredients – most dishes are less than 2000 CFP. Chow down on a succulent tuna carpaccio with pesto sauce or a flawlessly cooked grilled beef rib, and don't miss the devilish homemade *flan coco* (a custard-like dessert flavoured with coconut) for dessert. And oh, that view!

★ Chez Lili   INTERNATIONAL $$

(Map p148; ☑87 32 42 50; mains 1600-1700 CFP; ⊙11am-2pm Tue-Sun) For a menu that strays from the familiar 'raw fish in coconut milk' path, try this cute eatery at the eastern tip of Avatoru. Run by the energetic Lili, who is from Madagascar, it serves well-prepared daily specials, including chicken in Creole sauce and tuna tartare with mango.

Wash it all down with a glass of invigorating *citronnade au gingembre* (lime and ginger juice; 500 CFP). It's not right on the water's edge, but the open-air dining room has partial lagoon views.

Le Maitai Rangiroa –
Le Lagon Bleu   FRENCH, TAHITIAN $$
(Map p148; ☑40 93 13 50; mains 1600-2800 CFP; ⊙11.30am-1.30pm & 6-9pm) Familiar French fare with a local twist – salads, pasta and fish dishes – won't inspire devotion, but the atmosphere is relaxed, the half-tropical, half-contemporary decor appealing and the lagoon views spectacular. Bonus: nonguests who have their meal here can use the swimming pool.

Snack Rio   TAHTIAN, FRENCH $$
(Map p148; ☑40 96 04 56; mains 1700-2400 CFP; ⊙11.30am-2pm Mon-Sat) Prices are a bit steep for such a casual eatery with an unassuming position along the road (no sea views), but the chef, who worked for many years in a local resort, prepares a colourful assortment of palate pleasers such as tuna sashimi, beefsteak in spicy sauce and juicy burgers.

Chez Obelix   FRENCH $$
(Map p148; ☑40 96 02 07; mains 1600-1900 CFP; ⊙11am-2pm & 6-9.30pm; ☎) Big appetite? Make a beeline for this casual eatery run by Charly, a former French legionnaire. Although there's nothing out of the ordinary on the menu and the roadside setting isn't spectacular, it's a great place to tuck into generous cuts of meat and fish dishes served with rice, fries or vegetables. Free wi-fi. It's closed for several months of the year.

Kia Ora Resort & Spa –
Te Rairoa   INTERNATIONAL $$$
(Map p148; ☑40 93 11 11; mains 1600-3500 CFP; ⊙noon-2pm & 6.30-9pm) Rangiroa's standout resort restaurant is in the Kia Ora Resort. Nab a seat on the lovely overwater dining deck and look forward to interesting combinations of Pacific, European and Asian flavours. Another reason to visit it is the twice-weekly island night and buffet (7500 CFP), where you can take your pick of great dishes while enjoying a spectacular dance show.

🍸 Drinking & Nightlife

All hotel bars are open to nonguests.

Te Mao   LOUNGE
(Map p148; ☑87 26 05 25; ⊙5-10pm Tue-Thu & Sun, 5-11pm Fri & Sat; ☎) A happening bar in Rangiroa? No, you're not dreaming. Run by a Parisian couple who fell in love with the atoll, this venture with a boho vibe and loungey feel will stun you with its relaxing atmosphere, wide choice of beers and cocktails

(1200 CFP) and excellent tapas (from 800 CFP). It attracts tourists and locals alike.

🛍 Shopping

Rairoa Création   HANDICRAFTS
(Map p148; ☑40 96 02 41; www.arnotahiti.com; ⊙10am-6pm) A good find. Artist Arno is renowned for high-quality earth paintings that represent traditional designs. It also sells shirts as well as shell necklaces and bracelets.

Gauguin's Pearl   JEWELLERY
(Map p148; ☑40 93 11 30; www.gauguinspearl. com; ⊙8am-5pm Mon-Fri, 9am-noon & 3-5pm Sat) Has an excellent selection of set and loose pearls directly from the pearl farm, which is on the premises. Employs professional, English-speaking staff. You can be picked up for free from your place of lodging.

Ikimasho   JEWELLERY
(Map p148; ☑40 96 03 91; www.tahitigemfair. com; ⊙9am-5pm Mon-Sat) Has an interesting selection of creative local jewellery, including earrings, necklaces, pendants and rings, some of which are made of pearl and bone. It's in the eastern outskirts of Avatoru village.

ℹ Information

Note that there are only two ATMs on Rangiroa.

Banque de Tahiti (Map p148; Avatoru; ⊙7.30-11.30am & 1-4pm Mon-Fri) Currency exchange. In the village.

Banque Socredo (Map p146; Avatoru; ⊙7.30-11.30am & 1.30-4pm Mon, Wed & Fri, 1.30-4pm Tue & Thu) Currency exchange. Has two 24-hour ATMs. Beside the airport terminal.

Centre Médical d'Avatoru (Map p148; ☑40 96 03 75; ⊙7.30am-3.30pm Mon-Fri) Medical centre. There are also two private doctors in Avatoru.

Eleuthera (Map p148; per hr 200 CFP; ⊙8am-5pm; ☎) Wi-fi access. At Eleuthera diving centre.

Pharmacy (Map p148; Avatoru; ⊙7am-12.30pm & 2.30-6.30pm Mon-Sat, 10.30am-12.30pm Sun) In Avatoru village.

Post Office (Map p148; Avatoru; ⊙7am-3pm Mon-Thu, to 2pm Fri; ☎) Internet and wi-fi access (with the Manaspot network).

ℹ Getting There & Away

AIR
Within the archipelago, Rangiroa is the major flight hub. The airport is smack in between Avatoru (to the west) and Tiputa (to the east). **Air Tahiti** (☑40 86 42 42; www.airtahiti.pf) offers two to three flights daily between Pape'ete and Rangiroa (one hour, 24,200 CFP). Rangiroa is

also connected by air to Bora Bora and other atolls in the Tuamotus. One-way fares on offer include Bora Bora to Rangiroa 31,500 CFP, Rangiroa to Tikehau 9500 CFP, Rangiroa to Fakarava 9500 CFP, and Rangiroa to Mataiva 9500 CFP. If you're island-hopping, your best bet is to purchase an air pass (p234).

BOAT

The **Mareva Nui** (p236) and **Saint-Xavier Maris-Stella** (p236) are the only cargo ships serving Rangiroa (p236) that take passengers, besides the **Aranui** (p237), which stops on Rangiroa on its way back from the Marquesas.

❶ Getting Around

A sealed, entirely flat road runs the 10km from Avatoru village at the western end of the string of islets to the Tiputa Pass, at the eastern extremity. There's no public transport on Rangiroa, but there's a rather casual approach to hitchhiking (which is never entirely safe, although you'd be unlikely to run into problems on Rangiroa): if you're walking along in the hot sun, someone will often stop and offer you a ride.

TO/FROM THE AIRPORT

If you have booked accommodation, your hosts will be at the airport to welcome you. If your *pension* is near the airport, transfers will probably be free; places further away tend to charge (ask when you book).

BIKE, CAR & SCOOTER HIRE

The easiest way to get around is to hire a bicycle or scooter, but keep in mind that the road is not lit at night. Car hire is also available.

Arenahio Location (Map p148; ☑87 73 92 84) Hires out cars/scooters/bicycles for 8500/5200/1300 CFP for a full day.

Eleuthera (Map p148; ☑40 96 05 55; ☺8am-5pm) At Eleuthera diving centre, at the eastern end of the atoll. Rents bikes for 250 CFP per hour or 2000 CFP per day.

Rangi Rent a Car (☑40 96 03 28) Car hire from 6500 CFP per day.

BOAT

Nova Transport (Map p148; ☑87 26 78 06; ☺7am-5pm) Offers a shuttle service between Ohotu wharf and Tiputa village for 600 CFP return; taking a bicycle over costs 500 CFP extra. The crossing takes about five minutes.

TIKEHAU

POP 529

Tikehau is a joy. Its unparalleled beauty, endless coral beaches and low-key yet reasonably developed tourist infrastructure make it a real charmer. Time has eroded the ring of coral into sweeping, twisting *motu* of white and pink sands that engulf little bays, craggy nooks and the vivid turquoise lagoon. Idyllic picnic spots abound and the atoll's secluded shores are some of the best in the Tuamotus for lounging, loafing and lollygagging. And unlike on Rangiroa, you don't have to travel far to find that perfect strip of strand. Below the turquoise waters, a vast living world beckons divers of all levels.

◉ Sights

Les Sables Roses   BEACH
(Pink Sands) The southeast shores of the atoll are fringed with truly amazing 'Pink Sands Beaches' that really do glow a light shade of pink, a result of finely pulverised coral.

Tuherahera   VILLAGE
Most islanders live in Tuherahera, in the southwest of the atoll. Find peace in this pretty village, bursting with *uru* (breadfruit), coconut trees, bougainvillea and hibiscus. Fancy a dip? Head to one of Tuherahera's coral beaches. The best one lies east of the village, near the airstrip. The sand is wide and the waters are calm and translucent. Another beauty lies at the western tip of the village; this strip is lapped by a glassy turquoise channel and has pinkish sands.

Tuherahera also has an uncommon variety of churches, including Catholic, Sanito, Seventh Day Adventist and Protestant.

Motu Puarua   ISLAND
(Île aux Oiseaux, Bird Island) Lying almost in the middle of the lagoon, the rocky Motu Puarua hosts several species of ground-nesting birds including brown noddies and *uaau* (red-footed boobies).

Île d'Eden   FARM
(Eden Island) 🏴 Île d'Eden is not a traditional tourist site per se, but a working farm operated by a handful of families belonging to the Church of the New Testament. They have created a vibrant, organic garden in the infertile sands of their superb *motu*. Most visitors to Île d'Eden arrive on an organised tour, usually in combination with Motu Puarua and Les Sables Roses.

🏃 Activities

Diving & Snorkelling

On the diving scene, Tikehau has long played second fiddle to the better-marketed Rangiroa or Fakarava, but it's getting increasingly popular. The extraordinary Tuheiava Pass (p38), to the west of the atoll, about 30 minutes by boat from Tuherahera village, is an unspoilt underwater idyll teeming with all sorts of fish and marine life. Inside the lagoon, you'll have the chance of diving with manta rays at La Ferme aux Mantas (p38).

Diving Safari Tikehau DIVING
(☑87 24 60 65; Tuherahera; introductory/single dive 8000/7000 CFP) Run by a French couple, Diving Safari Tikehau offers small-group boat dives and certification courses. Two-tank dives in the morning cost 14,000 CFP. Snorkelling is also possible (4900 CFP). It's based at Tikehau Village. Free pick-ups.

Tikehau Plongée DIVING
(☑40 96 22 44, 87 32 62 56; introductory or single dive 8000 CFP) This small yet well-organised dive outfit is based in the village and also runs an annex at Tikehau Pearl Beach Resort. It offers two-tank dives (14,000 CFP) in the morning and has three/five/two-tank-dive packages (39,500/61,200 CFP). At most dive sites, snorkelling is also possible (3500 CFP). Free pick-up.

Tikehau Plongée is a member of Te Moana Pass (www.temoanadiving.com), an inter-island dive pass that's accepted in 16 dive shops in French Polynesia.

Lagoon Excursions
The easiest way to get a broad look at the delights around the lagoon is to take a one-day tour. All *pensions* and hotels can organise excursions, sometimes through an outside operator, and trips cost from 8500 CFP per person. They usually take in La Ferme aux Mantas, Motu Puarua and Île d'Eden, and include a barbecue picnic on one of many paradisiacal *motu* dotted along the Sables Roses.

🛏 Sleeping

🛏 Tuherahera Village & Around

Coconut Beach GUESTHOUSE, CAMPGROUND $
(☑40 96 23 86; pension.coconutbeachtikehau@ gmail.com; campsite for 2 persons 5500 CFP, s/d 7500/15,000 CFP, bungalow s/d 8500/17,000 CFP; 🛜) Jean-Louis, your friendly host, rents out two compact yet colourful and neat rooms in his modest house. For more privacy, opt for the snug bungalow (with private facilities) next door. The real appeal is the location – the property fronts a superb stretch of pinkish sand at the westen end of the village. Campers can pitch their tent right on the beach.

Tikehau

⊙ Sights
1 Île d'Eden...............................B1
2 Les Sables Roses..................B2

⊙ Activities, Courses & Tours
Diving Safari Tikehau .... (see 14)
3 La Ferme aux Mantas (Mantas' Farm)...............................A2
4 Le Trou aux Requins...........................A2
5 Tikehau Plongée A1
6 Tuheiava Pass A1

🛏 Sleeping
7 Chez Justine...........................A1
8 Coconut Beach........................A1
9 Hotu..A1
10 Ninamu....................................A1
11 Relais Royal Tikehau B1
12 Tikehau Bed & Breakfast.....................A1
13 Tikehau Pearl Beach Resort...............A2
14 Tikehau Village A1

⊗ Eating
15 Magasin Henriette A1
16 Snack Gilbert.....................................A1
17 Snack Ohina A1
18 Snack Perarai – Chez Rowena............ A1
Tikehau Pearl Beach Resort.. (see 13)
Tikehau Village........................... (see 14)

Note that bathrooms have cold-water showers. The daily rate includes half-board, the use of kayaks and bikes as well as wi-fi access, except for campers, who'll have to pay extra. Cash only.

Chez Justine PENSION, CAMPGROUND $
(☑87 72 02 44, 40 96 22 87; campsite for 2 persons 3500 CFP, bungalows incl half-board s 7500-8600

LA FERME AUX MANTAS

Every morning or so, several manta rays (up to four individuals) congregate around a lagoon site aptly named La Ferme (p38) – there was a pearl farm here before – in order to be cleaned by wrasses that feed on parasites from the mantas' wings. Snorkellers and divers can easily approach these majestic creatures in less than 10m of waters. One downside: as the sea floor is sandy, the water clarity is not exceptional – underwater photographers may be disappointed. Most lagoon tours stop here on their way to Motu Puarua and all dive centres offer dives to this site on a regular basis. Note that it's not a zoo – sightings can't be guaranteed.

CFP, d 15,000-17,200 CFP; 🕿) This family-run *pension* offers a divine location, on a wide beach lapped by topaz waters. Ask for one of the four beachfront bungalows here, which are slightly more expensive than the four basic, humbly furnished rooms tucked away behind (there are plans to refurbish them). Campers can pitch tents on a sandy, shady plot just 10m from the lagoon – bliss!

Campers also have a communal kitchen at their disposal or they can order a meal (1000 CFP to 2500 CFP). Kayaks and (rusty) bikes are complimentary.

Tikehau Bed & Breakfast   BUNGALOW, DORM $
(🖵 40 96 23 33; www.pensionhotu.com; dm incl breakfast 3700 CFP, bungalows d incl breakfast 12,500 CFP; 🕿) This is the only *pension* in the village. You have two options here. The four bungalows won't knock your socks off but are in good nick. For solo travellers, the spacious six-bed dorm fits the bill, but expect plenty of mosquitoes – mercifully, mosquito nets are provided. The property opens onto the lagoon, but the shore here is fronted by some craggy coral formations.

The ablution block (with cold water) is OK, and there's a communal kitchen. The name 'Bed & Breakfast' is misleading – the owners don't live on the premises, so you won't find the family atmosphere that's typical of other *pensions*. Wi-fi costs extra. A few rusty bikes are available.

★ Tikehau Village   PENSION $$
(🖵 87 76 67 85, 40 96 22 86; tikehauvillage@mail. pf; bungalows s/d incl half-board 15,000/22,000

CFP; 🕿) You can't argue with the location. It's right on the beach, so your biggest worry is tracking sand into your bungalow. Beautiful views are augmented by simple yet well-appointed bungalows that are made from woven coconut thatch and other natural materials. The shady terraces look out over white-sand and turquoise-lagoon bliss. There are kayaks and bikes for guests' use. Some English is spoken. Facilities include a well-regarded restaurant and a dive centre.

Hotu   BUNGALOW $$
(🖵 40 96 22 89; www.pensionhotu.com; bungalows s/d incl half-board 9700/19,400 CFP; 🕿) Occupying a divine stretch of sand, Hotu is a great place to enjoy the coral beach in low-key surroundings. It features five fan-cooled bungalows with private facilities, but the bathrooms don't have doors; they're teeny and feel a little past their prime on the inside, but get the job done. The daily rate includes the use of bikes and kayaks.

🛌 Private Motu

Relais Royal Tikehau   BUNGALOW $$
(🖵 40 96 23 37; www.royaltikehau.pf; s/d 13,000/ 23,000 CFP, bungalows s 18,000-20,000 CFP, d 28,000-30,000 CFP; 🕿) This upscale *pension* sits on a secluded *motu* about a 20-minute walk across some shallow waterways from the village. The property is lapped by a glassy turquoise channel on one side and fronted by a swath of pinkish sand on the other side – the magical setting will help you forget that this place is a tad overpriced.

Bungalows are big and comfy but simply furnished and don't have air-con. Avoid the rooms in a separate building, which are much less exciting and have no views. The whole place is run on solar and wind power. Airport transfers are 1200 CFP per person return. Free kayaks, but wi-fi is extra. Minimum two-night stay; half-board is included.

★ Ninamu   BUNGALOW $$$
(🖵 87 28 56 88; www.motuninamu.com; bungalows s/d incl full board 38,000/76,000 CFP; 🕿) 🦮 Anchored on a private white- and pink-sand *motu* a 10-minute boat ride from the village, this Australian-run venture is the kind of haven stressed-out city slickers dream about. The massive bungalows are built from gnarled hunks of wood, coral stonework and coconut thatch, and the restaurant is another Crusoe-with-style masterpiece. There are only six units, which ensures intimacy.

The feel is much more of a private club than a resort here, with most things, from snorkelling equipment to use of the kayaks, being free. Prices also include daily excursions. The ethos here is laid-back, ecological – everything is powered by wind and sun – and activity-oriented. Ninamu appeals to honeymooners, families and outdoorsy types in equal measures – a winning formula. One weak point? The *motu* is really small.

Tikehau Pearl Beach Resort   RESORT $$$
(☑ 40 96 23 00; www.spmhotels.com; bungalows d from 45,000 CFP; ❋ 🛜 ❄) A hot favourite with honeymooners, this intimate resort (there are only 38 units) boasts a stunning position between endless swaths of white- and pink-sand beaches and bright blue waters. The overwater suites offer the extra bonus of privacy and are so exquisitely designed that you might never want to leave your private dock. All options except the over-the-water standard bungalows have air-con.

There are free shuttle boats to the village four times a day, so you won't feel captive here. Amenities include a dive centre, a restaurant and a bar.

✗ Eating

Magasin Henriette   SUPERMARKET $
(Tuherahera; ⏲ 7am-noon & 1-7pm Mon-Sat, 7am-noon & 3-7pm Sun) A relatively well-stocked supermarket, right in the village.

Snack Ohina   TAHITIAN $
(☑ 87 70 65 33; Tuherahera; mains 1000-1500 CFP; ⏲ 11am-2pm & 6-9pm Mon-Sat) There aren't too many options at this family-run eatery, but there are always invigorating Tahitian favourites such as grilled *mahimahi*, tuna carpaccio and raw fish. Bonus: there's an enticing, shady terrace.

Snack Perarai – Chez Rowena   TAHITIAN $
(☑ 87 74 94 08; Tuherahera; mains 700-1100 CFP; ⏲ 11am-2pm & 6-9pm Wed-Mon) This local-style eatery at the western end of the village serves voluminous portions of good chow mein and *steak frites* (steak and chips). Burgers are also available.

Tikehau Village   TAHITIAN $$
(☑ 40 96 22 86; set menu 2500-3500 CFP) The restaurant at the Tikehau Village is one of the prettiest spots around, overlooking the water with cool breezes and a social vibe – nonguests are welcome (by reservation). The set menu is good value and it makes for

a pleasant change from the standard fare served at most *pensions*.

Snack Gilbert   TAHITIAN $$
(☑ 87 74 86 25; Tuherahera; mains 2000 CFP; ⏲ 11am-2pm Mon-Sat) Lovely setting, right by a beach overlooking a turquoise *hoa* at the western end of the village. What to expect? Simple meals incorporating organic ingredients. Call ahead, as the eponymous Gilbert can be a little grumpy when people drop by unannounced. He also sells shell souvenirs.

Tikehau Pearl Beach Resort   INTERNATIONAL $$$
(☑ 40 96 23 00; Tuherahera; mains 1400-3300 CFP; ⏲ 11am-2.30pm) Call for the shuttle times to lunch at this swanky resort. Light meals are available, and you can enjoy the fabulous setting without breaking the bank.

ℹ Information

There is no bank or ATM on Tikehau. There's wi-fi access (with the Manaspot network) near the post office.

ℹ Getting There & Away

Tikehau lies 300km northeast of Tahiti and 14km north of Rangiroa.

AIR

The airport is about 1km east of the village entrance. **Air Tahiti** (☑ 40 86 42 42; www.air-tahiti.pf) has daily flights between Pape'ete and Tikehau (24,500 CFP, one hour). There are also several weekly flights between Rangiroa and Tikehau (9600 CFP, 15 minutes). If you're island-hopping, air passes (p234) are available.

BOAT

For the adventurous, the cargo ships **Mareva Nui** (p236) and **Saint-Xavier Maris-Stella** (p236) offer transport from Pape'ete to Tikehau (p236).

ℹ Getting Around

A 10km track goes around Tuherahera, and passes by the airport. If you've booked accommodation, you'll be met at the airport.

MATAIVA

POP 280

Like stepping into a time machine, this tiny, picturesque atoll is the sort of hideaway that you search for your whole life to discover. Despite the limited tourist infrastructure, it provides a delightful holiday escape and is becoming one of the more popular spots in the archipelago. There are superb coral

THE TUAMOTUS MATAIVA

Mataiva

0 ———— 2 km
0 ———— 1 mile

La Passe
Toa Tere
PAHUA
Mataiva Village
Ariiheevai; Mataiva Plongée
La Piscine
Rocher de la Tortue
Île aux Oiseaux
Marae Papiro
SOUTH PACIFIC OCEAN

beaches, numerous snorkelling spots, two well-priced *pensions*, lots of fish and one of the few noteworthy archaeological sites in the Tuamotus.

The structure of the Mataiva lagoon gives it an unusual appearance: the coral heads create walls 50m to 300m wide that form about 70 basins with a maximum depth of 10m. Seen from the plane it looks like a mosaic of greens. Unforgettable.

⊙ Sights

Pahua   VILLAGE

The tiny village of Pahua is divided by a pass a few metres wide and no deeper than 1.5m, suitable only for very small boats. A bridge spans the pass and links the village.

Marae Papiro   ARCHAEOLOGICAL SITE

Marae Papiro is a well-kept *marae* (traditional temple) on the edge of a *hoa,* about 14km from the village. In the centre of this *marae* you can see the stone seat from which, according to legend, the giant Tu guarded the pass against invasion.

The *hoa* is good for swimming and snorkelling and there are a few appealing coral beaches close by.

Île aux Oiseaux   BIRD SANCTUARY

(Bird Island) To the east of the lagoon, a crescent-shaped coral spit covered in small shrubs is a favourite nesting place for *oio* (brown noddies), *tara* (great creasted terns) and red-footed boobies.

Rocher de la Tortue   NATURAL SITE

(Turtle Rock) The Rocher aux Tortues refers to a big coral outcrop lying about 4.5km north

of the village on the exterior reef. Its base has been undercut by water erosion, fashioning it into a peculiar mushroom shape.

🏃 Activities

All activities and excursions are organised by the two *pensions*, which run daily trips to the various sites by motor boat and by car. If you wish to dive on Mataiva (p38), there's a dive centre, which offers a couple of uncomplicated reef dives, including La Passe (p38), near the village.

La Piscine   SWIMMING

(The Pool) This artificial pool was originally carved into the shoreline to extract phosphate. It's now a great spot for swimming, although it's pretty deep and the water is milky.

Mataiva Plongée   DIVING

(☑87 76 75 17, 40 96 32 84; www.mataivaplongee.com; introductory/single dive 8000/7500 CFP) Based at Ariiheevai *pension*, this small yet respectable dive shop specialises in small groups and offers dive trips to the pass and beyond. Two-tank dives are 13,000 CFP, and six-/10-dive packages cost 37,500/55,000 CFP. Snorkelling trips (3000 CFP) and whale-watching outings (between August and October, 5000 CFP) can also be arranged.

🛏 Sleeping & Eating

The two *pensions* are in the village. Prices include airport transfers. There are several small shops with basic food supplies.

★ Ariiheevai   PENSION, DORM $

(☑40 96 32 50, 87 76 73 23; pensionariiheevai@gmail.com; dm incl breakfast 3500 CFP, bungalows incl full board & excursions s/d 8500/17,000 CFP; ❄🤙) This place is one of the best deals in the Tuamotus. Rates include daily activities and excursions (flower-garland making, picnics on a secluded islet, visits to Bird Island and a fish park, swimming at La Piscine) and all meals – a winning formula. Digs are in 10 well-organised bungalows scattered on a well-tended property abutting the white-sand-fringed emerald lagoon.

It's a particularly great find for families as four bungalows comfortably sleep four. For shoestringers or solo travellers, there's a comfy six-bed dorm with its own facilities (and air-con!), but excursions cost extra. The food is great and served buffet-style. Kayaks and a few (rusty) bikes are free. Reserve well in advance as it's very popular with Tahiti residents. Cash only. The local dive centre is based at the *pension*.

Mataiva Village PENSION, CAMPGROUND **$**
(☑ 40 96 32 95, 87 78 36 05; campsite per person incl breakfast 1700 CFP, bungalows incl full board & excursions s/d 8500/17,000 CFP; ✳ 🛜) This place is a great find if you're working to a tight budget – it's an all-inclusive formula, with daily excursions to the most scenic spots on the island. The eight comfortable bungalows, two of which have direct lagoon views, grace the pass, but there's not really a beach. A small plot is set aside for campers, who have their own ablution block.

Kayaks and bikes are free if you stay in a bungalow; campers pay 500 CFP per day. Cash only.

ⓘ Information

Bring stash of cash for there is no bank on the atoll. Pahua has a post office.

ⓘ Getting There & Away

Mataiva is 350km northeast of Tahiti and 100km west of Rangiroa.

AIR

Air Tahiti (☑ 40 86 42 42; www.airtahiti.pf) has two Pape'ete to Mataiva flights (22,500 CFP one way) a week. One flight is via Rangiroa (9600 CFP one way). Maitaiva is not part of the Air Tahiti island-hopping passes.

BOAT

The **Mareva Nui** (p236) and the **Saint-Xavier Maris-Stella** (p236) are the only cargo ships serving Mataiva that take passengers. Coming from Pape'ete, Mataiva is usually the first port of call in the Tuamotus (p236).

ⓘ Getting Around

A track goes almost all the way around the island through the middle of the coconut plantation for about 28km. Both *pensions* will take you around the island. They also have a few rusty old bikes for guests.

FAKARAVA

POP 820

One of the largest and most beautiful atolls in French Polynesia, Fakarava is the stuff of South Seas fantasy. Heavenly white and pink sand, ruffled coconut trees and an unbelievable palette of lagoon blues are the norm here. The atmosphere is supremely relaxed

and the infrastructure is quite good, with an assortment of well-run *pensions*.

Fakarava is a great place to unwind, but for those looking for more than a suntan, it offers a number of high-energy distractions. The fantastic diving and snorkelling are legendary among divers, who come for a truly exhilarating experience in the two passes.

Whatever your inclination, one thing is sure: after several days here, you'll find it difficult to pack and leave.

⊙ Sights

★**Les Sables Roses** BEACH
(Pink Sands) A double crescent of dreamy beaches split by a narrow spit of white-and-pink coral sands, Les Sables Roses seems to come right out of central casting for tropical ideals. The turquoise water laps both sides of the sandy strip and there's only one boat: yours. It's perfect for relaxing, swimming and evening up your sunburn. It's near the southernmost tip of the atoll, not far from Tetamanu, and is reached only on lagoon-excursion boats.

Lagon Bleu (Motu Tehatea) NATURAL SITE
(Blue Lagoon) Simply divine. Near the north-western corner of Fakarava, Lagon Bleu features an indescribably lovely stretch of white-sand coral beach, turquoise-blue water, palm trees leaning over the shore – and not a soul in sight. It's a fantastic place for a picnic or a bout of snorkelling and swimming. You'll need to take a boat tour to get to Lagon Bleu. One proviso: it's usually *nono* (gnat)-infested.

> ### ⓘ DIVING: HOW TO THE MAKE THE MOST OF FAKARAVA
>
> If you're based in or near Rotoava, day trips to Tumakohua Pass are organised on a regular basis by the local dive shops, but they're weather- and tide-dependent and require a minimum number of divers. Check what is planned closer to the time of your visit.
>
> If you stay in one of the three *pensions* near Tumakohua Pass, it's super-easy to dive this pass, but you won't be able to dive the Garuae Pass as the local dive centre doesn't organise trips there. The solution? Plan a combined stay – spend a few days in northern Fakarava followed by a couple of days in southern Fakarava, allowing you to dive both passes.

Fakarava

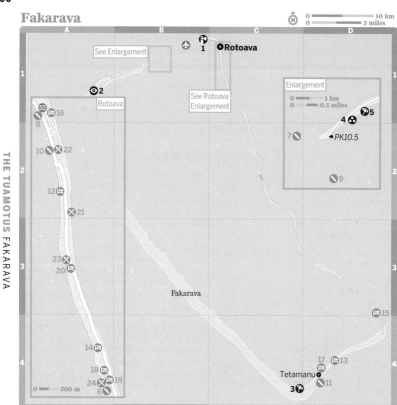

Rotoava
VILLAGE

Most islanders live in Rotoava village at the northeastern end of the atoll, 4km east of the airport. Aside from Rangiroa's Avatoru, this is the most developed and busiest town in the Tuamotu, but it's still pretty quiet by most people's standards. With only a few streets, a couple of churches and stores, a town hall and a school, it's easy to explore.

On the ocean side, the **Phare de Taputavaka** is worth a gander. This pyramid-shaped lighthouse built of stones is one of the oldest in French Polynesia, said to be more than 80 years old.

Ancien Phare de Topaka
LIGHTHOUSE

(PK2.5) This photogenic 15m-tall grey turret (dating from 1957) looks as if it's on loan from a medieval castle. The lighthouse is no longer in operation. To get here, follow the road to the airport and look for PK2.5 *(point kilométrique)*, from where a dirt track leads to the lighthouse.

Marae Tahiri Vairau & Beach
ARCHAEOLOGICAL, BEACH

(PK9.4) This partly restored *marae* built of coral slabs sits in a coconut grove beside a lovely strip of coral sand, about 400m past Plage du PK9. The beach offers shimmering waters and is great for sunbathing, picnicking, swimming and snorkelling. Beware of falling coconuts.

PK10.5
NATURAL SITE

(PK10.5) This marker is located at the end of the dirt road, just on the edge of the phenomenal Garuae Pass. By incoming or outgoing current, the pass gets really rough, with waves that can easily exceed 2m in the middle.

Tetamanu
VILLAGE

A handful of inhabitants also live in Tetamanu village, a tiny settlement on the edge of Tumakohua Pass, which is as backwater as backwater gets (despite the growing

Fakarava

Sights

1 Ancien Phare de Topaka B1
2 Lagon Bleu (Motu Tehatea) A1
3 Les Sables Roses C4
4 Marae Tahiri Vairau & Beach D1
5 Plage du PK9 .... D1

Activities, Courses & Tours

6 Dive Spirit A4
7 Garuae Pass C2
8 Kaina Plongée A1
9 Pufana (The Red Buoy) D2
10 Topdive A2
11 Tumakohua Pass D4

Sleeping

12 Havaiki Pearl Lodge A2
13 Motu Aito Paradise D4
14 Paparara A4
15 Raimiti D3
16 Relais Marama A1
17 Tetamanu Village D4
18 Tokerau Village A4
19 Vaiama Village A4
20 Veke Veke Village A3

Eating

21 Faka Délices A2
22 Faka Faapu A2
Havaiki Pearl Lodge .... (see 12)
23 Snack Elda A3
24 Snack Kori Kori A4

numbers of divers who stay in the nearby *pensions*). It has a cute coral chapel built in the 19th century and an old graveyard with coral tombstones.

Activities

Diving & Snorkelling

Fakarava is an outstanding dive destination (p38). Both Garuae Pass (p38) and Tumakohua Pass (p39) offer some of French Polynesia's most exciting dives. Divers rave about the fabulous array of fish life – especially grey sharks, blacktip sharks, manta rays, tuna and barracuda – that can be found in both passes. Good news for novice divers: most sites are accessible with an Open Water certificate. Another draw is the coral, which is much healthier than on Rangiroa. The catch? The two passes are 60km away from one another, which makes logistics a bit tricky if you want to dive the two passes in a limited period of time.

Kaina Plongée — DIVING

(📞 87 73 38 22; PK0, Rotoava; introductory/single dive 7500/7000 CFP) This low-key outfit specialises in small groups and offers dives to Garuae Pass. When conditions are optimal (usually between November and April), it may organise day trips to the neighbouring atoll of Toau (22,000 CFP including two dives and lunch) – don't miss it. Day trips to Tumakohua Pass are 22,000 CFP. Cash only.

Dive Spirit — DIVING

(📞 40 98 41 40, 87 32 79 87; www.divespirit. com; PK4.2; introductory/single/2-tank dive 8500/8500/15,000 CFP) Run by an efficient French-Spanish couple, this diving operation offers high standards and excellent service. It has regular outings to Garuae Pass as well as regular day trips to Tumakohua Pass (23,000 CFP, including two dives and lunch). Note that the boat doesn't have a roof, though. Six-/10-dive packages cost 42,000/68,000 CFP. Good English is spoken. Free pick-up.

Dive Spirit is a member of Te Moana Pass (www.temoanadiving.com), an inter-island dive pass that's accepted in 16 dive shops in French Polynesia.

Topdive — DIVING

(📞 87 29 22 32, 40 98 43 76; www.topdive.com; PK1, Rotoava; introductory/single dive 10,000/9,800 CFP) This reputable outfit in Rotoava also has an annex on a *motu* near Tetamanu (which caters for *pensions* in the south). Six- and 10-dive packages go for 50,000/80,000 CFP and can be used at any of the Topdive centres in French Polynesia (Tahiti, Bora Bora and Rangiroa). Day trips to Tumakohua Pass cost 31,000 CFP including lunch. Free pick-up. Prices are high, but Nitrox dives are offered at no extra cost.

Lagoon Excursions

As in other atolls, here organised tours are the only way of exploring the idyllic, remote spots on the lagoon, including Lagon Bleu, Tetamanu (if you're based in the north) and Les Sables Roses. Usually a minimum of four to six people is required.

Half-/full-day trips to Lagon Bleu cost around 7000/8500 CFP. A full-day excursion taking in Les Sables Roses, Tetamanu and a snorkelling stop in the southern pass usually costs 12,000 CFP, including a barbecue lunch at Tetamanu. All bookings can be made through your hotel or *pension*.

Note that it's at least a 90-minute boat ride to get to the southern sites from

ARATIKA & KAUEHI

Few visitors have heard about the atolls of Aratika and Kauehi, which lie northeast of Fakarava. With only two *pensions* and limited infrastructure, these two morsels of paradise are a dream come true for those looking to come down a few gears. Both are served once or twice weekly from Pape'ete by Air Tahiti (p233).

Pension Oterekia (✆87 75 03 16; www.pension-oterekia.com; bungalows incl half-board per person 12,000 CFP; ☐) This *pension* has a welcoming local-style atmosphere and is a great place to decompress. The six bungalows are spacious (they can sleep up to four people) and have lots of local charm, though the best thing they offer is the lullaby of the wavelets. From their small raised terraces, it's only a short dash into the turquoise lagoon. Meals including local specialities are served in the *fare potee* (open traditional house), where there's also a bar. Various activities are offered, including kayaking (free), snorkelling, fishing trips and various excursions on the atoll.

Kauehi Lodge (✆87 73 20 46; www.kauehi-lodge.com; s/d incl half-board 18,000/30,000 CFP; ☐) This lovely retreat on a peaceful *motu* has a clutch of good-looking bungalows that hover at the edge of a skinny coral and sand beach lapped by turquoise waters. Your biggest quandary here: a bout of snorkelling (or kayaking), a fishing trip or a lagoon tour? A great escape.

Rotoava. For Lagon Bleu, it takes about 30 minutes by boat from Rotoava.

🛏 Sleeping

🛏 Rotoava & Around (Northern Fakarava)

A couple of places are in the village; the others are a few kilometres to the south. Unless otherwise noted, they accept credit cards and offer free airport transfers.

Relais Marama BUNGALOW, CAMPGROUND **$**
(✆40 98 42 51, 87 76 12 29; www.relais-marama. com; campsite per person 2800 CFP, bungalows without bathroom s/d 7000/14,000 CFP; ☐) On the ocean side of Rotoava (no beach), this backpackerlike option is a great deal for solo travellers; eight no-frills, teeny but practical bungalows in a verdant compound, two well-scrubbed ablution blocks (with hot water) and a convenient location. Campers share the same facilities as the bungalows.

The bungalows are well spaced out and catch lots of breeze. All prices include breakfast and for other meals you can use the tip-top communal kitchen or go to nearby eateries. Rates include the use of bikes and wi-fi. Laundry service is also available.

⭐**Havaiki Pearl Lodge** RESORT **$$**
(✆40 93 40 15, 87 26 26 05; www.havaiki.com; PK2, Rotoava; garden bungalows s/d incl half-board 16,000/23,000 CFP, beach bungalows s/d incl half-board 26,000/33,000 CFP; ❄☐) At the south-

ern end of Rotoava, this petite resort-style venue is the fanciest option in the north of the atoll, with 10 small but immaculate bungalows that offer a lovely lagoon frontage. They have been renovated in a modern, clean, white-and-brown colour scheme. There are also three garden units, which are built on stilts (nice views), but they don't have air-con.

Amenities include two restaurants, a bar and a pearl shop. Bikes and kayaks are free. Good English is spoken and airport transfers cost 2000 CFP return. Wi-fi costs extra. There's a three-night minimum stay.

Veke Veke Village PENSION **$$**
(✆40 98 42 89, 87 70 45 19; www.pension-fakarava.com; PK4.1; bungalows s/d incl half-board 12,800/19,000 CFP; ☐) What an exquisite spot! Imagine a small, sandy bay fringed with coconut palms and lapped by turquoise waters. Choose between two family-sized semi-overwater bungalows or four smaller bungalows right on the beach. The dining area with coral-gravel floor is pleasingly simple, and there's also a picturesque, sunset-friendly pontoon. Kayaks and bikes are complimentary. Airport transfers are 1100 CFP return.

All options are on the old side but are generally well maintained. One quibble: bathrooms have cold-water showers.

Vaiama Village PENSION **$$**
(✆40 98 41 13, 87 70 81 99; www.fakaravavaia-ma.com; PK6.8; bungalows s/d incl half-board

12,700/19,700 CFP; 🕾) Each of the four bungalows here is crafted from a variety of local materials. Although they're packed rather closely together, they enjoy a splendid location, just steps from a fine ribbon of beach. All have attached bathrooms with coral-gravel floors and ferns for a tropical-oasis effect. There are also two garden bungalows with lagoon views.

There's a pontoon and good snorkelling and swimming out the front. The food is reputedly good, too. Airport transfers cost 2100 CFP return. Free kayaks.

Tokerau Village   PENSION **$$**
(✉40 98 41 09, 87 70 82 19; www.tokerauvil-lage.com; PK6.7; bungalows s/d incl half-board 15,200/27,800 CFP; 🕾) This comfortable *pen-sion* is run by Flora, who spends her days fine-tuning the garden and making sure there's not a speck of dust in any of the four well-proportioned bungalows, two of which have direct lagoon views. Kayaks are free and there are bikes available for hire. Some English is spoken. Airport transfers are 2000 CFP.

Each bungalow has a big terrace and mosquito net, but for the price you'd expect air-con. The food is delicious. If only the dining room was positioned near the lagoon, life would be perfect. It's 7km south of Rotoava.

Paparara   PENSION **$$**
(✉40 98 42 66; www.fakarava-divelodge.com; PK6; bungalows s/d incl half-board 12,600/22,600 CFP; 🕾) This *pension* offers four rustic bungalows made from natural materials in a delightful location on the lagoon. They maintain a fair level of comfort but are over-priced for the simplicity of the furnishings and the lack of hot water. The food here is good, plentiful and eaten family-style. Free kayaks.

Avoid the slightly cheaper unit that shares a cold-water bathroom – it's really basic. For families, there's also a quirkily laid out bungalow on a pontoon. Airport transfers cost 2000 CFP return, and wi-fi is extra (500 CFP per hour).

🛏 Tetamanu & Around (Southern Fakarava)

At the other end of Fakarava, a 90-minute boat ride from the airport, you'll find three accommodation options. Divers, be aware that if you base yourself here, you won't be able to dive Garuae Pass.

★**Raimiti**   BUNGALOW **$$$**
(✉87 71 07 63; www.raimiti.com; bungalow incl full board for 2 nights s 54,000-61,000 CFP, d 99,000-112,000 CFP) Travellers in search of romance enthuse about this Crusoe-chic and very isolated spot with only nine units – five rustic but tastefully decorated lagoonside cabins constructed from local materials as well as four larger oceanside dark-wood bungalows. Food is a highlight, with refined meals. Prices include excursions and transfers (be warned that it's an open boat, which can be uncomfortable in bad weather).

There's no electricity, but you'll come to love your oil lamps lighting the scene at night. Unfortunately, Raimiti sits beside a rocky stretch of lagoon shoreline, but there's good swimming and snorkelling out the front. Kayaks and snorkelling gear are free. No internet access.

Motu Aito Paradise   PENSION **$$**
(✉87 74 26 13; www.fakarava.org; bungalows s/d incl full board 15,000/30,000 CFP) The *motu* is really nothing special (and there's not even a beach), but the owners have built such beautiful coconut-thatch structures and planted enough flowers that they've transformed the land into something appealing. Prices are for a three-night minimum stay and include daily excursions. Airport transfers (by car and by boat) may take up to 1½ hours (be prepared to get wet if it's raining) and cost 3000 CFP. There's excellent snorkelling just offshore. Cash only. No internet access.

Tetamanu Village   PENSION **$$**
(✉87 77 10 06; www.tetamanuvillage.pf; Teta-manu; bungalows d incl full board per 3/4 days 114,000/140,000 CFP) This place is a real heartbreaker. It sits on a paradisiacal *motu*

DON'T MISS

PLAGE DU PK9

A bit of a local's secret, Plage du PK9 is – you guessed it – 9km west of Rotoava (go past the airport and follow the dirt track towards the northern pass; at the PK9 marker, take the path to the left). It's a thin, laid-back stretch of white coral sand backed by palms and lapped by sparkling turquoise waters. It's equally good for sunning and swimming and there's excellent snorkelling not far offshore. Bring plenty of water. Beware of falling coconuts.

overlooking the stunning Tumakohua Pass, with exceptionally healthy coral reefs just metres away. It comprises five local-style, rustic bungalows overlooking the lagoon and a delightful overwater dining room. Alas, we've heard reports of irregular service and lack of maintenance. There's a two-night minimum stay. No internet access.

An annex called **Tetamanu Sauvage** on a nearby *motu* connected to the 'Village' by a makeshift wooden bridge harbours another cluster of no-frills beachfront units. Overall, it's great for unfussy divers (there's an on-site dive centre) who want to be close to Tumakohua Pass; less so for holidaymakers.

✖ Eating

Snack Kori Kori TAHITIAN $
(☑87 79 57 46; PK4.2; mains 900-1500 CFP; ⊘11.30am-2pm) A very pleasant spot for lunch, this family-run affair boasts an ace location right on the edge of the turquoise lagoon and whips up simple yet tasty meals as well as copious sandwiches and paninis (from 350 CFP).

Faka Délices FRENCH, DESSERTS $
(☑40 98 41 82; PK2.5; mains 1200-1300 CFP; ⊘10am-1pm daily, pizzas 5-8pm Mon-Fri, desserts 7.30am-5pm Fri & Sat, 7.30am-noon Sun) A native from Brittany, Pascaline, the elderly owner, cooks simple but delectable French dishes as well as pizzas (evenings only). Her desserts (from 280 CFP) are delicious; try the passionfruit mousse or the melt-in-your-mouth *millefeuilles*. You can eat on the small terrace (there's one table) or take away. Good English is spoken (the owner has lived in New Zealand). Also on offer are excellent homemade jams.

Faka Faapu SUPERMARKET $
(☑87 32 56 78; PK1, Rotoava; ⊘7am-2pm Mon-Sat, 8am-noon Sun) For fruit and vegetables, stop at this roadside stall in Rotoava village.

Snack Elda TAHITIAN $$
(☑87 23 66 42, 40 98 41 33; PK4.1; mains 1500-1900 CFP; ⊘11.30am-1pm & 6.30-8pm) This unfussy little eatery could hardly be better situated: the dining deck is right on the lagoon. The menu concentrates on simply prepared seafood and meat dishes served in generous portions. Call ahead to make sure it's open. Free pick-up.

Havaiki Pearl Lodge INTERNATIONAL $$
(☑40 93 40 15; PK2, Rotoava; mains 1600-1800 CFP; ⊘11.30am-2pm) One of the pleasures of Fakarava is eating at this surprisingly hip beachfront restaurant with fantastic lagoon views, cool breezes and great food. A few tables are literally in the water – where else could you devour grilled fish, tuna sashimi or a burger while sitting in a translucent lagoon?

ℹ Information

Post Office (OPT; Rotoava; ⊘7-11.30am & 1-2.30pm Mon, Thu & Fri, to 2pm Wed; ☎) Internet and wi-fi access (with the Manaspot network). Also has one 24-hour ATM, but we recommend bringing enough cash with you in case it's empty or not functioning.

ℹ Getting There & Away

The atoll is 488km east-northeast of Tahiti.

AIR

Air Tahiti (☑40 86 42 42; www.airtahiti.pf) flies from Pape'ete to Fakarava five times weekly (24,200 CFP one way), three times weekly from Rangiroa to Fakarava (9500 CFP) and once or twice weekly from Fakarava to Rangiroa (9500 CFP). If you're island-hopping, air passes (p234) are available.

BOAT

Cargo vessels serve the Tuamotus (p236). The cargo ships **Saint-Xavier Maris-Stella** (p236), **Cobia III** (p236) and **Mareva Nui** (p236) stop at Fakarava and take passengers.

ℹ Getting Around

The airport is 4km west of Rotoava. A scheduled visit by former French president Jacques Chirac (he never actually showed up) brought funding to pave a 20km road from the airport to the southeast side of the atoll. From the airport, a dirt track goes as far as the edge of Garuae Pass, about 5.5km away to the west.

Fakarava Yacht Services (☑87 75 34 84; Rotoava) hires out bikes (1500 CFP per day) and delivers to your *pension*.

Tetamanu is accessible by private boat only or during a lagoon excursion.

AHE

POP 552

This 20km-long by 10km-wide ring of coral is a charmer. The many hues of its pure aqua-blue water, the foaming breakers around the reef and the thin strips of coral-sand beach of its many deserted *motu* make for an enchanting scene. It is less developed than many surrounding atolls because of its geography. The only pass is at the northwest of the atoll; the village of Tenukupara is in the far southwest and the airport is at the northern extremity. The atoll's beauty draws in a large number of yachties between May and August.

The aim of the game on Ahe is to relax – but if you're keen to get the blood flowing, there are excellent options available, including snorkelling, fishing and diving.

◉ Sights & Activities

Activities on offer at the pensions range from cruising around the *motu* and snorkelling spots to kayaking and fishing. Pearl-farm visits are also popular. Cocoperle Lodge can arrange deep-sea-fishing charters and spearfishing trips.

There are also some excellent diving opportunities to be had near Tiareroa Pass (p39). Abundant marine life, dramatic seascapes and a sense of wilderness – this pass has it all.

Motu Manu   ISLAND
A great way to get a feel for Ahe is to visit this islet, which has the only remaining patch of primary forest in the Tuamotus, which consists of imposing *Pisonia grandis*.

Dive N'Co   DIVING
(☑87 22 14 80; www.divenco-ahe.com; introductory or single dive 7500 CFP) This husband-and-wife team provides personalised service and works in close cooperation with Ahe's two *pensions* and yachties. They run daily trips to Tiareroa Pass, a 30-minute boat ride away from the dive shop. Dive N'Co is a member of Te Moana Pass (www.temoanadiving.com), an inter-island dive pass that's accepted in 16 dive shops in French Polynesia. Cash only.

🛏 Sleeping & Eating

Cocoperle Lodge   PENSION **$$**
(☑40 96 44 08; www.cocoperlelodge.com; bungalows s incl half-board 12,100-14,600 CFP, bungalows d incl half-board 24,200-29,200 CFP) 🐾 This

haven of peace is set in a coconut plantation facing the lagoon and a lovely *hoa*. The six bungalows are made with local materials and have private bathrooms (with hot water; two of the bathrooms, though private, are outside), fans and mosquito nets. Refined (but hardly copious) meals are served in a local-style *fare* (traditional-style house) by the lagoon.

The more expensive bungalows offer more privacy than the cheaper ones. Swimming, kayaking and snorkelling off the 140m-long pontoon are popular pastimes here, but there's also a whole menu of worthwhile excursions on offer, as well as fishing trips. There's a green ethos: the lodge packs its rubbish to Pape'ete for proper disposal. Credit cards are accepted, and some English is spoken. No internet access.

Chez Raita   PENSION **$$**
(☑87 22 14 80; www.pension-raita.com; bungalows s/d incl half-board 10,700/21,400 CFP) If you're hoping to partake in the Tuamotuan *pension* experience, look no further – Raita and her husband offer local hospitality at its finest. Digs are in four well-maintained bungalows that lip out onto the blue-on-blue vista of lagoon and sky. Various excursions can be organised, including line fishing in the lagoon and snorkelling. Free kayaks. Credit cards are accepted. No internet access.

🛈 Getting There & Away

AIR
The atoll is 450km east of Tahiti. **Air Tahiti** (☑40 86 42 42; www.airtahiti.pf) flies from Pape'ete to Ahe three to four days weekly (24,200 CFP one way, one hour).

BOAT
Cargo ships (p236) service Ahe. The **Saint-Xavier Maris-Stella** (p236) and **Mareva Nui** (p236) stop at Ahe from Pape'ete.

The Marquesas

POP 9264

Includes ➜

Nuku Hiva.................. 168
Taiohae.......................169
'Ua Huka.....................176
'Ua Pou 180
Hiva Oa.......................182
Atuona & Around 183
Tahuata 189
Fatu Hiva 191

Best Places to Stay

➜ Temetiu Village (p185)

➜ Keikahanui Nuku Hiva Pearl Lodge (p173)

➜ Hotel Hanakéé Hiva Oa Pearl Lodge (p186)

Best Archaeological Sites

➜ Iipona (p188)

➜ Kamuihei, Tahakia & Teiipoka (p175)

➜ Tohua Koueva (p169)

Why Go?

Grand, brooding and powerful, nature's fingers have sculpted the Marquesas Islands into sharp silhouettes that jut up dramatically from the cobalt-blue ocean. Waterfalls taller than skyscrapers trickle down vertical canyons, the ocean thrashes towering cliffs, basalt pinnacles project from emerald forests, and scalloped bays are blanketed with desert arcs of white or black sand.

Some of the most inspirational hikes and horseback rides in French Polynesia are found here, allowing walkers and horse riders the opportunity to explore the islands' rugged interiors. Here the past is almost palpable, thanks to a wealth of archaeological remains dating from pre-European times.

Another highlight is the culture. In everything from cuisine and dances to language and crafts, the Marquesas do feel different from the rest of French Polynesia. But don't expect turquoise lagoons, swanky resorts and an electric nightlife – the Marquesas are an ecotourist's dream, not a beach-holiday destination.

When to Go

➜ Closer to the equator than the rest of French Polynesia, the Marquesas' climate is a bit different. Temperatures and humidity tend to be slightly higher than in Tahiti.

➜ There is no bad time to visit: in theory, June to September sees heavier rain while November to March is drier (exactly opposite from the rest of French Polynesia) and experiences calmer seas (better for boat excursions and diving).

➜ In odd number years in December, try to catch the Marquesas Festival or mini Marquesas Festival.

History

Among the first islands to be settled by the Polynesians during the great South Pacific migrations, the Marquesas served as a dispersal point for the whole Polynesian triangle from Hawai'i to Easter Island and New Zealand. Estimates of the islands' colonisation vary from prehistory to between AD 900 and 1100.

The Marquesas' isolation was broken in 1595 when Spanish navigator Don Alvaro de Mendaña y Neyra sighted Fatu Hiva by chance. Mendaña's fleet sailed along past Motane and Hiva Oa, and anchored for around 10 days in Vaitahu Bay on Tahuata. Mendaña christened these four islands Las Marquesas de Mendoza in honour of his sponsor, the viceroy of Peru, García Hurtado de Mendoza.

In 1774, James Cook lingered for four days on Tahuata during his second voyage. Joseph Ingraham, the American commander of the *Hope*, 'discovered' the northern group of the Marquesas in 1791, arriving slightly ahead of Frenchman Étienne Marchand, whose merchant vessel took on fresh supplies at Tahuata and then landed on 'Ua Pou. In 1797, William Crook, a young Protestant pastor with the London Missionary Society (LMS), landed on Tahuata, but his attempts at evangelism were unsuccessful.

French interest in the region grew as a means of countering English expansion in the Pacific. After a reconnaissance voyage in 1838, Rear Admiral Abel Dupetit-Thouars took possession of Tahuata in 1842 in the name of French King Louis-Philippe.

Under the French yoke, the Marquesas almost fell into oblivion – the French administration preferred to develop Pape'ete on Tahiti, which they thought had a more strategic value. Only the Catholic missionaries, who had been active since their arrival on Tahuata in 1838, persevered, and Catholicism became, and still is, firmly entrenched in the Marquesas.

Upon contact with Western influences, the foundations of Marquesan society collapsed. Whaling crews brought alcohol, firearms and syphilis. The population plummeted from around 18,000 in 1842 to 2096 in 1926.

In the 20th century the Marquesas were made famous by Hiva Oa residents Paul Gauguin and Belgian singer Jacques Brel. Slow but sure development of infrastructure has helped lessen the archipelago's isolation, while archaeological surveys are uncovering a culture that was lost only a comparatively short while ago.

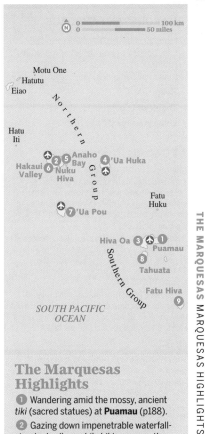

The Marquesas Highlights

1 Wandering amid the mossy, ancient *tiki* (sacred statues) at **Puamau** (p188).

2 Gazing down impenetrable waterfall-streaked valleys while hiking across the **Nuku Hiva** (p170) heartland.

3 Clip-clopping across the fecund interior to marvellous vistas in **Hiva Oa** (p185).

4 Searching for the rare and beautiful aquamarine lorikeet on **'Ua Huka** (p178).

5 Hiking or boating to the white beaches and jagged peaks of **Anaho Bay** (p174).

6 Raising your head high to see the tallest falls in the country in the stunning **Hakaui Valley** (p174).

7 Settling into island life under the striking, towering basalt spires of **'Ua Pou** (p180).

8 Enjoying a picnic on a secluded white-sand bay of **Tahuata** (p189).

9 Forgetting what day it is on lost and lush **Fatu Hiva** (p191).

MARQUESAN LANGUAGE

Marquesan is very different from Tahitian. Don't *ia ora na* (hello) or *mauruuru* (thank you) anyone out here; make friends by using the Marquesan instead.

Hello *Kaoha*

Thank you *Koutou*

Enjoy your meal *Kaikai maitai*

❶ Getting There & Away

AIR

The Marquesas are connected to Pape'ete. There aren't any direct services to other archipelagos – you'll have to go via Pape'ete. All flights are handled by **Air Tahiti** (☑ 40 86 42 42; www.airtahiti.pf).

Nuku Hiva and Hiva Oa are well connected with Tahiti, with daily direct flights from Pape'ete. Pape'ete–Nuku Hiva costs approximately 35,000 CFP one way while Pape'ete–Hiva Oa is around 39,000 CFP.

A smaller Twin Otter aircraft runs several times per week connecting 'Ua Pou and 'Ua Huka to each other as well as Hiva Oa and Nuku Hiva. Fares run around 16,000 CFP per leg.

BOAT

The *Taporo IX* and Aranui (p172) service the Marquesas, departing from Pape'ete and travelling via the Tuamotus (Fakarava and/or Rangiroa). The *Taporo IX* doesn't take passengers.

❶ Getting Around

Given the lack of public transport, it's still a bit of an adventure to get around the Marquesas, but that can be part of the fun. An absolute minimum of eight days is required if you plan to visit the two main islands (Nuku Hiva and Hiva Oa) plus one secondary island.

BETWEEN ISLANDS

The easiest and quickest way to island-hop within the archipelago is by regular Air Tahiti flights. *Bonitiers* (skipjack boats) can be individually chartered and you can hop on the cargo ship *Aranui* if your timing is right (ask about arrival dates). Tahuata and Fatu Hiva are only accessible by boat and it takes some ingenuity to organise this.

❶ TIME ZONE

Be sure to adjust your watch when you arrive in the Marquesas, as they are half an hour ahead of Tahiti. When it's noon in Tahiti, it's 12.30pm in the Marquesas.

ON THE ISLANDS

Guides and taxis are the main modes of transport for getting around the islands' web of 4WD tracks (and, increasingly, surfaced roads). It is possible to hire your own vehicle on Nuku Hiva and Hiva Oa. On Tahuata, Fatu Hiva and 'Ua Pou, you'll have to charter a 4WD with driver.

NUKU HIVA

POP 3151

This huge, sparsely populated island (the second largest in French Polynesia after Tahiti) boasts a terrain of razor-edged basaltic cliffs pounded by crashing waves, deep bays blessed with shimmering, Robinson Crusoe–like beaches, dramatically tall waterfalls and lush, green valleys that feel like the end of the world. Timeless little Taiohae, with its bay bobbing with sailboats and tattooed locals trotting through town on horseback, is the marvellous 'capital' of the Marquesas.

The island has a fascinating portfolio of archaeological sites, with more *tiki* and *tohua* (open-air gathering places) than you can count, while the ancient, rock-pile ruins of house foundations called *pae pae* seem to inhabit every stretch of forest. Horse riding is top notch, there's exceptional hiking and there are some beautiful handicrafts available to help you remember it all.

With daily flights from Pape'ete and good connections to other islands in the archipelago, there's no excuse not to spend at least three days here to do the island justice.

❶ Getting There & Away

The **Air Tahiti** (☑ 91 02 25, 92 01 45, 86 42 42; www.airtahiti.pf; ☺ 8am-noon & 1.30-4.30pm Mon-Thu, 8am-noon & 1.30-3.30pm Fri) office is in the centre of Taiohae.

The **Aranui** (p172) cargo ship makes a stop at Taiohae.

❶ Getting Around

Slowly but surely the roads of Nuku Hiva are being paved. At the time of writing, a sealed road ran from Taiohae to the airport and most of the way to Hatiheu.

TO/FROM THE AIRPORT

It takes a minimum of one hour to reach the airport from Taiohae along a winding road, longer if it has rained and the ground is muddy. Licensed 4WD taxis generally wait for each flight. It is nevertheless wise to book through your hotel or pension. Transfers to Taiohae cost 4000 CFP per person.

Nuku Hiva

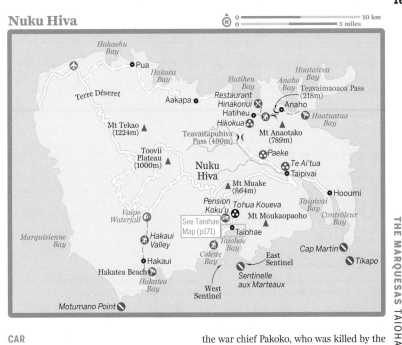

CAR

4WDs without driver can be hired from 11,300 CFP to 13,600 CFP per day. Rates include insurance and unlimited kilometres but not petrol. Contact the hotel **Moana Nui** (☑40 92 03 30; pensionmoananui@mail.pf) in Taiohae.

Taiohae

POP 1800

Sitting peacefully at the base of soaring mountains, Taiohae spreads gracefully along a perfectly crescent-shaped bay. This may be the Marquesas' 'capital', but Taiohae oozes the kind of sunny languor you'd associate with a tropical port, and it's impossible not to wind down a few gears here. Spend your Sunday morning in church to enjoy the booming harmonies, take a stroll along the laid-back seafront, meet a few woodcarvers and toss back a cool Hinano at sundown. Taiohae also offers useful services, including a tourist office, ATMs, internet access, a few shops and a handful of accommodation options. This is the obvious place to base yourself in Nuku Hiva.

⊙ Sights

★ **Tohua Koueva**   ARCHAEOLOGICAL SITE

It's believed that this extensive communal site, with its paved esplanade, belonged to the war chief Pakoko, who was killed by the French in 1845. Today it is a peaceful spot full of massive banyan trees and flowers. All the stone carvings are contemporary. This massive *tohua* is just over 1.3km up the Pakiu Valley on the Taipivai road, and 700m along a dirt track. Turn east from the main road at the 'Koueva' sign.

Notre-Dame Cathedral of the Marquesas Islands   CHURCH

This striking building is built from wood and stones on a former sacred site venerated by the ancient Marquesans. The stones come from the archipelago's six inhabited islands. Pop in to see Marquesan carved religious figures or come for Sunday service at 8am for hauntingly beautiful harmonies.

Pae Pae Piki Vehine   ARCHAEOLOGICAL SITE

Rebuilt for the 1989 Marquesas Festival, this *pae pae* (traditional meeting platform) contains modern sculptures and a dozen magnificent *tiki* made by the island's sculptors and artisans from Easter Island. Its central, breezy location makes it a popular hang-out for local kids.

Musée Enana   MUSEUM

(☑40 92 03 82; Hee Tai Inn; ⊙8-11.30am & 2-4.40pm Mon-Fri, 8-11.30am Sat) This little museum has a few documents and some

> **DON'T MISS**
>
> ## HIKING ON NUKU HIVA
>
> Nuku Hiva has a couple of exceptional walks that take in some awe-inspiring viewpoints, without another traveller in sight. A guide is essential because trails are not marked and it's easy to get lost. All routes have deteriorated in the last few years so be aware that being able to hike anywhere on Nuku Hiva will depend on trail upkeep and the weather (rain will mean mud and slippery terrain).
>
> **Tehaatiki** Explore the ridges around the southeastern part of Taiohae Bay. There are magnificent views of the bay and the coastline, but few shady areas. About five to six hours, moderate.
>
> **Peaks & cliffs near Aakapa & Hatiheu** A very scenic hike. Starting from Toovii Plateau, the path snakes its way through a primary forest on the plateau. Right on the plateau rim, the view over the Aakapa peaks and the northern coastline will be etched in your memory forever. It's mostly flat and shady. Keep an eye out for endemic birds, including the Marquesan imperial pigeon and the white-capped fruit dove. About six hours, moderate.
>
> **Big Z** An altogether different atmosphere. The western part of the island is barren. Starting from Toovii Plateau at an altitude of about 1000m, you follow a volcanic ridge to the west. Highlights include a lookout over a 'hidden valley', featuring snaggle-toothed peaks tangled together. Expect to see wild goats, white-capped fruit doves and white-tailed tropicbirds. No shade, but lots of breeze. About six hours, moderate.
>
> The hike to the **Vaipo Waterfall** is another stunner. DIYers have two good options for solo walking: **Colette Bay** and from **Hatiheu** to **Anaho**. For guides, contact the following:
>
> **Kimi Randonee** (☑ 87 75 39 69; kimi.rando@hotmail.fr; per full day 8000 CFP) Kimi is an ex-legionary, local fireman and all around jovial character who's a certified hiking guide with a good 4WD vehicle to get to the trailheads.
>
> **Richard Deane – Terama** (☑ 87 74 86 78, 87 28 08 36; per half-day from 3500 CFP) This guide specialises in walks near Taiohae and Taipivai.

beautiful ancient Marquesan artefacts. It also doubles as a small craft shop. Entry was free at the time of writing, but the owner may ask for a small fee in the future to help pay for air-conditioning and maintenance.

Monument to the Dead MONUMENT
On the seafront, you can't miss this obelisk fronted by a cannon constructed in honour of Étienne Marchand.

🏃 Activities

Horse Riding
Horse riding is a good way to soak up the drop-dead-gorgeous scenery.

Sabine Teikiteetini HORSE RIDING
(☑ 40 92 01 56, 87 25 35 13; half-day rides incl transfers 10,000 CFP) Sabine is a qualified guide who can arrange lovely rides on Toovii Plateau. You don't need any riding experience, as Sabine caters to all levels of proficiency. Rides last about three hours.

Nuku Hiva a Cheval HORSE RIDING
(☑ 87 25 44 87; nukuhivaacheval@gmail.com; day trips from 10,000 CFP) Roberto runs beautiful day tours around Hatiheu and Anaho for 10,000 CFP and two-day bivouac tours from 18,000 CFP per person. He's based in Hatiheu so you'll have to arrange a transfer to get there from Taiohae. These trips are best avoided in rainy weather when the trails become very slippery.

Island Tours & Dolphin-Watching
Marquises Excursions DOLPHIN-WATCHING
(☑ 87 73 23 48, 40 92 08 75; www.marquises-excursions.net; half-day cruise for 2 people 17,000 CFP) This small outfit runs dolphin-watching excursions. While an encounter is not guaranteed, the operator claims a success rate of 50% to 70% depending on the season. One caveat: the one-hour journey, along Nuku Hiva's pounded sea cliffs, will probably be cancelled if the sea is too choppy – as such, outings are rare.

Nuku Hiva Tours TOUR
(☑ 87 22 68 72, 87 79 13 69) Offers boat and hiking tours to Hakaui Valley and Vaipo Waterfall (for one/two/three people 14,000/7250/6500 CFP per person) and to see the melon-headed whales (one/two/four people 18,000/11,000/9000 CFP per person).

Taiohae

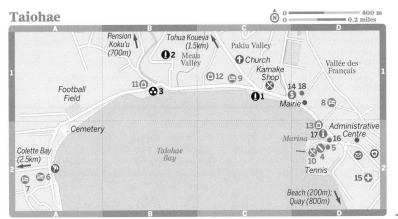

Taiohae

◉ Sights
1 Monument to the Dead	C1
Musée Enana	(see 6)
2 Notre-Dame Cathedral of the Marquesas Islands	B1
3 Pae Pae Piki Vehine	B1

◈ Activities, Courses & Tours
4 Centre Plongée Marquises	D2
5 Thierry Tekuataaoa	D2

◉ Sleeping
6 Hee Tai Inn	A2
7 Keikahanui Nuku Hiva Pearl Lodge	A2
8 Mave Mai	D1
9 Moana Nui	C1

◈ Eating
10 Café Vaeaki	D2
Hee Tai Restaurant	(see 6)
Keikahanui Nuku Hiva Pearl Lodge	(see 7)
Moana Nui	(see 9)
Snack Tuhiva	(see 13)

◉ Shopping
11 Damas Taupotini	B1
12 Edgar Tamarii	C1
13 Fare Artisanal	D2

ℹ Information
14 Banque Socredo	D1
15 Hospital	D2
16 Moetai Marine – Yacht Services	D2
17 Tourist Office	D2

ℹ Transport
18 Air Tahiti	D1

Jocelyne Henua Enana Tours DRIVING TOUR
(☑87 78 68 61; www.marquisesvoyages.com.pf; 4WD tour per person 6500 CFP) Jocelyne knows just about everything there is to know about Nuku Hiva. She is one of the only guides available on Sundays and speaks English. Her 4WD day tours offer a good overview of the island. Cash only.

Diving

There are a dozen magnificent diving sites, which are very different from those of the Society group or the Tuamotus. The Marquesas don't boast coral reefs, peaceful lagoons or crystalline waters. The water is thick with plankton and visibility is reduced (generally 10m to 20m). These specific conditions guarantee regular sightings of very unusual creatures, such as scalloped hammerheads and melon-headed whales, which are not encountered elsewhere in French Polynesia. All kinds of rays – mantas, eagles and stingrays – also swim close to the shore.

Since Nuku Hiva is devoid of any protective barrier reefs, divers should be prepared to cope with often difficult conditions, particularly the swell, to get to the sites. Most sites require a half-hour or so boat trip.

Centre Plongée Marquises DIVING
(☑40 92 00 88; marquisesdives@mail.pf) This small operation runs on a charter basis only. An outing costs around 50,000 CFP for up to three or four divers. Prices include

THE ARANUI

If there's an iconic trip in French Polynesia, it's the **Aranui** (☑ 40 42 62 40; www.aranui.com). For more than 25 years, this ship has been the umbilical cord between Tahiti and the Marquesas and a hot favourite with tourists. Its 14-day voyage, departing from Pape'ete, takes it to Takapoto Atoll in the Tuamotus and the six inhabited islands of the Marquesas. It does about 17 trips a year.

The *Aranui* has been supplying the remote islands of the Marquesas since 1984 and that is still its primary mission. Its front half looks just like any other cargo ship of its size, with cranes and holds for all types of goods. The back, however, is like a cruise ship, with cabins, several decks and a swimming pool. There's nothing glitzy about it – everything is simple and functional. Unless you're on a yacht, there's simply no other way to visit so many islands in the Marquesas (along with a Tuamotu atoll thrown in as a bonus) in such a short period. The plus is that you get the chance to see island life that few others ever will. Note that this is an organised journey; if you don't like to be tied to a schedule or forced to live with a group, it may not be for you.

There are four classes of accommodation, from staterooms (from 540,000 CFP per person) and suites (from 720,000 CFP per person) to dorm-style beds with shared bathroom facilities (330,000 CFP per person). All the accommodation has air-con, and prices include all meals, guided excursions and taxes. It is also possible to join the *Aranui* on Nuku Hiva for eight days in the Marquesas.

While the ship is unloading and loading freight – a major event on the islands – passengers take excursions ashore, which typically include picnics, scuba diving, snorkelling, 4WD trips to archaeological sites and remote villages, horse riding and stops at craft centres, where they can meet craftspeople and make purchases. No nights are spent ashore; all shore visits last just a day or half-day and include multilingual guides. European and North American art-history experts, archaeologists and ethnologists are invited on the cruise, providing cultural insights.

You may try to use the *Aranui* as a means of transport from one island in the Marquesas to another, but it's at the captain's discretion; don't rely too much on this option.

Bookings are essential, and peak periods (July, August and December) are booked up months in advance.

equipment and two successive dives. Dives are not guided, so you need to be experienced, but there's a comprehensive briefing before each dive. Book ahead.

🛏 Sleeping

Credit cards are accepted unless noted.

Moana Nui   HOTEL **$**
(☑ 40 92 03 30; pensionmoananui@mail.pf; s incl breakfast/half-board 6360/10,110 CFP, d incl breakfast/half-board 9890/17,390 CFP; ❄🐝) All eight rooms are clean, well organised (air-con, a small balcony, private facilities, hot shower, daily cleaning) and utilitarian. Rooms 1 and 2 have good views of the bay and all are decorated in local fabrics and woven bamboo. The location doesn't get any more handy, right in the middle of the bay. The on-site restaurant is an added bonus.

Car rentals are available here and the staff will call and arrange tours, although no one here is going to hold your hand. Best for independent types.

Pension Koku'u   PENSION **$**
(☑ 87 33 25 64 40 92 07 74; pensionkokuu@gmail.com; r per person with breakfast/half-board 4885/6500 CFP; 🐝) Here's a family-run place that embraces you like a big, warm Marquesan hug. Rooms are simple and not very private, but they are clean, tiled and have hot-water bathrooms. The location, a few kilometers uphill from Taiohae is inconvenient, but you come here more to dine, sing and be taken on adventures by the lovely Alvarado family.

The family will shuttle you down to town for free whenever you want. Meals from fresh produce are served at a big communal table.

Hee Tai Inn   HOTEL **$$**
(☑ 40 92 03 82; www.marquesas-hinn.com; r from 10,000 CFP; ❄🐝) Hee Tai Inn has the eight tidiest rooms in town, all in a plain but comfortable motel-like building at the back of a garden teeming with endemic plants. The real draw here, however, is the owner, Rose Corser, an American woman who has spent

decades learning and teaching others about all things Marquesan, from art history to botany.

Like all great characters, Rose has lots of opinions and if you stay here you will most probably hear them. Ask for the upstairs rooms which have views over the bay. The on-site, seaside Hee Tai Restaurant focuses on Marquesan specialties and is a real plus. The demi-*pension* plan of breakfast and dinner costs 3500 CFP per person.

Mave Mai PENSION $$
(📋 40 92 08 10; pension-mavemai@mail.pf; s/d incl breakfast 9000/11,000 CFP, incl half-board 11,000/15,000 CFP; ❄️ 🛜) Peacefully reposed over sloping grounds above the marina, this *pension* features eight rooms in a two-storey motel-style building. They're plain and not terribly Polynesian, but they're light and well appointed, with private facilities (hot water) and air-con, as well as a kitchenette in two of the rooms. The real draw is the small terrace (or balcony upstairs) overlooking the bay. The owners don't live on the premises so guests have the place to themselves most of the time.

Keikahanui Nuku Hiva Pearl Lodge HOTEL $$$
(📋 40 92 07 10; www.pearlodge.com; bungalows d 26,500-32,000 CFP; ❄️ @ 🛜 🏊) Nuku Hiva's only upmarket option, the Keikahanui occupies a wonderfully peaceful domain at the tip of Colette Bay. Digs are in Polynesian-style bungalows hidden in a sea of greenery on a hillside. They are commodious and decked out with tapa and woodcarved panels. Each bungalow has a private balcony with an eye-popping view over the bay.

There's a gorgeous but small swimming pool overlooking the bay, a bar and a good restaurant.

✖️ Eating & Drinking

You'll find several well-stocked little shops on the seafront, as well as a bakery, a small market and a few *roulottes* (mobile food vans) – your best bargain for cheap eats.

Café Vaeaki TAHITIAN $
(mains 800-1100 CFP; ⏰ 5am-9pm; 🛜) This friendly little godsend for yachties is right on the quay and offers simple but fresh dishes such as sashimi, grilled fish and chow mein alongside free wi-fi. There's also fresh juices and ice cream. Cash only.

Snack Tuhiva TAHITIAN $
(mains 1000-1200 CFP; ⏰ breakfast & lunch Mon-Sat) This low-key venue inside the market is a good spot to catch local vibes. Devour a comforting breakfast or munch on well-prepared fish dishes at lunchtime. It was being sold to a new owner when we passed but should continue to do more of the same. Cash only.

Moana Nui TAHITIAN $$
(📋 40 92 03 30; mains 1000-3200 CFP, pizzas from 1200 CFP; ⏰ 11am-9pm Mon-Sat; 🛜) Basking in a convivial buzz, the restaurant at this hotel has an eclectic menu, from salads and burgers to fish and meat dishes. Or opt for a pizza cooked in a wood-fired oven (evenings only).

Hee Tai Restaurant TAHITIAN, MARQUESAN $$
(mains 1200-1600 CFP; ⏰ 11.30am-2pm & 6-9pm Mon-Sat) In a lovely setting at the quiet western end of Taiohae Bay, this place takes pride in serving dishes from roast chicken to occasional roast pig feasts. There's also a full bar, perfect for cocktail hour.

Keikahanui Nuku Hiva Pearl Lodge INTERNATIONAL $$$
(📋 40 92 07 10; mains 2100-4600 CFP; ⏰ 11am-10pm) The chef at this upscale hotel fuses quality local ingredients with Gallic know-how. The Marquesan goat with coconut milk will certainly win your heart and there's even a dedicated vegetarian menu. Bag a table on the terrace and savour the views of the bay and the twinkling stars. Light meals are available at lunchtime.

It's also a great place for a sunset cocktail. If you're on a sailboat or staying at another *pension*, a shuttle can take you to the restaurant from the main road of Taiohae or the quay for 500 CFP return.

WORTH A TRIP

ANAHO & HAATUATUA BAY

The sublime Anaho Bay, on Nuku Hiva's northeast coast, is an arc of beach framed by surreal green hillsides that's completely disconnected with the outside world. It's only accessible by speedboat (15 minutes from Hatiheu; 7000 CFP) or a little less than 1½ hours by foot (also from Hatiheu). A few families make their living harvesting copra among the swaying coconut plantations; there is a tiny chapel and not much else. It's a popular anchorage for visiting yachts and, with the only coral reef on Nuku Hiva, the bay is lagoon-like and inviting. It's no wonder that back in 1888 Robert Louis Stevenson was inspired to write many pages describing its unsettling beauty.

Plenty of day tours go to Anaho, but if you're on your own, take the paved road at the end of Hatiheu up towards the valley. About 300m uphill there's a small clearing and a well-marked trail to the left. From the Teavaimaoaoa Pass (218m), reached after about 45 minutes, Anaho Bay appears like a mirage. Both the ascent from Hatiheu and descent to Anaho are quite steep, but the track is in good condition and is well marked. Bring mosquito repellent and plenty of water.

If Anaho's not remote enough for you, head to Haatuatua Bay, a 30-minute stroll to the east, on an easy-to-follow trail. This crescent-shaped bay fringed with a yellow scimitar of sand, framed by lofty volcanic ridges, is the epitome of an island paradise... except for a few wicked *nono* to bring you back to reality.

Shopping

Fare Artisanal HANDICRAFTS

(⊗ 8.30am-2.30pm Mon-Fri) Next to the tourist office, the *fare artisanal* (craft centre) is a good place to stock up on *monoi* (fragrant oil), necklaces, bracelets and carvings.

Damas Taupotini HANDICRAFTS

Master carver Damas Taupotini has a workshop across the road from Pae Pae Piki Vehine. He carves pieces from bone, wood and stone.

Edgar Tamarii HANDICRAFTS

(☑ 87 92 01 67) Another renowned carver is Edgar Tamarii, whose workshop is located near Moana Nui hotel. He specialises in woodcarvings.

Information

Banque Socredo (⊗ 7.30-11.30am & 1.30-4pm Mon-Fri) Currency exchange, as well as two ATMs.

Hospital (☑ 40 91 20 00) Has a dentist, too.

Moetai Marine – Yacht Services (☑ 40 92 07 50; ⊗ 8-11am & 12.30-3.30pm Mon-Fri; ☎) On the quay. Has laundry service (1000 CFP) and can help yachties with formalities. It's open extra hours 1 April to 30 July.

Post Office (⊗ 7-11.30am & noon-3.30pm Mon-Thu, 7-11.30am & noon-2.30pm Fri; ☎) Internet access and wi-fi (with the Manaspot card).

Tourist Office (☑ 40 92 08 25; ⊗ 7.30am-12.30pm Mon-Sat) Has a few brochures and can help with simple queries.

Hakaui Valley

Of all the marvels that Nuku Hiva offers, few equal the awe-inspiring majesty of the Hakaui Valley, which slices through the basaltic land mass, west of the island. On either side of the canyon, vertical walls rise to nearly 800m and **Vaipo Waterfall**, the highest in French Polynesia at 350m, plummets into a natural swimming pool at the end of the valley. In the drier months, the volume of the falls lessens and can be reduced to a mere trickle.

The valley was once the fiefdom of King Te Moana and Queen Vaekehu, and the ancient royal road follows the river past numerous ancient sites, namely *pae pae* and *tohua,* hidden behind a tangle of vegetation. Next to the Hakaui Valley, in Hakatea Bay, you'll find the magnificent **Hakatea Beach**. Waters are generally calm and good for swimming, but you'll have to deal with *nono* (biting flies). Bring lots of repellent.

Marquises Excursions (p170), Nuku Hiva Tours (p170) and **Thierry Tekuataaoa** (☑ 87 79 69 69; Yacht Service) can arrange guided trips to the waterfall. Expect to pay 14,000 CFP for two people for the full-day excursion without lunch. From Taiohae, it takes about 40 minutes by speedboat to reach Hakatea Bay, where the boat anchors. From the bay, allow about 2½ hours to reach the waterfall on foot. The path is flat and follows the river (be prepared to get wet) and includes stretches of the ancient paved royal road.

Note that it's not advised to walk the last 300m or so because the narrow canyon is subject to falling rocks. Back in Hakatea Bay, you can recharge the batteries on Hakatea Beach before returning to Taiohae.

Toovii Plateau

The Toovii Plateau spreads out over an average altitude of 800m at the heart of the island. With its conifer forests and vast pastures where cattle graze, it seems straight out of a Brothers Grimm fairy tale. At times, ghostly mists add a touch of the bizarre and the temperatures up here are markedly cooler than on the coast. Toovii used to supply the whole archipelago with meat, dairy produce and timber, but serves now as a playground for various activities including horse riding and hiking.

Taipivai

In July 1842, the American whaler *Acushnet* put in at Taiohae and a certain Herman Mellville jumped ship and escaped into the bush only to be captured and held captive (in a friendly sort of way) for three weeks by the feared cannibal tribes of Taipivai; Melville wrote about his amazing experiences in his novel *Typee* (1846). Later he went on to write *Moby Dick*, which has passages and a character obviously inspired by the people he lived with on Nuku Hiva. While there is much talk of developing tourist sites associated with Melville, there's really not much of interest as of yet, but the story itself makes this little valley more interesting.

Nowadays Taipivai is a charming village that carpets the floor of a river valley. At the eastern end of the village the river rushes into the majestic Contrôleur Bay.

It takes about half an hour by 4WD on a paved road in good condition to reach Taipivai from Taiohae.

Most tours stop in Taipivai to visit the Paeke archaeological site, which lies on a hillside at the exit of the village on the way to Hatiheu (the path that leads to the site is not signed, so ask around). It features two well-preserved *me'ae* (traditional sacred sites) flanked by a set of brick-coloured *tiki*. The *me'ae* further up the hill has a pit into which human remains were thrown. From the main road, it's a 20-minute walk uphill on a path.

Other sites include the new Te Ai'tua *mea'a* built for the 2011 Marquesas Festival and decked out in interesting modern, mostly cement *tiki*. A lesser visited highlight is the road leading to the village of Hooumi from where you can see an abundance of ancient *pae pae* dotting the landscape and some even being used as modern house foundations. The road ends at a beautiful grey-sand beach teeming with *nono*.

Hatiheu

Hatiheu is a graceful little village dominated by a crescent of black sand, soaring peaks and immaculate, colourful gardens; it's no wonder that Robert Louis Stevenson was so charmed by this setting when he passed through in 1888. On one of the peaks to the west, at a height of 300m, is a white statue of the Virgin Mary, erected in 1872.

From Taipivai, follow the main road 7.5km as it climbs to the impressive Teavaitapuhiva Pass (490m), from which there are magnificent views over Hatiheu Bay.

⊙ Sights

★ **Kamuihei, Tahakia & Teiipoka**   ARCHAEOLOGICAL SITE

About 300m towards Taipivai from the Hikokua site, these connecting sites make up the largest excavated archaeological area of Nuku Hiva. A team led by the archaeologist Pierre Ottino began restoration in 1998.

The importance and sheer number of these structures testify to the dense population this valley once sheltered.

COLETTE BAY

Colette Bay, about 3.5km from Taiohae, was the suffer-fest base camp for *Survivor Marquesas* (2002) but today it's simply a nice place for a gentle stroll or a picnic. Take the track going up to the Keikahanui Nuku Hiva Pearl Lodge, at the western side of the bay. Instead of branching left to the hotel, keep right and continue for about 2km. The track zigzags along the western side of the cove up to a pass, where you'll see a cattle fence, to the left. Open the gate and follow the dirt road that descends to the pebble beach at Colette Bay, which sometimes can be occupied by a herd of cows. Bring plenty of insect repellent.

With its large moss-covered basalt rocks and huge banyans, the largest of which has been estimated to be more than 600 years old, Kamuihei exudes *mana* (spiritual power).

At the foot of the largest banyan is a deep pit, presumably dug for the remains of sacrifices or for taboo objects. Other pits are scattered about the site; these are mostly *ua ma,* which stocked the all-important breadfruit. A little higher, on Teiipoka, are two large rocks about 2.5m high by 3m wide and decorated with petroglyphs that represent turtles, fish and the eyes of a *tiki,* along with human figures. It's estimated that the valley contains more than 500 other petroglyphs like these.

On the other side of the track is the restored *tohua* Tahakia, one of the biggest in the Marquesas, as well as some *pae pae.*

Hikokua   ARCHAEOLOGICAL SITE

One of the most powerful archaeological sites in the Marquesas, Hikokua was discovered by the archaeologist Robert Suggs in 1957 and has been restored and maintained by Hatiheu locals since 1987. It dates from around AD 1250 and was in use until the 1800s. The vast, central *tohua* was used for dance performances at community festivals.

It's flanked by tiers of small flat basalt blocks that were once used as steps for the spectators. On the terrace stand two modern stone carvings by a local artist, and a flat rock that was used for various purposes, including solo dances and rituals associated with puberty. Near the centre of the esplanade are nine Christian tombs. They probably date from the time of the first missionaries' arrival, after the abandonment of the site. The platform at the bottom, on the northern side of the esplanade towards the ocean, was the *tuu* (ceremonial activity centre), upon which sacrifices and displaying of the victims' bodies took place. The chief's residence stood at the northeast corner of the esplanade.

Hikokua is just off the dirt road, at the entrance to the village.

Archaeological Museum   MUSEUM

FREE This modest yet well-organised archaeological museum does a good job of explaining the archipelago's history and culture. It features artefacts, exhibits and replica. The detailed signs in English are very informative. Ask for the key at Restaurant Hinakonui, next door.

Tours

Given the scarcity of explanatory signs, it makes sense to hire a knowledgeable guide to visit Hatiheu's archaeological sites. Contact Jocelyne Henua Enana Tours (74 42 23, 92 08 32; www.marquisesvoyages.com.pf) in Taiohae or Restaurant Hinakonui in the village.

Eating

★Restaurant Hinakonui   MARQUESAN $$

(Chez Yvonne; 40 92 02 97; mains 1800-2900 CFP; ⊙11am-1pm Mon-Sat, dinner by reservation) This authentic Marquesan restaurant is a relaxing spot, with an open-air thatched terrace opening onto the seafront. Signature dishes include lobster flambéed with whisky (from February to October) and a truly fantastic goat with coconut milk. Most meals come with a side of breadfruit and cassava. Bookings are recommended, otherwise you might find the kitchen closed if there aren't enough customers.

Avoid the five boxy bungalows, which show too many signs of wear and tear, including saggy mattresses and sombre bathrooms.

DOLPHIN-WATCHING AROUND NUKU HIVA

At sea, Nuku Hiva is home to a bewildering 'event': dozens (and at times, hundreds) of melon-headed whales (a type of dolphin, also called electra dolphins, *Peponocephala electra)* congregate off the east coast in the morning. They usually stay at the surface, vertically or horizontally, sometimes playing, sometimes basking motionless. Though their habits remain largely unknown, some experts think that the east coast is their resting area during the day. The site itself is impressive, since it's anywhere between 100m and 1km off the coast, in a deep-blue sea.

'UA HUKA

POP 630

This low-key, little-visited island feels entirely clean of the troubles of the world; the trees are heavy with fruit, wind whips over the mostly bare hills, surf swishes against the rocky cliffs – and good luck getting a signal on your cell phone outside of Vaipaee. Woodcarving is the main activity here and this is the land of masters. There are only three villages, and after a day or two the small communities here seem to absorb you like a giant, friendly sponge. Watch the artisans at work; zigzag up the flanks of an extinct volcano to reach mysterious archaeological sites in the jungle; look for one of the world's rarest and most beautiful birds; and delve right into Marquesan life.

◎ Sights

Vaipaee VILLAGE
The island's main town is at the end of a very deep, narrow inlet, about 1km long and rightly named Invisible Bay. You'll find two stores, lots of fruit and flowers, and a few local carvers' studios tucked back down the side roads.

Arboretum BOTANICAL GARDEN
(⊙Mon-Sat) FREE A wide variety of plants, including 200 species of citrus fruits, are cultivated in these botanical gardens halfway between Vaipaee and Hane. The species best adapted to the climate are used for reforestation where the vegetation has been destroyed by wild goats and horses.

Te Tumu AREA
Built for the 2013 Mini Marquesas Festival, this beautiful site holds a large performance area and the island's main museum. The Marquesas's largest *tiki*, carved in 2013 from local red tuff, watches over the main event area. Also look for the several *pamuera* (whale *tiki*), unique to the island of 'Ua Huka. It's located just above the airport.

The museum was under construction when we passed but will display pestles, *tiki*, finely carved sculptures, *pahu* (drums), jewellery and period photos.

Manihina BEACH
Near the airport, Manihina Beach is a wonderfully scenic pebbly beach framed by basaltic cliffs. Sadly there are lots of *nono*. It's accessible by a dirt road.

Hane VILLAGE
Experts believe that the first Polynesian settlement on the Marquesas was here, tucked away in a bay protected on the east by the impressive **Motu Hane**. The white house on the seafront contains the excellent village **craft centre** as well as a modest **marine museum** (admission free), which shows the evolution of traditional *pirogues* (outrigger canoes) as well as other artefacts.

Get the key to the museum from the carving studio beyond the back corner of the craft centre, across the concrete playing field.

'Ua Huka

◎ Sights
1 Arboretum B2
2 Manihina...A2
3 Meiaute B2
4 Te Tumu A2
5 Vaikivi Petroglyphs A1

◉ Activities, Courses & Tours
6 Epo Epo (Big Crater) A2
7 Tahoatikihau (Small Crater) A2

◉ Sleeping
8 Chez Maurice et Delphine...................B2
9 Le Reve Marquisien A2
10 Mana Tupuna Village..........................A2

Meiaute ARCHAEOLOGICAL SITE
High up in the valley of Hane, the site of Meiaute includes three 1m-high, red-tuff *tiki* that watch over a group of stone structures, *pae pae* and *me'ae,* which are partly overgrown. Two of these *tiki* have projecting ears, one has legs and a phallus, while the other two have only a head and trunk.

The clearing forms a natural lookout with magnificent views of Hane Bay on one side and the caldera on the other. It's a 25-minute walk from the village of Hane. You don't really need a guide to get there; follow the main road inland, until you reach a concrete stairway on your right, 30m after a sharp bend. Climb the steep hill to the *pae pae*. A little higher up, in a clearing, you will find the *tiki*. If you're not sure, villagers will point you in the right direction.

Hokatu VILLAGE
Tiny and scenic Hokatu, about 3km east of Hane, lies in a sheltered bay edged with a

pebble beach pounded by azure seas with direct views of imposing, sugar-loafed Motu Hane. On the waterfront there's a small **museum** (admission free) that displays well-presented photographs of the petroglyphs around the island and just beyond is the **craft centre** – the island's biggest.

Motu Teuaua   ISLAND
Thousands of *kaveka* (sooty terns) nest year-round on these islets and lay thousands of eggs daily.

Access to Motu Hemeni is prohibited in order to protect the species. Teuaua, the neighbouring islet, is accessible by speedboat when the sea is calm. If the conditions are right (a rarity), you can accompany the islanders when they gather the eggs, which are considered a delicacy.

It's not for the fainthearted – you'll need to jump on to a rocky ledge and clamber up the rock using a rope. As you approach the nests, the *kaveka* swoop at you and their cries are deafening. If, despite all this, the experience still attracts you, wear a hat.

Vaikivi Petroglyphs   ARCHAEOLOGICAL SITE
This little-visited archaeological site on the Vaikivi Plateau is well worth the detour, if only for the walk or horse ride to get there. A guide is essential, ask at your *pension*. The petroglyphs represent an outrigger canoe, a human face, an octopus and various geometric designs.

🏃 Activities

Birdwatching

'Ua Huka is one of the few Pacific islands (Rimatara is the only other inhabited French Polynesian island) not yet colonised by the European rat, which is responsible for destroying much of the endemic birdlife elsewhere. As such, the island is blessed with two birds found nowhere else in the world, the Iphis monarch (*Pomarea iphis*) and the ultramarine lorikeet (*Vini ultramarina*). The latter is the most well-known thanks to its stunning blue and green plumage, while the former is a small grey bird that gets much less publicity.

Villagers report seeing more and more of both species in recent years. Fun fact: in order to protect the island from rats, 'Ua Huka has invested in a terrier from New Zealand named Dora who is trained to sniff out vermin as boxes arrive via the supply boat.

'Ua Huka's resident bird expert (and Dora the terrier's adopted mom) **Hinapootu**

Sulpice, (📞87 31 79 05) in Hokatu doesn't speak English, but she's an excellent source of info in French. All the *pensions* can also help with birdwatching. The birds are found in valleys around the island but your best bet is the Hokatu Valley at around 5am or 4pm. Sightings are likely any time of year. See also boxed text, Birdwatching in the Marquesas.

Walking

Any chunk of the coastal route between Haavei Bay to the west and Hokatu to the east offers views over jagged volcanic spires and steel-colored seas. For other walks, a guide is essential because the trails are unmarked. Ask at your *pension* for a guide; the usual cost is about 5000 CFP, picnic included.

Vaikivi Petroglyphs   WALKING
From Hane, it's a three-hour walk inland to the Vaikivi petroglyphs. A steep path wiggles up to the edge of the caldera, from which you'll get cardiac-arresting views of Hane Bay (plan on one hour from Hane). You can save this section by getting there by 4WD from Vaipaee. Then it's another two hours or so, well inland, amid a variety of landscapes – from thick vegetation to tree ferns and a dramatic finish of hacking through pandanus.

Tahoatikihau   WALKING
(Small Crater) A lovely, easy walk around the rim of an ancient volcano, located east of Vaipaee. Lunar landscapes and fantastic views. About 1½ hours.

Epo Epo   WALKING
(Big Crater) This hike takes you around the rim of the big crater west of Vaipaee. About four hours.

Hokatu to Hane   WALKING
There's an inland track connecting the two villages. It goes over a small pass. If the trail has been cleared, a guide may not be necessary.

Horse Riding

A fantastic ride is from Vaipaee to Hane, passing the arboretum, airport and windswept plateaus before reaching the coastal road, which plunges down towards Hane. If you want to explore the interior and reach a secluded archaeological site, then nothing beats the ride from Hane to the Vaikivi petroglyphs.

Horse-riding trips can be organised through your *pension*. A ride typically costs 6000 CFP for a half-day or 10,000 CFP for a full day, including a guide.

BIRDWATCHING IN THE MARQUESAS

Serious birdwatchers rate the Marquesas as a top birding hot spot, where you can spot rare species that are found nowhere else in the world. Here are just a few feathered friends to look out for:

Fatu Hiva monarch *(Pomarea whitneyi)* Fatu Hiva; forest-dwelling, 19cm, glossy purple-black; approximately 25 birds left in existence.

Iphis monarch *(Pomarea iphis)* 'Ua Huka; forest-dwelling, small light brown body, estimated population 1000–2500.

Marquesan imperial pigeon *(Ducula galeata)* Nuku Hiva and 'Ua Huka; 55cm and arboreal with a dark grey body with bronze-green reflections; approximate population 300.

Marquesan kingfisher *(Todiramphus godeffroyi)* Tahuata; beautiful white crown, blue eye stripe and blue-green back; population 400 to 500.

Ultramarine lorikeet *(Vini ultramarina)* 'Ua Huka; 18cm, flashy blue and aqua green with small orange beak; estimated population around 2000.

White-capped fruit dove *(Ptilinopus dupetithouarsii)* Throughout the archipelago; 20cm, greyish-white crown and olive green body; population unknown.

For more information, go to www.manu.pf and www.birdlife.org.

☞ Tours

Pension owners have 4WDs and can take you to visit the island's villages (about 5000 CFP per day depending on your itinerary).

🛌 Sleeping

Chez Maurice et Delphine　PENSION **$**
(☑ 40 92 60 55; Hokatu; bungalows half board per person 6500 CFP) This *pension* has five very ramshackle but spacious bungalows on a little knoll in Hokatu, with sweeping views of Hokatu Bay and Motu Hane. Try to book the bungalow Mata Otemanu – lying on your bed you can see the bay and the *motu*. Meals are locally sourced and delicious; think: lobster, breadfruit and chicken soup and flambéed bananas for dessert.

The delightful hosts, Maurice, is a master carver (his living room looks like a sculpture museum) and he can teach you some of his techniques, while his wife Delphine (who can get by in English) keeps the whole operation together and also runs the Hokatu crafts centre.

Mana Tupuna Village　PENSION **$**
(☑ 40 92 60 08; manatupuna@mail.pf; Vaipaee; s/d incl half-board 7500/13,500 CFP; 🖥) These four clean and brightly coloured bungalows on stilts are perched on the side of a flowery hill. There are beautiful views over the valley from the bungalows and also from the restaurant/common area where they're framed by giant *tiki* carved by the owner, Raphael.

The *pension* is run by Raphael's hip son Raiarii, who keeps it updated and fresh.

If you're looking for a convenient location (it's two steps outside Vaipaee) plus comforts such as hot water and wi-fi on 'Ua Huka, this place is your best bet. Meals use local fish and produce, and are simple but delicious.

Le Reve Marquisien　PENSION **$$**
(☑ 87 79 10 52; revemarquisien@mail.pf; Vaipaee; bungalows s/d incl half-board 16,400/21,000 CFP) Set in a secluded clearing surrounded by a lush coconut grove, this relaxed place has four comfortable bungalows with wooden floors, firm beds, hot water and TV. It's exactly what it promises: a dream escape, but its isolated location, about 2km from Vaipaee, makes it difficult in all respects to leave – especially if the road is muddy.

Airport transfers are free.

ℹ Information

Infrastructure is very limited on 'Ua Huka. Bring a wad of cash – there's no bank and no ATM, and credit cards are not accepted.

Comite de Tourisme Tupehe Nui Ua Huka
(☑ 40 92 61 16; Vaipaee; ⊙ 8-11am Tue & Thu; 🖥) Helpful office promoting 'Ua Huka's tourism. There's often someone there weekdays even though Tuesday and Thursday are the only posted hours.

Post Office (⊙ 7-11am Mon-Fri; 🖥) In Hane, has internet and wi-fi access (with the Manaspot card).

DON'T MISS

THE MARQUESAS ARTS FESTIVAL

Powerful, grandiose, visceral – words do little justice to the Marquesas' premier festival, which lasts about one week and is held once every four years (usually in December) either on 'Ua Pou, Nuku Hiva or Hiva Oa. The last one was held in 2015 on Hiva Oa, so you'll have to wait until December 2019 for the next, on 'Ua Pou. If you don't have the patience, 'mini festivals' are held on the smaller islands (on Fatu Hiva in 2017) in between two 'big' festivals.

The Marquesas Arts Festival revolves around a series of music, dance and cultural contests, with dance performances being the highlights. Groups from all the Marquesan islands demonstrate their skills at traditional dances, including the spine-tingling Haka Manu (Bird's Dance) and Haka Pua (Dance of the Pig). Groups from other Polynesian archipelagos are invited and they join the contests, too. Most dancing contests take place on restored archaeological sites, which strengthens the visual appeal of the performances. Events also include traditional Marquesan meal preparations as well as arts and crafts displays.

This is your top chance to immerse yourself in traditional Marquesan culture and islanders take it very seriously. Book your Air Tahiti flight a few months in advance.

❶ Getting There & Away

Air Tahiti (☑ 40 91 60 16, 40 92 60 44, 87 86 42 42; www.airtahiti.pf) has offices at the airport and in Vaipaee.

The **Aranui** (p172) cargo ship stops at Vaipaee. Speedboats can be hired to travel to 'Ua Pou and Nuku Hiva (from 55,000 CFP).

❶ Getting Around

A surprisingly good 13km road links Vaipaee to Hokatu via Hane.

'Ua Huka's airport is on an arid plateau midway between Vaipaee and Hane. *Pensions* charge 2000 CFP return for airport transfers.

'UA POU

POP 2300

'Ua Pou's geology is fascinating. A collection of 12 pointy pinnacles seem to soar like missiles from the basaltic shield. Almost constantly shrouded in swirling mist and flecked by bright sunlight, they form one of the Marquesas' most photographed scenes. Completing this natural tableau of otherworldly proportions are a few oasislike valleys bursting with tropical plants, as well as a handful of tempting beaches.

'Ua Pou's jewel-like natural setting will frame everything you do here, from hiking and horse riding across the island to visiting secluded hamlets. For culture buffs, the island musters up a handful of powerful archaeological sites.

❶ Getting There & Away

There is an office for **Air Tahiti** (☑ 87 86 42 42, 40 91 52 25; www.airtahiti.pf; ⊗ 7.30am-noon & 1.30-

3.30pm Mon-Fri) in Hakahau. The **Aranui** (p172) cargo ship stops at Hakahau and Hakahetau.

❶ Getting Around

One dirt 4WD track runs most of the way around the island, with the only inaccessible bit being the section between Hakamaii and Hakatao.

The airport is at Aneou, about 10km west of Hakahau. Your hosts will come to collect you if you have booked accommodation; it usually costs 4000 CFP per person return.

Ask at your *pension* about hiring a 4WD with driver; expect to pay 15,000 CFP to 20,000 CFP per day.

Hakahau

'Ua Pou's largest settlement, Hakahau is blessed with a photogenic location. A huge bite chomped out of the fretted coastline of 'Ua Pou's northern coast, Hakahau Bay resembles a giant mouth about to swallow up its prey, with the iconic basalt peaks in the background. Hakahau is a relaxed coastal town blessed with a sweeping black-sand beach – fairly suitable for a dip – and wicked waves that keep local surfers happy. With a couple of *pensions* and useful services, it's a convenient base. Don't miss the **crafts centre** (⊗ 8am-3pm Mon-Fri) if you want to buy local woodcarvings.

◉ Sights

Hakahau Bay　　　　　　　　　　　NATURAL SITE
For a beautiful view of Hakahau Bay head east from Pukuéé *pension* along a track until you reach a small pass. Here take the right fork and climb steeply for about 10 minutes until you reach a small flight of

steps leading to a white cross, which you can see from the quay.

Anahoa Beach
BEACH

From Hakahau, it's a 30-minute walk east to deserted Anahoa Beach. From the Hakahau quay, follow the sign for Pukuéé *pension* and continue along the paved road beyond the restaurant.

Catholic Church
CHURCH

Right in the centre of town is this enticing church made of wood and stone. Inside you'll find some fantastic woodcarvings of religious figures with a distinctly Marquesan touch.

🏃 Activities

The activity of choice on 'Ua Pou is walking. Without a guide you can walk along the 4WD tracks that connect the villages (but there's no shade). For deeper exploration, it's advisable to hire a walking guide since it's easy to get lost. Ask at Pukuéé *pension*. A full-day guided walk is about 12,000 CFP for two.

Hakahau–Hakahetau
WALKING

The cross-island path from Hakahau to Hakahetau takes three to four hours. It ends at Hakahetau where you can take a dip at the waterfall. Easy to moderate.

Poumaka Loop
WALKING

More challenging than 'Ua Pou's other hikes, the Poumaka loop takes about four hours and goes around Mt Poumaka. It affords hauntingly beautiful panoramas of the iconic basaltic 'pillars' that jab the skyline.

🛏 Sleeping & Eating

Pukuéé
PENSION, RESTAURANT **$$**

(☑87 72 90 08, 40 92 50 83; http://pukuee.free.fr; s/d incl half-board 10,500/19,800 CFP; 🔊🏊) Reliable, friendly and fabulously situated on a hillside with swooning views of Hakahau Bay, Pukuéé offers two rooms in a wooden house surrounded by greenery. Owner Jérôme is great with arranging excursions, and his wife Elisa is a real cordon-bleu cook.

Pension Vehine
PENSION **$$**

(☑87 70 84 32, 40 92 53 21; r incl breakfast/half-board per person 8800/17,600 CFP) In the centre of Hakahau, this *pension* offers two simple rooms with shared bathroom (hot-water showers) in a house and two beautifully finished bungalows in the garden (alas, no views). Meals are served at Snack Vehine, the family's restaurant. Cash only.

'Ua Pou

'Ua Pou

◉ Sights
1 Anahoa Beach B1
2 Cascade Vaiea A3
3 Catholic Church B1
4 Tetahuna A3

🛏 Sleeping
5 Pension Leydj A3
6 Pension Vehine B1
7 Pukuéé B1

🍴 Eating
Snack Vehine ....(see 6)
8 Ti' Piero A3

ℹ Information
9 Banque Socredo B1

ℹ Transport
10 Air Tahiti... B1

Snack Vehine
TAHITIAN **$**

(☑40 92 50 63; mains 1100-1900 CFP; ⏰11am-1.30pm & 6-8.30pm Mon-Sat) This casual eatery is your spot for chow mein, grilled or raw fish and steaks.

ℹ Information

Banque Socredo (⏰7.30am-noon & 1-3pm Mon-Fri) Currency exchange and an ATM.

DON'T MISS

PLAGE AUX REQUINS (SHARK BEACH)

Shortly beyond the airport at Aneou, Hakanai Bay appears like a mirage from around a sharp bend: a long curve of wave-lashed beach, and the only footprints to be seen other than your own are those of crabs and insects (except at weekends, when locals enjoy picnics here). It has been named Plage aux Requins (Shark Beach) because of the sharks that are occasionally seen in the cove (it's safe for a dip nonetheless).

Medical Centre In the south of the village this small medical centre has a doctor and dentist.
Post Office (⊙7-11.30am & 12.15-3pm Mon-Thu, 7-11.30am & 12.15-2pm Fri) On the seafront. Internet and wi-fi access (with the Manaspot network). Has an ATM.

Hakahetau

This tranquil village springs up like an oasis after driving along the west coast on a dusty track. There aren't many things to see, but the addictive peaceful atmosphere could hold you captive longer than expected.

◉ Sights

Cascade Vaiea   WATERFALL
At the entrance of the village a sign marks the mountainside track to a waterfall. It has a deep round bathing pool that looks like something out of a tonic-drink advert.

Tetahuna   ARCHAEOLOGICAL SITE
At the far end of the village, make a beeline for this grandiose *tohua*, which hosted numerous dance and cultural performances during the 2007 Marquesas Arts Festival. The grandiose site consists of several stone platforms where many ceremonies and rituals would have been performed in pre-European times. It sits next to an uncommonly clear river.

⛏ Sleeping & Eating

Pension Leydj   PENSION $
(✎40 92 53 19; maka@mail.pf; r incl half-board per person 6900 CFP) In a plum setting on a hill at the edge of Hakahetau, this mellow *pension* offers clean, well-swept yet impersonal rooms at a nice price. Bathrooms (hot water) are shared. Owner Tony is a renowned carver and the living room is like a small art

gallery – you won't find a better place to buy high-quality souvenirs.

Some seriously good Marquesan meals are served on the terrace with a view of the bay. Various excursions can be organised.

★**Ti' Piero**   MARQUESAN, FUSION $$
(✎40 92 55 82; mains 1800 CFP; ⊙by reservation Mon-Sat; 🛜) This family-run eatery does a wonderful job of preparing well-executed international specialities with a true Marquesan touch. Go the *chèvre de sept heures* (goat cooked for seven hours) and breadfruit rolls. A good place to recharge the batteries after the Hakahau–Hakahetau walk. Free wi-fi.

Hakamaii

At the end of the 4WD track from Hakahetau, on the west coast, this one-street village stretches along the Kahioa River. The facade of the town's stone church, facing the ocean, has unusual yellow, blue and red wooden panels that are meant to imitate stained-glass windows. A path running up the hill next to the church leads up to a ridge for fantastic views.

Hohoi

Tranquillity reigns supreme in this little charmer, located about 12km southeast of Hakahau, and nobody's complaining. Apart from its lovely setting and peaceful ambience, Hohoi is a definite must-see for those who want to experience traditional village life and explore some ancient vestiges.

Situated above the village, the magnificent **Tohua Mauia** comprises a huge L-shaped stone platform as well as numerous *pae pae* dotted around the main complex. Even if your interest in ruins is only slight, the enchanting setting and the almost mystical hush are reason enough to come here.

Further down in the village, look for the pagoda-shaped **Catholic church**. Continue to the beach; if you are lucky, you might come across *pierres fleuries* (flowering stones) – pieces of phonolite that have crystallised to form amber-coloured flower shapes.

HIVA OA

POP 2447
This serpentine island holds a heady, dramatic mix of lush jungle, sea-battered coastal cliffs and towering volcanic peaks.

The bays that fret the coastline are lined with white-sand, black-sand or pebble-stubbled beaches that are lapped by indigo waters and fringed by nodding palms. Behind sit silent, pastel Marquesan hamlets where time has stood still. After a few days, you'll understand why the artist Paul Gauguin and the Belgian singer Jacques Brel chose to escape the modern world here and make it their home. Hiva Oa has a wild feeling that inspires shutting off your wi-fi and focusing more on important things, like enjoying a perfect mango or sunset.

Hidden like Easter eggs in this tropical jungle dreamland are some of the most intriguing and enigmatic archaeological sites in the South Pacific, including massive, moss-covered stone *tiki* and unexplained petroglyphs that will keep you pondering about their meanings for days.

Hiva Oa is also the optimal launching pad for exploring Tahuata and Fatu Hiva.

ℹ Getting There & Away

The *Aranui* cargo ship stops at Atuona and Puamau and, less frequently, at Hanapaaoa and Hanaiapa. To get to Tahuata, you can charter a private boat and share the costs with any other passengers (you're looking at about 20,000 CFP from Atuona to Vaitahu) or hop on a tour from Atuona.

Air Tahiti (☑ 40 86 42 42, 40 92 70 90; www.airtahiti.pf)

ℹ Getting Around

TO/FROM THE AIRPORT

The airport is 13km from Atuona. If you have booked your accommodation, your host will come and collect you for about 3600 CFP return. You can also hitch a ride to town.

CAR

Atuona Rent-a-Car (☑ 40 92 76 07, 78 72 17 17) and **Hiva Oa Location** (☑ 40 92 70 43, 78 24 65 05) have 4WDs for hire (without driver) for about 10,000 CFP to 15,000 CFP per day, with unlimited kilometres.

Atuona & Around

POP 1762

Winding around the mouth of a flower-laden bay, Atuona is the southern Marquesas group's tiny administrative capital. The village is framed at the back by forested mountains that give the whole place a close-in, cosy feel. It's the only town with any sort of bustle (by Marquesan standards) on Hiva

THE SMILING TIKI

Hiva Oa's most bizarre statue, the Smiling Tiki, can be found near the road to the airport, about 10km from Atuona. About 1m in height, it stands alone in a clearing. Its two clearly outlined eyes resemble big glasses, and its curved lips suggest a smile – it looks like a friendly critter that almost inspires a hug. To find it (no sign), ask your hosts to draw you a map or ask for the little sketch map that's sold at the tourist office (it's surprisingly reliable).

Oa, and it has a small selection of restaurants and guesthouses. Neat, modern houses cling like limpets to a rocky peninsula that separates the town centre from the majestic Tahauku Bay to the east, a favourite anchoring place among yachties.

Atuona is particularly famous for having once been home to Paul Gauguin and Belgian singer Jacques Brel, whose memories are kept alive by a regular trickle of visitors. Both lend even more romance to this enchanting little town.

◉ Sights

Espace Culturel Paul Gauguin MUSEUM
(adult/child 600/300 CFP; ⊗8-11am Mon-Fri, 2-5pm Mon-Thu, noon-4pm Fri) A homage to Gauguin that traces the artist's life through locally painted reproductions of his art. The main signs are translated into English but the detailed info with tidbits about the individual works, alas, are only in French. The Maison du Jouir (House of Pleasure) is an abandoned-looking replica of Gauguin's house with a lifelike statue of the artist inside.

Centre Jacques Brel MUSEUM
(adult/child 500/250 CFP; ⊗8-11am Mon-Fri, 2-5pm Mon-Thu, noon-4pm Fri) Behind the Espace Culturel Paul Gauguin you'll find a big aircraft hangar. In the centre is Jacques Brel's plane, *Jojo*; faded posters tracing the musician's life adorn the walls and his music plays dreamily over the sound system. There's not a word of English in any of the explanations.

Calvaire Cemetery CEMETERY
A must-see for Gauguin and Brel devotees is the Calvaire Cemetery, perched on a hill overlooking Atuona. You will find this frangipani-filled graveyard an appropriately colourful place for Paul Gauguin's tomb.

Hiva Oa & Tahuata

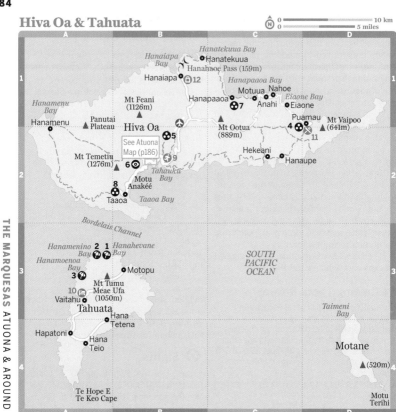

THE MARQUESAS ATUONA & AROUND

Hiva Oa & Tahuata

◎ Sights
1 Hanahevane Bay	A3
2 Hanamenino Bay	A3
3 Hanamoenoa Bay	A3
4 Iipona	C1
5 Tehueto Petroglyphs	B2
6 Tevitete Ancient Cemetery	B2
7 Tiki Moe One	C1
Tohua Pehe Kua	(see 11)
8 Tohua Upeke	B2

◎ Activities, Courses & Tours
9 Hamau Ranch – Chez Paco	B2

◎ Sleeping
10 Amatea	A3

◎ Eating
11 Pehekua – Chez Marie-Antoinette	D2

◎ Shopping
12 Jean & Nadine Oberlin	B1

While most of the tombs are marked with white crosses, Gauguin's is a simple round stone with his name painted in white. Right behind, a replica of his statue *Oviri* (meaning 'wild') stands guard.

Jacques Brel's grave is a bit below, near the access steps, on the left. The gravestone, lovingly planted with flowers, is adorned with a medallion depicting the singer with his companion, Madly.

To get there, head north on the road just east of the *gendarmerie* (police station). Continue for about 600m until you reach a fork in the road and follow the sign to the cemetery 100m further on. It takes about 20 minutes on foot.

Tehueto Petroglyphs ARCHAEOLOGICAL SITE
Anyone with an interest in ancient Marquesan civilisation shouldn't leave Atuona without a visit to the Tehueto petroglyphs. You'll find a massive rock with prolific carvings on two sides, including stylised human figures.

Hidden high up in the Tahauku Valley, the petroglyphs are a good walk from Tahauku Bay (approximately 2.5km inland), but it's usually quite overgrown and the path is confusing; we suggest hiring a guide (ask at your *pension*).

Tevitete Ancient Cemetery   HISTORIC SITE
This isolated, poignant site about 2km up in a valley (ask for directions) features a series of tombs made of stones; note the small *tiki* that are carved in bas-relief on a few tombs. At the back of the cemetery, a big trunk is carved in the shape of a *tiki*. There are great views of the valley and Atuona.

Catholic Church   CHURCH
The Catholic church, right in the centre of Atuona, is worth a peek for its elegant architecture that combines wood and stone.

Tohua Pepeu   ARCHAEOLOGICAL SITE
Restored for the 1991 Marquesas Arts Festival, the Tohua Pepeu faces Banque Socredo in the centre of town. It's used today as a festivities centre, where dances and cultural activities are performed.

Atuona Beach   BEACH
Framed by basaltic cliffs, this wide curve of black sand is very scenic – it inspired painter Paul Gauguin, which is saying a lot – but it's not appropriate for swimming because of strong currents. The road and area around have recently been upgraded making this a lovely short walk from town.

🏃 Activities

Hiking
There are some truly excellent hiking possibilities on Hiva Oa, including the strenuous cross-island trek from Atuona to Hanamenu (about 11 hours). Sadly, there's no way-marked trail and no guide was available on the island at the time of writing. Ask at your *pension* or contact Hamau Ranch – Chez Paco or Jeremie Kehuehitu, who may organise something for you with advance notice.

Horse Riding
Seeing the island from the saddle is a typical Hiva Oa experience and a low-impact way to imbibe the majestic scenery. A network of trails leading to some of the most beautiful sites can be explored on horseback. Reserve as far in advance as possible.

Hamau Ranch – Chez Paco   HORSE RIDING
(📞40 92 70 57, 87 28 68 21; hamauranch@mail.pf; rides 7000-14,000 CFP) Paco organises three-

hour jaunts on the plateau near the airport. No previous experience is necessary. The ultimate is a full-day ride to Hanatekuua Bay, to the north of the island, along undulating ridges and the coastline. Riders must be at least six years old. Transfers can be arranged.

Jeremie Kehuehitu   HORSE RIDING
(📞87 36 84 11, 87 23 01 58) Jeremie is a young dynamic guy offering both horse riding and hiking from three-hour jaunts to much longer.

Boat Excursions
Taking a boat excursion to nearby Tahuata will be one of the main highlights of your visit to Hiva Oa and it's well worth the expense (especially given the lack of reliable boat services to Tahuata). Day-long trips usually include stops at Hapatoni and Vaitahu and a picnic lunch at Hanamenino Bay or Hanahevane Bay. Your *pension* will make arrangements with a local operator or contact **Mofitu Transport** (📞87 24 64 77). Plan on 8500 CFP per person.

👉 Tours
Day-long excursions by 4WD cost about 8500 CFP for two people. Plan on two days if you want to take in Taaoa, Hanaiapa, Hanapaaoa and Puamau. For information, contact *pension* owners. Guides have a very limited knowledge of English and act more as drivers than proper guides, so don't expect in-depth historical comments.

🛏 Sleeping
Accommodation options on Hiva Oa are fairly limited. All places are in (or near) Atuona, bar one in Puamau. Unless otherwise noted, credit cards are accepted.

★ Temetiu Village   PENSION $$
(📞40 91 70 60; www.temetiuvillage.com; Tahauku Bay; bungalows standard per person 9000 CFP, large bungalows per person 11,000 CFP per person; 📶❄) This well-run and friendly *pension* has four shiny-clean bungalows perched scenically on a lush hillside, each enjoying wraparound views of Tahauku Bay. There are also two older (and slightly cheaper) bungalows, that are definitely less luxurious (linoleum floors instead of wood etc) but are more private and perfect for an unfussy couple or single traveler. The food is well respected. Breakfasts cost 1100 CFP and lunch or dinner is 3000 CFP.

Atuona

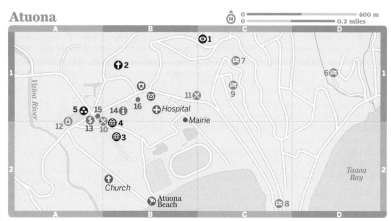

Atuona

⊙ Sights
1 Calvaire Cemetery C1
2 Catholic Church B1
3 Centre Jacques Brel B2
4 Espace Culturel Paul Gauguin B2
5 Tohua Pepeu A1

⊖ Sleeping
6 Hotel Hanakéé Hiva Oa Pearl
   Lodge D1
7 Pension Kanahau – Chez Tania C1
8 Relais Moehau C2
9 Temetiu Village C1

⊗ Eating
Hotel Hanakéé Hiva Oa
   Pearl Lodge .... (see 6)
Relais Moehau .... (see 8)
10 Salon de The Chez Eliane &
   Cyber Cafe B2
11 Snack Make Make B1
Temetiu Village .... (see 9)

⊕ Shopping
12 Crafts Centre A2

⊕ Information
13 Banque Socredo A1
14 Tourist Office B1

⊕ Transport
15 Air Tahiti A1
16 Air Tahiti B1

Pension Kanahau – Chez Tania   PENSION **$$**
(☑ 87 70 16 26, 40 91 71 31; http://pensionkanahau.
com; Tahauku Bay; s/d incl breakfast 10,600/13,500
CFP; ☜) Tania, your chirpy host, does a
superb job of keeping her place shipshape.
Location-wise, this *pension* plays in the
same league as nearby Temetiu Village,
with a flower-filled garden and stupendous
views of Tahauku Bay and the mountain
amphitheatre. The four bungalows are well
furnished, spacious and sparkling clean (hot
water is available); two units are equipped
with cooking facilities.

Tania may prepare meals, or she'll drive
guests to town for lunch or dinner for free.
Cash only.

Relais Moehau   HOTEL **$$**
(☑ 40 92 72 69; www.relaismoehau.pf; Atuona;
s/d incl breakfast from 8000/12,955 CFP; ☜)
Small and friendly like a *pension*, yet offering more independence, this classic South
Pacific–feeling place is across the road from
the waterfront and a short walk from town.
The front rooms are light-filled and face a
wide, bay-view terrace; those at the back face
a dark hill. All rooms are pint-sized, but airy
and have hot water, fan and plump bedding.

There's a good restaurant downstairs.

Hotel Hanakéé Hiva Oa
Pearl Lodge   HOTEL **$$$**
(☑ 40 92 75 87; www.pearlodge.com; bungalows
d 24,000-33,000 CFP; ✳@☜✷) A secluded
property on a mound overlooking Tahauku
Bay, with Mt Temetiu as a backdrop, the 14
well-designed bungalows sit in a blooming
garden. There's a small pool and a good
restaurant. Some units have views of the bay
while others face the valley and the moun-
tains. One minus: it's quite isolated.

✕ Eating

Most restaurants provide free transport for
their dinner guests (call ahead). You will

find several well-stocked grocery stores in Atuona.

Relais Moehau TAHITIAN, PIZZA $$
(☑40 92 72 69; mains 1300-2000 CFP; ⏱11.30am-1.30pm & 6-9pm) Headliners here include *chaud froid de thon* (seared tuna), grilled wahoo, and marinated raw shrimp with coconut sauce – but the pizzas (available dinner only) are very good too. The tiled terrace overlooking Atuona bay is breezy and lovely. Credit cards are accepted (minimum 5000 CFP).

Snack Make Make TAHITIAN, INTERNATIONAL $
(☑40 92 74 26; mains 950-1850 CFP; ⏱7.30am-1.30pm Mon-Thu, till 8.30pm Fri, occasionally Sat) Opposite the post office, this long-standing, very friendly joint serves everything from burgers and chow mein to curried goat and garlic shrimp. Smaller (read: normal-sized) portions are available of many dishes for only 950 CFP. Cash only.

Salon de The Chez Eliane & Cyber Cafe CREPERIE $
(Crêpes from 950 CFP; ⏱7.30am-5.30pm Mon-Fri, to 3.30pm Sat; 🛜) A cosy little lounge with wi-fi (500 CFP per hour) and a little snack bar serving crêpes (sweet and savory), burgers, coffee and ice-cold coconuts. It's right next to the Espace Culturel Paul Gauguin.

Hotel Hanakéé Hiva Oa Pearl Lodge INTERNATIONAL $$
(☑40 92 75 87; mains 1500-4200 CFP; ⏱lunch & dinner) Probably the number-one spot for fine dining in Hiva Oa, and certainly the most suitable place for a romantic soirée. The sweeping views from the terrace are impressive enough, but the excellent French-influenced cuisine is better still, and makes imaginative use of the island's rich produce. The Sunday brunch (3300 CFP) is a steal.

Temetiu Village MARQUESAN $$$
(☑40 91 70 60; set menu 3000 CFP; ⏱lunch & dinner by reservation) With panoramic views from the open-air dining room, a convivial atmosphere and delectable (and copious) Marquesan specialities, such as seafood or goat, this place is worth the short drive. Credit cards are accepted.

🛍 Shopping

Crafts Centre HANDICRAFTS
(⏱8am-5pm) This relatively large centre has a good selection of local woodcarvings, bone earrings, *pareu* (sarong-type garment) and tapa, and a lot of friendly ladies who enjoy chatting with newcomers.

ℹ GETTING A TATTOO

Marquesan tattooists rank among the best in the South Pacific and specialise in the Marquesas own, very distinct and increasingly popular geometric patterns. Ironically, most Marquesan tattooists are not in the Marquesas, but work either on more touristy islands in French Polynesia (especially Tahiti, Mo'orea and Bora Bora) or abroad. But no worries, you can still find good artists out here. On Nuku Hiva, ask for **Brice Haiti**; on Hiva Oa, **Louis Bonno** has a good rep. No two tattooists do the same designs. Both of these artists work to high-quality standards and use sterile needles.

ℹ Information

The best place for wi-fi besides the *pensions* and hotels is the **Salon de The Chez Eliane & Cyber Cafe**.

Banque Socredo (☑40 92 73 54; ⏱7.30-11.30am & 1.30-4pm Mon-Fri) Currency exchange. Has a 24-hour ATM.

Cyberservices (☑40 92 79 85, 87 23 22 47; VHF 11) Laundry service, wi-fi and can help yachties with formalities (call to be picked up).

Hospital (☑40 91 02 00) Small but well equipped; it's behind the mayor's office.

Post Office (⏱7am-noon & 12.30-3pm Mon-Thu, 7am-noon & 12.30-2pm Fri; 🛜) Internet and wi-fi access (with the Manaspot card, available at the counter). Has an ATM, too.

Tourist Office (☑40 92 78 93; ⏱8.30-11.30am & 2-4pm Mon-Fri) Right in the centre of town. Hands out useful brochures and sells sketch maps of most tourist sights. Opening hours are erratic.

Taaoa

This is a sweet, picturesque hamlet about 7km southwest of Atuona. Accessed by a scenic paved road, Taaoa really feels like the end of the line. It boasts a marvellous setting, with jagged green mountains as the backdrop, and an extensive archaeological site.

About 1.5km from Taaoa, high up in an uninhabited valley, **Tohua Upeke** doesn't have the impressive *tiki*, as at Iipona near Puamau, but its sheer size makes it just as interesting. Surrounded by thick overhanging trees (including huge banyan trees), it's not hard to imagine the power such sacred sites once had for the pre-Christian islanders. On arrival at the site, you will find yourself facing a vast *tohua* built on several levels. Try to find the well-preserved *tiki* more than 1m in height sitting on a platform under big banyan trees. From a distance it looks like a plain block of basalt, but as you get closer you can clearly pick out the contours of the eyes and mouth.

Puamau

Most tours visit this east-coast settlement to visit the Iipona archaeological site lying on the outskirts of the village. Puamau itself is a delightful, timeless village that occupies a coastal plain bordered by a vast amphitheatre of mountains. On the way from Atuona you'll pass through the picturesque hamlets of Motuua and Nahoe and the incredibly scenic Eiaone Bay.

Sights

★ Iipona   ARCHAEOLOGICAL SITE
(admission 300 CFP) Iipona is one of the best-preserved archaeological sites in French Polynesia. You'll be moved by its eeriness and impressed by the five monumental *tiki* – it pulsates with *mana*.

As you advance towards the first platform, you'll first notice the reclining Tiki Maki Taua Pepe, representing a woman lying on her stomach, her head stretched out and arms pointing to the sky. Experts believe she represents a woman giving birth. The petroglyphs on the pedestal represent dogs but their meaning is unknown.

Tiki Takaii, at 2.67m, is the largest ancient *tiki* in French Polynesia; it's named after a warrior chief renowned for his strength. Tiki Te Tovae E Noho is to the left of Takaii, on a lower platform. Less finely worked than the others, its upper torso is hard to make out and the head has disappeared. Note that its hands each have six fingers. Further back stands Tiki Fau Poe. Measuring about 1.8m, it is sitting with its legs stretched out, a position typical of women when they work in the fields. Experts believe it to be Takaii's wife. Tiki Manuiotaa is in complete contrast to the others: less massive, its proportions are harmonious and balanced. The hands are clearly recognisable, as is its female sex. It was decapitated, but its head has been replaced by archaeologists.

Known to ethnologists and archaeologists in the 1800s, the Iipona site was extensively restored in 1991 by French archaeologists Pierre and Marie-Noëlle Garanger-Ottino.

To reach the site from Puamau, follow the track directly back from the seafront, next to the football ground, and continue for about 1.5km. You will need to pay 300 CFP to the person who maintains and guards the site.

Tohua Pehe Kua   ARCHAEOLOGICAL SITE
On the property of the restaurant Pehekua – Chez Marie-Antoinette, shortly before the Iipona site, is a small graveyard with the tomb of the valley's last chief and his partner, who died early in the 20th century. One of the four tombs at the site is flanked by two *tiki*. You'll also find an imposing *pae pae*.

Eating

Pehekua – Chez Marie-
Antoinette   MARQUESAN $$$
(☑40 92 72 27; set menu 2700 CFP) Most visitors on a day trip from Atuona usually have lunch here (by reservation only). The dining room looks tired but the real hit is the tasty Marquesan food (fresh fish, goat, pork). The *tohua* Pehe Kua is in its grounds. You can also purchase vanilla pods. The rooms feel too neglected to be recommended. Cash only.

Hanapaaoa

It's a winding but scenic 1½-hour journey by 4WD to wild and beautiful Hanapaaoa from Atuona. The track passes the airport and then splits shortly after; the first turn-off goes to Hanaiapa and the second one leads to Hanapaaoa and Puamau. About 14km after the first turn-off, a 4WD track branches hairpinlike on the left. Soon the track snakes along the coast, offering ethereal vistas around every other bend – indigo-blue ocean, plunging cliffs and stunning bays – before reaching the hamlet of Hanapaaoa.

In Hanapaaoa, ask a local to take you to the Tiki Moe One, hidden on a hillside. One of the quirkiest statues in the Marquesas, it features a carved crown around the head and is said to be endowed with a strong *mana*. It's modestly sized at under 1m in height. According to legend, the inhabitants used to take it down to the beach every year where they bathed it and coated it with *monoi* (fragrant oil) before putting it back in place.

Hanaiapa

Picturesquely cradled by striking mountains carpeted with shrubs and coconut trees, Hanaiapa is a gem. Stretching for more than

ARCHAEOLOGY IN THE MARQUESAS

You don't need to have a PhD to appreciate the archaeological remains that are typical of the Marquesas, but a few explanations will greatly enhance your trip.

Tohua

Tohua are paved rectangular platforms with several tiers of basalt block rows on either side. The *tohua* were used as meeting places and also hosted festivals and dance performances.

Me'ae

The *me'ae* is the Marquesan equivalent of the Tahitian *marae*. *Me'ae* are religious sites built from basalt blocks placed side by side and piled up. Generally found in the valleys and away from secular places, the *me'ae* was a place of worship, burial and human sacrifice. Access was restricted to a few priests or chiefs endowed with *mana* (spiritual power). *Me'ae* were also used for cannibalistic rituals. They were generally built near a banyan, a sacred tree.

Pae Pae

Pae pae are platforms of stone blocks, on which *ha'e* (human habitations) were built from native plants and wood. The *pae pae* was divided into two sections. The front level was reserved for daily activities, while the back section, which was covered and slightly raised, served as a sleeping area. The roof was made of leaves from the *uru* (breadfruit) tree and coconut palm. Foundations of *pae pae* are ubiquitous in the Marquesas. Some modern houses are even built on them!

Tiki

Enigmatic *tiki* are carved humanlike statues, the height of which varies from a few dozen centimetres to almost 3m. Since they were generally erected on or near a holy place, experts believe *tiki* had a religious and symbolic function, possibly representing deified clan ancestors. They also marked the boundaries of places that were *tapu* (forbidden). Sculpted in the form of statues, *tiki* were also carved in bas-relief, on weapons, paddles and dugout canoes. According to many locals, some *tiki* are still possessed of *mana* and have a potential for evil that can manifest itself if they are moved or handled.

Petroglyphs

Petroglyphs are designs carved on stones. They feature sharks, turtles, whales, outrigger canoes, facial features and geometric patterns... Ancient works of art? Possibly, according to local experts.

1km along a single street, this neat and flower-filled village feels like the end of the line. The majestic Hanaiapa Bay is fringed with a pebble beach. An imposing rock sits in the middle of the bay.

Hanaiapa is a cul-de-sac, but you can walk to Hanatekuua Bay. At the entrance of the village (coming from Atuona), about 200m off the main road, to the right, you'll find some well-preserved **petroglyphs**. A big boulder sports elaborate geometric patterns. It's not easy to find (no signs); ask passers-by if you're stuck.

Arts and crafts lovers should definitely stop at **Jean & Nadine Oberlin's** (✆40 92 76 34) workshop. The couple from Alsace fell in love with Hanaiapa long ago and make lovely tapa (with a contemporary twist) as well as engraved calabashes. Look for the 'Artisanat' sign at the entrance of the village.

TAHUATA

POP 720

Just as lush but not as steep, Tahuata is Hiva Oa's shy little sister. Separated from Hiva Oa by the 4km-wide Bordelais Channel, it is the smallest inhabited island in the archipelago.

Most travellers visit Tahuata on a day tour from Hiva Oa, which is a shame as it deserves a couple of days to do it justice. So stretch that schedule and meet the bone carvers and tattoo artists at work, splash about on a deserted beach and explore the archaeological sites.

◎ Sights & Activities

The track that joins Vaitahu and Motopu in the northeast, a distance of about 17km, is suitable for walking.

★ **Hanahevane Bay** BEACH
This glorious bay is caressed by jade-green waters and is studded with a broad strand of golden sand. It's a good picnic spot (despite a number of pesky *nono*) and has shallow, calm waters and a few coral formations, making it suitable for snorkelling. It's accessible by boat only.

Vaitahu VILLAGE
This tiny village, built against the steep slopes of the central ridge, retains a few vestiges of its stormy past. On the seafront stands a modest **memorial** topped by a rusty anchor, recalling the first meeting between Admiral Dupetit-Thouars and Chief Iotete in 1838.

Near the post office is a tiny **museum** (admission free) with some archaeological items including fish hooks and stone pestles. There are no set opening hours – just ask at the *mairie* (townhall) next door.

The monumental stone **Catholic church** is opposite the seafront. Opened with great pomp and ceremony in 1988, it recalls the importance of Tahuata in the evangelisation of the archipelago. The church has beautiful stained-glass windows and some interesting woodcarvings.

Vaitahu is a good place to have a wander. Copra-drying sheds are dotted here and there, and brightly coloured traditional outrigger canoes (known locally as *vaka*) line the shore.

WORTH A TRIP

HANATEKUUA BAY

This impossibly scenic bay, fringed with a pristine stretch of white-sand beach and backed by a lovely coconut grove, is accessible only on foot or by boat. From Hanaiapa, it's a fairly easy 90-minute walk, although the path is not marked. Ask locals to show you the trailhead. After an ascent of about 20 minutes, you'll reach the **Hanahaoe Pass** (159m), from where there are superb views in all directions. From here the path veers due south along a ridge (don't take the path that descends into a small valley to the east). Some 45 minutes of relatively easy walking after leaving the pass, the bay of Hanatekuua comes into view – a fantastic sight. From here it's less than 30 minutes, downhill all the way, to the beach. Enjoy!

Hapatoni VILLAGE
Hapatoni curves around a wide bay and is accessible by boat in less than 15 minutes from Vaitahu, or by a track.

The **royal road** is the village's main attraction. Built on a dyke on the orders of Queen Vaekehu II in the 19th century, this paved road, lined with 100-year-old tamanu trees, extends along the shore.

At the promontory a path leads up to a **lookout**, with a magnificent view of the bay.

In the middle of the village there's a lovely *me'ae*. Next to it, you'll find a **church** built from stones, and a cemetery.

Hanamoenoa Bay BEACH
This quiet, sheltered bay is popular with yachties. It's fringed by a ribbon of white sand, lapped by multihued waters and backed by lush hills.

Hanamenino Bay BEACH
Another secluded bay lined with a golden-sand beach, Hanamenino is also used for picnics. Access is by boat only.

🛏 Sleeping

Every village has one or two small shops. Tahuata has only one place to stay.

Amatea PENSION **$**
(☑ 78 76 24 90, 40 92 92 84; Vaitahu; d 6000 CFP, d incl half-board per person 7500 CFP) This property is secure and well maintained, with helpful hosts and a good location near the seafront in Vaitahu. The four rooms share two bathrooms (cold water). The owners can help arrange activities and also transport to and from Tahuata.

ℹ Information

Tourist infrastructure is scarce on Tahuata. Bring cash, as there is no bank. The post office is in Vaitahu.

ℹ Getting There & Away

Tahuata is accessible only by boat (there's no landing strip) from Hiva Oa. There's no regular service, but locals frequently travel by boat between the two islands – ask around and hook onto a shared boat ride. Pension Amatea can also help arrange passage with private boats but it's much more expensive. You can also try to board the *Aranui* cargo ship at Hiva Oa.

By far the most convenient option is to take an excursion from Hiva Oa, which includes visits to Hapatoni, Vaitahu and a picnic on a beach at Hanamenino or Hanahevane for around 8500 CFP per person.

❶ Getting Around

A 17km track, accessible to 4WD vehicles, crosses the island's interior to link Vaitahu with Motopu and Vaitahu with Hapatoni. A 4WD costs 10,000 CFP for a day's hire with driver.

Hapatoni is less than 15 minutes from Vaitahu by speedboat. It costs about 6000 CFP to hire a boat between Vaitahu and Hapatoni, and 7000 CFP to 10,000 CFP between Vaitahu and Hanahevane Bay.

FATU HIVA

POP 630

As far away from the rest of the world as it's possible to get in these modern times (despite mobile phones and satellite TVs), Fatu Hiva is a marvellous 'stop the world and get off' place. When arriving by boat (there's no landing strip), expect a visual shock: wrinkled cliffs tumble into the ocean and splendid bays, including the iconic Bay of Virgins, indent the coastline.

There are only two villages, one good *pension* and one dirt track, so there are plenty of opportunities to move into slow gear. For some cultural sustenance, a couple of giant petroglyphs – the biggest in French Polynesia – hidden in the forest beckon.

It's a bit challenging to get to Fatu Hiva, but for travellers who relish the idea of being marooned for a few days, this hard-to-reach island way off most people's radar (bar yachties) is hard to beat.

◎ Sights

Omoa   VILLAGE

Time moves at a crawl in Omoa. The most striking monument is the Catholic church, with its red roof, white facade and slender spire. It makes a colourful scene on Sunday morning, when it's bursting at the seams with a devout congregation neatly dressed and belting out rousing *himene* (hymns).

Omoa is famous for its two giant petroglyphs, which are in two different locations. The first site is easily accessed after a 10-minute walk from the main road (ask around) and features a huge fish (probably a dorado) as well as a few small anthropomorphic designs inscribed on big basaltic boulders. The second site is a 20-minute walk from Chez Lionel Cantois. It has a clearly outlined whale incised on a big slab – an eerie sight. To get there, you'll need a guide (Lionel will be happy to show you the site).

Hanavave   VILLAGE

Hanavave boasts a splendid setting, at the mouth of a steep-sided valley, best enjoyed from the sea (lucky yachties!). When the setting sun bounces purple halos off the towering basaltic cones of Baie des Vierges, with a cluster of yachts at anchor, it's a hallucinatory wonderland.

Truth is, these cones resemble giant phalluses protruding out of the ocean. This risqué natural tableau was originally (and aptly) named Baie des Verges in French (Bay of Penises). Outraged, the missionaries promptly added a redeeming 'i' to make the name Baie des Vierges (Bay of Virgins).

There's a small, sober church with an elaborate wooden altar in the village, as well as a waterfall at the end of the valley (ask for directions).

North of Hanavave, the stunning Vaipo Cave is carved into black cliffs. It's accessible only by boat.

🏃 Activities

Most activities on Fatu Hiva are of the DIY variety, including walking and horse riding. Follow the 17km-long track that links Omoa to Hanavave via the interior for a four-hour walk that's not too difficult and you can't get lost. The first part of the walk goes up the Omoa Valley along a cliff-top path with sweeping views over the village below. The trail then crosses through the island's interior. It's a steep descent to Hanavave and there's not much shade along the way, but the views of the village and the dramatic coastline are well worth the effort. Horse-riding along the track is also possible – ask at your *pension*.

Fatu Hiva

MARQUESAN HANDICRAFTS

If there is one place in French Polynesia where it's really possible to spend some cash, it's the Marquesas. *Tiki*, pestles, *umete* (bowls), adzes, spears, clubs, fish hooks and other items are carved from rosewood, *tou* (dark, hard-grained wood), bone or volcanic stone. These treasures are pieces of art, items you will keep for a lifetime. Less expensive buys include seed necklaces and *umu hei,* an assortment of fragrant plant material such as ylang-ylang, vanilla, pieces of pineapple covered in sandalwood powder, and various other fruits and plants, held together with a plant fibre. Fatu Hiva prides itself on being the only island in French Polynesia to have perpetuated the manufacture of tapa (cloth made from beaten bark and decorated with traditional designs). Before visiting the Marquesas, be sure to check the customs regulations in your home country regarding things like woodcarvings or tapa.

In most villages there is a small *fare artisanal* where you can shop around. They may open only when requested or when the *Aranui* is in port. It's also well worth approaching craftspeople directly. Some work is done to order only, so if you stay several days on an island it's worth making a visit as soon as you arrive.

Bring enough cash because you cannot pay by credit card. Prices may be relatively high, but they're still lower than in Pape'ete and are well worth it for the time and artistic effort put into the works. Expect to pay at least 2000 CFP for a small tapa piece (up to 15,000 CFP for a piece 1m long), 3000 CFP for a small 15cm *tiki* (and up to 100,000 CFP for a large one) and 5000 CFP for a bowl or plate of about 50cm. Bargaining is not a Pacific tradition so don't expect to be able to beat the prices down very much.

🛏 Sleeping

Chez Lionel Cantois   PENSION $
(☑ 78 70 03 71, 40 92 81 84; chezlionel@mail.pf; Omoa; s/d incl breakfast 4500/6500 CFP, bungalow s/d incl breakfast 6500/9500 CFP; @) Basking in familial warmth, this *pension* at the far end of Omoa has an air of *Little House on the Prairie*. Lionel, who is from Normandy and who is a mine of local information (his English is passable), can take you virtually anywhere on the island, while his Marquesan wife Bernadette is a good cook (dinner from 1500 CFP).

The bungalow with bathroom (hot water) in the manicured garden is comfy and cosy, but if funds are short, the two rooms in the owners' house are a less expensive alternative (the walls don't make it to the ceilings, though). Not a bad place to get stuck on Fatu Hiva (fear not, Lionel will help you arrange transport back to Hiva Oa). Transfers to the quay cost 1000 CFP return.

🛍 Shopping

Fatu Hiva is renowned for its tapa and *umu hei*, carved coconuts and woodcarvings.

ℹ Information

Bring a stash of cash – there's no bank on the island and credit cards are not accepted. There is a post office in Omoa.

ℹ Getting There & Away

Fatu Hiva is the most difficult island to get to in the Marquesas, but sorting out transport is manageable if you're flexible.

In Hiva Oa, find out if boat charters to Fatu Hiva are being organised during your stay and you may be able to share the costs. There's no regular service; it all depends on the needs of locals (for instance, going back to Fatu Hiva after medical consultation in Atuona).

Another option is to hop on the *Aranui* cargo ship when it stops at Atuona, Omoa or Hanavave, although they are getting increasingly sticky about hop-on passangers. If you've got the dough, you can charter a private *bonitier* (about 50,000 CFP for the whole boat). Also contact Lionel at Chez Lionel Cantois, who's well clued up on the subject.

The crossing between Hiva Oa and Fatu Hiva takes anything between three and five hours depending on conditions and can be very uncomfortable if the sea is choppy.

ℹ Getting Around

The only dirt road is 17km long and links Hanavave with Omoa, but it's quicker (and cheaper) to hire a speedboat to travel between the two villages (about 7000 CFP per boat).

Enquire at your *pension* about hiring a 4WD; expect to pay 15,000 CFP a day with driver.

The Australs & the Gambier Archipelago

Includes ➜

The Australs............... 194
Rurutu 194
Tubuai.........................197
Raivavae..................... 198
The Gambier
Archipelago................ 201
Mangareva 201

Best Places to Stay

➡ Manotel (p196)

➡ Teautamatea (p196)

➡ Raivavae Tama (p199)

➡ Maro'i (p202)

Best Outdoor Experiences

➡ Walking to the top of Mt Hiro (p199)

➡ Exploring caves (p195) in Rurutu

➡ Swimming off Motu Piscine (p198)

➡ Lagoon touring in Tubuai (p197)

➡ Horse riding (p197) on the ridges of Rurutu

Why Go?

Isolated and straddling the Tropic of Capricorn, the magnificent and pristine Austral Islands are arguably French Polynesia's most underrated destination. The climate here is temperate, but everything else befitting a tropical paradise is here: flower-filled jungles, sharp peaks, outrageously blue water and genuinely friendly people. The islands here have had less of a history with Europeans and less influx from the outside world, so have kept their culture alive.

If, after visiting the Australs, you still feel the urge for more off-the-beaten-track adventures, consider travelling to the Gambier, where visitors are an absolute rarity. All the makings of an island holiday paradise can be found in this jaw-droppingly beautiful archipelago, but it's so far away (about 1700km southeast from Tahiti) and expensive to get to that it remains one of the best-kept secrets in French Polynesia.

When to Go

➡ During the dry season (May to October), the climate is significantly cooler than in other parts of the country.

➡ With average daily temperatures around 20°C, which can drop to a low of 15°C at night, the June to September period is not the best time to visit if you're hoping to laze around on a beach, but is an ideal time for hiking.

➡ The islands are hottest in January and February.

➡ The Australs have two important religious festivals: the Tere, which is held in early January, and the Me, which is celebrated in May.

➡ The whale-watching season runs from July or August to October.

THE AUSTRALS

Fly south towards the Tropic of Capricorn to find the blustery Austral Archipelago, where it's cool enough to grow peaches yet warm enough for bananas, coconut palms and turquoise, coral-laden lagoons. On these outrageously fertile islands, you'll find some of the most authentic Polynesian culture in all of French Polynesia. Best of all, they are wonderfully varied, from the limestone caverns of Rurutu and the Bora Bora–like lagoon of Raivavae to the windy bays of Tubuai and the alluring coastline of Rimatara.

What you shouldn't expect, though, is a thriving nightlife. These are quiet islands. There are no resorts, just a smattering of welcoming family-run guesthouses where visitors can sample delicious local-style meals and genuinely interact with their hosts.

History

The Australs were the last of the Polynesian islands to be settled; the first arrivals were believed to have come from Tahiti between AD 1000 and AD 1300. The islands came to European attention during the second half of the 18th century.

Apart from a colourful chapter in the *Bounty* saga, when the mutineers unsuccessfully tried to establish themselves on Tubuai, contact with Europeans and the Western world was limited until the late 19th and 20th centuries. This long period, during which English missionaries (or more frequently their native representatives) held sway, has ensured that Protestantism remains strong to this day.

Rurutu

POP 2400

The island's geology makes it unique; Rurutu is one of the South Pacific's largest raised atolls *(makatea)*. Vertical limestone cliffs pockmarked with caves line the coast, while the volcanic interior is a fertile, mind-bogglingly abundant jungle. While there's very little fringing reef, there are a few

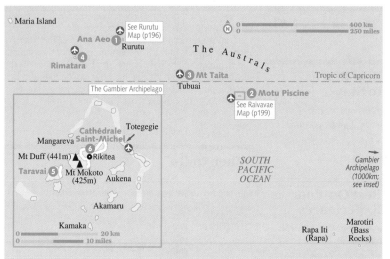

The Australs & The Gambier Highlights

❶ Exploring the surreal limestone cave of **Ana Aeo** (p195) on Rurutu.

❷ *Motu*-hopping in the radiant Raivavae lagoon and picnicking on idyllic **Motu Piscine** (p198).

❸ Scaling **Mt Taita** (p197) and feasting your eyes on 360-degree views of the lagoon.

❹ Watching the magnificent Rimatara lorikeet in its natural habitat on **Rimatara** (p200).

❺ Taking a lagoon and island tour to **Taravai** (p201) in the Gambier.

❻ Marvelling at the imposing **Cathédrale Saint-Michel** (p201) of Rikitea.

white-sand beaches where you can flake out. Feeling active? Various activities and lots of unique natural attractions will keep you busy.

⊙ Sights

Rurutu has a circumference of about 32km, but the road cuts inland through the mountains, making the island feel much bigger. Apart from the Moerai to Marae Tararoa section, which is practically flat, the circle-island route is very hilly.

Of the three main coastal villages, **Moerai** is the largest. A sealed road runs about a third of the way around the island, linking the airport with Moerai and the village of **Auti**. Another sealed road climbs over the centre of the island to link Moerai with **Avera**, the third main village.

Ana Aeo   CAVE
This cave, with its massive, oozy-looking stalactites and stalagmites, is the most stunning on the island. It's 500m north of the Teautamatea *pension*; there's a signposted track going to the right that leads to the cave.

Ana Tane Uapoto   CAVE
On the eastern outskirts of the village of Moerai, near Arei Point, you'll find this large roadside cavern with stalactites and stalagmites. Traditionally this cave was used to salt (for preservation) and divide whale meat among the islanders.

Te One Roa   BEACH
Beach bums in search of a place to wallow will make a beeline for this picture-perfect, white-sand beach on the western coast. Here the lagoon is deep enough for a proper swim. There's no sign – it's about 200m south of the Teautamatea *pension*.

Toataratara Point   BEACH
This is a sweet, picturesque spot at the southern end of the island. You'll find a series of photogenic little coves fringed with white-sand beaches. A great spot for a picnic.

🏃 Activities

Walking
The interior is perfect for walking. A network of tracks criss-crosses the Tetuanui Plateau (200m), leading to the peaks of Taatioe (389m), Manureva (385m) and Teape (359m) – you'll be rewarded with cracking views. You don't need a guide if you stay on the main tracks.

Reti Mii   HIKING
(📞87 22 12 45; 3000 CFP) Reti Mii is a professional guide who specialises in half-day hiking tours and cave tours to some otherwise hard-to-access caves north of Auti.

Whale-Watching
The whales come to Rurutu from around late July to mid-October to reproduce before heading back to the icy waters of the Antarctic. There are no promises that you will see any (it's not uncommon to experience a few weeks in a row with no sightings), but the best chance of seeing the whales is in August and September – check with the local operators.

Rurutu actually has fewer of these mammals visiting its coastlines each year than Mo'orea or Tahiti, but what makes this an ideal place to see them is the absence of a lagoon, which causes the whales to come closer to shore. The incredible visibility makes the experience all the more impressive.

Whales can often be seen from the two whale-watching platforms that have been built by the road between the airport and Auti. You can also take a whale-watching and whale-swim tour on offer from August to October. Be aware that the water may be chilly and the sea quite rough.

Tareparepa Baleines   WILDLIFE WATCHING
(📞87 79 48 86, 87 25 02 62; half-day tours 8500 CFP) A well-trained operator who has plenty of experience. Small groups only.

Toatai Baleines   WILDLIFE WATCHING
(📞40 94 04 23, 87 26 78 46; half-day tours 7500-8500 CFP) Offers professional whale-watching tours. Small groups only.

Rurutu

N 0 ——————— 2 km
0 ——————— 1 mile

Tétuanui Plateau
Ana Aeo
Tiare Hinano
MOERAI
Teautamatea
Snack Piareare
Arei Pt
Viriamu
Banque Socredo
Te One Roa
Ana Tane Uapoto
Mt Manureva (385m)
Mt Teape (359m)
Mt Taatioe (389m)
Manotel
PEVA
AVERA
SOUTH PACIFIC OCEAN
AUTI
Mt Erai (289m)
PAPARAI
Mt Rairiri (263m)
(160m)
NAAIROA
Toataratara Point

Tours

The two *pensions*, Manotel and Teautamatea, offer worthwhile full-day island tours for around 5000 CFP, usually with guides who are very knowledgeable about the history and flora of the island.

Sleeping & Eating

Manotel BUNGALOW $$
(40 93 02 25; www.lemanotel.com; bungalows s/d incl half-board 11,500/16,400 CFP;) Run by a French-Rurutu couple, Manotel has seven pretty bungalows with fans, good bathrooms and particularly inviting terraces; it's across the road from a long stretch of white beach (not suitable for swimming due to the fringing reef) about 3km south of Moerai. The garden is blooming with colours and the owner runs reputable island tours.

Bikes are available for hire. There's a 20% discount outside the whale-watching season. Airport transfers are 1000 CFP return and credit cards are accepted.

Teautamatea PENSION $$
(87 70 34 65, 40 93 02 93; www.teautamatea. blogspot.com; s/d incl half-board 9000/13,800 CFP;) A more congenial place you'll be hard-pressed to find. Viriamu is from Rurutu, his wife Elin is Welsh, and you'll get the best of both worlds. There are three clean, well-swept and uncluttered rooms. They are in the owners' home but offer enough privacy.

It's in a stunning setting in front of a *marae* and just across the road from one of Rurutu's best beaches. Gourmet palates, you're in luck: Elin will treat you with the freshest island ingredients at dinner. Great breakfast, too, with homemade tropical jams. Airport transfers are free. Cash only.

Snack Piareare TAHITIAN $
(40 94 04 95; Moerai; mains 1200-1300 CFP; 11.30am-2pm Mon-Fri, 5-9pm Sun) The decor is nonexistent at this no-frills eatery hidden behind a gate right across from the boat quay in Moerai, but the food is seriously good. The menu is limited to a couple of daily specials, but they're savoury and sizzling hot value.

Tiare Hinano CHINESE $
(40 94 05 00; Moerai; mains 1100-1500 CFP; 10.30am-2pm & 5-8pm Tue-Sat, 5-8pm Sun) The vast dining room might not be terribly Polynesian, but it's a great place to sample Chinese staples as well as local favourites.

Information

Banque Socredo (Moerai; 7.30-11.30am & 1.30-4pm Mon-Fri) Changes major currencies and has an ATM outside.

Post Office (Moerai; 7am-noon & 1-3.30pm Mon-Thu, to 2.30pm Fri;) Internet and wi-fi access (with the Manaspot network). Has an outdoor ATM.

Getting There & Around

Air Tahiti (40 86 42 42; www.airtahiti. pf) flies between Rurutu and Tahiti (23,600 CFP, 1½ hours, three to five flights weekly), Tubuai (13,000 CFP, 40 minutes, once or twice weekly), and Rimatara (10,800 CFP, once weekly, 35 minutes). For Raivavae, you'll need to change on Tubuai.

If you want to combine several islands, it's cheaper to buy an 'Australs Pass', or you can also add an 'Australs extension', which includes Rurutu, Rimatara, Raivavae and Tubuai to some Air Tahiti passes (p234).

The cargo ship **Tuhaa Pae IV** (p237) makes two to three trips a month between Pape'ete and Rurutu.

If you've booked accommodation you'll be picked up at the airport. The best way to get around the island is to take a tour.

Tubuai

POP 2300

With its spreading, fertile plains, low hills and temperate climate, Tubuai is the fruit bowl and vegie patch of French Polynesia. Although it lies in the shadow of Raivavae and Rurutu, this very scenic island is blessed with sandy beaches, a string of idyllic *motu* (islets), a fantastic lagoon and a few archaeological sites. Two mountain ranges slope down to the flat plains by the sea and a low-lying central region bisects the two.

⊙ Sights

Marae Raitoro, Haunarei & Harii ARCHAEOLOGICAL SITE

More than 200 *marae* have been found in Tubuai and the few that have been cleared are among the most fascinating in the country. Raitoro and Haunarei Marae are two connected *marae* that were for birthing and umbilical-cord-cutting ceremonies respectively. Nearby is Marae Harii, which once served as a meeting place for chiefs. It also has several upright stones. You'll need a guide to find this archaeological site.

Fort George HISTORIC SITE

The *Bounty* is remembered by a sign on the northeastern corner of the island marking the site of Fort George, where the mutineers attempted to set up camp for two months in 1789.

🏃 Activities

Lagoon excursions offered by the *pensions* allow you to get out to those idyllic *motu*. They cost anything between 5000 CFP and 7000 CFP per person, with a picnic provided. The most scenic spots, including the sandy spit of Motu One and the paradisiacal Motu Toena, which is fringed by white beaches, are at the northeastern end of the lagoon.

Mt Taita HIKING

Mt Taita (422m) commands sensational views of the lagoon and the island. You don't need a guide to climb up it – the route is signposted along the cross-island road and the trail is well maintained. It's mostly shady. Count on three hours return.

👉 Tours

Wilson Doom CULTURAL TOUR

(📞87 73 10 02, 40 93 22 40; per person 3200 CFP) For history buffs who can speak French, very

HORSE RIDING

Viriamu (📞87 70 34 65, 40 93 02 93; 2/3hr rides 5000/7500 CFP), from the Teautamatea pension, leads superb horse-riding excursions, suitable for all levels (children are welcome). The three-hour ride, during which you'll pass stunning viewpoints in Ruturu's interior and clip-clop along the lagoon on the western coast, is truly enchanting. For experienced riders, the ultimate is a two-day excursion that takes in the eerie landscape south of the island (15,000 CFP per day) – book well in advance.

interesting *marae* tours (3200 CFP) are run by effervescent Wilson Doom from Wipa Lodge. They take three hours and visit the best-preserved *marae*.

🛏 Sleeping & Eating

There is one supermarket in Mataura, plus a scattering of smaller stores around the island.

Toena BUNGALOW $

(📞40 95 04 12, 87 73 81 84; www.toena.pf; s/d without bathroom incl half-board 5000/10,000 CFP, bungalows s/d incl half-board 7500/15,000 CFP; 📶) Perched on a small plateau in the hills that dominate the eastern part of the island, this *pension* feels a bit isolated, but it's the perfect place to decompress. The two bungalows are very neat and tidy and have stupendous lagoon views. If funds are short, there are also two plain rooms with shared bathroom in the owners' home.

Bikes and cars are available for hire, and airport transfers are included. Cash only.

Mara'ai – Le Spot BUNGALOW $

(📞40 95 08 32, 87 73 62 20; maraai.le.spot@gmail.com; Tamatoa; d/tr 3600/5400 CFP) A very simple but well-maintained plank-wood

BASKETRY IN THE AUSTRALS

The Australs are renowned for their mats, hats and baskets woven from pandanus. There are a few artisanal shops on Rurutu, Raivavae and Tubuai, including the ones at the airports. On Rimatara, locals will point you to families who produce such items.

MOTU PISCINE

Raivavae's stunning lagoon, brimming with marine life and ringed by ironwood-covered *motu*, is one of the treasures of the South Pacific. Motu Piscine (Motu Swimming Pool; Motu Vaiamanu) is the best-known *motu*, fringed with white beaches and divided from its neighbour by a glassy turquoise channel that's teeming with tropical fish. Fa-bu-lous. All *pensions* can arrange a lagoon tour, including a picnic, on Motu Piscine.

bungalow with an outside bathroom (hot water). It can sleep three people – a good deal for budgeteers. Great news if you don't understand French: Ina, who has lived in California, speaks good English. Free kayaks and bikes. Airport transfers cost 2000 CFP return per carload. Cash only (euros and US dollars are accepted).

Wipa Lodge   BUNGALOW $$
(☑40 93 22 40, 87 73 10 02; maletdoom@mail.pf; bungalows s/d incl half-board 13,500/18,500 CFP; 🛜) This well-run *pension* has five bungalows that were built in late 2015. They're modern, comfortable and well equipped, and the garden setting is very pleasant. Best of all, there's a great beach across the road. Airport

THE TERE & THE ME FESTIVALS

The Australs have two important religious festivals: the **Tere**, which is celebrated in early January in Rururu and Rimatara to celebrate the new year; and the **Me**, which is held in May (the three first weekends) in Rururu, Rimatara and, to a lesser extent, Raivavae.

Visitors are welcome; it's a great way to learn more about local customs and culture as all the population gathers to pray, sing and partake in a traditional meal. For the Tere and the Me, men collect taro – a staple throughout the South Pacific – in the taro fields scattered around the island. Lots of starchy taro will be used for the *ahimaa* (cooking pit), along with other tubers, pigs and fish. If you plan to attend one of these festivals, it's best to book your accommodation well in advance.

transfers are 1200 CFP return and there are cars for hire. Bikes are free. Cash only.

All activities can be organised, including *marae* tours (p197) run by Wilson, the owner. His wife Gisèle does a good job of cooking delicious French-inspired meals. It's on the coast west of Mataura.

Mara'ai – Le Spot   INTERNATIONAL $
(☑40 95 08 32, 87 73 62 20; maraai.le.spot@gmail.com; Tamatoa; mains 1100-1500 CFP; ◷11am-9pm, closed 2 months Jun-Sep; 🛜) Run by French Hervé and his Tahitian wife Ina, Mara'ai – Le Spot is the only independent restaurant on Tubuai. With a sand floor and a palm-frond roof, this is a cool and rustic place for a drink or a relaxed meal any time of the day. Tuck into flavoursome fish and meat dishes, pizzas, pasta, burgers and salads at puny prices.

It's in the village of Tamatoa, southeast of the island.

ⓘ Information

Mataura, on the north coast about 4km east of the airport, is the main village.
Banque Socredo (Mataura; ◷8am-noon & 1.30-4pm Mon-Fri) Changes major currencies and has an ATM outside.
Post Office (OPT; Mataura; ◷7.30am-noon & 12.30-3.30pm Mon-Thu, to 2.30pm Fri; 🛜) Internet and wi-fi access (with the Manaspot network). Has a 24-hour ATM.

ⓘ Getting There & Around

Tubuai is 600km south of Tahiti. **Air Tahiti** (☑40 86 42 42; www.airtahiti.pf) flies between Tubuai and Tahiti (26,000 CFP, 1½ hours, three to five flights weekly), Rururu (13,000 CFP, 45 minutes, twice weekly) and Raivavae (12,800 CFP, 40 minutes, once or twice weekly). For Rimatara you'll need to change on Rururu.

You can also add an 'Australs extension', which includes Rururu, Rimatara, Raivavae and Tubuai to some Air Tahiti passes (p234), or buy an 'Australs Pass'.

The cargo ship **Tuhaa Pae IV** (p237) makes two to three trips a month between Pape'ete and the Australs.

If you've booked accommodation, you'll be picked up at the airport. The two *pensions* have cars for clients' use.

Raivavae

POP 977

Visitors to Raivavae (ra-ee-va-va-eh) rave that this is what Bora Bora must have been

Raivavae

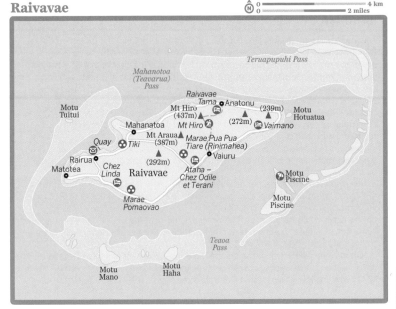

like 50 or even 75 years ago. It's a paradise not only because of the sweeping blue lagoon, idyllic white-sand *motu* and the green mountainous interior dominated by square-topped Mt Hiro (437m), but also because the warm Polynesian welcome and traditional way of life you'll find here are the most authentic and heart-warming in all of French Polynesia. Amazingly, the island receives only a small trickle of tourists.

⊙ Sights & Activities

All *pensions* offer lagoon tours and excursions to *motu* (5500 CFP to 7000 CFP) plus a tour of the island by car (about 1500 CFP).

Although the lagoon is the main highlight, Raivavae also has a few archaeological sites that are worth a peek.

Tiki
ARCHAEOLOGICAL SITE

The only remaining *tiki* (carved humanlike statue) on the island stands in a private garden just to the west of the village of Mahanatoa. About 1m in height, it has highly stylised hands and chest as well as clearly outlined eyes. Its curved lips suggest a smile. It's not signed; ask around or look for the small supermarket Magasin Florès Louise – it's 50m to the west.

Marae Pomaovao
ARCHAEOLOGICAL SITE

Across the road from the airport, this *marae* (traditional sacred site) features a large paved platform and a massive upright stone standing more than 2m high. According to legend, this stone was used to measure the height of warriors.

Marae Pua Pua Tiare
ARCHAEOLOGICAL SITE

(Rinimahea) This well-maintained *marae* can be found about 1km from the Vaiuru entrance of the cross-island road (ask for directions as it's not easy to find). It features large upright stones that enclose a paved area.

Mt Hiro
HIKING

It's a fairly tough climb to reach Mt Hiro (437m), the impressive rocky wall that looms above the eastern part of the island, but the 360-degree panorama at the summit is well worth the effort. There are two access trails; one starts from Anatonu and the other from Vaiuru. Allow three hours for the return trip.

The path is relatively well marked, but it's best to go with a guide – contact your *pension* for securing one (about 3500 CFP).

⊨ Sleeping & Eating

Raivavae Tama
BUNGALOW $

(☑ 40 95 42 52, 87 31 24 73; www.raivavaetama. com; Anatonu; d incl half-board per person 6500

RIMATARA

This low-key island, blissfully isolated about 600km south of Tahiti and 150km west of Rurutu, remains something of a 'secret'. Here time moves at a crawl, the atmosphere is supremely relaxed, and the traditional way of life is among the most authentic in French Polynesia. What sets its apart from most other Polynesian islands is its unique geology. Like Rurutu, Rimatara is a raised atoll, or *makatea* – a hilly, volcanic island walled in by a fringing reef (a fossilised coral limestone shell) and circled by beautiful white-sand beaches. The circle-island road that connects the three villages is fun for exploring by bike.

Air Tahiti began servicing the island in 2006, but it has yet to register on the tourist radar. The exception is birders, who visit in search of the exquisitely coloured Rimatara lorikeet and the more discreet Rimatara reed-warbler. Even for non-birdwatchers, it's an amazing experience to walk through the forest and sight a pair of eye-catching lorikeets perched on a banana leaf.

Run by retired school teacher Aline Kato, **La Perruche Rouge** (☑ 87 74 66 13, 40 94 42 88; www.laperrucherouge.com; bungalows s/d incl half-board 9900/14,000 CFP; ☏) eases you right into the peaceful lifestyle of Rimatara. The four bungalows are soothingly positioned on a hillside just above the owner's home, near the airstrip. They're bright and come with private terraces, and two of them afford cracking ocean views. Dinners are copious and come in for warm praise.

Various tours and activities can be organised, including visits to a taro plantation, bird-watching, pandanus-weaving courses and guided walks. Cash only. **Air Tahiti** (☑ 40 86 42 42; www.airtahiti.pf) flies to/from Pape'ete three times a week (27,500 CFP, 1¾ hours).

CFP, bungalows s/d incl half-board 8500/15,000 CFP; ☏) Three rustic, coconut-thatched bungalows with bathrooms sit on a skinny stretch of white sand, with fabulous lagoon views; there are also two boxy rooms with shared bathroom in the family's home (which is across the road) and two comfortable bungalows in the garden at the back. The local-style food and welcome here are extraordinary and excellent English is spoken.

Kayaks and bikes are available for hire (1000 CFP) and wi-fi costs 1000 CFP for the duration of your stay. Credit cards are accepted.

Chez Linda BUNGALOW $
(☑ 40 95 44 25, 87 78 80 24; www.pension-lindaraivavae.pf; s/d incl half-board 8500/12,500 CFP, bungalows s/d incl half-board 10,600/14,000 CFP; ☏) This is a reputable place with four Polynesian-style bungalows with private bathrooms and two adjoining tiny rooms at the back of the property. Food is a highlight, with delicious traditional dishes served at dinner. The lagoon is just across the road but swimming is not great, with shallow, murky waters. Bikes are available for hire and kayaks are free. Cash only.

Ataha – Chez Odile et Terani BUNGALOW $
(☑ 40 95 43 69, 87 28 92 35; www.pensionataha. com; Vaiuru; s/d incl half-board 8600/13,200 CFP)

Ataha has a spacious room in the owner's house (with its own private entrance) as well as seven adjoining rooms in a separate building; they're small and lack character but get the job done. Odile and Terani, the affable owners, serve excellent *Ma'a Tahiti* (traditional Tahitian food). The lagoon is just across the road but there's no beach and swimming is poor.

Kayaks and bikes are complimentary. For a back-to-nature escape, consider spending a night or two at Ataha Sauvage, a rustic hut on stilts situated alone on a *motu* of white sand. No internet access. Cash only.

Vaimano BUNGALOW $$
(☑ 40 95 43 03, 87 20 42 33; vaimano@outlook. fr; bungalows s/d incl half-board 12,000/22,000 CFP) Owner Clarisse is a respected *tifaifai* (quilts) maker and rents four well-appointed bungalows that are perched on a hillside and offer memorable views of the lagoon. There's no swimmable beach nearby, but guests can make use of the kayaks to explore the lagoon – Motu Piscine is within paddling distance. No internet access. Cash only.

❶ Information

Rairua, on the north coast, is the main village. There's only one ATM on the island and credit cards are only accepted at one *pension* – bring enough cash.

TARAVAI, AUKENA & AKAMARU

Got a fantasy of a deserted island with idyllic beaches? You've just pictured Taravai, Aukena and Akamaru. They not only fit the picture-postcard ideal, but they also have some fascinating historic buildings. For tours, ask at your *pension*.

Taravai had a population of 2000 when the missionaries arrived, but today only about five people live here. The 1868 Église Saint-Gabriel (Church of St Gabriel), with its gorgeous shell decoration, is well maintained and has a picturesque arch that welcomes you from the shore.

Aukena has reminders of the missionary period, including the hexagonal lookout tower, still used as a landmark, the former seminary and the lime kiln. The white-sand beach leading to the tower is one of the prettiest in all of French Polynesia.

Akamaru was the first island to be visited by Laval, and his majestic 1841 Église Nôtre-Dame-de-la-Paix (Our Lady of Peace Church) still stands on the sparsely inhabited island. Groups from Mangareva occasionally come over to hold services.

Post Office (OPT; Rairua; ⊘7am-noon & 12.30-3pm Mon-Thu, to 2pm Fri; 🛜) Internet and wi-fi access (with the Manaspot network). Has a 24-hour ATM.

ℹ Getting There & Around

Raivavae is 650km southeast of Tahiti and 200km southeast of Tubuai. **Air Tahiti** (📞40 86 42 42; www.airtahiti.pf) operates flights to/from Pape'ete three days a week (28,500 CFP, two hours), sometimes via Tubuai (13,000 CFP, 40 minutes). You can also add an 'Australs extension', which includes Rurutu, Rimatara, Raivavae and Tubuai to some Air Tahiti passes (p235), or buy an 'Australs Pass'.

The cargo ship **Tuhaa Pae IV** (p237) makes two trips a month between Pape'ete and the Australs.

Pensions provide free airport transfers and bike hire. Cycling the flat 22km of coast road is easy.

THE GAMBIER ARCHIPELAGO

POP 1421

The geology here is unique: one reef, complete with sandy *motu*, encircles a small archipelago of lush high islands dotting an exquisitely blue lagoon that's as clear as air. Adding to the allure are some of the eeriest and most interesting post-European structures in the country, a legacy of the Gambier's history as the cradle of Polynesian Catholicism. Today the archipelago is known for producing some of the finest and most colourful pearls in Polynesia.

History

The Gambiers were populated in three waves from the 10th to the 13th centuries, and they may have been a stopping point on the Polynesian migration routes to New Zealand or Easter Island.

The Sacred Heart Congregation, the first Catholic mission in French Polynesia, was established here in 1834 and Father Honoré Laval and his assistant François Caret became virtual rulers of the archipelago. Laval ran the islands like his own personal fiefdom until persistent complaints about his behaviour led to his exile on Tahiti in 1871.

Moruroa lies just 400km northwest of Mangareva and between 1966 and 1974, when above-ground nuclear tests were conducted, the population of the island was herded into fallout shelters (now demolished) if winds threatened to blow towards the Gambier.

Mangareva

Most of the population lives on Mangareva, in and around the minuscule, fruit-tree-fringed village of Rikitea.

◎ Sights & Activities

All the *pensions* can help organise day-long lagoon tours for 8000 CFP to 9000 CFP per person.

Cathédrale Saint-Michel CATHEDRAL
(Rikitea) Fully restored in 2011, the imposing Cathedral of St Michael was built between 1839 and 1848 and was Laval's most ambitious project. It makes a colourful scene on

Sunday morning, when it is bursting at the seams with a devout congregation singing moving *himene* (hymns).

Couvent Rouru   RUIN
(Rikitea) The eerily beautiful remains of Rouru Convent, which once housed 60 nuns, stands south of the cemetery and is quickly becoming engulfed by weeds. It's said that Laval hid the entire female population of the island in the convent whenever whaling ships paid a visit.

Motu Tauna   ISLAND
Picture this: there's a white-sand beach lapped by turquoise waters, palm trees leaning over the shore, and great snorkelling options. This deserted islet is certainly Mangareva's most idyllic spot. All *pensions* can arrange picnics on Motu Tauna.

Mt Duff   HIKING
A hiking trail to Mt Duff is signposted about 2km north of Rikitea and it's about a 1½-hour climb to the peak (441m) from this point. It's a pretty steep ascent, but nearly the entire route is shaded. You'll be rewarded with cardiac-arresting views.

🍴 Sleeping & Eating

Maro'i   BUNGALOW $
(☑87 70 36 55, 40 97 84 44; www.pensionmaroi. com; bungalows 1-3 people 8000-9500 CFP; 🛜) Mangareva's best option lies in a super-quiet property edging a lovely bay on the opposite side of the island from Rikitea. There are four immaculate bungalows laid out on a grassy, fruit tree–studded lawn fringed with a narrow white beach. They can sleep three to four people and are suitable for families. Free bikes and kayaks.

Marie and her husband, the warm and happy owners, serve excellent meals (2700 CFP) in an open-air dining room overlooking the water and can organise lagoon tours and a visit to their pearl farm. Credit cards are accepted.

Chez Bianca & Benoît   BUNGALOW $$
(☑40 97 83 76; www.chezbiancaetbenoit.pf; Rikitea; s/d incl half-board 11,100/17,000 CFP, bungalows s/d incl half-board 13,300/17,000 CFP; 🛜) You have two options here: one of four bungalows with bamboo-woven walls and decks with views over Rikitea and the lagoon, or four immaculate yet sterile rooms in a separate building. Food is a definite plus, with copious meals using local ingredients (*korori* salad, anyone?). It's perched

on a small hill, about 1km north of Rikitea. Credit cards are accepted.

Chez Teava   TAHITIAN $
(☑40 97 82 51; Rikitea; mains 1000-1500 CFP; ⏲11am-1pm & 5.30-8pm Mon-Sat, 5.30-8pm Sun) This is Rikitea's best spot for lunch or dinner. Local ingredients and freshly caught seafood are the staples of the simple menu. Voluminous sandwiches (from 200 CFP) too. Near the cathedral.

Pizza Atomic   PIZZA $
(☑40 97 83 09; Rikitea; mains 1000-1300 CFP; ⏲5.15-9pm Fri-Sun) Serves glowing-hot pizzas to eat in or take away. The Rumarei, with cheese and *korori* (the adductor muscle of the oyster), is particularly original.

Snack Jojo   TAHITIAN $
(☑87 76 36 24; Rikitea; mains 1000-1500 CFP; ⏲11am-2pm Mon-Sat, 6.30-9pm Fri-Sun; 🛜) It's hardly haute cuisine at this modest joint, but the fine choice of sandwiches (from 400 CFP) alongside the mainstream Tahitian dishes provide easy midday or evening fuel. The owners also rent a spacious, well-appointed bungalow (one/two people including half-board 9900/15,000 CFP) at the back of the property, right on the water's edge (but there's no beach). Credit cards are accepted.

🛍 Shopping

**Centre Educatif de
Développement**   HANDICRAFTS
(CED; ☑40 97 82 89; Rikitea; ⏲8-11.30am & 1-3pm Mon-Fri) To check out Mangareva's famous mother-of-pearl carvings, head to this venture, just downhill to the left from the intersection above Cathédrale Saint-Michel, where you can watch students as they engrave shells. You can buy finished products including small pendants and barrettes at the on-site shop.

ℹ Getting There & Around

AIR
Mangareva is 1700km southeast of Tahiti. **Air Tahiti** (☑40 86 42 42; www.airtahiti.pf) flies to/from Pape'ete once or twice weekly (78,000 CFP return, about 3½ hours). The airport is on Motu Totegegie, on the northeastern side of the lagoon. A communal ferry from Mangareva (1000 CFP, 45 minutes) meets every flight.

BOAT
From Tahiti, the cargo ship **Nuku Hau** (p237) is the only one serving the Gambier that takes passengers. It sails once a month.

Understand
Tahiti & French
Polynesia

TAHITI & FRENCH POLYNESIA TODAY.........204

Polynesian culture makes a comeback while the economy takes a nosedive.

HISTORY 206

From prehistoric voyages across oceans to warring missionaries and nuclear explosions, French Polynesia's past reads like an adventure novel.

ENVIRONMENT............................. 215

Beyond blue water and white sands are fragile coral reefs, a plethora of marine species and a nuclear footprint.

ISLANDER LIFE 218

Take it slow, tuck a *tiare* flower behind your ear and get your boogie on, and you'll fit right in.

FRENCH POLYNESIA IN POPULAR CULTURE...222

Since the mid-1800s, French Polynesia has attracted some of the world's greatest writers and artists.

FOOD & DRINK.............................224

Raw fish, cooked fish, shellfish, fruit and even some meat are the superstars of French Polynesian dining.

Tahiti & French Polynesia Today

Even though French Polynesia is far from everywhere aside from other Pacific nations, it's closest ties are with France and thus, the TV news is a mix of local reporting and emissions from Europe. Major events in France hit Tahiti deeply, but daily talk is usually about local issues ranging from corrupt politics to school sports. Recently the country has fostered closer relations with the rest of Polynesia (from Hawai'i to New Zealand), but overall French Polynesia is disconnected from its sister cultures, a real island unto itself.

Best in Film

The Ultimate Wave Tahiti (2010) The Teahupoo monster in IMAX.
The Last Reef (2012) Gorgeous underwater footage.
Blood & Ink (2012) Exploration of tattoos.
Les Possédés de Faaite (2009) Reporting into scary, real-life witch hunts.

Best in Print

Mutiny on the Bounty (1932; Charles Nordhoff and James Norman Hall) The classic, fictionalised tale of the real-life mutiny in the late 1700s.
Breadfruit (2000; Celestine Hitiura Vaite) The first book in a series of three that vividly brings the reader into Tahitian culture via strong female protagonist Materena Mahi.
To Live in Paradise (1996; Renée Roosevelt Denis) Autobiography of an extraordinary woman's life on Mo'orea.
Piracy in the Pacific (1976; Henri Jacquier) Fascinating and entertaining account of islands' only ever mother-of-pearl pirates.

Best in Modern Music

Tikahiri Goth punk amazingness fronted by hunky tattooed twins from the Tuamotus.
Pepena Tahiti's favorite live band plays covers and their own style of Tahitian-inspired rock and roll.

Cultural Renaissance

Culturally, French Polynesia is rediscovering itself. In the last 25 years, the Tahitian language has been reclaimed as a subject now required in schools and as a university-level discipline. Tahitian dance is flourishing, tattoos have become the norm and *Ma'a Tahiti* (traditional Tahitian food) has been transformed into haute cuisine. Even a few pre-European Tahitian events are being resuscitated, such as the Matari'i i Ni'a in November, marking the beginning of the 'season of abundance' – Westerners more pessimistically call this the 'wet season'.

Government Gymnastics

While technically a part of France, French Polynesia is, for the most part, self-governing. Since 2004 the government has been in turmoil as the main political parties battle it out and try to woo members of the assembly to flip-flop the balance of power. While democratic elections decide how many assembly seats go to each party, once there the members can switch allegiances. When it's a fragile majority, which is usually the case, one or two changes can overturn the entire government. From 2004 to 2014 this happened 13 times, but Édouard Fritch is blowing the trend by remaining president since September 2014.

Tourism in Free Fall

While elsewhere in the Pacific tourism is back on the rise, Tahiti's stats fell and now are rising only slightly; this makes the number of visitors per year not much greater than those of 1996 (around 150,000, compared to 180,000 visitors in 2014). This is a harsh blow to a country whose primary industry is tourism. Many blame the costly airfare, but the country's reputation as a high-end-only destination may also be to blame. Another thing to think about, a large part of tourism is on cruise ships that don't impact local economies very much. It's sad, because the destination has so much more to offer than its packaged image suggests.

Plentiful, Unprofitable Pearls

The 1990s were the gold-rush years for Tahitian pearls. But the country's infrastructure wasn't able to deal with the business that was generated. A lack of government regulation meant there were no production limits or quality guidelines. Buyers became wary; worse, an imposed export tax made pearls more expensive. Add a global recession and the availability of cheap Chinese-produced pearls, and the market collapsed. Today, with the price of a Tahitian pearl at one-quarter of what it was in 2000, only a few larger farms and a scattering of family-run farms are still in business.

Le Fiu

All these puzzle pieces make the big picture bad news for the French Polynesian people. They no longer have faith in their politicians or political systems, the economy is failing and France seems less and less inclined to offer large sums of money to keep everything afloat. There's a word for this in the Tahitian language: *Fiu*, meaning fed up, over it or just plain tired. There is hope that a new generation of politicians will come along who will bring the country forward instead of stagnation, but so far these saviors are nowhere to be seen.

POPULATION: **280,000**

LAND-MASS: **3500 SQ KM**

TOTAL AREA:
2.5 MILLION SQ KM

NUMBER OF ISLANDS: **118**

HIGHEST POINT:
MT OROHENA (2241M)

TIARE FLOWERS HARVESTED PER DAY: **300,000**

DISTANCE FROM PARIS:
15,700KM

if French Polynesia were 100 people

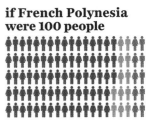

78 would be Polynesian
12 would be Chinese
10 would be French

belief systems
(% of population)

Protestant Roman Catholic

Other

population per sq km

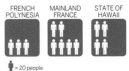

FRENCH POLYNESIA   MAINLAND FRANCE   STATE OF HAWAII

≈ 20 people

History

The isolated islands of Polynesia were among the last places on Earth to be settled by humans and were also some of the last places to be colonised by Europeans. Without written language, little is known of the islands' history before Europeans arrived. When Western explorers first visited in the late 1700s, word of an idyllic way of life turned the region into a dream destination that, in many ways, retains the same allure today.

Getting There Is Half the Fun

The Great Polynesian Migration is one of the world's most outlandish yet mysterious historical events. Early Polynesians (hailing, it's believed, from either Taiwan or Southeast Asia) some 3000 to 4000 years ago tossed chickens, dogs, pigs, vegies and the kids into canoes and sailed into the wild blue yonder. And they found islands, lots of them. Using celestial navigation as well as now-forgotten methods of reading cloud reflections, wave formations and bird-flight patterns, Polynesians could find islands in the vast Pacific far better than we could find a last-minute seat on Air Tahiti during Christmas holidays.

Nothing remains of the boats used to make these voyages, so we have to make do with descriptions given by 18th-century Europeans. Forerunners of the catamaran, the canoes had two parallel hulls fused together by cross beams or platforms; they could be driven by sail, paddle or both. They could carry up to 70 people – the plants, seeds and animals needed to colonise the new land were carried on the connecting platform.

The first settlers in French Polynesia landed in the Marquesas, having journeyed via Samoa, sometime around 200 BC. From here they went on to discover the Society Islands around AD 300.

Paradise: Behind the Scenes

The Polynesian islands were blessed with a situation unique in history: habitable, fertile islands where the pioneers could create their own society and religion in a place nearly devoid of danger. What this society was like before European contact is up to speculation, but for most of their history, Polynesians would have lacked very little. Music, dance and the arts were revered and a big part of life.

Top Archaeology Sites

Marae Taputapuatea (p106), Ra'iatea

Opunohu Valley (p83), Mo'orea

Maeva (p97), Huahine

Iipona (p188), Hiva Oa

Hikokua, Kamuihei & Tahakia (p175), Nuku Hiva

Marae (p69) around the Relais de la Maroto, Tahiti

TIMELINE	1500 BC	200 BC–AD 400	AD 1520
	Polynesia's westernmost islands of Samoa and Tonga are populated via Melanesia. This Great Polynesian Migration is believed to have originally begun in Taiwan or Southeast Asia.	Eastern islands, including French Polynesia, Hawaii and Easter Island, are populated. It is also theorised that during this time there was trade between these islands and South America.	Ferdinand Magellan (Spanish), the first European to sail across the Pacific Ocean, sights Puka Puka in the northeast Tuamotus but manages to miss the rest of French Polynesia.

WHAT'S A MARAE?

Scattered throughout the islands, the most visible remains of ancient Tahitian culture are in its *marae,* open-air places of worship. Today Polynesians have fully embraced Christianity and many of these temples have been destroyed in the name of agriculture, dismantled to construct churches, used as house foundations or simply left to become engulfed by vines and weeds.

Births, deaths and family events were celebrated at simple family *marae;* larger *marae* were temples of chiefs where village meetings, sacrifices and wider religious ceremonies were practised. The largest and most important temples were the royal *marae,* such as Ra'iatea's Taputapuatea, which had influence over the whole of Polynesia, attracting chiefs from afar who would pledge allegiance to the kings.

Yet it wasn't free from problems. Overpopulation caused shortages of farming areas, particularly for taro, and wars frequently broke out between clans. The outcome of these wars was cruel: the defeated were often massacred and their *marae* destroyed. The victors would then take possession of the defeated clan's lands.

Society also wasn't as sweet as European explorers perceived it. Underneath the smiles was an extremely hierarchical, structured and aristocratic system that was nearly feudal in nature and heavily ritualised. High chiefs known as *ari'i* ran the show and their positions were inherited; *tahua* were the priests; middle-class landowners were called *raatira;* the *arioi* were a group of itinerant artist-troubadours whose role it was to entertain everyone; and last were the *manahune,* which consisted of the bulk of the population including fishermen, farmers and servants. Human sacrifices were occasionally needed in religious rituals and these would invariably come from the *manahune.* Infanticide was also practised in circumstances where a girl of lower stature got pregnant by an *ari'i.* The *arioi* were not allowed to have children at all, so would practise infanticide if primitive birth-control or abortion methods didn't work.

Despite this dark side, the unanimous reports from the first European explorers told of an exceptionally happy population who were uninhibited in showing emotions; they were as quick to cry as they were to laugh.

Paradise & Its Droll, Wanton Tricks

Imagine months at sea in cramped, squalid quarters, with many of the crew suffering from scurvy, and happening upon a mountainous isle exploding with fruit, water and women. It was in these circumstances that, around 1500 years after the islands were settled, the first European explorers ventured into the region.

1567	1615–16	1767	1768
Alvaro de Mandaña (Spanish) comes across the northeast Polynesian islands and names them Las Marquesas de Mendoza after the viceroy of Peru. His visit is bloody and without cultural connection.	Dutch captain Jacob Le Maire sails through the Tuamotus. It isn't until 1722 that the Society Islands are sighted by another Dutchman, Jacob Roggeveen, who 'discovers' Maupiti.	Samuel Wallis arrives in Tahiti, kills many Tahitians and names the island 'King George's Land'. He sets up the first trade with the islanders and claims the island for England.	Louis-Antoine de Bougainville visits Tahiti, ogles the women and begins the myth of 'New Cythera'. Not knowing that Wallis had already been there, Bougainville claims Tahiti for France.

BOENECHEA & THE FIRST MISSIONARIES

In 1772, Don Domingo de Boenechea, a Spaniard, sailed the *Aguilla* from Peru and anchored in the lagoon off Tautira on Tahiti Iti. Boenechea installed two missionaries and established Tautira as the first long-term European settlement on the island.

In 1775, the *Aguilla* again returned from Peru. The two Spanish missionaries, who had been spectacularly unsuccessful at converting 'the heathen', and who from all reports were terrified of the islanders, were more than happy to scuttle back to Peru. Boenechea died on Tahiti during this visit, and thus ended the Spanish role on Tahiti. He is buried by the Catholic church that today bears his name in Tautira on Tahiti Iti.

Captain Wallis

First came Captain Samuel Wallis on his ship the *Dolphin*, which he anchored at Matavai Bay in Tahiti's lagoon in late June 1767. A quarter of the crew was down with scurvy and Wallis himself was incapacitated during most of his visit. Initially the arrival was greeted with fascination as hundreds of canoes surrounded the ship, including canoes carrying young women 'who played a great many droll wanton tricks'. But the locals' fascination turned to fear and they attacked the *Dolphin*. Wallis retaliated by firing grapeshot at the Tahitians and then sending a party ashore to destroy homes and canoes. Following this, a trade relationship somehow developed: the crew was desperate for fresh supplies and the Tahitians, who had not yet discovered metals, were delighted to receive knives, hatchets and nails in exchange.

Back in Europe, Wallis's official report of Tahiti focused on the geographical beauty of the region; this was soon overshadowed by gleeful rumours of uninhibited and beautiful women greeting the sailors with 'lascivious gestures'.

Captain Bougainville

With his ships *La Boudeuse* and *L'Etoile*, Louis-Antoine de Bougainville arrived on Tahiti in April 1768. At this time Wallis was still homeward-bound, so Bougainville was completely unaware that he was not the first European to set eyes on the island. His visit only lasted nine days, but unlike Wallis, Bougainville had no unfriendly clashes with the Tahitians.

Bougainville explained that the Tahitians 'pressed us to choose a woman and come on shore with her; and their gestures, which were not ambiguous, denoted in what manner we should form an acquaintance with her'. Bougainville's reports of Venus-like women with 'the celestial form of that goddess', and of the people's uninhibited attitude towards sexual matters, swept through Paris like wildfire. Captain James Cook, who arrived a year after Bougainville, was less florid, but his reports

1769	1772	1776–80	1789
Captain James Cook makes his first voyages to Tahiti to observe and record the transit of Venus, but his equipment proves unworthy of the job.	Don Domingo de Boenechea dispatches missionaries at Tautira; the missionaries, fearing the Tahitians, lock themselves inside and scarcely come out till their Peru-bound boat picks them up in 1775.	Cook brings Omai back to Huahine, leaves many gifts that ultimately estrange Omai from his people, then later 'discovers' the Hawaiian Islands where the captain is killed and possibly eaten.	Fletcher Christian sets Captain Bligh adrift in a small boat then returns to Tahiti on the *Bounty*. Some mutineers remain on Tahiti while the rest sail away to Pitcairn Island.

confirmed the view that Tahitian women would 'dance a very indecent dance' while 'singing most indecent songs'.

Sex, Lies & Venereal Diseases

In reality, Polynesian women were probably not hanging around waiting to seduce a shipload of strange white men. Sex was a natural part of everyday life, so it wouldn't have been surprising that Polynesian women wanted to check whether these funny-looking guys had all the right bits and pieces. Serge Tcherkézoff in his book *Tahiti 1768: Jeunes Filles en Pleur* (Young Girls in Tears) theorises that the girls sent to the ships were not seducing sailors for their own curiosity, but had been given orders by Tahitian priests to become pregnant by the strangers in order to capture their essence. Alexander H Bolyanatz in his book *Pacific Romanticism: Tahiti and the European Imagination* takes another angle and says that the women's overtly sexual behaviour was defensive since the Tahitians had learned early on to fear European weaponry; by seducing the sailors, the islanders would have more power over their often violent visitors.

Whatever the case, this uninhibited approach to sex was soon exploited by sex-starved sailors, whalers and traders, who began buying sex with nails (coveted by the locals for making fish hooks), clothes and alcohol, creating a demand for prostitution, spreading European diseases and palpably contributing to the rapid decline of the Polynesian culture.

The Expeditions of Captain Cook

History depicts Captain James Cook as one of the greatest explorers of all time. Indeed, Cook's navigational and surveying skills, his ability to control unruly crews and keep them healthy and, above all, his cultural understanding, did set him apart. He is described as having been a dispassionate and tolerant man; it's often claimed he did not want to harm or offend the islanders, and that he made concerted efforts to befriend them.

In three great expeditions between 1769 and 1779, Cook filled out the map of the Pacific so comprehensively that future expeditions were reduced to joining the dots. Cook had been sent to the Pacific with two ambitious tasks. One, which was for the Royal Society, was to observe the transit of Venus as it passed across the face of the sun. By timing the transit from three very distant places it was hoped that the distance from the Earth to the sun could be calculated. Tahiti was selected as one of the three measuring points (the other two were in Norway and Canada). Cook's second objective was to hunt for the mythical great continent of the south.

The instruments of the time proved to be insufficiently accurate to achieve Cook's first objective, but Cook's expeditions did yield impressive scientific work. As a result, Cook's voyages communicated the wonders not only of Tahiti but also of New Zealand and Australia to an appreciative European audience.

Best History Museums

Musée de Tahiti et des Îles (p64), Tahiti

Espace Culturel Paul Gauguin (p183), Hiva Oa, the Marquesas

House of James Norman Hall (p55), Tahiti

Musée Gauguin (p65), Tahiti

1797	1803	1819	1827
The London Missionary Society arrives with 25 missionaries at Pointe Vénus in Tahiti – the Tahitians are welcoming but hard to convert, so only a few of the missionaries stay.	Death of the Tahitian King Pomare I, who is succeeded by his son Pomare II who appeals to British Protestants to help him gain influence.	The Code of Pomare is established, forming a Christian alliance between the Leeward Islands; governing is based entirely on the scriptures establishing an unofficial missionary rule.	After Pomare III's reign of six years comes to an end, the young Queen Pomare IV takes the throne and continues to rule for the next 50 years.

TUPAIA & OMAI: POLYNESIAN DIPLOMATS

Europeans explorers were enchanted and fascinated by Tahiti and its people, and they were both thrilled and honoured when the opportunity arose to take adventurous islanders on as shipmates.

On James Cook's first voyage, Tupaia, a high priest of noble lineage, joined the HMS *Endeavor* near Tahiti (with his servant Taiata) and sailed onward with the ship's exploration of the Pacific. A highly educated man and brilliant navigator, Tupaia also proved to be a skilled diplomat and linguist. The Tahitian language was similar enough to other Polynesian languages that Tupaia was able to announce the European's intentions on their arrival to new island groups. His noble stature also impressed his Polynesian cousins – in New Zealand he was welcomed as a near god and in Maori oral history, Tupaia is remembered and mentioned far more than Cook. Unfortunately Tupaia never made it to Europe – he died, along with a huge number of Cook's usually healthy crew, of dysentery in Batavia (modern day Jakarta) on the long trip back to Britain.

During Cook's second Pacific voyage, the mission's flagship HMS *Adventure* took aboard Omai (although it's now thought his name was just Mai), an islander from Ra'iatea. Omai sailed back with the ship to England where he lived for two years before returning to Polynesia on Cook's third voyage. During his stay in London, Omai became popular with the aristocracy, not only for his exotic background but for his charm and good looks. His most famous encounter is a meeting with King George III whom Omai greeted with 'How do King Tosh!'

It's said that when Omai returned to live in Huahine that his many European possessions instilled jealousy in his fellow Polynesians and that the adventurer was never able to fully reintegrate back into island life. When Captain Bligh visited Tahiti on the HMS *Bounty* (before the mutiny) in 1789, he was told that Omai died about two and a half years after Cook's departure.

But Cook's composure was far from impenetrable. During his last voyage in particular, his footsteps were not as light as he had claimed he wanted them to be. Stories of the voyage show that the once-tolerant man became less so – in particular he was angered deeply by any sort of theft and in one instance even ordered an islander's ear be cut off for stealing the ship's property.

The reasons for Cook's death and possible consumption (his remains were 'cooked', although no one is sure if he was eaten) in Hawai'i have been debated. His journal, in which he had dutifully written for almost every instance of his journeys, remains uncharacteristically blank in the period before his death. Some speculate a cultural misunderstanding may have occurred, while others say Cook had become increasingly tyrannical and insensitive. Whatever the case, even though he was

1842	1864	1877	1888
Herman Melville deserts his whaling ship on Nuku Hiva and spends three weeks in remote Taipivai Valley – his book about the escapade, *Typee,* is published in 1846.	The first 329 Chinese immigrants arrive to work at American-run cotton fields on Tahiti. Workers continue to arrive from China through the 20th century and will eventually become successful merchants.	Queen Pomare IV is succeeded by King Pomare V, who isn't interested in the job and effectively abdicates to the French four years later; then he drinks himself to death.	The French annex the Society Islands as part of the colony after plenty of battles and hostility from the islanders, particularly on Huahine.

murdered, the captain's bones were distributed among Hawaiians in a manner usually reserved for the highest chiefs.

Paradise Lost

Once the Europeans came on the scene, traditional Polynesian society took a beating. It was a three-pronged affair: a jab to the ribs with high-tech European weaponry, a blow to the head by an influx of diseases and hard liquor and, finally, a kick in the groin by some Old World Christianity.

Guns

First enter the guns. At the time of first contact, islands consisted of chiefdoms that warred with each other over resources. This was quick to change once the Tahitians realised the power of European weaponry. Most explorers resisted when clans pressed them to take sides in local conflicts, but the *Bounty* mutineers, along with whalers and traders, were happy to offer themselves as mercenaries to the highest bidder. The highest bidders were the Pomares, one of a number of important families, but by no means the most important at that time.

The mutineers and their weapons helped create the political environment where one group could control all of Tahiti. Pomare I, the nephew of Obarea, the 'fat, bouncing, good looking dame' whom Wallis had assumed was the island's chief in 1767, already controlled most of Tahiti when he died in 1803. His son, Pomare II, took over and today the Pomares still consider themselves the royal family of French Polynesia.

Disease

But guns weren't the only problem. Whalers and traders began frequenting Tahiti from England and the USA in the 1790s, escaping their harsh shipboard life, buying supplies, introducing alcohol and spreading diseases. Traders also started to appear from the convict colonies in Australia; they exchanged weapons for food supplies, encouraged prostitution and established stills to produce alcohol.

Listless and plagued by diseases against which it had no natural immunity, the Polynesian population plummeted. The population of Tahiti in the late 1760s was estimated around 40,000; in 1800 another estimate put the population at less than 20,000; by the 1820s it was down to around 6000. In the Marquesas the situation was even worse: it has been estimated the population dropped from 80,000 to 2000 in one century.

Whiskey & God

In March 1797, 25 members of the London Missionary Society (LMS) landed at Pointe Vénus. While the new religion wasn't quick to catch on, the missionaries were able to closely associate themselves with King Pomare II,

Western Vestiges

Paul Gauguin's tomb, Calvaire Cemetery (p183) Hiva Oa, the Marquesas

Cathédrale Saint-Michel (p201), Gambier Archipelago

WWII coastal defence guns (p122), Bora Bora

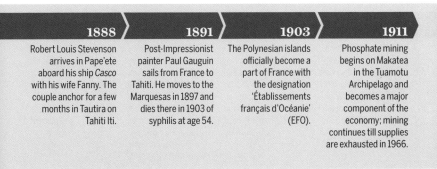

1888	1891	1903	1911
Robert Louis Stevenson arrives in Pape'ete aboard his ship *Casco* with his wife Fanny. The couple anchor for a few months in Tautira on Tahiti Iti.	Post-Impressionist painter Paul Gauguin sails from France to Tahiti. He moves to the Marquesas in 1897 and dies there in 1903 of syphilis at age 54.	The Polynesian islands officially become a part of France with the designation 'Établissements français d'Océanie' (EFO).	Phosphate mining begins on Makatea in the Tuamotu Archipelago and becomes a major component of the economy; mining continues till supplies are exhausted in 1966.

MUTINY ON THE BOUNTY

There have been some colourful chapters in the history of European exploration in the Pacific, but none captures the imagination like the mutiny on the *Bounty*. It all started when Captain William Bligh, an expert navigator who had learnt his trade under James Cook and had already visited Tahiti, was sent off to transport breadfruit from Tahiti to the Caribbean after someone had the bright idea that breadfruit would be a good food source for Caribbean slaves.

Bligh's expedition started late in 1787. After an arduous 10-month voyage, he arrived at a time when breadfruit-tree saplings could not be transplanted. The crew remained on Tahiti for six long, languorous months. Eventually, with the breadfruit trees loaded on-board, the *Bounty* set sail, westbound, for the Caribbean.

Three weeks later, on 28 April 1789, when passing by Tonga, the crew, led by first mate Fletcher Christian, mutinied and took over the ship. The storybook version has Bligh depicted as a tyrant who deserved mutiny, but it's speculated that the reasons for the crew's takeover could have been due to Christian's mental instability or that a good portion of the crew had fallen in love with Tahitian women.

Bligh was pushed onto the *Bounty's* launch with 18 faithful crew members and set adrift. Proving his unmatched skill as a champion navigator, Bligh sailed his overloaded little boat across the Pacific and amazingly made landfall in Timor after a 41-day, 5823km voyage that was promptly written into the record books. By early 1790, Bligh was back in England; an inquiry quickly cleared him of negligence and a ship was dispatched to carry British naval vengeance to Tahiti.

Meanwhile, Christian and his mutineers returned to Tahiti before sailing off to find a more remote hideaway. Ultimately 16 mutineers decided to stay on Tahiti while a small-er group left with Christian and the *Bounty* to inhabit Pitcairn Island. Today, thanks to Fletcher Christian's mutiny, the odd Tahitian-British colony still on Pitcairn Island is one of the last vestiges of the British Empire.

Vengeance arrived for the mutineers on Tahiti in 1791 in the shape of Captain Edward Edwards, who made Bligh look like a thoroughly nice guy. He quickly rounded up mutineers and informed the men's new Tahitian wives that the men were going back to Britain to get their just desserts.

Bligh himself was back on Tahiti in 1792, this time in command of HMS *Providence* and with 19 marines to ensure there was no repeat performance. Bligh duly picked up his breadfruit saplings and transported them in record time to the Caribbean. As it turned out, the slaves never developed a taste for the fruit.

and Christianity was established as the dominant religion in 1815 and carried through the reign of Queen Pomare IV who ruled for 50 years.

The missionaries were an unyielding bunch and, although they had the best intentions, smothered many important, ancient customs with a rigid interpretation of Protestantism. A century later, the English

1918	1942	1947	1957–58
An influenza pandemic thought to have origi-nated in the USA kills approximately 20% of Tahiti's population. The disease spreads around the Pacific and is still considered one of the deadliest in history.	Five thousand Ameri-can soldiers descend on Bora Bora to build the territory's first airstrip. The American military uses the island as their supply base through WWII.	Thor Heyerdahl makes his voyage to the Tuamotus from Peru aboard a balsa raft to prove Polynesians came from South America. His journey is a success but his theory is later disproved by genetics.	The territory is officially named French Polynesia and votes to remain part of France amid riots in Pape'ete. Pouvana'a a Oopa, leader of the separatist movement, is exiled to France.

writer Robert Keable, who had been a vicar with the Church of England, commented about pioneering missionary William Ellis that 'it was a thousand pities that the Tahitians did not convert Mr Ellis'.

Although the missionaries get a bad rap for destroying so much of the beauty of the Polynesian culture, in certain ways they very much helped the Polynesians by creating a spiritual framework in which to deal with the new challenges (such as alcohol and prostitution) being introduced by less savoury Europeans. Today, Christianity is the country's best advocate and tool in the fight against alcoholism, domestic violence and incest, as well as providing exceptionally strong support for community.

Enter the French

The French takeover of what is now French Polynesia was essentially a war of the missionaries. British clergy were an unofficial colonial power via the Pomare clan in the Society Islands, the Australs and the Tuamotus, but the French Catholic missionaries were in firm control in the Gambier Archipelago from 1834 and the Marquesas from 1838. In 1836, two French missionaries from the Gambier Archipelago were quietly dropped off near Tautira at the eastern extremity of Tahiti Iti; they were promptly arrested and deported by the British.

The deportation of the two French missionaries was considered a national insult to the French. Demands, claims, counterclaims, payments and apologies shuttled back and forth until 1842, when Rear Admiral Dupetit-Thouars arrived in *La Reine Blanche*, pointed his guns at Pape'ete and took power. Queen Pomare IV was forced to yield to the French.

The queen, still hoping for British intervention, fled to Ra'iatea in 1844 and a guerrilla rebellion against the French broke out on Tahiti and other islands. The presence of French forts around Tahiti confirms that it was a fierce struggle, but eventually the rebels were subdued, and by 1846 France had control over Tahiti and Mo'orea. In 1847, Queen Pomare was persuaded to return to Tahiti, but she was now merely a figurehead.

Queen Pomare died in 1877 and was succeeded by her son, Pomare V. He had little interest in the position and effectively abdicated power in 1881; he drank himself to death in 1891.

The Nuclear Era

French Polynesia continued to be a valuable strategic port for the French, especially when the islands' economies of vanilla, cotton, copra and mother of pearl were flourishing during WWI, and during WWII, when American forces used Bora Bora as a military base. Postwar, as the territory's exports declined, another usage of it was devised. In 1963 Moruroa and Fangataufa, atolls in the Tuamotus, were announced to become France's nuclear test sites. Atmospheric nuclear explosions began in 1966. The Centre

A fire tragically destroyed half of the town of Pape'ete in 1884. After the disaster it became illegal to use local building materials within city limits.

HISTORY ENTER THE FRENCH

In 1918, an influenza epidemic wiped out approximately 20% of Tahiti's population. There were so many dead, the bodies were burned in great pyres.

1961	1963	1982	1984
Faa'a International Airport is constructed on landfill covering a coral reef. French Polynesia is opened up to the world and the tourism industry takes off.	French Centre d'Expérimentation du Pacifique for nuclear testing opens on Moruroa and Fangataufa. The first atmospheric tests begin in 1966; in 1981, underground shafts are dug for underground testing.	Gaston Flosse begins his first term as president of French Polynesia. He remains in control on and off until 2004 but becomes president a few times again after that.	French Polynesia gains internal autonomy from France, which is later expanded in 1990 and again in 1996. In 2004 it gains the unique French status of 'Overseas Collectivity'.

d'Expérimentation du Pacifique (CEP; Pacific Experimentation Centre) soon became a major component of the French Polynesian economy.

Over the next 30 years, 193 tests were performed on the two atolls and more than 130,000 people worked for the CEP. In 1981, 17 years after the USA, Britain and the USSR agreed to halt atmospheric testing, the French drilled bomb shafts under the central lagoons of the atolls and finally moved the tests underground. In 1995 French president Jacques Chirac announced a new series of underground tests, and a storm of protest erupted worldwide. Rioting broke out in Pape'ete but fell on deaf ears in France. The final rounds of tests were concluded in early 1996, and it was announced there would be no further testing in the Pacific.

International opposition to nuclear testing was also growing. In 1985 French secret service agents bombed and sank the Greenpeace ship *Rainbow Warrior*, in Auckland Harbour, New Zealand, killing four people. The ship was on its way to protest testing on Moruroa Atoll. Only two of the agents were caught by New Zealand authorities and, although they were found guilty, France pressured them to release the prisoners to a Club Med–style prison on Hao, in the Tuamotus. France reneged on the agreement after two years and the bombers were sent back to France.

For many years the French government denied that the tests posed any ecological threat to the region. Finally, in 1999 a French study reported that there had been radioactive leakage into underground water, and later that same year the existence of cracks in the coral cones of Moruroa and Fangataufa were also acknowledged. A 2006 study conducted by the French Polynesian Territorial Assembly concluded that Tureia in the eastern Tuamotus and the Gambier Archipelago would have been exposed to nuclear fallout during atmospheric testing; because there were never any dosimeter measurements taken on these islands, what the levels of radiation would have been has not been proved.

In November 2008, the French defence minister announced a bill setting the standards for nuclear-test workers' compensation, which passed in 2010. Still, two associations, the Association of Nuclear Test Veterans (AVEN), which is made up of former French military personnel, and Moruroa e Tatou, which has more than 4000 French Polynesian members, have been lobbying the French government for any compensation for well over a decade, with little – or no – gains. On top of this, the environmental impacts of the tests have been disregarded by the legislation.

In January 2012, France approved a motion that would restore Moruroa and Fangataufa (previously under control of the French defence ministry) to French Polynesia's public domain. The bill would, among other things, let French Polynesia monitor radiation levels rather than rely on French reports, which it has come to mistrust. Pundits say this bill has little chance of passing.

TV wasn't in French Polynesian homes until the early 1980s, when RFO (Radio France Overseas) began the first local broadcasts.

Income tax was only introduced to French Polynesia in 1994, although it is still very low compared to France or even the US.

1985	1995–96	2006	2011
French secret agents blow up the New Zealand–based Greenpeace ship *Rainbow Warrior* as it prepares for a protest voyage to the nuclear test site on Moruroa.	Rioting against nuclear testing breaks out in Pape'ete and at Faa'a International Airport. The testing continues despite worldwide criticism until the series is complete in 1996.	Gaston Tong Song is elected president and becomes a part of a constant flip-flopping of power, now mostly between himself and Temaru, over the next five years.	During one of his longer terms of presidency, Temaru, supported by his Assembly, champions decolonisation of French Polynesia from France.

Environment

It's impossible to talk about the French Polynesian landscape without clichés. From the lush slopes of the high islands to the white-sand, palm-ruffled atolls with lagoons bluer than well, anything, this is the place that stereotypical ideals of paradise come from.

The Landscape

French Polynesia's 118 islands are scattered over an expanse of the Pacific Ocean stretching more than 2000km – an area about the size of Western Europe. Still, the islands and atolls make up a total land mass of barely 3500 sq km (less than one-third the size of the US state of Connecticut). Five archipelagos, the Society, Tuamotu, Marquesas, Austral and Gambier, divide the country into distinct geological and cultural areas.

High islands – think Tahiti, Mo'orea and Bora Bora – are essentially mountains rising out of the ocean that are often encircled by a barrier reef. A protected, shallow lagoon, with that flashy blue colour of postcards and brochure fame, is formed by the reef.

An atoll is a ring of old barrier reef that surrounds a now-sunken high island. Over time the reef was built up and mini-islands called *motu* were formed. These *motu*, which encircle the lagoon, reach a maximum height of 6m and are usually covered in low bushes and coconut palms. *Motu* are separated by shallow *hoa* (channels) that link the inner lagoon to the ocean. A *hoa* that's deep enough for boats to pass through is called a 'pass'.

> For information about French Polynesia's birdlife, check out www.manu.pf, the official site of SOP Manu, the Tahitian organisation for the protection of bird species.

Land Animals

The bulk of the Pacific's fauna originated in Asia/Melanesia and spread east; the further east you travel, the less varied it becomes. Don't come looking for wildlife safaris here, unless they're underwater.

Basically, any fauna that couldn't swim, float or fly to French Polynesia has been introduced. The first Polynesians, knowing they would be settling new lands, brought pigs, chickens and dogs in their canoes. They also brought geckos and the small Polynesian rat, probably as stowaways.

PROTECTION OF FLORA & FAUNA

Marine reserves in French Polynesia in the past have been few; BellinScillyghausen (remote islands in the Leeward group of Society Islands) and eight small areas within Mo'orea's lagoon are the only ones that have been protected long-term by the country itself. Fakarava and its surrounding atolls (Aratika, Toau, Kauehi, Niau, Raraka and Taiaro) are a Unesco biosphere reserve. This is changing, however, with the likelihood of the creation of a 1 million sq km reserve around the Austral Islands; it's expected that this will become a reality by 2020. Another 700,000 sq km area around the Marquesas Islands is hoped to be protected by 2017.

The only terrestrial reserves are the Marquesan Nature Reserves, which include the remote uninhabited islands of Motu One, Hatutu, Eiao and Motane. Several species are protected and there are limits placed on the fishing of some fish and crustaceans. Unfortunately, fish continue to be caught indiscriminately and shells are still collected. Although turtles are highly protected, they continue to be poached for their meat and their shells.

Europeans introduced horses and goats, which can be found around the islands, but are most present in the Marquesas Islands where they often roam free. A few more types of rats and birds have also been introduced, often to negative effect on the environment. Birds that have been brought in, such as the Indian Myna, aggressively compete for food and territory, which has led to the extinction of many French Polynesian endemic species. Meanwhile the European rat has devastated local bird populations by feasting on their eggs.

The endemic birdlife of French Polynesia is as fragile as it is fabulous. Of the 29 land species, 12 are introduced and have driven many local species to near extinction. The 27 species of sea birds, including terns, noddies, frigates and boobies, make French Polynesia one of the richest tropical areas for marine species.

Common Deep-Sea Fish

Tuna

Mahimahi (dorado)

Bonito

Wahoo

Swordfish

Sea Creatures

Any dismay about the lack of animal diversity on land is quickly made up for by the quantity of underwater species – it's all here.

Large Marine Life

At the top of the food chain, sharks are found in healthy numbers throughout the islands. Blacktip and whitetip reef sharks are the most common and pose little danger. More aggressive and sometimes unnervingly curious, the grey reef shark is common in the Tuamotus. Large sleeper or nurse sharks, distinguished by their broad head and oversized dorsal fins and tail, look daunting but generally keep to themselves on the bottom of channels and sandy banks.

Other large creatures you are likely to encounter are graceful manta rays; smaller, spotted leopard rays; stingrays; and moray eels. Five of the seven species of sea turtle (all endangered) make their home in French Polynesia, but you're most likely to see the green and hawksbill turtles, which often come to feed in the lagoons.

Between July and October, humpback whales can be seen primarily off the shores of Tahiti, Mo'orea and Rurutu. There are actually at least 24 species of whale that pass through French Polynesia, but startlingly few species other than the humpbacks are ever observed. Dolphins can be seen year-round, especially spinner dolphins. Electra dolphins are a major attraction around Nuku Hiva, where they gather in groups of several hundred, a phenomenon seen nowhere else in the world.

Fish, Shells & Crabs

Hundreds of species of fish of all colours, shapes and sizes flutter about the reefs. Lobsters, slipper lobsters and crabs are found on the outer slopes of reefs or the bottom of caves and cliffs. Black-lipped pearl oysters and *pahua* (giant clams) are found on reefs inside the lagoons. Porcelain and cat-eye kauri are valued by collectors, but as shells are so scarce in French Polynesia, it is not advised to take any living shells.

WATER HAZARDS

➡ Cone shells have a deadly poisonous stinger that protrudes from the hole at the cone's bottom.

➡ Pencil urchins live in crevices by day and dot the reefs at night – watch your feet, as stepping on the spikes can cause extreme pain. Urinating on the wounds can soothe them.

➡ Stonefish are French Polynesia's biggest, most prolific shallow-water hazard, yet are so well camouflaged they're nearly impossible to see; if you get stung, apply heat immediately and head for the hospital. Wearing plastic, waterproof sandals provides the best protection.

NUCLEAR LEFTOVERS

The environmental repercussions of French nuclear testing are still hotly debated. It was confirmed in 1999 that Moruroa and Fangataufa were fissured by tests and that radioactivity has been allowed to escape from cracks in the atolls' coral cones. Evidence has been found of low-level activity in certain areas of the Gambiers, but long-ranging conclusive evidence has yet to come forth. Travellers can rest assured that any radiation threat (which was only ever present in remote areas of the Tuamotu and Gambier Archipelagos) has long since passed.

The comedians of the islands are hermit crabs. They are very fashion-conscious and will quickly swap their old shells for prettier ones; they act tough and threaten to pinch you, and will try to eat your sandwich off your picnic blanket if you're not careful. In the Tuamotus the enormous and impressively colourful *kaveu* (coconut crab) feeds at night and is prized for its coconut-flavoured flesh. *Tupa* (land crabs) are found on all of the islands and have a penchant for getting squashed by cars.

Plants

Before human habitation, the variety of vegetation was limited to the seeds and spores that could travel by means of wind, sea or bird droppings. Polynesians brought *uru* (breadfruit), coconut, taro and bananas, and early missionaries introduced sugar cane, cotton, pineapples, citrus fruits, coffee, vegetables and other staples. Over the years, botanists and enthusiasts have brought in various tropical plant species, which have thrived in the favourable climate. Today, visitors will encounter all of the sumptuousness of a tropical paradise: papayas, star fruit, mangos, avocados, guavas, pomelos and rambutan grow among birds of paradise, hibiscus and allamanda.

The *tiare,* a small, white, fragrant gardenia, is the symbol of French Polynesia. The significance of this flower runs deep. It is the first thing visitors are offered on arrival at Faa'a airport, it is used in many traditional medicines, it's used as a perfume and it is the classic flower to string as a *hei* (flower crown or necklace) or wear behind your ear.

The *uru* tree was the lifeline of ancient islanders, who used the bark for tapa (paperlike cloth), the trunk for canoes, the roots and leaves for medicine, and of course the fruit was the dietary staple. Taro, a root vegetable, is the secondary staple; the leaves of yellow taro resemble spinach when cooked, and this is called *fafa.*

The atolls are a stark contrast to the lush high islands. Made up primarily of sand and coral rock, the land lacks the minerals to support much vegetation. Coconut palms and an endemic shrub, the small-leafed, red-barked *miki miki,* dominate the landscape. Adding grace and much-needed shade to the atolls is the grand *kahaia* tree with its large, glossy leaves and fragrant white flowers.

The Tahitian language has at least seven words for the coconut; each describes a different stage of the nut's maturity.

Environmental Issues

Atolls and high islands are ecologically fragile, but French Polynesia has been slow to implement environmental protection. Despite a limited number of 'green' establishments that are springing up, and the rigorous requirements of public buildings and hotels to blend in with the landscape, pollution is steadily chipping away at the picture of paradise.

Although there are many low-lying atolls in French Polynesia, the effects of climate change, including rising sea levels, have so far been minimal. Higher water temperatures are one of the biggest threats to the health of the country's coral reefs and, during El Niño years in particular, huge amounts of coral die, which affects the entire ecosystem.

Islander Life

If French Polynesia had a national slogan it might be *haere maru* (take it slow). It's hard not to reduce your speed several notches out here. With one road encircling most islands, you'll often get caught driving behind an old pick-up truck at 50km/h with no chance of passing, the internet takes an eternity (if it works at all) and it seems holidays shut all the shops every week or so. Yet, somehow, everything works out.

Family & Multiculturalism

Islander Etiquette

....

Do eat Tahitian food with your fingers.

....

Do remove shoes off before entering a home.

....

Don't tip unless there's a sign or service is exceptional.

The traditional Tahitian family is an open-armed force that is the country's backbone. Although modern girls are increasingly less likely to stay home and have baby after baby, an accidental pregnancy is considered more of a blessing than a hindrance, and babies are passed along to another eager, infant-loving family member. *Faamu* (adopted children) are not thought of as different to blood brothers and sisters, although the birth mother, and occasionally the father, sometimes remains a peripheral part of the child's life. Once a child is in a family, he or she is in no way obligated to stay; children move about to aunties, uncles and grandparents as they wish.

This family web is vitally important to an individual. When people first meet, the conversation usually starts with questions about family and most people are able to find a common relative between themselves within minutes. This accomplished, they are 'cousins' and fast friends.

But it's not all roses in what appears to be such a warm, fuzzy family framework. Domestic violence and incest are prevalent. This is closely connected with high rates of alcoholism. The government has launched programs addressing these issues but little progress has been made.

The majority of the population claims to be Polynesian (although most have some other ethnicity in the mix), 12% of the population is Chinese and the rest is European. Racial tension is rare but does exist. A few insults exist for each race, although they are usually only uttered on drunken binges or in schoolyards. Outward displays of racism are usually from Polynesians to French, while the more insidious kind goes from the French to the Polynesians. The Chinese generally try to stay out of it.

GENDER BENDER

You'll find that some women serving food in restaurants or working in hotels or boutiques aren't actually women at all. *Mahu*, males who are raised as girls and continue to live their lives as women, were present when Europeans first arrived on the islands. Although the missionaries attempted to halt this 'unnatural crime', nowadays *mahu* are an accepted part of the community. In today's lingo, another category of *mahu,* called *raerae,* refers to more flamboyant cross-dressers. These people face more discrimination than their *mahu* counterparts, who act more like very effeminate men.

It remains unclear whether this practice has a sexual or social origin, but it is generally assumed to be the latter, as *mahu* don't necessarily have sex with men. *Raerae,* however, do prefer men.

HAWAIKI NUI CANOE RACE

The sporting spectacular that has French Polynesians glued to their TV sets and talking passionately about favourites and challengers is a canoe race. The three-day, four-island Hawaiki Nui va'a (*pirogue*, or outrigger-canoe) race pits around 60 of the islands' best *pirogue* teams against each other and against anyone brave enough from overseas.

The 116km race, held in late October or early November, starts on Huahine, heads across the open sea to Ra'iatea, then to Taha'a and then finally on to Bora Bora. Check out www.hawaikinuivaa.pf (in French) for more details.

Sport

The national sport is, without dispute, *va'a* (*pirogue,* or outrigger-canoe) racing. You can admire the *pirogue* teams training on any lagoon, and if you're around in late October or early November, you can catch the Hawaiki Nui canoe race.

During the Heiva and a few scattered cultural festivals, Polynesians pull some interesting traditional sports out of their hats, including *amoraa ofae* (rock lifting), *patia fa* (javelin throwing), fruit-bearing races and coconut-husking competitions.

Surfing was an ancient Tahitian sport. The Billabong Pro international surf competition, held every August at the nearly mythically scary wave at Teahupoo on Tahiti Iti, brings worldwide coverage to Tahitian surfing.

Polynesians are great believers in *tupapau* (ghosts) and most people will have a good story to tell about the supernatural if you ask them.

Religion

Historically, Polynesians were polytheistic, worshipping *atua* (gods) who were surrounded by a pantheon of secondary gods. The main gods were Ta'aroa (god of creation), Tu (man god), Tane (god of craftsmen), 'Oro (god of war) and Hiro (god of thieves and sailors).

The arrival of Protestant missionaries at the end of the 18th century, followed soon after by the Catholics, marked the suppression of traditional religious beliefs. The missionaries changed the religious and cultural landscape forever, and today French Polynesia has a surprising number and variety of churches relative to its population. This includes a few takes on Mormonism, but around half of the population is Protestant and 30% are Catholic.

A few pre-Christian rituals and superstitions still exist alongside Christianity. Christian Polynesians continue to respect and fear ancient *tapu* (taboo) sites, and nothing would persuade a Polynesian to move a *tiki* (sacred statue) or *marae* (traditional temple) stone. On occasion, a *tahua* (faith healer or priest) is still consulted, and *raau tahiti* (traditional herbal medicine) is making a comeback – there's a vendor or two selling cures at the Pape'ete Central Market.

Go to www. maisondela-culture.pf (in French) for information on upcoming and past performances, exhibitions and all things cultural.

Arts

The zealous work of the missionaries managed to rid the existing Polynesian art and culture of many of its symbols and practices. Among other things, temples and carvings were destroyed, and tattooing and dancing were banned. Fortunately, some traditions survived this period, and in recent years there has been a revival of Polynesian culture.

Dance

Tahitian dance is not just a tourist attraction, it's a vibrant expression of Maohi (Polynesian) culture. The dances that visitors see are not created for tourists – they are authentic performances that take months of rehearsals and are based on rigorously standardised choreography depicting specific legends. In this land of oral traditions, dance is not merely an aesthetic medium but also a means of preserving the memory of the past.

Tahitian dance is taught in the schools from a young age and those who become serious about it (and there are many) can continue on in a local troupe or at private dance schools. These schools and troupes foster a lot of community since the dancers end up spending from three to 20 hours together per week practicing the choreography and hand crafting their elaborate costumes from local foliage.

Many luxury hotels offer quality dance shows about twice a week. On Tahiti and Mo'orea they are performed by semiprofessional groups and range from small groups dancing to piped-in music (in the worst cases) to theatrical extravaganzas with live orchestras. These shows include a buffet and are open to all.

Polynesian Playlist

Bobby *Dreamy*

Te Ava Piti *Ukulele riffs*

Angelo Neuffer *Poetic*

Ester Tefana *Ukulele mood*

Tapuarii Laughlin *Modern classics*

Fenua *Traditional-techno fusion*

Trio Kikiriri *Synth/ukulele*

Music

Traditional Polynesian music, usually performed as an accompaniment to dance, is heard reverberating across the islands. Ukuleles and percussion instruments dominate, and the music is structured by a fast-paced and complex drum beat. Sunday *himene* (hymns) at churches feature wonderful harmonies.

Drums are the Maohi instruments par excellence and the most common is the *toere*, a cylindrical, hollowed-out piece of wood with a narrow slit down its length. String instruments are of European origin, though the ukulele (mini guitar with four strings), comes by way of Hawaii.

Modern Polynesian music by local artists is the blaring soundtrack to everyday life, whether it's in a bus, at a cafe or on the radio – some groups also perform in hotels and bars. This music ranges from rock to folksy ballads usually accompanied by a guitar or ukulele. A current popular local group (highly recommended) that you may see playing on Tahiti and Mo'orea is called Pepena.

Sculpture, Woodcarving & Tapa

Traditionally, the best sculptures and woodcarvings have come out of the Marquesas, where fine *tiki,* bowls, mortars and pestles, spears and clubs are carved from rosewood, *tou* (dark, hard-grained wood) or stone. You can find these pieces in the market of Pape'ete, as well as gift shops around the islands, but the best deals are had in the Marquesas themselves.

Some woodwork sold in French Polynesia is actually made elsewhere (usually Indonesia), so if you see several of the same item, chances are it wasn't made in the country. Ask around to ensure you are getting the real thing.

THE HEIVA

Each year for a month, from late June to late July, islanders from all of the archipelagos join together for a full program of festivities in Pape'ete (Tahiti), and on some of the other islands. The emphasis is on traditional-dance contests (both professional and amateur) and singing competitions, but there is a huge range of other activities on offer. Craft-making demonstrations include *niau* (woven coconut-palm leaves) and tapa (paperlike cloth) and a stone-carving competition. There's a procession of floral floats, a vote for Miss Heiva and Mr Heiva, a funfair, fireworks, fire walking and tattoo displays. Meanwhile, there's an outrigger-canoe race and traditional-sports competitions.

Reservations for the evening dance contests can be made from May onwards at the kiosk at Pl Toata in Pape'ete. You can also enquire at the tourist office. Official dates can be found on the Tahiti Tourisme website (www.tahiti-tourisme.com). The evening will set you back between 1000 CFP and 4000 CFP. Dance performances take place at Pape'ete's Toata Amphitheatre.

MONOI

What can't *monoi* do? This local concoction, made from coconut oil and *tiare* (fragrant gardenia, and the national flower), is deliciously perfumed with sandalwood, vanilla, coconut or jasmine. It's used liberally as hair oil, ointment, sunscreen and even mosquito repellent. It costs from 400 CFP to 800 CFP a bottle, is great on the skin after a day of sizzling in the sun and makes a great gift (although it does solidify in cooler climates).

Traditionally made throughout the Pacific, tapa (paperlike cloth) is a nonwoven fabric made from the bark of *uru* (breadfruit), banyan or *aute* (paper mulberry) trees. It was the semidisposable clothing fabric of pre-European Polynesia. Finished pieces are dyed with the sap of various plants or decorated with traditional artwork. Today, designs are sometimes just drawn on with ink.

Plaiting & Basketwork

Baskets and hats, and the panels used for roofing and the walls of houses, are made by women. Coconut-palm leaves are used for the more rough-and-ready woven work, while pandanus leaves or thin strips of bamboo are used for finer hats, bags and mats, which are often decorated with flowers or shells. Some of the finest work comes from the Australs.

Flowers & Shells

Flowers are omnipresent in French Polynesia. When you arrive at the airport, you'll be presented with a *tiare* (Tahiti's national flower) to sniff as you brave the customs queues. Both men and women tuck a *tiare* or other flower behind their ear in the world's most simple yet graceful gesture of physical adornment. Traditionally, a flower behind the left ear meant you were taken or married, while a blossom tucked behind your right ear meant you were available; while Tahitians love to tell tourists about this practice, in reality no one will try and deduce your relationship status in this way.

Hei (flower crowns or necklaces) are given as gifts on arrival while shell necklaces are given on departure.

Tattoos

Since the early 1980s, tattooing has enjoyed a strong revival, becoming one of the most expressive and vibrant vehicles of Polynesian culture.

Modern tattooing is completely for the sake of style or beautification; in ancient times it was a highly socially significant and sophisticated art. It was a symbol of community or clan membership and geographic origin; it was also an initiation rite, a symbol of social status and an aesthetic adornment that played a part in the seduction process. Finally, tattooing served to intimidate: in the Marquesas, warriors tattooed their faces to make themselves look terrifying.

Today, you'll find talented tattoo artists throughout the islands who will be happy to create an unforgettable souvenir on your skin.

Types of Dance

Otea
Fast hip action

Aparima
Free-flowing, graceful

Hivinau
Inspired by anchor hoisting

Paoa
Seated legend recitation

Fire dance
Juggling flaming torches

French Polynesia in Popular Culture

For more than 300 years, French Polynesia has been painted as paradise via art and media. Throughout this time the clichés haven't changed much, but new Polynesia-based artists are starting to unearth the subtleties of their stereotype-ridden home.

Literature

Author Zane Grey spent many months in French Polynesia in the 1920s and 1930s. While there, he caught the first game fish (a marlin) to exceed 1000lb (over 450kg); he tells this story and more in his book *Tales of Tahitian Waters* (1931).

Polynesia has been getting the Western pen flowing since the first European explorers returned with accounts of paradise. Early writers also offered valuable historical and ethnological details. Most modern fiction by non-Polynesians veers more towards fantasy, based only slightly on reality.

English-Language Writers

Through the 1800s and early 1900s, several great authors travelled to French Polynesia looking for adventure. Herman Melville was the first, giving a fascinating account of his experiences living with an isolated cannibalistic tribe on Nuku Hiva in his book *Typee* (1846). He followed this with *Omoo* (1847), about his time on Tahiti. Robert Louis Stevenson came through the islands in the late 1880s before continuing through the Pacific. His book *In the South Seas* (1908) chronicles his voyage and his many encounters with local peoples. Jack London followed the footsteps of his idols Melville and Stevenson in 1906, visiting many of the places his heroes had written about. His travels inspired much of his writing, including *South Sea Tales* (1911). In 1917, Somerset Maugham visited Tahiti to research *The Moon and Sixpence* (1919), loosely based on Paul Gauguin's life.

The most famous books with a French Polynesian backdrop remain the *Mutiny on the Bounty* (1932) trilogy, by James Norman Hall and Charles Nordhoff. Both authors lived on Tahiti for a good portion of their lives and the books evoke all of the colours of the landscape and culture while telling one of the world's greatest adventure tales – it's based on a true story.

James Michener's *Tales of the South Pacific* (1947) and *Return to Paradise* (1951) contain a few stories based in French Polynesia, particularly during WWII. From the 1960s, literature became dominated by French authors, but from the 2000s Polynesia began to appear more

---

MUTINY IN THE CINEMA

The uprising on the *Bounty* has been embellished by filmmakers three times in 50 years. If another version is made, audiences could be forgiven for having a mutiny of their own.

Mutiny on the Bounty (1935) Starred Charles Laughton as Captain Bligh and Clark Gable as Fletcher Christian. Very little was actually shot on Tahiti.

Mutiny on the Bounty (1962) Trevor Howard played Bligh and Marlon Brando was Christian. Filmed on Tahiti and Bora Bora.

Bounty (1984) Filmed mostly on Mo'orea; Anthony Hopkins played Bligh and Mel Gibson was the more-handsome-than-ever Christian.

in romance and adventure genres, including books by Clare Coleman, Ferenc Máté and Suzanne Enoch.

A must-read, *The Signature of All Things* (2013) by Elizabeth Gilbert takes readers on a perfect-in-its-detail voyage to Tahiti via a female botanist in the 1800s. It's a delicious adventure and a glimpse into the island's past.

Australian writer Sarah Turnbull writes about her experiences as an expat on Tahiti alongside her many trials of trying to conceive a child in *All Good Things: From Paris to Tahiti: Life and Longing* (2013).

Polynesian & French Writers

Oral recitation was the fountain pen of the Pacific, and the written word only came into being after missionaries began producing texts in Tahitian in the 19th century. This dependence on the spoken word means that literature by Polynesians has only recently begun to grace bookshelves.

A number of Polynesian writers are slowly changing the literary landscape; few have been translated into English, but you can find them. Search for books by Henri Hiro, Turo Raapoto, Hubert Bremond, Charles Manutahi, Michou Chaze, Chantal Spitz and Louise Peltzer.

The *Materena* (2006) series, by Celestine Hitiura Vaite, a Tahitian living in Australia, is a trilogy of novels available in English about a headstrong but poor woman in contemporary Tahiti. Meanwhile, Franco American writer Alex du Prel (editor of Tahiti's French news monthly, *Tahiti Pacifique*) has been in French Polynesia so long he's an honorary local. His *Tahiti Blues* (2011) series recounts fascinating modern tales of the islands.

Painting

Even today, painting in the South Pacific is synonymous with Paul Gauguin, the French post-Impressionist painter. Gauguin spent much of his later life in Polynesia, and presented Europe with images of the islands that moulded the way Europeans viewed Polynesia. In his wake, a number of predominantly European artists have sought inspiration in the region.

Henri Matisse made a short visit to Tahiti, but his work on Polynesia is eclipsed by Jacques Boullaire, a French artist who first travelled to Tahiti in the 1930s. He produced magnificent watercolours, and reproductions of his work are readily available.

Other artists who have influenced the art scene locally and internationally include Christian Deloffre, François Ravello, Michèle Dallet, Bobby (also a singer and musician; he died in 1991), André Marere, Jean Masson, Maryse Noguier and Erhard Lux. In the islands you can visit the studios of several renowned painters, including Melanie Shook Dupre (Huahine), GOTZ (Mo'orea), Garrick Yrondi (Bora Bora) and Alain Despert (Bora Bora). Up-and-coming artists to look out for in the local galleries include Hel Ton Jon and Andrea Dietloff.

Cinema

Until the recent comedy *Couples Retreat* (2009), mostly filmed at the St Régis Resort on Bora Bora, French Polynesia's role as a movie backdrop is almost exclusively tied up with *Mutiny on the Bounty*. But times are a changing. The IMAX movie *The Ultimate Wave Tahiti* (2010) brought surfing Teahupoo to the really big screen. There's stunning footage but, perhaps in an attempt to adhere to stereotypes, the film has a Hawaiian-music soundtrack and even the dancing has non-Tahitian choreography. As a result, the cultural parts feel canned. Then in 2015, Tahiti got another cinematic jolt highlighting the wave at Teahupoo once again in the big Hollywood remake of *Point Break*.

Tabu, released in 1931, was filmed on Bora Bora. This work of fiction explores the notions of *tapu* (taboo), and although it remains an interesting slice of history, it was a flop in its era. James Michener's *South Pacific* may have been about Polynesia, but it was filmed in Malaysia.

In the footsteps of Somerset Maugham, Peruvian author Mario Vargas Llosa wrote *The Way to Paradise* (2003), a story that mirrors the life of Gauguin with his feminist-socialist grandmother Flora Trist.

Jacques Brel's 1977 song 'Les Marquises' inspired a generation of French dreamers of the South Seas.

FRENCH POLYNESIA IN POPULAR CULTURE PAINTING

Food & Drink

Polynesians like to eat and they like it when you eat. Luckily the food on offer is a pleasure on the palate. French Polynesia is a seafood-lover's paradise, vegetarians will be in fruit heaven and carnivores will be pleased to find New Zealand's best cuts served around the country.

Bounty of the Islands

Just as you'd expect, these lush islands are bursting with tropical fruits and fresh seafood.

It's illegal and highly discouraged to bring local fruit and vegetables from Tahiti to islands in other archipelagos, since you might also be bringing unwanted insect pests that could disrupt the balance of these fragile ecosystems.

Seafood

Think open-sea fish like tuna, wahoo, swordfish and *mahimahi*, or lagoon fish – from snapper to jackfish. It's served incredibly fresh. No matter how you feel about seafood, you should give it a try at least once while in the islands.

Korori (pearl oyster meat) is gaining popularity in raw and cooked dishes, with a meaty flavour and tender texture. Lobsters appear on many menus especially at fine restaurants. Fresh and saltwater prawns are found in abundance because they are farmed on Tahiti. Other, more hard-to-find shellfish to look out for include the *varo* (mantis shrimp), *kaveu* (coconut crab) and mud crabs (mostly on Raiatea and Huahine).

Meat

Pua (pork) is the preferred meat for traditional Polynesian food, while chicken (which is mostly imported despite how many you see running around) is found everywhere and in a huge variety of dishes. Most beef is imported from New Zealand and is of very high standard.

In the Marquesas Islands, goat takes pride of place and is hunted locally. It's delicious served in the traditional style with coconut milk.

Fruits & Vegetables

Tropical-fruit lovers rejoice. Mangoes, the world's sweetest pineapples, pomelos (called *pamplemousse* locally), avocados, bananas, papayas and a variety of other exotics like rambutans, soursop and star fruit are all widely available. The best season for fruit is between November and March.

Besides *uru* (breadfruit) and taro, vegetables don't play much of a role in traditional Polynesian cuisine. However, you'll find plenty of salads on menus (lettuce, carrots, peppers and tomatoes are all grown locally)

TRAVEL YOUR TASTEBUDS

Traditional Tahitian food uses a lot of fermentation. *Miti hue* (found at many supermarkets) is a mild example and is a thick, lumpy sauce made from fermented coconut milk. But the most challenging dish for visitors is reeking, fetid *fafaru*, made with raw fish that's briefly marinated in *mitifafauru* (seawater that's been infused with rotting fish for 10 days). The marination gives the fish a velvety texture but the smell – similar to roadkill wrapped in a sweaty sock – makes it extremely challenging to eat.

as well as vegetables that have mostly been imported frozen, like green beans, peas and sweet corn.

Staples & Specialities

Modern Tahitian food is a multicultural melange of French, Chinese and Polynesian influence: bechamel, soy sauce or coconut milk all have an equal chance of topping your meal.

Main Dishes

A handful of usual suspects appear on most budget to midrange menus alongside other simple dishes like hamburgers and pasta. However, there are four main dishes you're most likely to encounter.

First is *poisson cru*, which is raw fish marinated in lime juice, mixed with vegetables (usually tomato, cucumber, onions and shredded carrot) and then topped with coconut cream. Then there is sashimi, thinly sliced raw tuna (just like you'd find topping a lovely piece of maguro sushi, but using red or white tuna instead) that's piled atop a bed of shredded cabbage and served with white rice. Steak frites is a steak cooked to order served with a heaping portion of french fries and a sauce topping, such as barbecue, Roquefort (blue cheese and cream), vanilla (a light, creamy savoury-sweet cream sauce) or garlic butter. Last is chow mein, which is a classic dish of Chinese fried wheat noodles with a variety of ingredients from shrimp, Chinese sausage and chicken to bok choi and onions. Chow mein can usually be made vegetarian.

Beyond these common choices, expect to find fish and meats grilled and served with a variety of sauces, plus some inventive internationally inspired twists that mix local fare with foreign flavours from India to the Caribbean.

Ma'a Tahiti

Ma'a Tahiti (traditional Tahitian food) is a heavy mix of starchy taro and *uru*, raw or cooked fish, fatty pork, coconut milk and a few scattered vegetables. On special occasions the whole lot is neatly prepared and placed in a *hima'a* (cooking pit) where a layer of stones and banana leaves separate the food from the hot coals beneath. The food is covered with more banana leaves then buried so that all the flavours and juices can cook and mingle for several hours. The result is a steamy, tender abrosia of a meal.

Quick Eats

Small, local restaurants in French Polynesia are called *snacks*. But don't worry, you get far more than snack-sized portions at these homey little joints. This is where the locals eat and you should too, especially if you're on a budget. Expect the normal offerings of *poisson cru* to burgers and grilled fish plus cheap baguettes at lunch.

Even smaller and offering similarly priced, copious fare, *roulottes* are mobile food vans. These places usually specialise in a few items – maybe crêpes or pizza – or they may offer a few classics. The Place Vaiete *roulottes* in Pape'ete are the most well known, but you'll find little roadside vans all over the islands.

Restaurant Dining

There is a wondrous array of restaurants on Tahiti where you can experience the finest French cuisine, Italian, fusion and much, much more. The rest of French Polynesia has much more limited options. On outer islands many of the best restaurants will likely be found in the hotels and *pensions*. The finest hotels will often have internationally acclaimed chefs who whip up amazingly creative concoctions inspired by what's available locally.

It's a good idea to reserve at fine restaurants, especially for dinner.

Tipping is not expected, however, it's becoming more common in touristy places and can be a nice way to show appreciation for good service.

FOOD & DRINK STAPLES & SPECIALITIES

Drinks

Vin de Tahiti produces wines from grapes grown on the coral atoll of Rangiroa. They are unique and worth a try. Find them in fine restaurants and supermarkets.

Hinano beer is the classic and now comes in three varieties: lager (the well-known refresher), amber (full-bodied with more hops) and gold (a more malty, flavoursome lager). In most places you'll only find the lager. A bottle of Hinano at the supermarket costs 250CFP and count on 500CFP at a bar. Tabu is the other local brand, which offers a basic lager, and a lager mixed with vodka. International beers, including Heineken and Corona, are widely available.

The classic cocktail is the *maitai* (rum, orange Curacao and fruit juices) although plenty of other tropical creations are on offer as well. Tahiti Drink, found in most supermarkets, is like a *maitai* in a carton.

Most supermarkets and restaurants also stock a wide selection of mostly French wines with a few international choices as well. It can be excellent, but if you happen upon some from a crate that spent time in the hot sun at the port, it can be completely ruined. Expect to pay at least 1000 CFP for a decent bottle at a store, or 1800 CFP at a restaurant.

Fresh fruit juices can be found in many small to fancy restaurants. Real coffee is gaining popularity, especially in Pape'ete, but in more remote islands you will often be served instant coffee. Fine restaurants will often have an espresso machine. Tea is less popular but still widely available.

The tap water is safe to drink only in very small pockets of the country, so ask the locals or stick to bottled water (or better, bring a travel water filter to cut plastic usage).

Survival Guide

DIRECTORY A–Z 228

Accommodation 228
Business Hours 228
Climate 228
Customs
Regulations 228
Embassies
& Consulates 228
Electricity 229
Food 229
Insurance 229
Internet Access 229
Legal Matters 229
LGBT Travellers 229
Money 230
Post 230
Public Holidays 230
Safe Travel 230
Telephone 231
Time 231
Tourist
Information 231
Travellers with
Disabilities 231
Visas 231
Women Travellers 232
Work 232

TRANSPORT 233

GETTING THERE
& AWAY 233
Entering the Country 233
Air 233
Sea 233
GETTING AROUND 234
Air 234
Bicycle 235
Boat 235
Local Transport 237

HEALTH 239

LANGUAGE 242

Directory A–Z

Accommodation

There is a wide variety of accommodation options (p28) in French Polynesia.

Business Hours

Typical business hours are as follows:

Banks 8am to noon and 1.30pm to 5pm Monday to Thursday, to 3pm Friday

Businesses 7.30am to 11.30am and 1.30pm to 5pm Monday to Saturday

Government offices 7.30am to noon and 1pm to 5pm Monday to Thursday, to 3pm Friday

Restaurants 11.30am to 2pm and 6.30pm to 9pm

Supermarkets 6.30am to 7pm Monday to Saturday, 6.30am to 11am Sunday

Customs Regulations

➡ The duty-free allowance for visitors entering French Polynesia includes 200 cigarettes or 50 cigars, 2L of wine and 2L of spirits and 50mL of perfume.

➡ No live animals can be imported (if they're on a yacht, they must stay on-board) and certification is required for plants.

➡ On the way out of the country you're allowed to bring up to 10 undrilled pearls plus as much mounted jewellery as you like, tax-free.

Embassies & Consulates

Given that French Polynesia is not an independent country, there are no foreign embassies, only consulates, and many countries are represented in Pape'ete by honorary consuls.

The following consulates and diplomatic representatives are all located on Tahiti. Many are just single representatives and do not have official offices, so you'll have to call or email them.

Australian & Canadian Consulate (☑40 46 88 53; virginie.kiou.petropol@mail.pf)

Austrian & Swiss Consulate (☑40 42 00 30; papeete@honrep.ch)

German Consulate (☑40 43 92 26; papeete@hk-diplo.de)

Italian Consulate (☑89 73 46 04; consolato_polinesia@yahoo.fr)

Japanese Consulate (☑40 45 45 45; nippon@mail.pf)

New Zealand Consulate (☑40 50 02 95; nzhonconsulate@mail.pf)

US Consulate (☑40 42 65 35; www.usconsul.pf)

Climate

Atuona

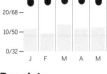

°C/°F **Temp** / Rainfall inches/mm

Pape'ete

°C/°F **Temp** / Rainfall inches/mm

Electricity

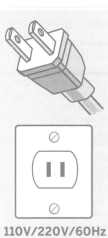

110V/220V/60Hz

110V/220V/60Hz

Food

There's no shortage fresh seafood and tropical fruit in the cuisine of French Polynesia. See p224 for more.

In this book, the following price indicators refer to a standard main course.

$ less than 1400 CFP

$$ 1400 CFP to 2400 CFP

$$$ more than 2400 CFP

Insurance

Worldwide travel insurance is available at www.lonely-planet.com/travel-insurance. You can buy, extend and claim online any time – even if you're already on the road.

➡ A travel-insurance policy to cover theft, loss and medical problems is highly recommended. Some policies specifically exclude 'dangerous activities', which can include scuba diving (p240) and even hiking. Make sure your policy covers you for your activity of choice.

➡ You should check if your insurer will pay doctors directly rather than requiring you to pay on the spot and claim later. If you have to claim later, keep all documentation. Check that the policy covers emergency medical evacuations by air.

Internet Access

➡ Thanks to the advent of smartphones, iPads and wi-fi, dedicated internet cafes have become a rarity in French Polynesia. Wi-fi access is increasingly the norm.

➡ Many post offices have internet posts, but don't count too much on it – they are usually ancient models that are often not functioning.

➡ Wireless is offered at many guesthouses and hotels (at least near the reception or the bar, if not always in each room, for which sometimes there's an additional charge) and at a number of restaurants and cafes. Some places still charge a fee.

➡ Connections are fairly fast and reliable in the Society Islands, which have broadband internet; elsewhere, slow connections are the norm.

➡ If you're toting your own device through the

BOOK YOUR STAY ONLINE

For more accommodation reviews by Lonely Planet authors, check out http://lonelyplanet.com/hotels/. You'll find independent reviews, as well as recommendations on the best places to stay. Best of all, you can book online.

Marquesas, the Australs or the Society Islands, consider buying a prepaid pass online (www.vinispot.pf) or from the local post office. This allows you to access the internet at 'Vini Spots' (wi-fi zones) located in post offices and at some hotels, restaurants and public areas.

Legal Matters

French Polynesia is a part of France, and is thus subject to that country's penal system. The police rarely hassle foreigners, especially tourists. Drunk driving is a real problem on the larger islands, and police sometimes set up checkpoints on Tahiti, Ra'iatea and Mo'orea.

LGBT Travellers

French laws concerning homosexuality prevail in French Polynesia, which means there is no legal discrimination against homosexual activity, however open displays of affection in public should be avoided.

French Polynesia does feel remarkably heterosexual, given the preponderance of honeymooning couples, but homophobia is uncommon. and you will meet lots of *mahu* (men living as women) working in restaurants and hotels (see box, p218).

Money

The unit of currency in French Polynesia is the *cours de franc Pacifique* (CFP; Pacific franc), referred to simply as 'the franc', and it's pegged to the euro.

ATMs

➡ Known as *distributeurs automatiques de billets* (DABs) in French, ATMs will give you cash via Visa, MasterCard, Cirrus or Maestro networks.

➡ International cards generally work only at Banque Socredo ATMs; luckily most islands have at least one of these. You'll need a four-digit pin number.

➡ There's a Socredo ATM at Faa'a International Airport.

➡ Some post offices are also equipped with ATMs.

Banks

➡ There are three major banks operating in French Polynesia: Banque de Tahiti, Banque de Polynésie and Banque Socredo. They change major foreign currencies, but a transaction fee applies – usually from 600 CFP to 950 CFP.

WITHDRAWAL LIMITS

Check with your bank before you leave home to ensure that the card you plan to use to withdraw cash doesn't have a low daily or weekly limit. Some travellers (particularly those with European cards) find that they are only able to take out 35,000 CFP per week in French Polynesia – not nearly enough if you plan on going to smaller guesthouses or restaurants that don't take credit cards.

➡ The best currencies to bring are US dollars and euros.

➡ All the main islands in the Society group, apart from Maupiti, have at least one banking agency. In the Tuamotus, only Rangiroa has a permanent banking service. In the Marquesas, there are Socredo agencies on 'Ua Pou, Nuku Hiva and Hiva Oa. In the Australs group, Rurutu and Tubuai have some banking services.

Credit Cards

All top-end and midrange hotels, restaurants, jewellery shops, dive centres and the bigger supermarkets accept credit cards, sometimes exclusively Visa or Master-Card, but they usually require a 2000 CFP minimum purchase. You can also pay for Air Tahiti flights with a card. Most budget guesthouses and many tour operators don't accept credit cards.

Tipping

Tipping is not a part of life in French Polynesia. The price quoted is the price you are expected to pay, which certainly simplifies things. In special circumstances, such as an excellent tour or great service by the hotel cleaning crew, a tip is appreciated.

Post

➡ The postal system in French Polynesia is generally quite efficient, and there are modern post offices on all the main islands.

➡ Mail to Europe, the USA and Australia takes about a week. Postcards or letters weighing up to 20g cost 100 CFP to France, 140 CFP to anywhere else.

➡ **FedEx** (Map p60; ☑40 45 36 45; PK2.5, Faa'a; ☺7.30am-4pm Mon-Fri) and **DHL Express** (Map p60; ☑40 83 73 73; www.dhl.com; PK4.8, Faa'a; ☺7.30am-4pm Mon-Thu, to 3pm Fri) have offices in Pape'ete. If you need to

send something fast from the outer islands, they can usually help – although it will probably involve sending the item by freight on Air Tahiti.

Public Holidays

Public holidays, when all businesses and government offices close, include the following.

New Year's Day 1 January

Arrival of the First Missionaries 5 March

Easter March/April

Labour Day 1 May

VE Day (Victory in Europe Day) 8 May

Ascension Late May

Pentecost & Pentecost Monday Early June

Internal Autonomy Day 29 June

Bastille Day 14 July

Assumption 15 August

All Saints' Day 1 November

Armistice Day 11 November

Christmas Day 25 December

Safe Travel

➡ Overall, French Polynesia is relatively safe compared with most Western countries, but occasional robberies do occur, and there has been a rise in muggings in Pape'ete in recent years. Avoid walking alone at night in the capital.

➡ Don't leave anything of value in a rental car or on the beach and ensure that your room or bungalow is securely locked.

➡ There are a lot of dogs roaming around French Polynesia; a few (especially when they're in packs) are aggressive. Pretending to throw a stone often discourages them.

➡ Swimmers should always be aware of currents and riptides. If you're not familiar with water conditions, ask around. It's best not to swim alone in unfamiliar places.

➡ When sunbathing or walking around a coconut grove, beware of falling coconuts – they can cause severe head injuries.

➡ French Polynesia has a bad record when it comes to road safety, which means that you must drive defensively at all times. Potential dangers include drunk drivers and excessive speed.

Telephone

➡ French Polynesia's country code is ☑689.

➡ There are no area codes in French Polynesia.

➡ To call overseas, dial ☑00 plus the country code followed by the phone number.

➡ From a landline, local phone calls cost 18 CFP per minute or 29 CFP per minute to a mobile phone.

➡ You can buy prepaid cards to call overseas at most post offices.

Mobile Phones

➡ There are two mobile phone operators in French Polynesia: **Vini** (www.vini.pf) and **Vodafone** (www.vodafone.pf).

➡ Mobile-phone services operate on 900 GSM and 98% of the inhabited islands have cellular coverage.

➡ Many foreign mobile services have coverage in Tahiti, but roaming fees are usually quite high.

➡ You can buy a local SIM card for around 1000 CFP and use it in your own phone if it's unlocked (check with your provider before you leave). Talk isn't cheap, however: calls from a mobile cost 30 CFP to 60 CFP per minute (and from 60 CFP to 110 CFP per minute if you call overseas).

➡ Both providers have offices in Pape'ete. Top-ups can be purchased online or at various shops and most post offices.

➡ If your phone is locked by your phone company, there are often good deals at Champion and Carrefour supermarkets on phones – you can get a basic phone plus SIM card for less than 5000 CFP.

➡ Local mobile-phone numbers begin with ☑87 or ☑89.

➡ 3G is available on Tahiti, Mo'orea, Huahine, Ra'iatea and Bora Bora.

Time

➡ TAHT (Tahiti Time) is 10 hours behind GMT/UTC. When it's noon in Pape'ete, it's 10pm in London, 2pm or 3pm in Los Angeles and 9am (the next day) in Sydney; the region is just two hours east of the International Date Line.

➡ There is no daylight-saving time.

➡ The Marquesas are a half-hour ahead of the rest of French Polynesia (noon on Tahiti is 12.30pm in the Marquesas).

➡ The Gambier Archipelago is one hour ahead of the rest of French Polynesia (noon on Tahiti is 1pm in the Gambier).

PRACTICALITIES

➡ **Newspapers** The weekly English-language tourist paper *Tahiti Beach Press* includes some local news. If you read French, there is one Tahitian daily, *La Dépêche de Tahiti* (www.ladepeche.pf), while *Tahiti Infos* (www.tahiti-infos.com) is published five times a week.

➡ **Radio** There are about 10 independent radio stations that broadcast music programs with news flashes in French and Tahitian along with the occasional interview. Among the best-known stations are Tiare FM (the pioneer nongovernmental radio station; 104.2 FM), NRJ (103 FM) and Radio Polynésie 1ere (95.2 FM).

➡ **TV** The local channels are Polynésie 1ere and TNTV.

➡ **Weights & Measures** French Polynesia follows the international metric system.

Tourist Information

The main tourist office is the **Office du Tourisme de Tahiti et ses Îles** (Tourist Office; Map p58; ☑40 50 40 30; www.tahiti-tourisme.com; ☺7.30am-5.30pm Mon-Fri, 8am-4pm Sat, 8am-noon Sun) in the centre of Pape'ete.

For information before you leave home, visit www.tahiti-tourisme.com, which has several international tourism office links.

Travellers with Disabilities

With narrow flights of steps on boats and difficult boarding facilities on Air Tahiti aircraft, French Polynesia resembles a tropical obstacle course for those with restricted mobility. What's more, hotels and guesthouses are not used to receiving guests with disabilities. However, all new hotels and public buildings must conform to certain standards, so change is happening.

Visas

Everyone needs a passport to visit French Polynesia. The regulations are much the

GETTING MARRIED IN FRENCH POLYNESIA

International visitors can legally get married in French Polynesia. You'll need to plan in advance, fill out forms and make reservations for a civil service at a city hall (for information, see www.tahiti-tourisme.com/weddings/tahitidestinationweddings.asp).

Following this, you can indulge in a traditional Polynesian wedding ceremony, which is now offered through most big resorts – a list of places is on the Tahiti Tourism website.

same as for France: if you need a visa to visit France, you'll need one to visit French Polynesia. Anyone from an EU country can stay for up to three months without a visa, as can citizens of Argentina, Australia, Brazil, Canada, Chile, Japan, Mexico, New Zealand and Switzerland.

Other nationalities need a visa, which can be applied for at French embassies.

Apart from permanent residents and French citizens, all visitors to French Polynesia need to have an onward or return ticket.

Visa Extensions

Stays by foreign visitors may not exceed three months. For longer periods, you must apply to the French consular authorities in your own country for a residence permit; you cannot lodge your application from French Polynesia unless you have a sponsor or get married to a permanent resident.

Formalities for Yachts

In addition to presenting the certificate of ownership of the vessel, sailors are subject to the same passport and visa requirements as travellers arriving by air or by cruise ship. Unless you have a return air ticket, you are required to provide a banking guarantee of repatriation equivalent to the price of an airline ticket to your country of origin.

Yachties must advise the **Police aux Frontières** (Border Police; Map p60; ☎40 80 06 00; pafport@mail.pf; Airport, Faa'a; ☷8-11.30am & 2-4.30pm Mon-Fri) of their final departure.

If your first port of call is not Pape'ete, it must be a port with a *gendarmerie* (police station). The *gendarmerie* must be advised of each arrival and departure, and of any change of crew.

Before arriving at the port of Pape'ete, announce your arrival on channel 12. Next, you'll need to report to the **Bureau des Yachts** (Harbour Master's Office; Map p58; ☎40 47 48 54; Blvd Pomare, Pape'ete; ☷9-11.30am & noon-3pm Mon-Thu, 9-11.30am & noon-2pm Fri), and complete an arrival declaration.

Women Travellers

➡ French Polynesia is a great place for solo women. Local women are very much a part of public life in the region, and it's not unusual to see Polynesian women out drinking beer together or walking alone, so you will probably feel pretty comfortable following suit.

➡ It is a sad reality that women are still required to exercise care, particularly at night, but this is the case worldwide. As with anywher, give drunks and their beer breath a wide berth.

➡ Perhaps it's the locals getting their own back after centuries of European men ogling Polynesian women, but there is reportedly a 'tradition' of Peeping Toms in French Polynesia, mainly in the outer islands. Take special care in places that seem to offer opportunities for spying on guests, particularly in the showers, and make sure your room is secure and locked at night.

Work

French citizens aren't required to comply with any formalities, but for everyone else – even other EU citizens (except those with very specialised skills) – it's difficult to work in French Polynesia. Unless you're a pearl grafter, a Chinese chef or a banking executive, you stand little chance. Authorisation to take up paid employment is subject to the granting of a temporary-residence permit, issued by the French state, and a work permit, issued by the territory.

Transport

GETTING THERE & AWAY

Entering the Country

Entry procedures for French Polynesia are straightforward. You'll have to show your passport, with any visa you may have obtained beforehand. You'll also need to present completed arrival and departure cards, usually distributed on the incoming flight. You may also be asked to show proof of a return airline ticket.

Air

Most visitors to French Polynesia arrive at **Faa'a International Airport** (Map p52; www.tahiti-aeroport.pf), on Pape'ete's outskirts, 5km west of the capital. It is the only international airport in French Polynesia. The international check-in desks are at the terminal's eastern end.

The national carrier is **Air Tahiti Nui** (Map p58; ☑40 45 55 55; www.airtahitinui.com), connecting French Polynesia internationally to France, the USA, Japan and New Zealand. It has an excellent safety record.

For Australia, you'll have to connect via Auckland.

A number of international airlines serve French Polynesia from different parts of the world and have offices in Pape'ete.

Air Calédonie International (Aircalin; Map p60; www.aircalin.nc) Has flights between Noumea (New Caledonia) and Pape'ete.

Air France (Map p58; www.airfrance.com) Has flights between Paris and Pape'ete via Los Angeles.

Air New Zealand (Map p58; www.airnewzealand.com) Flies between Pape'ete and Auckland (New Zealand).

Air Tahiti (www.airtahiti.pf) Has flights between Pape'ete and Rarotonga (Cook Islands).

Air Tahiti Nui (Map p58; ☑40 45 55 55; www.airtahitinui.com) French Polynesia's national carrier has flights to France, the USA, Japan and New Zealand. There's an extra 23kg baggage allowance for divers, surfers and golfers.

Hawaiian Airlines (Map p58; www.hawaiianair.com) Flies between Honolulu (Hawai'i) and Pape'ete.

LAN (Map p58; www.lan.com) Operates flights between Santiago (Chile) and Pape'ete via Easter Island.

Sea

Cargo Boat

Due to a lack of scheduled departures, getting to French Polynesia by cargo boat can be a real challenge; although cargo boats from the USA and Australia occasionally pass through for a day or so.

Yacht

Travelling to French Polynesia by yacht is eminently

CLIMATE CHANGE & TRAVEL

Every form of transport that relies on carbon-based fuel generates CO_2, the main cause of human-induced climate change. Modern travel is dependent on aeroplanes, which might use less fuel per kilometre per person than most cars but travel much greater distances. The altitude at which aircraft emit gases (including CO_2) and particles also contributes to their climate change impact. Many websites offer 'carbon calculators' that allow people to estimate the carbon emissions generated by their journey and, for those who wish to do so, to offset the impact of the greenhouse gases emitted with contributions to portfolios of climate-friendly initiatives throughout the world. Lonely Planet offsets the carbon footprint of all staff and author travel.

BAGGAGE ALLOWANCE

If you buy your ticket (online or at an Air Tahiti office) within French Polynesia, the baggage weight allowance is 10kg per passenger. Divers get an extra 5kg but must show their equipment and certification card at the check-in desk.

If you buy your ticket outside French Polynesia, whether online or via a travel agent, the baggage weight allowance is 23kg per passenger but the cost of your ticket is about 15% higher than the same ticket bought within French Polynesia.

feasible. Yachts heading across the Pacific from North America, Australia or New Zealand are often looking for crew and, if you're in the right place at the right time, it's often possible to pick up a ride. It's also possible to pick up crewing positions once in French Polynesia. Sailing experience will definitely score extra points, but so will the ability to cook soup when the boat's keeled over and waves are crashing through the hatch.

➡ On the eastern side of the Pacific, try the yacht clubs in San Diego, Los Angeles, San Francisco or Honolulu. On the western side, Auckland, Sydney and Cairns are good places to try. Look for notices pinned to bulletin boards in yacht clubs and yachting-equipment shops, and post your own notice offering to crew. Another great resource is the Latitude 38 (www.latitude38.com) crew list where you can post yourself as a potential crew member and peruse ships that are looking for crew.

➡ It takes about a month to sail from the US West Coast to Hawai'i and another month south from there to the Marquesas; with stops, another month takes you west to Tahiti and the Society Islands. Then it's another long leg – at least a month, without stops – southwest to Australia or New Zealand.

➡ There are distinct seasons for sailing across the Pacific in order to avoid cyclones. From the USA, late September to October and January to March are the usual departure times. From Australia and New Zealand, yachts tend to set off from around March and April.

GETTING AROUND

Getting around French Polynesia is half the fun. There are regular and affordable (and dramatic and scenic) connections between the larger islands by boat and aeroplane. Getting to the remote islands can be time-consuming and difficult, but never boring.

Air

Airlines in French Polynesia

➡ Air is the main way to cover long distances in French Polynesia. Domestic flights are run by the national carrier **Air Tahiti** (www.airtahiti.pf), which flies to 48 islands in all five of the major island groups. Window seats on its modern fleet of high-wing turboprop aircraft offer great views, but for the nervous flyer these flights can be rather hair-raising.

➡ Note that Pape'ete is very much the hub for flights within French Polynesia and, with only a few exceptions, you'll generally have to pass through Pape'ete between island groups.

➡ Flight frequencies ebb and flow with the seasons, and extra flights are scheduled in the July–August peak season. Air Tahiti publishes a downloadable flight-schedule, which is essential reading for anyone planning a complex trip around the islands.

➡ If you are making reservations from afar, you can reserve online and pay by credit card.

➡ The longest nonstop flight (between Pape'ete and the Gambier Archipelago) takes about 3½ hours, while the shortest flight (between Pape'ete and Mo'orea) is only seven minutes.

➡ Note that Air Tahiti and Air Tahiti Nui are different airlines: Air Tahiti Nui is the international carrier, while Air Tahiti operates domestic flights only (as well to the Cook Islands).

Air Passes

Because distances to the remote islands are so great, some of the full fares are quite high and the cheapest way to visit a number of islands by air is to buy one of Air Tahiti's air passes. These passes allow you to link up various islands within French Polynesia for less than you'd pay booking flights individually.

➡ Travel must commence in Pape'ete and you cannot connect back to Pape'ete until the end of the pass. You are only allowed one stopover on each island. If you stop at an island to change flights, it counts as a stopover.

➡ Passes are valid for a maximum of 28 days and all flights must be booked when you buy your pass. Once you have taken the first flight on the pass the routing cannot be changed and the fare is nonrefundable. The children's fares are for kids aged 12 and under.

➡ Most Air Tahiti passes are can be purchased online or at the Air Tahiti office in Pape'ete.

➡ Some passes are based on whether a flight is 'blue,' 'white' or 'red' – depending on the time of the day – and these flights are marked as such on the Air Tahiti schedule. In general the 'red' flights are the most popular and hence, the most expensive.

➡ You're entitled to a 20% discount if you travel on a 'blue' flight between Tahiti and one of the following islands (return trip): Huahine, Ra'iatea, Bora Bora, Maupiti, Rangiroa, Tikehau or Fakarava.

DISCOVERY PASS

The Discovery Pass (Pass Decouverte; adult/child 34,000/21,000 CFP) is the most basic pass and allows visits to Mo'orea, Ra'iatea and Huahine from Pape'ete.

BORA BORA PASS

The Bora Bora Pass (Pass Bora Bora; adult/child 42,000/26,000 CFP) allows you to visit the six main islands in the Society group: Tahiti, Mo'orea, Huahine, Ra'iatea, Bora Bora and Maupiti.

CORAL PASS

This pass (adult/child 45,000/35,000 CFP) allows visits to Ahe and Manihi from Pape'ete.

LAGOON PASS

The Lagoon Pass (Pass Lagons; adult/child 46,000/28,000 CFP) allows you to frolic in the vast lagoons of Mo'orea, Rangiroa, Tikehau and Fakarava.

BORA-TUAMOTU PASS

This pass (adult/child 65,000/40,000 CFP) allows you to enjoy the high islands of Mo'orea, Huahine, Ra'iatea, Bora Bora and Maupiti before heading to the atolls of Rangiroa, Tikehau and Fakarava.

MARQUESAS EXTENSION

You can extend the Society Islands and Tuamotu Islands passes to include the Marquesas (Nuku Hiva and Hiva Oa) for an extra 65,000/41,000 CFP per adult/child fare.

AUSTRALS EXTENSION

You can extend the Society Islands and Tuamotu Islands passes to include the Australs (Rimatara, Rururu, Raivavae and Tubuai) for an extra 59,000/36,000 CFP per adult/child fare.

MARQUESAS PASS

Visit wild and ancient Nuku Hiva, Hiva Oa, 'Ua Pou and 'Ua Huka for 81,000/50,000 CFP per adult/child.

AUSTRALS PASS

The Australs Pass includes Rurutu, Tubuai, Raivavae and Rimatara and costs around 59,000/36,000 CFP per adult/child.

NINAMU PASS

With this pass (29,000 CFP), you can visit Huahine, Ra'iatea and Mo'orea provided you travel on a 'white' or 'blue' flight. No child fare.

MOANA PASS

With this pass (34,500 CFP), you can visit Huahine, Ra'iatea, Bora Bora and Mo'orea provided you travel on a 'white' or 'blue' flight. No child fare.

Discount Cards

Air Tahiti has several cards available that let you buy tickets at reduced prices. You can get these discount cards at the Air Tahiti office in downtown Pape'ete. You'll need to show a passport, pay the fee and give them an ID photo. Reducations are based on whether a flight is 'blue', 'white' or 'red' – 'red' flights are usually the ones that go at peak hours while 'blue' flights go at the quietest times of the day.

Carte Jeunes (2500 CFP) 50% off 'blue' flights, 30% off 'white' flights and 10% off 'red' ones for those aged 12 to 25 years.

Cartes Marama (2500 CFP) 50% off 'blue' flights, 30% off 'white' flights and 10% off 'red' ones for those over 60 years old.

Carte Familles (3500 CFP) 50% off 'blue' flights for both parents and 75% off for children under 12. On 'white' and 'red' flights kids get 50% off. Parents get 30% off on the 'white' flights and 10% off the 'red'. Be aware that you'll need to produce a birth certificate for each kid.

Bicycle

Cycling around the smaller islands of French Polynesia is a sheer pleasure, particularly if it's not too hot. The distances are rarely great, the traffic is rarely heavy (except in Tahiti) and the coastal roads are rarely hilly. Bikes can be hired on many of the islands for about 2000 CFP a day, but you may find yourself riding an antique. Helmets are not provided. Consider bringing your own bike if you are a really keen cyclist. Bicycles are accepted on all the inter-island boats.

Boat

Boat travel within the Society group isn't as easy as you'd hope unless you're only going to Mo'orea or taking a cruise or sailboat. A number of companies shuttle back and forth between Tahiti and Mo'orea each day; other routes between the islands are less frequent but served at least twice a week by cargo vessels.

In the other archipelagos, travel by boat is more difficult. If you are short on time and keen to travel beyond the Society Islands, you may need to consider flying at least some of the way.

While cargo ships are principally involved in freight transport, some take passengers. However such a voyage can, depending on the circumstances, be anything from a memorable experience to an outright nightmare. The level of comfort is rudimentary: some ships don't have passenger cabins and you have to travel 'deck class', providing your own bedding to unroll on the deck and all your own meals. You may get wet and cold. And then there's seasickness... At the same time, the connection with the locals and the sheer street cred of travelling this way can make it worth it for a select few.

Cruise Ship

At the other end of the spectrum from rudimentary cargo ships are the luxury cruise ships that operate in the Society Islands. These ships are incredibly stylish and comfortable, and offer shore excursions at each stop – this is a long way from the leaky copra boats of traditional inter-island travel.

Paul Gauguin (☑in the US +1 425 440-6171; www. pgcruises.com) This very popular luxury cruise ship departs Pape'ete to visit the Society Islands and sometimes an atoll or two in the Tuamotus. Some itineraries may include the Marquesas. The standard cruise lasts a week. Prices start at US$4445 for a week, including round-trip airfares from Los Angeles.

Ferry & Cargo Ship
THE SOCIETY ISLANDS
Aremiti 5 & Aremiti Ferry 2 (☑Mo'orea 40 56 31 10, Pape'ete 40 50 57 57; www. aremiti.pf) These two boats jet between Tahiti and Mo'orea three to five times daily between 6am and 4.30pm. The trip takes about 35 minutes on the *Aremiti 5* or 45 minutes on the *Aremiti Ferry 2*. You can buy tickets (per person/car one way 1500/5000 CFP) at the ticket counter on the quay just a few minutes before departure.

Hawaiki Nui (Map p60; ☑40 54 99 54; Motu Uta, Pape'ete; ⊘7.30am-2pm Mon-Fri) Travels the Society Islands

circuit (Huahine, Ra'iatea, Bora Bora and Taha'a) on a twice-weekly schedule (Tuesday and Thursday at 4pm). It costs 2000 CFP in deck class and 6000 CFP in a cabin (one way). Reserve well in advance.

Maupiti Express 2 (☑87 72 30 48, 40 67 66 69) Has three-weekly trips between Bora Bora and Taha'a and Ra'iatea. Tickets (5400 CFP) can be purchased at the quay.

Te Haere Maru (☑40 65 61 33) This small passenger vessel runs between Ra'iatea and Taha'a every day except Sunday. The fare is from 730 CFP.

Taporo VII (Map p60; ☑40 42 63 93; Fare Ute, Pape'ete; ⊘7-11am & 12.30-3.45pm Mon-Fri, 7.30-11am Sat) This cargo ship makes two trips a week between Pape'ete and Bora Bora (via Huahine, Ra'iatea and Taha'a), leaving Pape'ete on Tuesday and Thursday around 4pm; it leaves Bora Bora on Wednesday and Friday. Note that it's pretty difficult for tourists to get passage as it's usually booked out by locals. It docks at the Farepiti quay, 3km north of Vaitape.

Terevau (☑40 50 03 56; www.terevau.pf) Runs four to six times daily between Pape'ete and Mo'orea (1200 CFP one way) and takes about 35 minutes. It costs 4200 CFP for a car.

THE TUAMOTUS
The cargo vessels that serve the Tuamotus Islands are true lifelines. Only the following take passengers (others take freight only), but their main purpose is to transport goods and petrol, and the standard of comfort is generally basic. Because of insurance changes in recent years there are limited places – usually 12 – available. Still, this is the way to go if you're looking for adventure and have plenty of time on your hands.

The routes and fares mentioned here are just an indication and are subject to change. The offices are all in the Fare Ute or Motu Uta port area in Pape'ete (take

bus 3 from the *mairie* – the town hall).

Cobia III (Map p60; ☑40 43 36 43; cobia@mail.pf; Motu Uta, Pape'ete; ⊘7.30am-3pm Mon, 8am-noon & 1-3pm Tue-Thu, 7.30am-3pm Fri, 8-11am Sat) A small boat (think lots more wave movement) that travels Pape'ete–Kaukura–Arutua–Apataki–Aratika–Fakarava–Pape'ete once a week; there are cabins but no meals are served. The fare is 7300 CFP. It usually leaves Pape'ete late afternoon on Monday and arrives on Kaukura the next day.

Kura Ora II (Map p60; ☑40 45 55 45; kuraora. yolanda@gmail.com; Motu Uta, Pape'ete; ⊘7.30am-noon & 12.30-4pm Mon-Thu, to 3pm Fri) These boats make a trip once a month to the remote atolls of the central and eastern Tuamotus, including Anaa, Hao and Makemo. Deck-class prices cost around 9000 CFP, plus around 3000 CFP per person per day for meals. The complete trip takes about three weeks.

Mareva Nui (Map p60; ☑40 42 25 53; contact@mareva nui.pf; Motu Uta, Pape'ete; ⊘7-11am & noon-4pm Mon-Thu, to 3pm Fri) Runs a circuit from Pape'ete taking in Makatea, Mataiva, Tikehau, Rangiroa, Ahe, Manihi, Takaroa, Takapoto, Fakarava, Niau, Raraka, Kauehi, Apataki, Arutua and Kaukura. Fares vary from 6200 CFP to 24,000 CFP (including meals) for a bunk; the complete trip takes nine days. There are two monthly departures.

Saint-Xavier Maris-Stella (Map p60; ☑40 42 23 58; maris-stella@mail.pf; Motu Uta, Pape'ete; ⊘7.30-11.30am & 1-4pm Mon-Fri, 7.30-11am Sat) Travels a circuit from Pape'ete every 15 days, taking in Mataiva, Tikehau, Rangiroa, Ahe, Manihi, Takaroa, Takapoto, Aratika, Kauehi, Raraka, Toau, Fakarava, Kauehi, Niau, Apataki, Arutua and Kaukura over 10 days. Departing from Pape'ete, fares vary from 7100 CFP to 15,000 CFP (deck class) depending on the distance travelled, and from 10,000 CFP to 37,000 CFP for an air-conditioned cabin. Meals are included.

This is the most comfortable option for the Tuamotus, but it's still pretty basic.

THE MARQUESAS

Aranui (Map p60; ☑40 42 62 42; www.aranui.com; Motu Uta, Pape'ete) More a cruise ship than a passenger boat, the *Aranui* runs from Pape'ete to the Marquesas. Prices start at €2305 for the 14-day voyage, and there are 17 trips per year.

THE AUSTRALS

Services between the Society Islands and the Australs are limited, so make sure you plan ahead.

Tuhaa Pae IV (Map p60; ☑40 41 36 06; snathp@mail.pf; Motu Uta, Pape'ete; ⊙7.30am-noon & 1.30-4pm Mon-Thu, to 3pm Fri) This large ship leaves Pape'ete twice a month. It stops at Rurutu and Tubuai on every trip, and Rimatara and Raivavae every other trip. You can choose between bunks and air-con cabins. From Pape'ete to Rururtu, Rimatara or Tubuai, a bunk costs 6300 CFP; to Raivavae it costs 9000 CFP. An air-con cabin is 11,000 CFP per night, plus 5200 CFP per day for meals.

THE GAMBIER

This archipelago is the farthest away from Tahiti and the hardest to get to, with limited boat services.

Nuku Hau (Map p60; ☑40 54 99 54; contact@snp. pf; Motu Uta, Pape'ete) Once a month this cargo ship takes a 15-day circuit from Pape'ete to Rikitea in the Gambier Archipelago via a few eastern Tuamotu atolls. Deck passage to Rikitea is 8400 CFP plus 2500 CFP per day for meals. Tickets are sold by the supercargo when the boat is anchored in Pape'ete.

Local Transport

French Polynesia doesn't have much of a public transport system; Tahiti is the only island where public transport is even an option.

Most islands in the Society group have one road that hugs the coast all the way around. Tahiti (where there is even a stretch of freeway), Mo'orea, Bora Bora, Ra'iatea, Taha'a and Huahine have paved and reasonably well-maintained roads. On all of these islands, tracks leading inland are often rough and ready, and almost always require a 4WD.

There are far more boats than land vehicles in the Tuamotus, although there is a sealed road running the length of Rangiroa's major island – all 10km of it – as well as a superb sealed road on Fakarava and Makemo.

Outside the towns there are hardly any sealed roads in the Marquesas. Tracks, suitable for 4WDs only, connect the villages, although bits and pieces are slowly being paved.

Sealed roads encircle both Tubuai and Raivavae in the Australs, and there are reasonable stretches of sealed road on Rurutu. Otherwise, roads in the Australs are fairly limited and little transport is available.

Bus

➡ The colourful, old *le trucks* (trucks with bench seats in the back for passengers) have now been replaced by a more modern fleet of air-con buses. Buses (often still called *le trucks*) stop at designated spots (which are marked with a blue sign) and supposedly run on a schedule – although times are hardly regular.

➡ Although there are official *le truck* stops, complete with blue signs, they are rather difficult to spot, and *le trucks* will generally stop anywhere sensible for anybody who hails them. Note that you pay at the end of your trip and that for many routes there is a set fare, irrespective of distance.

Car & Scooter

If you want to explore the larger islands of the Society group at your own pace, your best bet is to hire a car or a scooter, particularly given the price of taxis and the dismal state of public transport outside Pape'ete.

DRIVING LICENCE

Car-hire agencies in French Polynesia only ask to see your national driving licence, so an international driving licence is unnecessary.

HIRE

➡ There are many different car-hire agencies on the more touristy islands, but the prices really don't vary much. Compared with rental costs in the rest of the world, prices are high. For a small car expect to pay from 8000 CFP a day including unlimited kilometres and basic insurance – and that's not even including petrol. On some islands (Taha'a comes to mind) rentals start at 12,000 CFP. Rates drop slightly from the third day onwards. Fortunately, the cars available are pretty economical and you won't cover too many kilometres, no matter how hard you try. Off-road excursions into the interior are usually off limits to anything other than a 4WD.

➡ Most places offer four-, eight- and 24-hour rates, as well as two- and three-day rentals. At certain times of the year (July, August and New Year's Eve) it's wise to book vehicles a few days in advance; though at any time of year reserving in advance helps ensure that you get one in the price bracket you are hoping for.

➡ You'll need a credit card, of course.

➡ On Tahiti you will find the major international car-hire agencies such as Avis, Europcar and Hertz. On other islands such as Mo'orea, Huahine and Bora Bora, as well as on Rangiroa in the Tuamotus, the market is divided up between Avis and Europcar. Smaller local agencies exist on some islands, but the rates are almost as high.

➜ You can hire a car on Rurutu in the Australs, but in the Marquesas rental vehicles are mainly 4WDs with a driver (15,000 CFP to 20,000 CFP per day). Rental without a driver is possible only on Atuona (Hiva Oa) and Taiohae (Nuku Hiva).

➜ Avis and Europcar rent scooters on a number of islands. It's a good way of getting around the small islands, but bear in mind you won't be wearing protective gear, so this is probably not the place to learn to ride a scooter. You'll pay around 6000 CFP a day.

ROAD RULES

➜ Driving is on the right-hand side in French Polynesia.

➜ Although the accident statistics are pretty grim, driving here is not difficult, and the traffic is light almost everywhere apart from the busy coastal strip around Pape'ete on Tahiti. However, the overtaking habits of locals can sometimes get the heart rate up.

➜ Beware of drunk drivers at night, and of pedestrians and children who may not be used to traffic, particularly in more remote locations. Sometimes dodging sauntering dogs and chickens makes driving in Tahiti feel like a video game – take it slow.

Hitching

Hitching (*auto-stop* in French) is a widely accepted – and generally safe – way of getting around the islands in French Polynesia. Of course, hitching is never entirely safe and we don't recommend it, but if you're going to hitch, French Polynesia is an easy place to start. Usually, you'll never have to wait more than 15 or 20 minutes for a ride, plus you'll meet some interesting folks.

Always take the necessary precautions and use your judgement before jumping into a car; drunk drivers are likely to be your biggest problem. It's not recommended for women to hitch alone.

Health

You probably have less chance of getting sick in French Polynesia than in any major international city. There's no malaria, land snakes, poisonous spiders or crocodiles, and cold and flu bugs are brought in from elsewhere. Mosquitoes do exist in quantity, however, and dengue fever as well as chikungunya will be a concern when there is an outbreak. Your biggest worry will be sunburn and avoiding infection in minor cuts and scrapes.

AVAILABILITY & COST OF HEALTH CARE

Health facilities in the country are generally of a good standard but some less-populated islands will have little to no medical services.

French Polynesia has doctors and dentists in private practice, and standard hospital and laboratory facilities with consultants in the major specialities. The outer islands, of course, have more basic services. Private consultation costs from 3500 CFP to see a GP; specialists are more expensive and anywhere you go, the waiting times can be very long. Direct payment is required everywhere except where a specific arrangement is made, such as in the case of evacuation or where prolonged hospital stay is necessary; your insurer will need to be contacted by you.

Most commonly used medications are available, but private pharmacies are not allowed by law to dispense listed drugs without a prescription from a locally registered practitioner. It's best to have a sufficient supply of any regularly taken medication as a particular brand may not be available and sometimes quantities can be limited.

INFECTIOUS DISEASES

Chikungunya

This viral infection transmitted by certain mosquito bites was traditionally rare in French Polynesia until late 2014 when an epidemic hit the five archipelagos. Chikungunya (the unusual name means 'that which bends up' in the East African language of Makonde, a reference to the joint pain and physical distortions it creates in sufferers) is rarely fatal, but it can be, and it's always unpleasant. Symptoms are often flu-like, with joint pain, high fever and body rashes being the most common. It's important not to confuse it with dengue fever, but if diagnosed with chikungunya then expect to be down for at least a week, possibly longer. The joint pain can be horrendous and there is no treatment; those infected need simply to rest inside (preferably under a mosquito net to prevent reinfection), taking gentle exercise to avoid joints stiffening unbearably. At the time of writing the epidemic was over and should not be considered a major threat. Still, the best way to avoid it is to avoid mosquito bites, so bring plenty of repellent, use the anti-mosquito plug-ins wherever you can and bring a mosquito net if you're really thorough.

Dengue Fever

Dengue fever is a viral disease spread by the bite of a daytime-biting mosquito. It causes a feverish illness with headache and severe muscle pains similar to those experienced with a bad, prolonged attack of influenza. Danger signs include any sort of bruising or bleeding, vomiting or a blotchy rash – if you experience any of these alongside the fever get medical attention quickly. There is no preventive vaccine. Self-treatment involves paracetamol, fluids and rest. Do not use aspirin.

Leptospirosis

Also known as Weil's disease, leptospirosis produces fever, headache, jaundice and, later, kidney failure. It is caused by a spirochaete organism found in water contaminated by rat and pig urine. The organism penetrates skin, so swimming in flooded areas or in rivers near pig farms is a risky practice. If diagnosed early it is cured with penicillin. This disease is often confused with dengue fever; if you have blood in your urine consider leptospirosis, which is considerably more serious.

ENVIRONMENTAL HAZARDS

Threats to health from animals and insects are rare, but you need to be aware of them.

Bites & Stings

Poisonous jellyfish and sea snakes are virtually unheard of in French Polynesia. More of a worry are extremely well-camouflaged stonefish, prolific on coral reefs and rocky areas – they are nearly impossible to see and have poison-injecting spines along their backs. If you do get stung, apply heat immediately and head for the hospital. Wearing plastic, waterproof sandals provides the best protection.

Poisonous cone shells abound along shallow coral reefs. Stings can be avoided by handling the shell at its blunt end only and preferably using gloves. Stings mainly cause local reactions; nausea, faintness, palpitations or difficulty in breathing flag the need for medical attention. Also watch out for sea urchins, as the spines are long and sharp, break off easily and once embedded in your flesh are very difficult to remove.

On land, mosquitoes and noseums will be your biggest concern. Although there is no malaria in French Polynesia, there are occasional dengue-fever and chikungunya outbreaks spread by mosquitoes. Noseums (*nonos* in French Polynesia) aren't disease carriers but be careful not to over-scratch the bites or you'll risk severe infection.

Coral Cuts

Coral is sharp stuff and brushing up against it is likely to cause a cut or abrasion. Most corals contain poisons and you're likely to get some in any wound, along with tiny grains of broken coral. The result is that a small cut can take a long time to heal. As soon as you can, cleanse the wound thoroughly (getting out all the little bits of coral or dirt if needed), apply an antiseptic and cover with a dressing. You can get back in the water but healing time will be prolonged if you do. Change the dressing regularly, never let it sit wet and check often for signs of infection.

Skin & Ears

Coral ear is a fungal infection caused by water entering the canal. Apparently trivial, it can be very, very painful and can spoil a holiday. Apart from diarrhoea it is the most common reason for tourists to consult a doctor. Self-treatment with an antibiotic-plus-steroid eardrop preparation is very effective. Stay out of the water until the pain and itch have gone.

Staph infection of cuts and scrapes is very common and cuts from live coral are particularly prone to infection.

Water

The municipal water supply in Pape'ete and other large towns can be trusted, but elsewhere avoid untreated tap water. In some areas the only fresh water available may be rainwater collected in tanks, and this should be boiled or otherwise treated. Water at restaurants, particularly resort restaurants, is safe.

DIVING SAFETY

Decompression Sickness

This is a very serious condition – usually, though not always, associated with diver error. The most common symptoms are unusual fatigue or weakness; skin itch; pain in the arms, legs or torso; dizziness and vertigo; local numbness, tingling or paralysis; and shortness of breath. Signs may also include a blotchy itchy rash, staggering, coughing spasms, collapse or unconsciousness.

The most common causes of decompression sickness (or 'the bends' as it is commonly known) are diving too deep, staying at depth for too long or ascending too quickly. This results in nitrogen coming out of solution in the blood and forming bubbles, most commonly in the bones and particularly in the joints or in weak spots such as healed fracture sites.

Avoid flying after diving, as it causes nitrogen to come out of the blood even faster than it would at sea level.

The only treatment for decompression sickness is to put the patient into a recompression chamber so nitrogen bubbles can be reabsorbed. There is one recompression chamber on Tahiti, at the **Centre Hospitalier du Taaone** (Map p60; ☑40 48 62 62, 24hr emergencies 40 42 01 01; Pira'e).

Insurance

In addition to normal travel insurance, it's a very good idea to take out specific diving cover, which will pay for evacuation to a recompression facility and the cost of hyperbaric treatment in a chamber. **Divers Alert Network** (DAN; www.divers alertnetwork.org) is a nonprofit diving-safety organisation that offers a DAN TravelAssist policy that provides evacuation and recompression coverage. If you have not taken out insurance before leaving home you may be able to do so online with DAN.

OTHER CONDITIONS

Fish Poisoning

Ciguatera has been reported in many carnivorous reef fish, especially barracuda and very large jack, but also red snapper and napoleon fish; in French Polynesia it sometimes occurs in the smaller reef fish as well and this will vary from island to island.

There is no safe test to determine whether a fish is poisonous or not. Although local knowledge is not entirely reliable, it is reasonable to eat what the locals are eating.

Treatment consists of rehydration and, if the pulse is very slow, medication may be needed. Healthy adults will make a complete recovery, although disturbed sensation may persist for some weeks.

Heat

Sunburn is an obvious issue so use sunscreen liberally.

It's also important to stay hydrated; heat exhaustion is a state of dehydration associated to a greater or lesser extent with salt loss.

Heat stroke is more dangerous and happens when the cooling effect of sweating fails. This condition is characterised by muscle weakness and mental confusion. Skin will be hot and dry.

If this occurs, 'put the fire out' by cooling the body with water on the outside and cold drinks for the inside. Seek medical help.

Language

Tahitian and French are the official languages of French Polynesia, with Tahitian spoken more than it is written. Although French dominates, many of those working in the tourist industry can speak some English. If you venture to the more remote and less touristy islands, it's definitely useful to know some French, and even more so, a few Tahitian words which will be greatly appreciated. Other Polynesian languages on the islands include Austral, Marquesan and Tuamotuan.

TAHITIAN

Tahitian (also known as Reo Maohi) belongs to the group of Polynesian languages that includes Samoan, Maori, Hawaiian, Rarotongan and Tongan. There are several dialects of Tahitian, but the spread of Christianity through French Polynesia helped make the variety spoken on Tahiti the most widespread.

Most Tahitian sounds are also found in English. The vowels are pronounced as follows: a as in 'father', e between the 'e' in 'bet' and in 'they', i as in 'marine', o as in 'more' and u as the 'oo' in 'zoo'. All vowels have a longer version too, indicated in this language guide by a line over the vowel (ā, ē, ī, ō and ū). Note also that r is often rolled, and h is pronounced as in 'house' (but as the 'sh' in 'shoe' when preceded by i and followed by o). The apostrophe (') in this language guide indicates a glottal stop – the sound you hear in the middle of 'uh-oh'.

WANT MORE?

For in-depth language information and handy phrases, check out Lonely Planet's *South Pacific Phrasebook* and *French Phrasebook*. You'll find it at **shop.lonelyplanet.com**, or you can buy Lonely Planet's iPhone phrasebooks at the Apple App Store.

Basics

Hello./Good morning.	*Ia ora na, nana.*
Goodbye.	*Pārahi, nana.*
Welcome.	*Maeva, mānava.*
Thank you.	*Māuruuru.*
Excuse me./Sorry.	*E'e, aue ho'i e.*
No problem./Don't worry.	*Aita pe'ape'a.*
Yes.	*E, 'oia.*
No.	*Aita.*
Pardon?	*E aha?*
How are you?	*E aha te huru?*
My name is ...	*To'u i'oa 'o ...*
country	*fenua*
I don't understand.	*Aita i ta'a ia'u.*
Good luck!	*Fa'aitoito!*
I'm ill.	*E ma'i to'u.*

Accommodation & Food

bathroom	*piha pape*
bed	*ro'i*
breakfast	*tafe poipoi*
room	*piha*
Cheers!	*Manuia!*
beer	*pia*
coffee	*taofe*
food	*ma'a*
menu	*tāpura mā'a*
restaurant	*fare tāmā'ara'a*
water	*pape*

Shopping & Services

How much?	*E hia moni?*
bank	*fare moni*
chemist/pharmacy	*fare ra'au*
embassy	*fare tonitera rahi*
film (camera)	*firimu*
money	*moni*
police station	*fare mūto'i*
shop	*fare toa*
telephone	*niuniu paraparau*

Time & Numbers

When?	*Afea?*
What time is it?	*E aha te hora i teie nei?*
day	*ao*
now	*i teie nei*
today	*i teie nei mahana*
tonight	*i teie pō*
tomorrow	*ānānahi*

1	*hō'ē*
2	*piti*
3	*toru*
4	*māha*
5	*pae*
6	*ono*
7	*hitu*
8	*va'u*
9	*iva*
10	*'ahuru*
20	*piti 'ahuru*
100	*hō'ē hānere*
1000	*hō'ē tauatini*

Transport & Directions

bicycle	*pereo'o tāta'ahi*
boat	*poti*
bus	*pereo'o mata'eina'a*
car	*pereo'o uira*

Where is ...?	*Tei hea ...?*
address	*vahi nohoraa*
beach	*tahatai*
map	*hoho'a fenua*
plantation	*fa'a'apu*

TAHITIAN LEXICON

Although Tahitian borrowed a number of terms from English, it was not simply a case of adopting terms for items new to Tahitian culture. Tahitians use their own rich language to derive terms for words generated by modern technology. Some of the new terms are very colourful and expressive.

accelerator	*ha'a pūai ra'a pereo'o* (make-power-vehicle)
aeroplane	*manu reva* (bird-space)
airport	*tahua manu reva* (field-bird-space)
ambulance	*pereo'o ma'i* (vehicle-sick)
bank	*fare moni* (house-money)
bar	*fare inu ra'a* (house-drink)
battery	*'ōfa'i mōrī pata* (stone-light-switch on)
bedroom	*piha ta'oto* (room-sleep)
bicycle	*pereo'o tāta'ahi* (vehicle-pedal)
bra	*tāpe'a titī* (hold-breast)
camera	*pata hoho'a* (click-image)
can opener	*pātia punu* (stab-container)
car	*pereo'o uira* (vehicle-lightning)
cathedral	*fare pure ra'a rahi* (house-pray-big)
cheese	*pata-pa'ari* (butter-hard)
dentist	*taote niho* (doctor-tooth)
drawer	*'āfata 'ume* (box-pull)
fork	*pātia mā'a* (spear-food)
glasses	*titi'a mata* (filter-eye)
goat	*pua'a niho* (pig-tooth)
horse	*pua'a horo fenua* (pig-run-ground)
hose	*uaua pipi tiare* (rubber-water-flower)
hospital	*fare ma'i* (house-sick)
motorcycle	*pereo'o tāta'ahi uira* (vehicle-pedal-lightning)
office	*piha pāpa'i ra'a parau* (room-write-word)
post office	*fare rata* (house-letter)
refrigerator	*'āfata fa'a to'eto'e ra'a* (box-make-cold)
submarine	*pahī hopu moana* (ship-dive-ocean)
telephone	*niuniu paraparau* (wire-speak)
television	*'āfata teata na'ina'i* (box-cinema-small)
toilet	*fate iti* (house-small)

FRENCH

The sounds used in spoken French can almost all be found in English. There are a couple of exceptions: nasal vowels (represented in our pronunciation guides by o or u followed by an almost inaudible nasal consonant sound m, n or ng), the 'funny' u (ew in our guides) and the deep-in-the-throat r. Bearing these few points in mind and reading our pronunciation guides below as if they were English, you'll be understood just fine.

Basics

Hello.	*Bonjour.*	bon·zhoor
Goodbye.	*Au revoir.*	o·rer·vwa
Excuse me.	*Excusez-moi.*	ek·skew·zay·mwa
Sorry.	*Pardon.*	par·don
Yes./No.	*Oui./Non.*	wee/non
Please.	*S'il vous plaît.*	seel voo play
Thank you.	*Merci.*	mair·see

How are you?
Comment allez-vous? ko·mon ta·lay·voo

Fine, and you?
Bien, merci. Et vous? byun mair·see ay voo

You're welcome.
De rien. der ree·en

My name is ...
Je m'appelle ... zher ma·pel ...

Do you speak English?
Parlez-vous anglais? par·lay·voo ong·glay

I don't understand.
Je ne comprends pas. zher ner kom·pron pa

I'm ill.
Je suis malade. zher swee ma·lad

Accommodation & Food

campsite	camping	kom·peeng
guesthouse	pension	pon·syon
hotel	hôtel	o·tel
room	chambre	shom·brer
youth hostel	auberge de jeunesse	o·berzh der zher·nes
Cheers!	Santé!	son·tay
beer	bière	bee·yair
breakfast	petit déjeuner	per·tee day·zher·nay
coffee	café	ka·fay
grocery store	épicerie	ay·pees·ree
market	marché	mar·shay
menu	carte	kart
water	eau	o

Shopping & Services

How much is it?
C'est combien? say kom·byun

I'd like to buy ...
Je voudrais acheter ... zher voo·dray ash·tay ...

credit card	carte de crédit	kart der kray·dee
internet cafe	cybercafé	see·bair·ka·fay
post office	bureau de poste	bew·ro der post
tourist office	office de tourisme	o·fees der too·rees·mer

Time & Numbers

What time is it?
Quelle heure est-il? kel er ay til

When?	Quand?	kon
yesterday	hier	yair
today	aujourd'hui	o·zhoor·dwee
tomorrow	demain	der·mun

1	un	un
2	deux	der
3	trois	trwa
4	quatre	ka·trer
5	cinq	sungk
6	six	sees
7	sept	set
8	huit	weet
9	neuf	nerf
10	dix	dees
20	vingt	vung
100	cent	son
1000	mille	meel

Transport & Directions

boat	bateau	ba·to
bus	bus	bews
plane	avion	a·vyon
train	train	trun

Where's ...?
Où est ...? oo ay ...

I want to go to ...
Je voudrais aller à ... zher voo·dray a·lay a ...

At what time does it leave/arrive?
À quelle heure est-ce qu'il part/arrive? a kel er es kil par/a·reev

GLOSSARY

ahu – altar in a *marae*; in the *marae* of French Polynesia the *ahu* was generally a pyramid shape

aparima – dance with hand gestures

ari'i – high chief of the ancient Polynesian aristocracy; literally, 'king'

atoll – type of low island created by *coral* rising above sea level as an island gradually sinks; post-card atolls consist of a chain of small islands and reef enclosing a *lagoon*; see also *low island*

atua – god or gods

barrier reef – *coral* reef forming a barrier between the shoreline and the open sea but separated from the land by a *lagoon*

belvédère – lookout

bonitier – whaleboat or skipjack boat; used for fishing and for transferring passengers and cargo from ship to shore on islands that have no wharf or quay

breadfruit – see *uru*

caldera – volcano crater

CEP – Centre d'Expérimentation du Pacifique; the French nuclear-testing program

CFP – Cour de Franc Pacifique, usually known as *franc cour pacifique*; currency of French Polynesia

ciguatera – malady caused by eating infected reef fish

CMAS – Confédération Mondiale des Activités Subaquatiques; scuba-diving qualification; the Francophile equivalent of *PADI*

copra – dried coconut meat, used to make an oil

coral – animal of the coelenterate group which, given the right conditions of water clarity, depth and temperature, grows to form a reef

cyclone – tropical storm rotating around a low-pressure 'eye'; 'typhoon' in the Pacific, 'hurricane' in the Caribbean

demi-pension – see *half board*

fare – traditional Polynesian house; hotel bungalow

fare atua – house for the gods on *marae*; actually a small chest in the form of a statue

fare potee – chief's house or community meeting place; open dining room of a restaurant or hotel

fenua – country or region of origin

feo – coral outcrop

fringing reef – *coral* reef immediately alongside the shoreline, not separated from the shore by a lagoon as with a *barrier reef*

full board – bed and all meals (French: *pension complète*); see also *half board*

gendarmerie – police station

ha'e – traditional Marquesan house

half board – bed, breakfast and lunch or dinner (French: *demi-pension*); see also *full board*

hei – garland of flowers

heiva – celebration or festival; the Heiva is a huge festival of Polynesian culture (mainly dance) that takes place on Tahiti in July

high island – island created by volcanic action or geological upheaval; see also *low island*

hima'a – underground oven used for cooking traditional Polynesian food

himene – Tahitian-language hymn

Hiro – god of thieves who features in many Polynesian legends

hoa – shallow channel across the outer reef of an atoll, normally carrying water into or out of the central lagoon only at unusually high tides or when large swells are running; see also *pass*

kaveka – sooty tern

kaveu – coconut crab

lagoon – calm waters enclosed by a reef; may be an enclosed area encircled by a *barrier reef* (eg Rangiroa and Tetiaroa)

with or without *motu*, or may surround a *high island* (eg Bora Bora and Tahiti)

lagoonside – on the lagoon side of the coast road (not necessarily right by the lagoon); see also *mountainside*

le truck – public 'bus'; a truck with bench seats that operates a buslike service

leeward – downwind; sheltered from the prevailing winds; see also *windward*

LMS – London Missionary Society; pioneering Protestant missionary organisation in Polynesia

low island – island created by the growth and erosion of *coral* or by the complete erosion of a *high island*; see also *atoll*

ma'a – food

ma'a Tahiti – Tahitian or Polynesian food; Tahitian buffet

mahimahi – dorado; one of the most popular eating fish in French Polynesia

mahu – males who are raised as girls and continue to live their lives as women; see also *raerae*

mairie – town hall

maitai – local cocktail made with rum, pineapple, grenadine and lime juices, coconut liqueur and, sometimes, Grand Marnier or Cointreau

makatea – *coral* island that has been thrust above sea level by a geological disturbance (eg Rurutu, and Makatea in the Tuamotus)

mana – spiritual or supernatural power

manahune – peasant class or common people of pre-European Polynesia

manu – bird

Maohi – Polynesian

mape – Polynesian 'chestnut' tree

maraamu – southeast trade wind that blows from June to August

marae – traditional Poly-nesian sacred site generally constructed with an *ahu* at one end; see also *me'ae*

me'ae – Marquesan word for *marae*

Melanesia – islands of the western Pacific; Papua New Guinea, the Solomons, Vanuatu, New Caledonia and Fiji

Micronesia – islands of the northwest Pacific including the Mariana, Caroline and Marshall groups, Kiribati and Nauru

monoi – coconut oil perfumed with the *tiare* flower and/or other substances

motu – small islet in a lagoon, either along the outer reef of an *atoll* or on a reef around a *high island*

mountainside – on the mountain side of the coast road (not necessarily up in the mountains); see also *lagoonside*

nacre – mother-of-pearl; iridescent substance secreted by pearl oysters to form the inner layer of the shell; shell of a pearl oyster

navette – shuttle boat

niau – sheets of plaited coconut-palm leaves, used for roof thatching

noni – yellowish fruit with therapeutic properties, grown in the Marquesas and popular in the USA; also known as nono

nono – very annoying biting gnat found on some beaches and particularly prevalent in the Marquesas

nucleus – small sphere, made from shells found in the Mississippi River in the USA, which is introduced into the gonads of the pearl oyster to produce a cultured pearl

'Oro – god of war; the cult that was superseding the *Ta'aroa* cult when the first Europeans arrived

PADI – Professional Association of Dive Instructors; the most popular international scuba-diving qualification

pae pae – paved floor of a pre-European house; traditional meeting platform

pahu – drum

pahua – giant clam

pamplemousse – grapefruit/pomelo

pandanus – palm tree with aerial roots; the leaves are used for weaving hats, mats and bags

pareu – traditional sarong-like garment

pass – channel allowing passage into the *lagoon* through the outer reef of an *atoll* or the *barrier reef* around a *high island*; see also *hoa*

pension – guesthouse

pension complète – see *full board*

petroglyph – carving on a stone or rock

pirogue – outrigger canoe (Tahitian: *va'a*)

PK – *point kilométrique;* distance markers found along the roads of some French Polynesian islands

Polynesia – islands of the central and southeastern Pacific, including French Polynesia, Samoa, Tonga, New Zealand and the Cook Islands

raerae – sometimes applied to *mahu* who are transsexual or homosexual

roulotte – mobile diner; a food van operating as a snack bar

seaward – side of an *atoll*, island or *motu* that faces the sea rather than the *lagoon*

snack – snack bar

Ta'aroa – supreme Polynesian god whose cult was being superseded by worship of *'Oro*, god of war, at the time of the European arrival

tabu – alternative spelling of *tapu*

tahua – faith healer; priest of the ancient Polynesian religion

tamure – hip-jiggling version of traditional Polynesian dance

tapa – cloth made from beaten bark and decorated with traditional designs; worn by the people of pre-European Polynesia

tapu – sacred or forbidden; the English word 'taboo' comes from *tapu* or *tabu*

taro – root vegetable; a Polynesian staple food

tiare – fragrant white gardenia endemic to the Pacific; the flower has become symbolic of Tahiti

tifaifai – colourful appliquéd or patchwork material used as blankets, bedspreads or cushion covers

tiki – humanlike sacred sculpture usually made of wood or stone and sometimes standing more than 2m high; once found on many *marae*

tohua – meeting place or a place for festival gathering in pre-European Polynesia but especially in the Marquesas

tou – *Cordia subcordata;* tree, common in the Marquesas, that produces a dark, hard, grained wood popular with carvers

tupapau – irritating spirit ghosts of the ancient Polynesian religion, still much feared

tuu – ceremonial activities centre in the Marquesas

ua ma – Marquesan food pit

umete – traditional Tahitian wooden dish or bowl

uru – breadfruit; starchy staple food of Polynesia that grows on a tree as a football-sized fruit (French: *arbre à pain*)

va'a – outrigger canoe (French: *pirogue*)

vahine – woman

vanira – vanilla

windward – facing prevailing winds; see also *leeward*

Behind the Scenes

SEND US YOUR FEEDBACK

We love to hear from travellers – your comments keep us on our toes and help make our books better. Our well-travelled team reads every word on what you loved or loathed about this book. Although we cannot reply individually to your submissions, we always guarantee that your feedback goes straight to the appropriate authors, in time for the next edition. Each person who sends us information is thanked in the next edition – the most useful submissions are rewarded with a selection of digital PDF chapters.

Visit **lonelyplanet.com/contact** to submit your updates and suggestions or to ask for help. Our award-winning website also features inspirational travel stories, news and discussions.

Note: We may edit, reproduce and incorporate your comments in Lonely Planet products such as guidebooks, websites and digital products, so let us know if you don't want your comments reproduced or your name acknowledged. For a copy of our privacy policy visit lonelyplanet.com/privacy.

OUR READERS

Many thanks to the travellers who used the last edition and wrote to us with helpful hints, useful advice and interesting anecdotes:

Alex Bettenhauseno, Gilbert Block, Cindy Egan, Mark Galeck, John & Magic Garcia, William Gournac, Jim Haynes, Shirley Vandemaele, Bill Wotherspoon.

AUTHOR THANKS
Celeste Brash

Thanks to Patrick Humbert and Diana Hammer for sailing away in the 1970s, to my kids and husband for being the heart of the adventure and to all my Tahitian friends and family for laughter and love. In the islands, thanks to Melanie and Ray on Huahine, Lili Hunter, Valena and the emergency doctors on Ra'iatea, the Atges on Taha'a, Kimi on Nuku Hiva, all of 'Ua Huka (and bad weather), the Kaysers on Hiva Oa and the good people at Tahiti Tourisme in Pape'ete and in the US. Special shout out to my extraordinary colleague Jean-Bernard, the best co-author in the world, and to Tasmin Waby, our wily editor.

Jean-Bernard Carillet

Heaps of thanks to the South Pacific team at LP, especially Tasmin, for her trust and support, and to the editorial and cartography teams, including Diana Von Holdt. A heartfelt *māuruuru roa* to coordinating author Celeste, with whom I share the same passion for that trippy *fenua*. In French Polynesia, a special mention goes to my second family, the Peirsegaeles in Mahina – thanks Yan, Vai, Sean, Majo, Hubert for having open all doors and the infectious *aroha*. A big thanks also to all people who helped out and made this trip so enlightening, including Katou, Moearii, Manoa, Zelie, Isabelle, Lionel, Yves, Sébastien, Marco, Vladimir and Ludo. As always, a big *bisou* to Eva and Chris, who are always supportive.

ACKNOWLEDGEMENTS

Climate map data adapted from Peel MC, Finlayson BL & McMahon TA (2007) 'Updated World Map of the Köppen-Geiger Climate Classification', Hydrology and Earth System Sciences, 11, 163344.

Cover photograph: Woman wearing *hei* (floral garlands), Rurutu, Austral Islands; Cindy Hopkins/Alamy Stock Photo ©

THIS BOOK

This 10th edition of Lonely Planet's *Tahiti & French Polynesia* guidebook was researched and written by Celeste Brash and Jean-Bernard Carillet. The previous two editions were also written by Celeste and Jean-Bernard. This guidebook was produced by the following:

Destination Editor
Tasmin Waby

Coordinating Editors
Trent Holden,
Simon Williamson

Product Editor
Catherine Naghten

Senior Cartographer
Diana Von Holdt

Book Designer
Katherine Marsh

Assisting Editor
Helen Koehne

Assisting Cartographer
Hunor Csutoros

Cover Researcher
Naomi Parker

Thanks to Joel Cotterell, Laura Crawford, Elizabeth Heynes, Andi Jones, Lauren Keith, Karyn Noble, Kirsten Rawlings, Sarah Reid, Alison Ridgway, Kathryn Rowan, Ellie Simpson, Angela Tinson

Index

A

Aakapa 170
accommodation 28-32,
    228, *see also individual
    locations*
language 242, 244
activities 21, 31-2, *see also
    individual activities,
    locations*
Afareaitu 80
Ahe 39, 164-5
air travel 233, 234-5
Akamaru 201
Ana Aeo 195
Ana Tane Uapoto 195
Anaho Bay 174
Anau Cave 125
Ancien Phare de Topaka 160
animals 215-16, *see also
    individual species*
Apooiti Marina 109
Arahoho Blowhole 70
Aranui 12, 172, 237, **12**
Aratika 162
archaeological sites 18, *see
    also marae*, petroglyphs,
    tiki, tohua
Atuona 185
Hatiheu 175-6
Huahine 97, 99
Puamau 188
Raivavae 199
Taaoa 187
Taiohae 169
Taipivai 175
Tubuai 197
'Ua Huka 177
'Ua Pou 182
archaeology 189, 206
area codes 231
Arikitamiro Pass 151
art galleries, *see* museums
    & galleries
arts 19, 219-20, 222-3

Map Pages **000**
Photo Pages **000**

Atiha Bay 80
ATMs 230
Atuona 183-7, **186**
Aukena 201
Australs 46, 193, 194-201,
    196, 199
accommodation 193
activities 193
climate &
    travel seasons 193
highlights 194, **194**
history 194
Auti 195
auto-stop 238
Avatoru 146, **148-9**
Avea Bay 98
Avera 107, 195

B

Baie des Vierges 191
Bain de Vaima 64
banks 230
basketry 197, 221
beaches 20
Atuona 185
Bora Bora 122
Fakarava 159, 160, 163
Huahine 95, 98
Maupiti 138
Mo'orea 77
Nuku Hiva 174
Ra'iatea 112
Rangiroa 147
Ruturu 195
Taha'a 116
Tahiti 55, 64, 69, 71, 72
Tahuata 190
Tikehau 154
'Ua Huka 177
'Ua Pou 181, 182
beer 226
bicycle travel, *see* cycling
birds 179, 215, 216
birdwatching
Mataiva 158
Rimatara 200

Tikehau 154
'Ua Huka 178
bites & stings 216, 240
Bligh, Captain William 212
Blue Lagoon 159
boat tours
Bora Bora 123, 131
Fakarava 161-2
Hiva Oa 185
Huahine 99
Maupiti 139-40
Mo'orea 81-2
Ra'iatea & Taha'a 110
Tahiti Iti 72
Tikehau 155
Tuamotus 147-8
boat travel 17, 233-4, 235-7,
    see also boat tours,
    sailing
Aranui 12, 172, 237, **12**
Bora Bora 135
Fakarava 164
Huahine 104
Marquesas 168
Mataiva 159
Maupiti 142
Mo'orea 93
Ra'iatea 114
Rangiroa 154
Boenechea,
    Don Domingo de 208
Boenechea's grave 71
books 204, 222-3
Bora Bora 9, 45, 120-35,
    124-5, 129, 8
accommodation 120, 127-31
activities 37, 122-6
climate &
    travel seasons 120
drinking & nightlife 134
entertainment 134
festivals & events 126
food 120, 131-3
highlights 121, **121**
history 121
shopping 134

sights 122
tourist information 135
tours 126
travel to/from 135
travel within 135
Bougainville,
    Louis-Antoine de 208
Bounty 212, 222
Brando, Marlon 56
Brel, Jacques 183, 223
budget 17
family discounts 43
tours 127
bus travel 237
business hours 228

C

Calvaire Cemetery 183-4
canoe racing 219
car travel 17, 237-8
cargo ships 172, 233, 236-7
Cascade Vaiea 182
cathedrals, *see* churches
Catholicism 219
caves 64, 72, 125, 191, 195
cell phones 16, 231
cemeteries 183-4, 185
Centre Jacques Brel 183
chikungunya 239
children, travel with 41-3
Bora Bora 123
Mo'orea 82
Chinese Temple 54
Christian, Fletcher 212
churches
Atuona 185
Cathédrale
    Notre-Dame 54
Cathédrale
    Saint-Michel 201
Église de la Sainte
    Famille 80
Gambier Archipelago
    15, **15**
Hakahau 181
Hanavave 191

churches *continued*
Hapatoni 190
Hohoi 182
Mataiea 64
Notre-Dame Cathedral of the Marquesas Islands 169
Omoa 191
Papetoai 78
Protestant Temple 80
Temple de Paofai 51
Vaitahu 190
ciguatera 241
cinema, *see* films
climate 16, 21-3, 228, *see also individual regions*
climate change 233
Coastal Defence Guns 122
Code of Pomare 209
coffee 226
Colette Bay 175
cone shells 216, 240
consulates 228
Contrôleur Bay 175
Cook, Captain James 209-10
Cook's Bay 77, 84-5, **85**
coral cuts 240
coral ear 240
costs 17, 29, 40
Couvent Rouru 202
crabs 216-17
craft centres 177, 178, 187, 202
credit cards 230
cruise ships 236
culture 204-5
currency 16, 230
customs regulations 228
cycling 235
Bora Bora 135
Huahine 104
Mo'orea 93
Rangiroa 154

D
dance 19, 61, 219-20, 221
dangers, *see* safety
decompression sickness 240
dengue fever 239
disabilities, travellers with 231
discount cards 235
Distillerie et Usine de Jus de Fruits de Moorea 77

Distillery Huahine Passion 98
diving & snorkelling 18, 33-40
Ahe 39
Bora Bora 37, 122
costs 40
courses 38
decompression sickness 240
dive centres 40
Fakarava 38-9, 159, 161
Huahine 34-5, 98-9
live-aboards 40
Makemo 39
Marquesas 39-40
Mataiva 38, 158
Maupiti 37, 138-40
Mo'orea 34, 80-1
Ra'iatea 35, 109
Rangiroa 37-8, **36**
recompression chambers 240
responsible diving 37
Taha'a 35, 109, 116
Tahiti 33-4, 65-6, 72
Taiohae 171-2
Tikehau 38, 154
Toau 39
dolphins 176, 216
dolphin-watching 82
Nuku Hiva 176
Taiohae 170
Tuamotus 145
drinking water 226, 240
drinks 20, 226
driving, *see* car travel

E
ear infections 240
economy 204-5
Eiaone Bay 188
electricity 229
embassies 228
emergencies 17
language 243
environment 215-17
environmental issues 217
Espace Culturel Paul Gauguin 183
etiquette 218
events, *see* festivals & events
exchange rates 17

F
Faaha 116
Faaroa Bay 107

Faarumai Waterfalls 70
Faatemu Bay 107
fafaru 224
Faie 98
Fakarava 159-64, **160**
diving 38-9
families 218
Fare 95, 100-1, 103
Fatu Hiva 191-2, **191**
fauna 215-16
Fenua Aihere 72
Ferme Perlière Champon 115
ferries 236-7
festivals & events 21-3
Australs 198
Hawaiki Nui 219
Heiva 9, 22, 51, 126, 220, **9**
Marquesas 180
Fetuna 107
films 204, 222, 223
fish 216-17
fish poisoning 241
Fitii 98
food 20, 224-6, 229, *see also individual locations*
for children 42
language 242, 244
Fort George 197
French language 244
fruits 224

G
galleries, *see* museums & galleries
Gallery Umatatea 97
Gambier Archipelago 15, 46, 193, 201-2, **15**
accommodation 193
activities 193
climate & travel seasons 193
highlights 194, **194**
history 201
gardens, *see* parks & gardens
Garuae Pass 160
Gauguin, Paul 183, 223
Gauguin's Pearl 146
gay travellers 229
geology & geography 50, 215
Gilbert, Elizabeth 223
golf 66-7

H
Haamene 115
Haapiti 80, 88-9, 92

Haatuatua Bay 174
Hakahau 180-2
Hakahetau 182
Hakamaii 182
Hakanai Bay 182
Hakatea Beach 174
Hakaui Valley 174-5
Hall, James Norman 222
Hana Iti Beach 98
Hanahaoe Pass 190
Hanahevane Bay 190
Hanaiapa 188-9
Hanamenino Bay 190
Hanamoenoa Bay 190
Hanapaaoa 188
Hanatekuua Bay 190
Hanavave 191
handicrafts 63, 192, 197, 220-1
Hane 177
Hapatoni 190
Haranae Petroglyphs 138
Hatiheu 175-80
Hauru Point 78, 86-8, 91-2, **87**
Hawaiki Nui Canoe Race 23, 126-7, 219
health 239-41
heat stroke & exhaustion 241
hei 221, **19**
Heiva 9, 22, 51, 126, 220, **9**
hiking 18
Bora Bora 125
Fatu Hiva 191
Hiva Oa 185
Huahine 100
Mo'orea 83
Nuku Hiva 170
Ra'iatea 111
Rurutu 195
Taha'a 116
Tahiti 66, 73
'Ua Huka 178
Hikokua 176
history 18, 206-14, *see also individual locations*
European explorers 207-9
European settlement 211-12
French takeover 213
missionaries 211-12
nuclear testing 213-14
Polynesian Migration 206
hitching 238

Hiva Oa 182-9, **184**, **186**
Hohoi 182
Hokatu 177
holidays 230
honeymooners 123
Hooumi 175
horse riding
  Fatu Hiva 191
  Hiva Oa 185
  Huahine 100
  Mo'orea 84
  Ruturu 197
  Tahiti Iti 73
  Taiohae 170
  'Ua Huka 178
House of James Norman
  Hall 55
Huahine 11, 45, 94-104,
  96, **11**
  accommodation 94,
    100-3
  activities 98-100
  climate &
    travel seasons 94
  diving 34-5
  food 94, 103-4
  highlights 95, **95**
  history 95
  Huahine Iti 102-3
  Huahine Nui 95-8
  sights 95-8
  tourist information 104
  tours 100
  transport 104
Huahine Nui Pearls &
  Pottery 98
Hurepiti Bay 115

I
Iipona 188
Île aux Oiseaux 158
Île aux Récifs 145
Île d'Eden 154
immigration 233
influenza 213
insects 173, 240
insurance 229, 240-1
internet access 229
islets, see motu
itineraries 24-7, **24**, **25**, **27**

J
Jardins Botaniques 65
Jardins de Paofai 54
jellyfish 240
Joe Dassin Beach 116

K
Kamuihei 175-6
Kauehi 162
kayaking 82, 110, 140
Kings' Valley 125
kitesurfing 20, 83, 125

L
La Ferme aux Mantas 156
Lagon Bleu (Fakarava) 159
Lagon Bleu (Rangiroa) 146
lagoon excursions,
  see boat tours
Lake Fauna Nui 95
Lake Vaihiria 69
landscape 215
languages 16, 168, 242-6
Le Jardin de Corail 98
legal matters 229
leptospirosis 239-40
Les Sables Roses
  (Fakarava) 159
Les Sables Roses
  (Tikehau) 154
Les Trois Cascades 111
lesbian travellers 229
lighthouses 160
literature 204, 222-3
Love Here 115
luxury resorts 18

M
ma'a Tahiti 225
Maeva 97
Magical Mountain 77-8
Maharepa 90-1
mahu 218
Mairie de Pape'ete 55
Maison Blanche 77
Maison de la Vanille 115
Makemo 39, 151
Mangareva 201-2
Manihina 177
manta rays 128, 156
Mara'a Grotto 64
marae 207
  Haunarei Marae 197
  Marae Ahu-o-Mahine 81
  Marae Anapua 69
  Marae Anini 98
  Marae Arahurahu 64
  Marae Farehape 69
  Marae Fare-Opu 122
  Marae Harii 197
  Marae Hauviri 106
  Marae Manunu 97-8
  Marae Marae Taata 64
  Marae Matairea Rahi 99

Marae Nuutere 71
Marae Paepae Ofata 99
Marae Papiro 158
Marae Pomaovao 199
Marae Pua Pua Tiare 199
Marae Tahiri Vairau 160
Marae Tainuu 107
Marae Taputapuatea 15,
  106, **15**
Marae Tauraa 106
Marae Tefano 99
Marae Titiroa 81
Marae Vaiahu 138
Marae Vaitoare 69
Raitoro Marae 197
Marché de Pape'ete 51, **26**
marine reserves 215
Maroe 98
Marquesan language 168
Marquesas 46, 166-92,
  169, **171**, **177**, **181**, **184**,
  186, **191**
  accommodation 166
  climate &
    travel seasons 166
  diving 39-40
  food 166
  highlights 167, **167**
  history 167-9
  travel to/from 168
  travel within 168
Marquesas Arts Festival
  23, 180
Mataiea 64
Matairea Hill 99
Mataiva 38, 157-9, **158**
Matavai Bay 69
Matira Point 122, 127-8,
  133, **129**
Maupiti 13, 45, 136-42,
  139, **13**
  accommodation 136,
    140-2
  activities 37, 138-40
  climate &
    travel seasons 136
  food 136, 142
  highlights 137, **137**
  history 137
  sights 137-8
  travel to/from 142
  travel within 142
Me festival 198
me'ae 189
measures 231
medical services 239
Meiaute 177
Mellville, Herman 175, 222
Michener, James 222

Miss Tahiti 22
missionaries 211-12
miti hue 224
mobile phones 16, 231
Moerai 195
money 16, 17, 230
monoi 221
Monument to the Dead 170
Mo'orea 10, 44, 75-93,
  78-9, **85**, **87**, **10**, **26**
  accommodation 75,
    84-90, 88
  activities 80-4
  climate &
    travel seasons 75
  drinking & nightlife 92
  food 75, 90-2
  highlights 76, **76**
  history 76-7
  shopping 92
  sights 77-80
  tourist information 93
  tours 84
  travel to/from 93
  travel within 93
mosquitoes 240
motu
  Bora Bora 131
  Maupiti 138-40, 141-2
  Motu Auira 138
  Motu Hane 177
  Motu Iriru 107, 112
  Motu Manu 165
  Motu Miri Miri 112
  Motu Napahere 151
  Motu Nono 71
  Motu Oatara 107, 112
  Motu Paeao 138
  Motu Piscine 198
  Motu Pitihahei 138
  Motu Puarua 154
  Motu Tau Tau 116, **19**
  Motu Tauna 202
  Motu Tehatea 159
  Motu Teuaua 178
  Motu Tiapaa 138
  Motu Topati 99
  Motu Tresor 96
  Motu Tuanai 138
  Motu Vaiamanu 198
  Motu Vaiorea 99
Motuua 188
Mt Duff 202
Mt Hiro 199
Mt Mouaputa 83
Mt Ohue 125
Mt Otemanu 122, **8**
Mt Pahia 125

Mt Poumaka 181
Mt Rotui 84
Mt Taita 197
Mt Tapioi 111
Mt Teurafaatiu 140
multiculturalism 218
Musée de Tahiti et des
   Îles 64
Musée Gauguin 65
museums & galleries 209
   Archaeological
      Museum 176
   Centre Jacques Brel 183
   Espace Culturel Paul
      Gauguin 183
   Gallery Umatatea 97
   Hokatu 178
   House of James Norman
      Hall 55
   marine museum 177
   Motu Tresor 96
   Musée de la Perle 54
   Musée de Tahiti et des
      Îles 64
   Musée Enana 169-70
   Musée Gauguin 65
   Vaitahu 190
music 19, 204, 220
Mutiny on the Bounty
   212, 222

N
Nahoe 188
national parks & reserves,
   see marine reserves
newspapers 231
nonos 173
Nordby 109
Nordhoff, Charles 222
nuclear testing 213-14, 217
Nuku Hiva 168-76, 169, 171

O
Omai 210
Omoa 191
opening hours 228
Opoa 107
Opunohu Bay 77
Opunohu Valley 81

P
pae pae 189
Pae Pae Piki Vehine 169
Paeke 175
Pahua 158

Map Pages 000
Photo Pages 000

Painapo Beach 80
painting 223
Paopao 77, 81
Pape'ete 51-63, 58, 60
   accommodation 55-6
   activities 55
   drinking & nightlife 61
   emergencies 63
   entertainment 61
   food 57-61
   history 51
   shopping 62
   sights 51-5
   tourist information 63
   travel to/from 63
   travel within 63
Papenoo 70
Papetoai 78
parasailing 123
parks & gardens, see also
   wildlife sanctuaries
   Arboretum 177
   Bain de Vaima & Vaipahi
      Spring Gardens 64
   Jardins Botaniques 65
   Jardins de Paofai 54
passports 233
Pati 115
Patio 115
pearl farms 14, 98, 115, 146
pearls 62, 14
petroglyphs 189
   Fatu Hiva 191
   Hiva Oa 184, 189
   Maupiti 138
   Tahiti 72
   'Ua Huka 178
PK10.5 160
Plage aux Requins 182
Plage de Hitimahana 70
Plage de Taharuu 64
Plage de Toaroto 64
Plage de Vaiava 64
Plage du Mahana Park 64
Plage du PK9 163
Plage du PK23.5 64
Plage Lafayette 55
planning
   accommodation 28-32
   activities 31-2
   budgeting 17
   calendar of events 21-3
   children, travel with 41-3
   choosing an island 28-32
   climate 228
   diving 33-40
   French Polynesia basics
      16-17

French Polynesia's
   regions 44-6
   Gambier Archipelago 195
   internet resources 17
   itineraries 24-7, 24, 25, 27
   travel seasons 16, 21-3
plants 217
Pohue 151
Pointe du Taharaa –
   One Tree Hill 55
Pointe Vénus 69
poisson cru 225
politics 204-5
Polynesian Migration 206
Pomare family 211
population 205
postal services 230
Pouheva 151
Poutoru 115
Povai Bay 133
Prel, Alex du 223
Protestantism 219
Puamau 188
public holidays 230
public transport 237
Puohine 107
Puraha Waterfall 69

R
radio 231
Ra'iatea 45, 105, 106-15,
   108
   accommodation 105,
      111-13
   climate &
      travel seasons 105
   diving 35
   drinking & nightlife 113
   food 105, 113
   highlights 107, 107
   history 106
   shopping 114
   sights 106-9
   tourist information 114
   tours 110
   travel to/from 114
   travel within 114-15
Rainbow Warrior 214
Raivavae 198-201, 199
Rangiroa 10, 145-54, 146,
   148, 36
   accommodation 148-52
   activities 146-8
   diving 37-8
   drinking & nightlife 153
   food 152-3
   shopping 153
   sights 145-6

travel to/from 153
travel within 154
religion 205, 219
remote islands 20
responsible travel 128
restaurants 225
Rimatara 200
Rocher de la Tortue 158
Rotoava 160, 162-3
Rurutu 194-6, 196

S
safety 230-1
   bites & stings 216, 240
   hitching 238
sailing 110, 232, 233-4
sandflies 173
scenic flights 122
seafood 224
Sentier de Faaroa 111
sharks 128, 216
shopping, see individual
   locations
   language 243
skydiving 84
Smiling Tiki 183
snacks 225
snorkelling, see diving &
   snorkelling
spas 31, 32
sports 219
stand-up paddleboarding
   (SUP) 82
Stevenson, Robert Louis
   71, 222
stonefish 216
sunburn 241
surfing 20
   Huahine 100
   Mo'orea 83
   Tahiti 12, 65, 71, 73, 12
swimming 158

T
Ta'ahiamanu Beach 77
Taaoa 187-8
Taha'a 45, 105, 115-19, 108
   accommodation 105,
      116-18
   activities 35, 116
   climate &
      travel seasons 105
   drinking & nightlife 118
   food 105, 118
   highlights 107, 107
   shopping 119
   sights 115-16
   tours 116

travel to/from 119
travel within 115
Tahakia 175-6
Tahiti 44, 48-74, **52-3**,
 58, **60**
 accommodation 48,
  67-8, 70-1, 73
 activities 34, 65-7, 72-3
 climate &
  travel seasons 48
 diving 33-4
 food 48, 68, 70-1, 73-4
 geography & geology 50
 highlights 49, **49**
 history 50
 sights 64-5, 69, 70-2
 Tahiti Iti 70-4
 Tahiti Nui 63-70
 tours 69
 travel to/from 50
 travel within 50-1
Tahiti Billabong Pro 23, 71
Tahitian language 242-3
Tahuata 189-91
Taiohae 169-74, **171**
Taipivai 175
tapa 221
Tapuamu 115
Taravai 201
Taravao 70-4
tattoos 13, 221, **2**, **13**
 Marquesas 187
 Mo'orea 83
 Taha'a 119
Tautira 71
Te Ai'tua 175
Te One Roa 195
Te Pari Cliffs 72
Te Tumu 177
Teahupoo 12, 71, **12**
Teavaitapuhiva Pass 175
Tefarerii 98
Tehaatiki 170
Tehueto Petroglyphs 184
Teiipoka 175-6
telephone services 16, 231

Temae 89-90, 92
Temae Beach 77
Temehani Plateau 111
Tere 198
Tereia Beach 138
Tetahuna 182
Tetamanu 160, 163-4
Tetiaroa 56
Tevaitoa 107
Tevitete Ancient
 Cemetery 185
Three Coconut Trees
 Pass 83
tiare apetahi 110
Tikehau 13, 38, 154-7,
 155, **14**
Tiketike 151
tiki 189, 220
 Pae Pae Piki Vehine 169
 Raivavae 199
 Smiling Tiki 183
 Te Tumu 177
 Tiki Fau Poe 188
 Tiki Maki Taua Pepe 188
 Tiki Manuiotaa 188
 Tiki Moe One 188
 Tiki Takaii 188
 Tiki Te Tovae E Noho 188
time 168, 231
tipping 225, 230
Tiputa 146, **148-9**
Tiputa Pass 10
Tiva 115
Toataratara Point 195
Toatea Lookout 77
Toau 39
tohua 189
 Hikokua 176
 Tetahuna 182
 Tohua Koueva 169
 Tohua Mauia 182
 Tohua Pehe Kua 188
 Tohua Pepeu 185
 Tohua Upeke 187
Tombeau du Roi
 Pomare V 55

Toovii Plateau 175
Topatari Waterfall 69
tourism 204-5
tourist information 231
tours 32, *see*
 also individual
  locations, boat tours
travel to/from French
 Polynesia 233-4
travel within French
 Polynesia 234-8
trekking, *see* hiking
Tuamotus 46, 143-65, **146**,
 148, **155**, **158**, **160**
 accommodation 143
 climate &
  travel seasons 143
 food 143
 highlights 144, **144**
 history 145
Tubuai 197-8
Tuherahera 154, 155-6
Tupaia 210
tupapau 219
TV 214, 231

U
'Ua Huka 176-80, **177**
'Ua Pou 180-2, **181**
undersea walks 81, 123
urchins 216
Uturoa 106

V
vacations 230
Vaiare 80, 88-9
Vaiea 138
Vaiharuru Waterfall 69
Vaikivi Petroglyphs 178
Vaipaee 177
Vaipahi Spring Gardens 64
Vaipo Cave 191
Vaipo Waterfall 170, 174
Vaipoiri Cave 72
Vaitahu 190

Vaitape 122, 127, 132
Vaite, Celestine Hitiura 223
Vaitoetoe Ridge 116
Vallée de la Vanille 116
vanilla farms 115, 116, 119
vegetables 224
Vin de Tahiti 152
vineyards 152
visas 16, 231-2

W
walking, *see* hiking
Wallis, Captain Samuel 208
water sports 99-100, 110
waterfalls
 Hanavave 191
 Mo'orea 80
 Nuku Hiva 170, 174
 Ra'iatea 111
 Tahiti 11, 69, 70, **11**
 'Ua Pou 182
weather 16, 21-3, 228, *see*
 also individual regions
weddings 232
weights 231
whales 176, 216, **15**
whale-watching 15
 Mo'orea 82
 Nuku Hiva 176
 Rurutu 195
 Tahiti 65-6
wildlife 215-17, *see also*
 individual species
wildlife sanctuaries 158,
 215
wildlife-watching 128
wine 226
women travellers 232
woodcarvings 220
work 232
WWII relics 122

Y
yachting, *see* sailing

Map Legend

Sights
- Beach
- Bird Sanctuary
- Buddhist
- Castle/Palace
- Christian
- Confucian
- Hindu
- Islamic
- Jain
- Jewish
- Monument
- Museum/Gallery/Historic Building
- Ruin
- Shinto
- Sikh
- Taoist
- Winery/Vineyard
- Zoo/Wildlife Sanctuary
- Other Sight

Activities, Courses & Tours
- Bodysurfing
- Diving
- Canoeing/Kayaking
- Course/Tour
- Sento Hot Baths/Onsen
- Skiing
- Snorkelling
- Surfing
- Swimming/Pool
- Walking
- Windsurfing
- Other Activity

Sleeping
- Sleeping
- Camping

Eating
- Eating

Drinking & Nightlife
- Drinking & Nightlife
- Cafe

Entertainment
- Entertainment

Shopping
- Shopping

Information
- Bank
- Embassy/Consulate
- Hospital/Medical
- Internet
- Police
- Post Office
- Telephone
- Toilet
- Tourist Information
- Other Information

Geographic
- Beach
- Gate
- Hut/Shelter
- Lighthouse
- Lookout
- Mountain/Volcano
- Oasis
- Park
- Pass
- Picnic Area
- Waterfall

Population
- Capital (National)
- Capital (State/Province)
- City/Large Town
- Town/Village

Transport
- Airport
- Border crossing
- Bus
- Cable car/Funicular
- Cycling
- Ferry
- Metro station
- Monorail
- Parking
- Petrol station
- Subway station
- Taxi
- Train station/Railway
- Tram
- Underground station
- Other Transport

Note: Not all symbols displayed above appear on the maps in this book

Routes
- Tollway
- Freeway
- Primary
- Secondary
- Tertiary
- Lane
- Unsealed road
- Road under construction
- Plaza/Mall
- Steps
- Tunnel
- Pedestrian overpass
- Walking Tour
- Walking Tour detour
- Path/Walking Trail

Boundaries
- International
- State/Province
- Disputed
- Regional/Suburb
- Marine Park
- Cliff
- Wall

Hydrography
- River, Creek
- Intermittent River
- Canal
- Water
- Dry/Salt/Intermittent Lake
- Reef

Areas
- Airport/Runway
- Beach/Desert
- Cemetery (Christian)
- Cemetery (Other)
- Glacier
- Mudflat
- Park/Forest
- Sight (Building)
- Sportsground
- Swamp/Mangrove

OUR STORY

A beat-up old car, a few dollars in the pocket and a sense of adventure. In 1972 that's all Tony and Maureen Wheeler needed for the trip of a lifetime – across Europe and Asia overland to Australia. It took several months, and at the end – broke but inspired – they sat at their kitchen table writing and stapling together their first travel guide, *Across Asia on the Cheap*. Within a week they'd sold 1500 copies. Lonely Planet was born.

Today, Lonely Planet has offices in Dublin, Franklin, London, Melbourne, Oakland, Beijing and Delhi, with more than 600 staff and writers. We share Tony's belief that 'a great guidebook should do three things: inform, educate and amuse'.

OUR WRITERS

Celeste Brash

Celeste first visited French Polynesia in 1991, fell in love with the place and the man who would become her husband, and moved to the country in 1995. After five years pearl farming and raising babies on a remote atoll, she and her family moved to Tahiti where they spent the next 10 years surfing, dancing, swimming and, oh yeah, working. She now divides her time between Tahiti and Portland, Oregon. During all this moving about her award-winning writing has appeared in publications from the BBC to *National Geographic*. Find more about her at www.celestebrash.com.

Jean-Bernard Carillet

Paris-based journalist and photographer Jean-Bernard is a French Polynesia expert. So far, he has explored 29 islands in the five archipelagos and has clocked up more than 13 trips. For this gig he searched for the most idyllic *motu* (small islets), the best manta-ray encounters, the most thrilling lagoon tours, the tastiest *poisson cru*, the most romantic resorts and the best value accommodations. His favourite experiences included diving with hundreds of grey sharks on Fakarava, swimming in Makemo lagoon – the most translucent water he's ever seen – and climbing Mt Duff in the Gambier Archipelago.

Published by Lonely Planet Global Limited
CRN 554153
10th edition – December 2016
ISBN 978 1 78657 219 6
© Lonely Planet 2016   Photographs © as indicated 2016
10 9 8 7 6 5 4 3 2 1
Printed in China